THE COLLECTED CORRESPONDENCE AND LONDON NOTEBOOKS OF JOSEPH HAYDN

I Haydn. Wax bust by Thaller (Vienna City Museum).

The Collected Correspondence
and London Notebooks of

JOSEPH HAYDN

H. C. ROBBINS LANDON
AUTHOR OF
THE SYMPHONIES OF JOSEPH HAYDN

LONDON
BARRIE AND ROCKLIFF
1959

©

Printed by W. & J. Mackay & Co. Ltd, Chatham

PREFACE

THE LETTERS collected in this volume probably represent only a small fraction of those Haydn wrote and received during his long life; in a note to his young friend Joseph Eybler, for example, Haydn excuses himself for being so curt and adds, "this is the tenth letter I have to mail [today]" (see 22nd March 1789); of these ten, one has survived. The title "Collected Correspondence" is perhaps a little presumptuous, for even as recently as after World War II, a large and vitally important collection of hitherto unknown letters was discovered in the Esterházy Archives at Budapest, the "Acta Musicalia" of which are just now being thoroughly examined for the first time. It is doubtful whether we shall find another treasure trove of this magnitude, but it should be said that the present edition— the first attempt to collect all Haydn's letters within the covers of a book—cannot be complete. Several letters were sold by antiquarian booksellers and have since disappeared, and there are several others of which we have only the contents, or extracts. On the other hand, it is highly doubtful if more than a handful of undiscovered letters still exists, and thus the title "Collected Correspondence" is as justified as is possible in the present circumstances.

Readers may find the following notes useful. The † appearing at the head of some earlier letters is equivalent to the sign of the Cross. Maria Anna von Genzinger begins all her letters with the three-fold Cross, *i.e.* the Holy Trinity. The "m.p." "m.pr." or "m.pria" at the end of the letters means "manu propria". Generally I have not translated the different kinds of money referred to in the letters, and I have also left the abbreviations as they stand. Fl. = Viennese Gulden; X, Xr, or Kr. = Kreutzer. 1 ducat = 4.5 Gulden. The terms ducat and Fl. (Gulden) were often used in one and the same document (see 7th December 1792). The purchasing power of Viennese currency declined considerably after 1800, and Haydn's petitions for his musicians of this period constantly reflect the need for increased salaries "bey so theuren Zeiten". In 1786, a Viennese bachelor of the middle class could have lived on about 525 Fl.; in 1804, he would have required 1,200 Fl. See O. E. Deutsch, 'Austrian Currency Values and Their Purchasing Power (1725–1934)', *Music & Letters*, July 1934, pp. 236–238. £ 500 were then 5,883 Gulden.

The Castle at Esterháza is sometimes referred to as "Estoras", sometimes as "Esterház": I have not thought it necessary to standardize these terms. In Austrian dialect, the female sex was often (and still is, among the peasants) indicated by adding "-in" to the end of the name. Thus Haydn's soprano, Barbara Pilhofer, was referred to, even in official documents, as "Pilhoferin" or even the rather grotesque "Pilhofin"; Frau Kellerin = Frau Keller, and so forth. The most difficult problem of translation proved to be the formulae used at the beginning and the end of formal letters, *e.g.* to royalty, business associates, and in general persons with whom one was not on intimate terms. In fact they cannot be translated at all (a Prince was addressed as "Durchlaucht", for example, which literally means "Transparency"). At first I intended to leave them in the original German; but on second thoughts, it seemed very unfair to expect English readers to guess the meaning of "Durchläuchtig Hochgebohrner Reichs Fürst, Gnädigst Hochgebiethender Herr, Herr". So I have attempted to give the flavour of these formal addresses; I realize that "Nobly born Sir" and the like do not read well in the English language, but on the other hand it is wrong, I feel, to translate "Hoch Edlgebohrner, Insonders Hochzuverehrender Herr!" simply as "Sir" (as Lady Wallace and others have done). It is perhaps necessary to warn readers not to take these formulae too literally; neither the writer nor the recipient thought twice about the content. It meant no more to write (I translate literally) "High, nobly born, most especially respected Sir" than it does for us to write "Dear Sir" to someone whom we regard as anything but dear.

When drafts of letters have been included, I have always retained the final version; for obvious reasons it is not practicable to reproduce in translation the linguistic subtleties of a draft.

I have always given the addresses (so far as they are still extant) in the original language; and when one of the publishing firms (such as Artaria) made notes concerning the arrival of the letter and when it was answered, I have retained the original language of the dates, *etc.* if they were easily understandable (*e.g.* "Haydn/Esterház / 21 Februarii") and have simply translated such words as "beant." ("ans'd"). Words which are underlined in the original texts have been printed in small capital letters; capital letters have also been used to indicate passages written in a very large size (*e.g.* when Haydn addresses Prince Esterházy. (See illustration XIII.)

Haydn scholars will perhaps look in vain for the letters which Count Morzin wrote to Haydn in the late 1770's and 1780's (autographs in the Sándor Wolf Museum, Eisenstadt): the letters are forgeries—very cleverly done, with old ink on old paper, but thoroughly spurious. It would take more space than the subject warrants to explain all the points where the forger erred, and I will limit myself to three: Morzin asks for Haydn's opera *Flora*: (1) Haydn never wrote an opera of this name; (2) no such opera was ever performed at Esterháza; (3) no such opera is ever known to have been written by anyone. Morzin also asks for Haydn's opera *Alceste*: this is a clever touch, for Haydn actually did perform a marionette opera of this name by Carlos d'Ordoñez. The forger did not, however, know this: he took his information from the booklet, *Beschreibung des Hochfürstlichen Schlosses Esterhász . . .*, Pressburg 1784, wherein (p. 39) we read . . . "the eternal MARIA THERESIA gave her gracious approval to the opera *Alceste*", an *opera seria* performed at the marionette theatre in her presence. Finally Morzin talks in these letters of "Streichquartett" (string Quartet). The term did not exist in the eighteenth century (Morzin would have called it "Quadro", "Quartett", "Divertimento", or "Quartetto": the prefix "Streich-" does not appear until fifty years later).

The Esterházy Archives and other private and public libraries contain many receipts, either entirely in Haydn's handwriting, or drawn up by a clerk and signed by him. Receipts are certainly not letters, and thus I have included only a very few of them—those which I felt to be of exceptional biographical or musicological interest.

The only substantial collection of Haydn's letters ever published in the English language is Lady Wallace's translation of Nohl's *Musikerbriefe* (*Letters of distinguished Musicians . . .* London 1867). I have not hesitated to make free use of Lady Wallace's often rather quaint translation of Haydn's still quainter German: the source from which she translated, however, proved to be incomplete and inaccurate in many cases, and I hasten to add that, whereever possible, I have gone back to the autographs or other early sources (*e.g.* Pohl's MS. copies). The only other major English translation of the material in this book is Krebiehl's edition of the first two London notebooks which, though not quite complete and not always completely accurate, often proved most useful. The remaining translations are all my own, except for one Dutch source, which Baron van Pallandt of Geneva kindly translated for me at the instigation of Mr. Geoffrey Robinson. Translations are in some ways hopeless; they can never fully convey the subtleties of the originals. I can only assure readers that I have made every effort to show the difference, for example, between the ponderous verbosity of official documents (*e.g.* the letter of 1st April 1804, the original German of which actually consists of only three gigantic sentences) and between the pithy Italian of Haydn's letters to Polzelli.

In preparing the English translations of the London Notebooks, I have tried to retain the flavour of the original, in which the German is sprinkled with French, Italian and Latin words. Haydn learned English by hearing it spoken, and his spelling often reflects the sound of the word as it would have been written in German (*e.g.* "cahst" for cast). I have altered neither his English spelling nor his capitalization and spelling in other languages; when reproducing poetry, however, I have made the one concession of starting each line with a capital letter—a procedure which Haydn himself sometimes adopts. Where the translation was especially problematical, I have placed the original, in brackets, after my translation. I have retained the original languages of all the poetry and the aphorisms in these notebooks; a prose translation has been added in parentheses. Contrary to the letters, in which the commentary has been included in the form of footnotes (serially per letter), I found it more practical to use the Deutsch method for the London Notebooks: the commentary, when present, has been placed in smaller type directly after each entry. The reader is thus spared enormous numbers of unsightly footnotes; the final entry of the Fourth Notebook—a lengthy and very useful catalogue—could not, however, be treated in this way, and for this one entry I have returned to footnotes.

Several hundred letters to libraries, antiquarian booksellers and private collectors formed the basic attempt to collect Haydn's letters. Apart from personal contacts, there was a small response to "want letters" placed in newspapers and periodicals in England, the United States, the Continent and Australia. The autographs of Haydn's letters are spread over four continents and some fourteen countries, including Japan, Southern Rhodesia, most of Europe, England and the United States. In the arduous task of tracing private collections which might include Haydn sources, I was greatly assisted by some two dozen antiquarian booksellers, who provided me with the names and addresses of their clients; some of these booksellers actually went to the trouble of photographing Haydn's letters which happened to be in their possession, or they allowed me to consult the originals. My experience with these busy ladies and gentlemen has been of the very happiest, and I wish to thank them collectively as well as individually. The private collectors to whom I wrote proved exceptionally cooperative in all but one or two cases (and these, I regret to say, were Americans); without their generosity some dozen letters would be missing entirely, and the texts of another score would be inaccurate and incomplete. Of the many libraries who placed their sources at my disposal, I am particularly indebted to the National Museum at Budapest, who sent microfilms of all the Haydn letters thus far discovered in the Esterházy Archives; some of these documents are here published for the first time. Dr. Arisztid Valkó is in the process of transcribing all these fascinating letters in the original German, and the first series has recently (1957) been published (see Sources). Professor Dénes Bartha was kind enough to collate the texts of numerous letters in the National Museum, both in the manuscript department and in the Esterházy Archives. As a result of his kindness, half-a-dozen of Haydn's letters to Artaria can now be published for the first time complete and in textually accurate (though of course translated) form. Professor Bence Szabolcsi also arranged to have an important letter in the Esterházy Archives photographed for me before it was published in the afore-mentioned series of Dr. Valkó.

I have exchanged information and sources with two other scholars who have been collecting Haydn letters for many years: Dr. Antony van Hoboken, Ascona, who was good enough to send me photographs of the letters he owns and also of others which are at present unavailable; and Dr. E. H. M. von Asow, Director of the Internationales Musiker-Brief-Archiv, who also provided me with photographs of letters, the originals of which have in some cases disappeared or are now in unavailable private collections. I should like to express my gratitude to both these gentlemen for giving so unstintingly of their time and knowledge.

Dr. E. F. Schmid, Augsburg, General Editor of the New Mozart Collected Edition, kindly placed at my disposal his card catalogue of Haydn letters; he also drew my attention to a hitherto unpublished letter in a South German private collection. On two occasions Mr. Paul Badura-Skoda took the time, in the midst of a busy concert tour, to secure unpublished Haydn letters for me; I am most obliged to him. Professor Jan LaRue, as always, proved a useful and indefatigable collaborator. Count C.-G. Stellan Mörner, Stockholm, generously copied out two Haydn letters in Swedish private collections. Miss Emily Anderson, London, was kind enough to give me

all the addresses of private collections in which she had discovered
Beethoven material, as a result of which I gained five "new" autographs. Mr. John Pashby, of Sotheby & Co, took the great trouble
to send me a list of all the Haydn letters that had passed through the
firm's hands in recent years. I am also indebted to Mr. Albi Rosenthal, Oxford; Mr. Cecil Hopkinson, London; Miss Mary Benjamin,
New York City; Messrs. Lucien Goldschmidt, New York City;
Mrs. H. J. Laufer, London; Mr. Heinrich Eisemann, London; Herr
Heinrich Hinterberger, Vienna; and Messrs. V. A. Heck, Vienna—
those antiquarian booksellers who were particularly helpful to me
in my research.

The following public libraries answered queries, supplied photo-
graphs or allowed me to examine their material personally: the
Österreichische Nationalbibliothek, Vienna; the Gesellschaft der
Musikfreunde, Vienna; the Stadtbibliothek, Vienna; the Öster-
reichisches Staatsarchiv, Vienna; Archiv für Niederösterreich,
Vienna; the Haus- Hof- und Staatsarchiv, Vienna; Archiv der
Stadt Wien; the Archiv des Landesgerichtes, Vienna; the Benedic-
tine Monastery of Göttweig, Lower Austria; the Sándor Wolf
Museum, Eisenstadt; the Mozarteum, Salzburg; the Landesregie-
rungsarchiv, Salzburg; the Archivio di Stato, Naples; the Biblioteca
musicale di Conservatorio di Musica "G.B. Martini", Bologna
(Dr. Luigi F. Tagliavini kindly copied out a letter for me in
that library); Biblioteca Estense, Modena; Národní Museum v
Praže, Prague; the Westdeutsche Bibliothek, Marburg/Lahn
(Dr. Martin Cremer); the Deutsche Staatsbibliothek, Berlin; the
Goethe-Schiller-Archiv, Weimar; the Kästner Museum, Hanover;
Kungl. Musikaliska Akademiens Bibliothek, Stockholm; Narodna
i Univerzitetna Knjižnice v Ljubljani; Musée de Mariemont,
Mariemont (Belgium); Conservatoire Royal de Musique, de
Bruxelles (Dr. A. van der Linden); Bibliothèque Royale de Belgique,
Brussels; Universitätsbibliothek, Zürich; Bibliothèque Nationale,
Paris; Bibliothèque du Conservatoire de Musique, Paris; Maison
Pleyel, Paris; the British Museum, London; Stanford Memorial
Library, California; the Harvard College Library, Cambridge,
Mass.; the Boston Public Library; the New York Public Library
(Mr. Carleton Sprague Smith); the Historical Society of Penn-
sylvania, Philadelphia, Pa.; the Library of Congress, Washington;
the Gemeente-Archief, Amsterdam.

Apart from these listed above, the following private individuals
kindly sent photographs of their letters: S. L. Courtauld, Imbeza

Valley, Southern Rhodesia; *Studienprofessor* Filibert Boccali, Kempten (Allgäu); Frau Margarete Hummel, Florence; Dr. Felix Salzer, New York City; Dr. Max Thorek, Chicago; M. Henri Gouin, Royaumont (France); Mr. Toshitatsu Mayeda, Tokyo; Dr. Rudolf Floersheim, Bern; Mr. J. E. Kite, Hove, Sussex; Mr. Walter Hinrichsen, New York City; Mrs. Marguerite Manley, Scarsdale, N.Y.; Mr. Roger Barrett, Chicago; *Hofrat* Viktor Keldorfer, Vienna; Mr. Richard Franko Goldman, Amawalk, N.Y.; Frau E. Sarasin-Geigy, Basel; Herr Hugo von Mendelssohn-Bartholdy, Basel; and the Heineman Foundation, Greenwich (Conn.).

Many of my colleagues and friends answered questions, some of which were involved and required a great deal of time. Among others, I should like to single out Dr. Roger Fiske, London; Mr. A. Hyatt King, London; Mr. O. W. Neighbour, London; Mr. William Lichtenwanger, Washington (D.C.); Mr. Richard S. Hill, Washington (D.C.); Professor Karl Geiringer, Boston; Professor Oliver Strunk, Princeton; Professor O. E. Deutsch, Vienna; Mr. Bernard Herrmann, North Hollywood, California; M. François Lesure, Paris; Dr. H. von Hase, Wiesbaden; President Wilhelm Kux, Chur; Mr. Harold Acton (then in Naples); Dr. Edmund Schilling, London; Mr. Irwin Lubroth, Madrid; Dr. Angelo Filipuzzi of the Instituto Italiano di Cultura per l'Austria, Vienna; Professor Franz Stoessl, Vienna; and the National Maritime Museum, Greenwich (England). Christa Fuhrmann-Landon transcribed many of the letters and collated the texts of the London Notebooks with the autographs; and apart from this, she was of the greatest assistance to me throughout the preparation of this book.

Vienna, Autumn 1958　　　　　　　　　　　　　　　　H.C.R.L.

POSTSCRIPTUM

After having completed the manuscript of this book, the compiler made a three weeks' research trip to the Esterházy Archives in Budapest, where he was able to check various doubtful textual points with the autographs there. Professor Dénes Bartha and Professor Bence Szabolcsi kindly provided me with Dr. Arisztid Valkó's transcriptions of another dozen unpublished letters to and by Haydn which had just been discovered in the Esterházy Archives; and a number of useful facts could be gleaned from the "Eisenstäder Commissions Prothocol . . . von Jahr 1777 bis 1790" (Acta Musicalia, fasc. 2489), the "Index deren von Sr. hochfürstl. Durchlaucht bewilligten

Pensionen, Conventions, Vermehrungen und neuen Anstellungen von Monath Junio 1788 bis Ende 1790" (Acta Musicalia, fasc. 2499) and the "Prothocoll über verschiedene hochfürstl. Commissiones, Decretationes, Intima und andere Buchhaltereys Verordungen de Anno 1734 [et seq.]" (Acta Musicalia, fasc. 2488)—all of which are unpublished, and are of vital importance to Haydn research. I am most grateful to these gentlemen for allowing me to copy these documents, and grateful to my publishers for arranging, at the last minute, that the letters be included (galley proofs were ready by the time I could send the new material to London).

Budapest, 20th December 1958   H.C.R.L.

CONTENTS

LIST OF PLATES

INTRODUCTION

THE purpose of this Introduction is to introduce the reader to the principal persons figuring in Haydn's correspondence; it also serves the purpose of freeing the text from the long footnotes which would otherwise be necessary.

The scene opens, as it were, on Haydn's negotiations with his second Prince, Nicolaus ("The Magnificent") Esterházy, who acceded to the title in 1762 upon the death of his brother Paul Anton (often referred to simply by the second of his Christian names). With one or two exceptions, these fascinating letters were discovered in the Esterházy "Acta Musicalia" after World War II, and are herewith printed in English for the first time (see also Preface, *supra*, p. v); some of them—particularly the later ones to and from Nicolaus II—have never been printed at all. The documents will undoubtedly shock many readers, for it is clear that at the beginning of Haydn's tenure as *Vice-Capellmeister*, he was treated little better than a servant. Nicolaus was certainly highly musical and highly intelligent, but he was obviously a despot used to "profound submission" from his personnel. The astonishing thing about the letters is not only their obvious importance as documents of the age, but also the brilliant searchlight they throw on that which has always been regarded as the "dark period", biographically, in Haydn's life: the first thirty years of his service under the Esterházys. They reveal Haydn to be a master diplomat, clever enough to get his way with a Prince who could be as ruthless as the icy winter that often gripped the Hungarian countryside round Esterháza. Time after time the Prince intended to dismiss a member of the band, and Haydn, who loathed writing letters (as we know from his biographer Griesinger), would laboriously make the sign of the Cross and write His Serene and Noble Prince of the Holy Roman Empire, Dread Lord and Sire; in every case thus far recorded, Haydn had his way. And gradually, as the years passed, Haydn's relationship with the Prince became a very different affair: it is perhaps not an exaggeration to say that the mellowed Prince who appears in the 1780's was partly Haydn's creation. First we see the composer writing directly to the Prince; shortly afterwards, when Haydn saw that personal

interviews were more successful, he had the Princely *Secretaire*
Scheffstoss act as intermediary; and finally, Haydn seems to have
conducted such interviews himself. The famous story of the "Farewell" Symphony now appears in its proper context, as one of
Haydn's clever inspirations, designed, in this case, to get the Prince
to leave the icy marshes of Esterháza; it is obvious too, I think, that
the beautiful and lonely Symphony succeeded far better than any
letter could have done. Esterházy for his part soon realized that his
Capellmeister was a genius; he obviously wanted to keep Haydn
content, and thus never hesitated, for example, to lend him money,
and otherwise to satisfy his every-day needs.

In the year 1780, a new aspect of Haydn's personality begins to
appear: his business correspondence with the music-publishing house
of Artaria & Company, Vienna.[1]

The Artaria family came from Blevio on Lake Como. Five members
of the family left Blevio in 1759 and attended fairs in Frankfurt,
Leipzig and Würzburg. Two of them subsequently returned to
Italy, while three members of the family formed a company in
Mainz. The two cousins Carlo and Francesco then went on to
Vienna where, in 1770, they established a business in engravings,
optical goods and barometers. They soon imported music too, and
in August of 1778, they began to publish and print music themselves. Late in the year 1779, the firm and Haydn entered into a
relationship which was to prove highly profitable to both.

Haydn's letters to Artaria show the composer to have been a
shrewd business man. We must remember that music-publishing, on
a large scale, was a relatively new trade, at least in Central Europe.
Previously, music of all kinds had been circulated by manuscript
copies, which were cheaper and fairly quickly produced; side by
side with Artaria's new music-publishing activities, many music-
copying firms continued to thrive in Vienna till the end of the
century (*e.g.* L. Lausch, Traeg, Wenzel Sukowaty, *etc.*). Composers
received nothing for music distributed by these copyists, who often
bribed members of an orchestra to get, for instance, Haydn's and
Mozart's newest works; it was piracy of the worst sort, but there
was no such thing as a copyright law, and the composer was helpless
against the thieving and unscrupulous activities of these professional
musical gangsters. Haydn's letters to Artaria vividly reflect the

[1]The following notes on the firm are taken from the most recent source: the
excellent and far too little-known *Vollständiges Verlagsverzeichnis Artaria & Comp.*
by Alexander Weinmann (Vienna 1952), pp. 4*ff.*

"every-man-for-himself" attitude of composer, professional copyist and publisher. For years and years, Haydn must have watched with astonishment and frustration the mass of music published under his name in Paris, London, Berlin and Amsterdam—some of it spurious, but a good part of it genuine compositions, for the publication of which he received nothing. It is quite certain that there are whole *opera* of Haydn published in Paris the very existence of which the composer never even realized. Consequently Haydn, though obviously pleased and flattered at Artaria's interest in his music, regarded music publishers with a rather jaundiced eye. On the whole, Artaria turned out to be an exceptionally gentlemanly firm, who took great pains to keep one of their principal sources of income happy. The whole correspondence is not only interesting to students of Haydn, but it illuminates the entire field of music-publishing during the eighteenth century, and is indispensable to scholars of the period. Some of the problems have not changed a whit, and every composer will smile when he reads of Haydn's rage at a careless engraver, or his lament that nothing Artaria ever produced was without printers' errors.

Towards the middle of the 'eighties, Haydn began to enter into negotiations with other publishers—French (Boyer, Sieber) and English (Forster); he got into serious trouble with Forster for selling the same pieces to him and to Artaria, and when Haydn arrived in London, Forster sued Artaria's London agents, Longman & Broderip, and subpoenaed Haydn as a witness.

In 1789, Haydn began the well-known correspondence with Maria Anna von Genzinger.[1] Her husband, Peter Leopold von Genzinger, was a popular "Ladies' Doctor", whom the Empress Maria Theresia had raised to the nobility in 1780; in 1792, he became Rector of the Vienna *Hochschule*. For many years before that, he had been Physician in Ordinary to Prince Nicolaus Esterházy, in which capacity Haydn must have become friendly with him. Genzinger's wife, Maria Anna Sabina (1750–1793) was the daughter of Joseph von Kayser, Prince Batthyáni's Court Councillor, and Maria Anna, *née* von Hackher zu Hart, an old Austrian aristocratic family. She seems to have married Genzinger about 1772 and subsequently bore him five children, three boys and two girls. Her musical education must have been exceptional, for she was able to read full orchestral scores and transcribe them for the pianoforte. The Genzingers gave

[1]The notes on the Genzinger family are drawn from Karajan's charming book *J. Haydn in London*, Vienna 1861, pp. 2*ff*.

soirées to which Vienna's musical élite, including Mozart, was invited.

The correspondence began with a letter to Haydn (her German, incidentally, is several grades more appalling, orthographically, than Haydn's). In the course of the next half dozen letters, it becomes apparent that Haydn was very much attracted to the charming and cultivated "gnädige Frau". Karajan, in 1861, found someone—an acquaintance of Leopold von Sonnleithner—who had been alive at the time, and who reported as follows: "Haydn seems to have cherished not only respect for the artistic abilities of this lady, but also more tender feelings. Their contemporaries knew nothing of such an emotion being returned, however, and Frau von Genzinger's well-disposed attitude towards Haydn seems to have been based purely on friendly attention and on her respect for his artistic position".

In 1790, Prince Nicolaus died, and his successor, Anton, dismissed the band, retaining only music for the hunt and, as nominal *Capellmeister*, Haydn. As is well known, J. P. Salomon came to Vienna and persuaded Haydn to go to England, and the two travellers arrived in Dover on New Year's Day, 1791.

Haydn's London visits are vividly reflected in a number of ways: first, in the letters to his friends, acquaintances and Prince Esterházy in Austria; secondly, in the London Notebooks (see *infra*); and lastly, in the correspondence with his newly gained English friends. One of the principal recipients was Haydn's former mistress, Luigia Polzelli, a mezzo-soprano of mediocre talents whose character seems to have been commensurate with that of most mediocre operatic sopranos no longer in their prime. On 26th March 1779, the Polzelli couple had been engaged in the Esterházy *Capelle*: Antonio, already old, as a violinist, and Luigia, his wife, *née* Moreschi of Naples, then aged nineteen, as singer in the Opera Company. An Italian passport (which Pohl saw) describes her as having a small narrow face, olive skin and dark eyes, chestnut hair and eyebrows, and a graceful figure of medium size. The Prince dismissed them both from his service at the end of December 1780, but Haydn seems to have persuaded the Prince to retain them, even though Antonio was no longer able, because of illness, to fulfil his duties in the orchestra. There were three children, Pietro (born at Bologna in 1777), Antonia (born at Esterháza in 1780, died there two years later) and Aloysius Antonius Nikolaus (born at Esterháza in 1783). It was rumoured that Haydn was the father of the youngest son, but the letters to Luigia (in which there would have been no reason to conceal this fact) never suggest such a thing; moreover, Haydn's favourite seems to have been "Pietruccio".[1]

Upon his return to Vienna in 1795, following the second London visit, Haydn entered the service of Prince Nicolaus II Esterházy, who seems to have been the most unsympathetic of all four Esterházys whom Haydn served. On the one hand, Haydn no longer considered himself a lackey and on the other, Nicolaus seems to have ignored such matters as the French Revolution and to have treated his personnel with a cold, despotic ruthlessness which is sometimes quite appalling, even as reflected in the few documents included below. His charming and beautiful wife, however, won Haydn's heart, and looked after his interests. It was she who interceded with the Prince when matters between Haydn and His Highness were tense; and so, in time, this despotic tyrant, like his more cultivated namesake, became tamed and, towards the end of Haydn's life, almost human and friendly. One revealing story shows the relationship in the early stages: the Prince is said to have walked into one of Haydn's rehearsals and criticized something. "That, Your Highness," answered Haydn, "is my affair." The Prince, white with fury, turned on his heel and left the room. Haydn also insisted that he no longer be addressed like a lackey, in the third person, but as "Herr von Haydn" (the von, though properly indicating nobility, was also used as a term of respect).

The principal publishers during Haydn's declining years were Breitkopf & Härtel, the famous Leipzig house which still exists today, though but a shadow of its former self. As "middle man" between Haydn and Leipzig, Breitkopf & Härtel found an excellent representative in the person of Georg August Griesinger, tutor in the household of the Royal Saxon Legation's Councillor, Count von Schönfeld. Griesinger came to Vienna in 1799, and his letters to Leipzig and about Haydn (which the editor hopes to publish separately) show the famous, now ageing composer in quite a new light. Most of Haydn's correspondence with Griesinger and Breitkopf & Härtel has been preserved: it shows Haydn to be the clever business-man he always was, but also a man who could now afford to be generous with his publishers.

Haydn's contact with Artaria still continued, for having issued his string Quartets of Op. 76, they then took over the distribution of the *Creation*. The composer himself published the full score by subscription, and this venture as a *Selbstverleger* was responsible for

[1]Pohl II, 89*ff.*

many of the letters written and received around the turn of the century.

When Haydn was in the middle of composing the *Seasons*, he was approached by George Thomson, an enterprising Edinburgh publisher, to write the accompaniments to a number of Scottish Songs. In the Autumn of 1799, Thomson sent him a batch of melodies to harmonize; the Secretary of the British Legation in Vienna, Alexander Straton, acted as the go-between, and on 16th February 1800 he wrote to Thomson as follows:

> Dear Sir,
> Haydn called here yesterday and mentioned that he had already written to you and also begun the composition of the accompanyments to the scotch airs (15 in number) that you had sent him through me. He seemed desirous of having rather more than the two Ducats for each air, but did not precisely insist upon this point, which I therefore left undecided [,] exhorting him to proceed with his composition as speedily as its nature as well as that of his other occupations will admit of. This he solemnly promised but said he could not possibly determine a period for finishing the airs in question. Upon the whole he appears to be a rational animal, whereas all that can be said of the other, I mean Koz [eluch] is, that he is a Bipede without feathers.[1]
>
> [Pohl III, 159]

The correspondence with Thomson continued as long as Haydn was able to write letters. In the course of it, we have a tiny letter to Haydn's gifted pupil, Neukomm, hitherto unpublished (*cf.* 3 April 1803), which will be a considerable shock to Haydn scholars. (The letter also provides a neat example of a seemingly insignificant little

[1]Straton had had his troubles with Leopold Anton Koželuch (1752–1818), Court Composer to the Emperor Leopold II. The correspondence, which J. C. Hadden (*George Thomson*, London, 1898) describes as "in some respects rather diverting" shows Straton to have been a man of biting wit. Some years before, on 28th October 1797, he had written of an interview with Koželuch wherein the latter, misunderstanding the peculiar harmonic characteristics of Scottish national music, had "found most of [the songs] *une musique barbare* . . . courtier-like, [I] told M. Koželuch that . . . you would naturally be desirous of seeing a specimen of it in its new garb; and Mr. Koželuch having, by an extraordinary exertion of his mental faculties, fathomed the meaning of my observation, sent me this morning the enclosed paper."

As time went on, and "rude epistle[s]" went back and forth from Koželuch *via* Straton to Thomson, Straton bewails that Thomson's arguments, "however pointed in themselves and forcibly directed, were not tantamount to force a passage through the fated armour which encompasses our friend's intellect". It must have been with considerable relief that Straton turned from Koželuch to the civilized and courteous Haydn, whom he describes, on 19th June 1800, as "poor Haydn [who] laboured under so severe an illness during the course of this spring that we were not altogether devoid of alarm in regard to his discovery".

note revolutionizing our knowledge of the person or persons concerned.) The incongruous postlude to this pleasant exchange of letters occurred early in 1805, when Thomson, hearing the false news of Haydn's death, wrote a letter of condolence to Haydn's bankers in Vienna, Fries & Co. The bankers wrote back a letter, the gist of which Haydn dictated to them (6th February 1805).[2]

The official letters to and from musical societies at home and abroad constitute a considerable part of the letters written after the turn of the century. Most of them were probably drafted by Haydn's friends, such as Griesinger, or the *Abbé* Hofstätter (who is supposed to have written Haydn's reply to the Vienna City Magistracy in May 1803), and in them we miss the pithy personal quality of Haydn's own style. As the composer became steadily weaker, letter writing became more and more of a terrible burden to him, and after about 1805, his hand was too shaky to admit of his doing more than signing the letters.

The London Notebooks, which have been placed together at the end of the correspondence, are an extraordinary mixture of observations, naïve and shrewd, scraps of poetry, Latin aphorisms, addresses, descriptions of places he visited, "anecdotes", banal gossip, and trenchant wit—in short, the typical kind of eighteenth century "commonplace book". To provide the kind of commentary currently in favour with German musicologists would have swelled the notes to about three times the size of the original documents, and I have therefore tried to keep my commentary down to a minimum— the identification of Haydn's music, of the musicians and friends with whom he came in contact, but not, for instance, figures like the Prince of Wales, King George III, *etc.*, the details of whose lives can be found in any encyclopaedia.

Part of one notebook is filled with Haydn's copies of love letters he received from Rebecca Schroeter, widow of Johann Samuel Schroeter (Warsaw 1750—London 1788), J. C. Bach's successor as Master of the Queen's Music and a first-rate pianist. As a composer

---

[2]B.M. Add MS. 35263, f. 255 (French). The letter is not strictly Haydn's and thus had not been included in the main body of the text below:

"Kindly say to Mr. Thomson that Haydn is very sensible of the distress that the news of his alleged death has caused him, and that this sign of affection has added, if that be possible, to the esteem and friendship he will always entertain for Mr. Thomson . . . You will notice that he has put his name and the date on the sheet of music to give better proof that he is still in this base world. At the same time he begs to have the letter of condolence copied and the copy sent to him. . . . "

he was very much under the shadow of J. C. Bach (as who, in England at that time, was not?), and it must have been out of politeness to the widow that Haydn carted home to Vienna several of Schroeter's harpsichord Concertos. It is reported that Schroeter "married a young lady of considerable fortune, who was his scholar" (*Rees's Cyclopedia*), but the marriage seems not to have been a very happy one.

It is surprising that a love affair of these proportions, between the famous Haydn and a lady of London Society, managed to escape the gossip hounds of the day; it must have been conducted very discreetly indeed. It is also curious that Haydn copied the letters into his notebook: the explanation is perhaps that when Haydn left London the second time and for good, Mistress Schroeter demanded the letters to be returned, and Haydn, for whom the affair must have meant a good deal, too, wanted to keep copies of them. The letters date only from the first London trip, 1791 and 1792; but Haydn, during his second journey, lived within a short walking distance of Mrs. Schroeter, and perhaps it was no longer necessary to exchange letters; or perhaps Haydn made no copies of them. The affair probably did continue in 1794 and 1795, however, for the composer dedicated three of his most beautiful pianoforte Trios to her (Opus 73, Longman & Broderip 1795, Nos. 24–26 of the chronological list).

It is typical of Haydn's mentality that he should have made friends with so many English people (rather than keeping to the German speaking community which was quite numerous at that time in London). To judge from his notebooks, he seems to have had a very large circle of acquaintances, ranging from the Prince of Wales and other members of the nobility to "Mister March, . . . dentist, *Carossieur* [*sic*. Carrossieur = coachmaker] and dealer in wines." On the other hand, he seems to have been quite genuinely shocked at the heavy drinking in England, at the "miserable trash" played at the English opera and the "common people's" reaction to it, and at what he calls "English fanaticism". We shall probably never know why he finally returned to Vienna (where, for example, his arrival had been scarcely noticed in 1792), but possibly he felt, that at sixty-three, he could not keep up with the pace of London indefinitely.

Of the other letters, *i.e.* apart from those written to the principal recipients noted above, the editor would draw the reader's attention to one in particular, written on 23 November 1793 to the Elector of

Cologne. The letter concerns Haydn's pupil Beethoven, and extraordinary as it sounds, this highly significant document is all but
unknown in English-speaking countries (it was discovered and first
printed in 1935: see Sources). The letter is interesting for a number
of obvious reasons, but among others, it shows how much London
had changed Haydn; he could never have written such a letter before
experiencing the country which was then, as perhaps now, the only
true democracy in the world. Interested readers are invited to compare Haydn's early letters to Prince Esterházy with that to the mighty
Kurfürst, wherein (politely sprinkled among the usual formulae of
the day) Haydn raps the Serene Electoral knuckles in a way which is
quite unprecedented in Haydn's (and perhaps also in the *Kurfürst's*)
earlier correspondence. The letter also enables us in future to dispense
with pages of second- and third-hand trash concerning Haydn's
relationship to his young and brilliant pupil.

In closing, I would add a word concerning the illustrations. A
selection of Haydn's letters in German, French, English and Italian is
designed to show his handwriting in all these languages and further
to provide scholars with the possibility of comparing his handwriting from 1761 to 1805. Since there are no letters extant before
1765, I have placed side by side receipts of the years 1761, 1799 and
1804. One of Haydn's drafts (to his brother Michael) has also been
included, for a person's handwriting, when making notes for himself, can be considerably different from that appearing on the final fair
copy. As a striking example of such a difference, I have included
details from two copies of the same letter, one to Prince Nicolaus
Esterházy and one, a "cover letter" to the Princely *Secretaire*,
Scheffstoss, quoting the letter to the Prince and asking if it can be sent
in that form. Johann Elssler, the copyist-*cum*-valet, who plays such
an important rôle in Haydn's later years, is represented by three
documents: two addresses and the texts of a letter which Haydn
signed. A specimen page from one of the London Notebooks has
been included. Apart from these literary documents, I have
included *inter alia* a newly discovered profile of J. P. Salomon by
George Dance (whose Haydn drawing the composer considered the
best portrait made of him in England), and the beautiful wax bust of
Haydn by Thaller, which, for some curious reason, is not very well
known, though it is one of the best preserved likenesses. The name of
Mozart frequently appears in these pages: rather than reproduce one
of the Mozart portraits—all of which are known and have been
printed countless times—I have chosen one of the most touching

documents extant of Mozart's musical affection for his older friend. Professor Walter Senn recently discovered a contemporary MS. copy of Haydn's string Quartets Op. 17 with holograph corrections and additions in Mozart's hand. The source is part of a unique collection of Mozartiana owned by the Heilig-Kreuz-Kirche in Augsburg, whence it came from Leopold Mozart's legacy. Professor Senn, with whom the editor has been in friendly contact for many years, was kind enough to send me photographs of several specimen sheets, one of which graces these pages.

ABBREVIATIONS

Artaria-Botstiber: F. Artaria & H. Botstiber, *Joseph Haydn und das Verlagshaus Artaria*, Vienna 1909.

Brand: Carl Maria Brand, *Die Messen von Joseph Haydn*, Würzburg 1941.

Dies: A. C. Dies, *Biographische Nachrichten von Joseph Haydn*, Vienna 1810.

Griesinger: G. A. Griesinger, *Biographische Notizen über Joseph Haydn*, Leipzig 1810.

Hase: H. von Hase, *Joseph Haydn und Breitkopf & Härtel*, Leipzig 1909.

Hoboken: A. van Hoboken, *Joseph Haydn: Thematisch-bibliographisches Werkverzeichnis, Band I*, Mainz 1957.

Karajan: T. von Karajan, *J. Haydn in London, 1791 und 1792*, Vienna 1861.

Landon: H. C. Robbins Landon, *The Symphonies of Joseph Haydn*, London 1955.

Larsen: J. P. Larsen, *Die Haydn-Überlieferung*, Copenhagen 1939.

Marton Coll.: Copies of Haydn letters in the Esterházy Archives made by Dr. Eugen Marton (*Österreichische Nationalbibliothek*, Vienna).

Nohl: L. Nohl, *Musiker-Briefe*, 2nd ed., Leipzig 1873.

Pohl I: C. F. Pohl, *Joseph Haydn* (Vol. I), Berlin 1875.

Pohl II: ditto (Vol. II), Leipzig 1882.

Pohl III: *Joseph Haydn: Unter Benutzung der von C. F. Pohl hinterlassenen Materialien weitergeführt von Hugo Botstiber*, Leipzig 1927.

Pohl Denkschrift: C. F. Pohl, *Denkschrift aus Anlass des Hundertjährigen Bestehens der Tonkünstler-Societät . . .* Vienna 1871.

Pohl H. in L.: C. F. Pohl, *Haydn in London*, Vienna 1867.

(For monetary abbreviations, see Preface).

THE COLLECTED CORRESPONDENCE

THE COLLECTED CORRESPONDENCE

[To Prince Nicolaus Esterházy. *German*]
Serene Highness and Noble Prince of the Holy Roman Empire,
Gracious and dread Lord![1]

I have received with every submissive and dutiful respect Your Illustrious and Serene Highness' letter of the 8th inst. addressed to me, and I see from it that Your Highness has taken it very amiss that I protested against the detention of the *flauto traverso* player Frantz Sigl[2] to Herr von Rahier,[3] whose commands I am now admonished to follow, in order that I may behave better in the future, on penalty of the dread displeasure of my Serene Highness. Most Serene Highness! Gracious Lord! On behalf of the above-named *flauto traverso* player, because of whom the fire started, I went with the whole band to Herr von Rahier, and it was not on account of the detention, but only on account of the rude detention and the hard treatment of the subject that I protested, but with all proper respect, to Herr von Rahier. But we could not get anywhere with the administrator, and I even had to put up with his slamming the door in my face, he pushed all the others out, and threatened everyone with detention. Similarly, this very day Friberth[4] fled excitedly from the administrator (on account of not doffing his hat, which must have been an oversight), and does not dare to come home, because this same administrator pretends that the first-mentioned Friberth was rude to him, and that therefore he will mete out his own punishment. But I testify, as do all the other musicians, that Friberth did nothing else except that, when the administrator threatened all of us with detention—and without any reason—he said he had no other master but His Serene Highness, Prince Esterházy. I myself told the administrator to complain to Your Serene and Illustrious Highness if he felt his own person to have been insulted, but I was given the answer that the administrator is his own judge and will meet out the punishment himself. Everyone is very upset on this account, they find this treatment very unfair and hope that Your Serene and Gracious Highness' intentions certainly do not extend this far, and that for this reason you will graciously put a stop to such a procedure [*Potere*] whereby anyone can be his own judge without differentiating between guilty or not guilty.

The orders of the oft-mentioned administrator (as YOUR SERENE AND GRACIOUS HIGHNESS knows anyway) have been correctly carried out at all times, and as often as I receive through him an order of YOUR SERENE AND GRACIOUS HIGHNESS, I shall always execute it to the best of my ability; if therefore the administrator has complained in this regard, it must be the result of his angry pen. But moreover YOUR SERENE AND ILLUSTRIOUS HIGHNESS must yourself remember, in your graciousness, that I cannot serve two masters, and cannot accept the commands of, and subordinate myself to, the administrator, for YOUR SERENE AND ILLUSTRIOUS HIGHNESS once said to me: COME FIRST TO ME, BECAUSE I AM HIS[5] MASTER.

I am therefore confident that YOUR SERENE AND ILLUSTRIOUS HIGHNESS will not receive ungraciously this my most submissive and obedient letter, but will regard me and the whole band with gracious eyes, and, since everyone is desirous of this grace, that you will watch over us in fatherly protection. I hope for further marks of favour and grace from YOUR HIGHNESS and I remain ever, with every mark of profound respect,

YOUR SERENE AND GRACIOUS HIGHNESS'
most humble and obedient
Josephus Haydn.

Eisenstadt, 9th September 1765

[On the outside, in another hand, the date of the letter again and the following summary of its contents: "Excusatio Capellae Magistri Haydn adversus delationem Regentis de Rahier".]

[1] "Durchleuchtig Hochgebohrner Reichsfürst./Gnädigst Hochgebiettender Herr Herr!"

[2] FRANZ SIEGL was flautist in the Esterházy band from 1762 to 1769.

[3] *Wirthschaftsrath* and administrator ("Regent") of the Esterházy Castle at Eisenstadt.

[4] CARL FRIBERTH, tenor of the Esterházy band from 1759 to 1776. Friberth also arranged and translated libretti: he wrote the word-book for Haydn's opera, *L'incontro improvviso* of 1775.

[5] Esterházy would have addressed Haydn and any other servant in the third person. It was not until his return from London that Haydn forced his Prince (then Nicolaus II) to drop this degrading form of address.

[RAHIER TO PRINCE NICOLAUS ESTERHÁZY. *German*]

Most gracious Prince!

Yesterday *Kapellmeister* Haydn and Friberth came to see me; the latter humbly apologized for his unsuitable conversation recently and asked that it be forgiven him. I answered him that I had already informed Your Highness and that you would take any further action. But since he apologized so humbly, I respectfully suggest to Your Highness that this time you graciously leave it at the humble apology . . . Siegl has served his detention and has been set at liberty . . .

Rahier m.pr.

1765, 13th September.

[To Haydn. Draft of an order from Prince Nicolaus Esterházy. *German*]
Regulatio Chori Kissmartoniensis[1]

Inasmuch as the musicians of the Eisenstadt Chapel Choir have produced a great disorder in the choir-loft, because of indolence and lack of discipline, and have neglected the instruments through poor care and storage, *Capellmeister* Haydn [*sic*] is herewith earnestly enjoined as follows:

First, to prepare a catalogue, in three identical copies, of all the extant instruments in the choir-loft, as well as of the music, according to the enclosed formula, with indication of the composers, number of parts, *etc.*, and will deliver the same within eight days: one to us, the second to the bookkeeper's office, and the third to the choir-loft.

Secondly, to deliver the necessary music for each service to the schoolmaster Joseph Diezl,[2] put it in their proper order after the service, and have it returned to, and stored in, the cupboards wherein it belongs, so that nothing will be taken away or miscatalogued.

Thirdly, to see to it that the schoolmaster keeps all the instruments constantly in good repair and in proper order, to which end said schoolmaster should always appear in the choir-loft a quarter of an hour before the service begins.

Fourthly, to take especial pains to ensure that all the players appear regularly at the church services and fulfil their duty and obligations in a proper and disciplined way.

Fifthly, to hold in our absence two musical concerts [*Academien*] every week in the Officers' room at Eisenstadt, *viz.*, on Tuesdays and Saturdays from 2 to 4 o'clock in the afternoon. All the musicians shall appear and to assure that in future no one is absent without permission from the church services or concerts (as was the case hitherto), a written report will be delivered to us every fortnight, with the name of, and reason for, anyone presuming to absent themselves from duty.

Finally, said *Capel Meister* Haydn is urgently enjoined to apply himself to composition more diligently than heretofore, and especially to write such pieces as can be played on the gamba,[3] of which pieces we have seen very few up to now; and to be able to judge his diligence, he shall at all times send us the first copy, cleanly and carefully written, of each and every new composition.[4]

[Nicolaus, Prince Esterházy]

Süttör, the [blank = October or November] 1765.

[1]Kismarton, the Latin (and Hungarian) name for Eisenstadt.

[2]JOSEPH DIEZL (see also page 12), a tenor, was in charge of the church choir. He entered the Prince's service in 1753 and remained in it until his death, in 1777.

[3]The baryton, Prince Nicolaus's favourite instrument.

[4]Süttör was the hunting lodge which stood on the grounds later occupied by Estoras (Esterháza) Castle. The reason for the existence of this document is seen if we examine a letter, dated October 1765, which Haydn's superior, *Capellmeister* Gregorius Werner (who was to die the next year, and whose letter was "written from [his] sick-bed") sent to the Prince. Werner bitterly complains about Haydn's supposed lack of discipline and the chaotic conditions of the music in the choir-loft; the letter also contains an accusation that, as a result of Haydn's neglect, the instruments were being pilfered. The document (Esterházy Archives, Acta Musicalia, Fasc. I, 84) was published by J. Harich in *Muzicka* (Budapest), II, 1930, Nos. 4 and 5. Prince Esterházy's letter to Haydn is nevertheless a harsh reprimand, especially the last paragraph, wherein Haydn is "enjoined to apply himself to composition more diligently . . . ."—a grotesque accusation if we remember his enormous output from 1761–1765. But this despotic letter may have been the cause of Haydn's beginning his thematic *Entwurf-Katalog* (Draft Catalogue), which is so vital to establishing authenticity and chronology in his music. Haydn soon managed to satisfy the Prince, as is shown by an extract from Esterházy's letter to *Wirthschaftsrath* von Rahier, dated Esterháza Castle, 4th January 1766: " . . . This very moment I received 3 pieces from Hayden, and I am very satisfied with them. You will therefore see that he gets 12 ducats from the cashier's office in my name; tell him at the same time to write 6 more pieces similar to those he sent me, and also 2 Solo pieces, and to see that they are sent here at once . . ." See Pohl I, 248*f*.

[TO PRINCE NICOLAUS ESTERHÁZY. *German*]
MOST SERENE HIGHNESS AND NOBLE PRINCE OF THE HOLY ROMAN EMPIRE GRACIOUS AND DREAD LORD!

The most joyous occasion of your name day[1] (may YOUR HIGH-NESS celebrate it in divine Grace and enjoy it in complete well-being and felicity!) obliges me not only to deliver to you in profound submission 6 new Divertimenti,[2] but also to say that we were de-lighted to receive, a few days ago, our new Winter clothes—and submissively to kiss the hem of your robe for this especial act of grace: adding that, despite YOUR HIGHNESS' much regretted absence, we shall nevertheless venture to wear these new clothes for the first time during the celebration of High Mass on YOUR HIGHNESS' name day. I have received YOUR HIGHNESS' order to have the Diverti-menti I wrote (twelve pieces in all) bound. But since YOUR HIGHNESS has returned some of them to me to be altered, and I have not noted the changes in my score, I would respectfully ask you to let me have the first twelve you have at hand for three days, and then the others one after the other, so that apart from the required changes, they may be all neatly and correctly copied and bound: in this connection I would like to ask respectfully in which way YOUR HIGHNESS would like to have them bound?

Incidentally, the two oboe players report (and I myself must agree with them) that their oboes are so old that they are collapsing, and no longer keep the proper pitch [*Tonum*]; for this reason I would humbly point out to YOUR HIGHNESS that there is a master Rockobauer in Vienna, who in my opinion is the most skilful for this sort of work. But because this master is continually busy with work of this kind, and since it requires an exceptionally long time to complete a pair of good and durable oboes with an extra length of reed pipe (as a result of which, however, all the necessary notes can be produced)—for these reasons the cheapest price is 8 ducats. I therefore await YOUR HIGHNESS' gracious consent whether the abovementioned and most urgently needed two oboes may be constructed for the price indicated.[3] I hope for your favour and grace,

YOUR SERENE AND GRACIOUS HIGHNESS'
most humble
Joseph Haydn.

[5th December 1766][4]

[1]"Nahmens Fest" or "Namenstag" (the modern and more usual form): Festival of the anniversary of one's saint. St. Nicholas' Day falls on December 6th.

[2]Divertimenti for baryton, viola and 'cello. We cannot determine exactly which works are described, but they may have been among HV 21–31, of which HV 24 is dated 1766 (see Larsen, pp. 227*ff.*).

[3]MATHIAS ROCKOBAUER seems not to have delivered the oboes; at least the Esterházy Archives show no record of his having made them. One receipt, dated 30th December 1766 and countersigned by Haydn, lists only woodwind mouthpieces. Another, of 20th June 1767 (countersigned by Haydn a week later), also lists only mouthpieces for oboes and English horns; while a third, of 25th September 1767, concerns the repair of an English horn. The first document in the Marton Coll. (VNat), the other two in Astrid Valkó, p. 649.

[4]The date recorded on the letter by the Esterházy administration: the letter was probably delivered by a messenger the same day.

[To Anton Scheffstoss, "Secretaire" and Chief Bookkeeper of
the Esterházy Administration. *German*]

†

Eisenstadt, 20th March 1768.

Nobly born,
Highly respected Sir![1]

You will recall that last year I set to music with all my power the
highly esteemed hymn, called Stabat Mater, and that I sent it to the
great and world-celebrated Hasse[2] with no other intention than that
in case, here and there, I had not expressed adequately words of such
great importance, this lack could be rectified by a master so successful in all forms of music. But contrary to my merits, this unique
artist honoured the work by inexpressible praise, and wished nothing
more than to hear it performed with the good players it requires.
Since, however, there is a great want of singers *utriusque generis* in
Vienna, I would therefore humbly and obediently ask His Serene
and Gracious Highness through you, Sir, to allow me, Weigl and
his wife,[3] and Friberth[4] to go to Vienna next Thursday, there on
Friday afternoon at the FFr.:Miseric:[5] to further the honour of our
gracious prince by the performance of his servant; we would return
to Eisenstadt on Saturday evening.

If His Highness so wishes, someone other than Friberth could
easily be sent up. Dearest Mons. Scheffstoss, please expedite my
request; I remain, with the most profound veneration,

Your nobly born Sir's
most devoted
Josephus Haydn, [m.] pria.

P.S. My compliments to all the gentlemen. The promised Divertimenti[6] will surely be delivered to His Highness one of these next
weeks.

[1]"Wohl Edl Gebohrn/In Sonders HochgeEhrtester Herr!" Concerning
Scheffstoss, see also n.3 *infra*.
[2]J. A. Hasse (1699–1783), especially well known for his vocal music.
[3]Joseph Weigl, the 'cellist, who had joined the band in June, 1761. In 1764
he married Anna Maria Josepha, the daughter of Anton Scheffstoss, who
had been engaged as soprano in the church choir in 1760. Haydn was
devoted to the family and was godparent to their first child, Joseph (born
1766). See letter of 11 January 1794.
[4]See p. 3.
[5]The Order of the Brothers of Mercy (Ger.: Barmherzige Brüder), whose
Viennese convent in the Leopoldstadt (now 2nd district) is still extant.
[6]Baryton Trios. We cannot identify exactly which ones are referred to.

[LETTER TO AN UN-NAMED AUSTRIAN MONASTERY—PROBABLY
ZWETTL IN LOWER AUSTRIA—ACCOMPANYING THE SCORE OF
THE *Applausus* CANTATA (1768). *German*]
[Undated: but written in 1768][1]

Since I cannot be present myself at this *Applaus* [*sc.*: *Applausus*],
I have found it necessary to provide one or two explanations concerning its execution, *viz.*:

First, I would ask you to observe strictly the tempi of all the arias
and recitatives, and since the whole text applauds, I would rather
have the allegros taken a bit more quickly than usual, especially in
the very first ritornello and in one or two of the recitatives; but no
less in the two bass arias.

Secondly: for the overture all you need to play is an allegro and
an andante, for the opening ritornello takes the place of the final
allegro. If I knew the day of the performance, I might perhaps send
you a new overture by that time.

Thirdly: in the accompanied recitatives, you must observe that
the accompaniment should not enter until the singer has quite
finished his text, even though the score often shows the contrary.
For instance, at the beginning where the word "metamorphosis" is
repeated, and the orchestra comes in at "-phosis", you must nevertheless wait until the last syllable is finished and then enter quickly;
for it would be ridiculous if you would fiddle away the word from
the singer's mouth, and understand only the words "quae metamo
. . . ". But I leave this to the harpsichord player, and all the others
must follow him. N.B.: our scholars in Eisenstadt—and there are
very few—disputed a great deal over the word "metamorphosis";
one wanted the penultimate syllable short, the other long; and
despite the fact that in Italian one says "metamōrfosi", I have always
heard it pronounced "metamorphōsis" in Latin; should I have made
a mistake, the error can be easily corrected.

Fourthly: that the fortes and pianos are written correctly throughout, and should be observed exactly; for there is a very great difference between *piano* and *pianissimo*, *forte* and *fortiss[imo]*, between
crescendo and *forzando*, and so forth. It should be noted, too, when in
the score the one or the other *forte* or *piano* is not marked throughout
all the parts, that the copyist should rectify this when preparing the
performance material.

Fifthly: I have often been annoyed at certain violinists in various
concerts, who absolutely ruined the so-called ties—which are among
the most beautiful things in music—in that they bounced the bows

off the tied note, which should have been joined to the preceding note. And so I would point out to the first violinist that it would be silly to play the following (as found in bar 47)

—in which the first two notes are to be taken on one bow—in such a disagreeable and mistaken way as

all staccato, and as if there were no ties present.

Sixthly: I would ask you to use two players on the viola part throughout, for the inner parts sometimes need to be heard more than the upper parts, and you will find in all my compositions that the viola rarely doubles the bass.

Seventhly: if you have to copy two sets of violin parts, the copyist should see that they do not turn their pages at the same time, because this takes away a great deal of strength from an orchestra with only a few musicians. The copyist should also see that the *da capo* signs ⁏⁏ are written in one of the violin parts as in the score, but in the other he can put the *da capo* a couple of bars after the sign ⁏⁏, and then write the sign in its proper place.

Eighthly: I suggest that the two boys [soloists] in particular have a clear pronunciation, singing slowly in recitatives so that one can understand every syllable; and likewise they should follow the method of singing the recitation whereby, for example 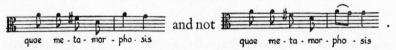 must be sung

The penultimate note "g" drops out entirely, and this applies to all similar cases. I rely on the skill of the tenor, who will explain such things to the boys.

Ninthly: I hope for at least three or four rehearsals for the entire work.

Tenthly: in the soprano aria the bassoon can be omitted if absolutely necessary, but I would rather have it present, at least when the bass is *obbligato* throughout. And I prefer a band with 3 bass instruments—'cello, bassoon and double bass—to one with 6 double basses and 3 'celli, because certain passages stand out better that way. Finally I ask everyone, and especially the musicians, for the sake of my reputation as well as their own, to be as diligent as possible: if I have perhaps not guessed the taste of these gentlemen, I am not to be blamed for it, for I know neither the persons nor the place, and that fact that they were concealed from me really made my work very difficult. For the rest, I hope that this *Applausus* will please the poet, the worthy musicians, and the honourable reverend *Auditorio*, all of whom I greet with profound respect, and for whom I remain

Your most obedient servant,

Giuseppe Haydn.

Maestro di Cap: di Sua Alt:

Sere: Prencipe d'Estorhazy.

[1]The autograph of the *Applausus* Cantata is dated 1768 (Gesellschaft der Musikfreunde, Vienna). For many years it was not known for which Austrian monastery the work was intended: Haydn himself, as an old man, believed Kremsmünster and added a note to this effect over the *incipit* of the work in his *Entwurf-Katalog*. Pohl, having discovered that Kremsmünster was the wrong place, decided on Göttweig (because a new abbot had been installed there in August 1768). Leopold Nowak, however, shows convincingly that *Applausus* was probably intended for the birthday celebration of the abbot of Zwettl Monastery (Lower Austria); this was where the autograph, the letter, and a set of parts were discovered. Previously, Haydn scholars had forgotten that *Applausus* was written, not for the installation of an abbot, but to celebrate a birthday, and had consequently overlooked the obvious choice of Zwettl because there was no installation of an abbot there during 1768. See Nowak's *Haydn*, p. 206. It is most curious that Haydn was not informed of the circumstances for which *Applausus* was intended as the *pièce de resistance*.

[To ANTON SCHEFFSTOSS, "SECRETAIRE" AND CHIEF BOOKKEEPER OF THE ESTERHÁZY ADMINISTRATION. *German*]

✝

Nobly born,

Highly respected Sir!

I send you herewith my petition to His Highness, reading as follows:

Your Serene Highness, etc.

Your Illustrious and Serene Highness graciously gave me to understand, not long hence, that not only was the Rent Collector

Frantz Nigst[1] found superfluous as a violinist, but also Joseph Diezl[2] as a member of the band; and moreover I was ordered to demand the 2 uniforms from the former. Concerning the former, *i.e.*, Franz Nigst, I must respectfully persuade Your Highness, and admit myself candidly, that the second violin section in all the operas hitherto produced was, with him, in the best possible hands, because he is the only one capable of leading the seconds: therefore if he were dismissed, one would fear for the future on account of the mistakes which would creep in—that is, unless Your Highness were minded graciously to engage another permanent second violinist, or to have one come from Vienna when we produce operas. Because there are no other players for the seconds except the horn players Frantz[3] and May,[4] with whom one is really not properly equipped. It is true that if the whole band goes to Esterház next year, he could not be in Esterház permanently on account of the rent office, but nevertheless it is my humble opinion that he should be brought to Esterház when the Imperial and Royal Court, or other high dignitaries, are present there. I humbly ask Your Highness, moreover, graciously to allow him the yearly 50 Gulden, and also the Winter and Summer clothes (in which he has already seen service in Esterház). Joseph Dietzl [*sic*] is in my opinion especially necessary in the choir loft if the whole band goes off to Esterház, so that the customary church services can be held by him, his *praeceptor* and the boy choristers who are in his apprenticeship. I hear from many people that he cannot possibly support himself with his position as schoolmaster. I ask you humbly to grant him in your graciousness enough so that he can live.

In case you find anything imprudent in the above, please kindly let me know of it at once. I flatter myself that through my petition and through your confirmation of it, something may have an effect on His Highness.

Apart from wishing you best greetings for the coming Holidays, and a happy farewell to the old and welcome to the new year, I am,

Highly respected Sir,
Your obedient servant,
Joseph Haydn [m.] pria.

Eisenstadt, 22nd December 1768.

[A second copy, to the prince, has instead of the last two paragraphs addressed to Scheffstoss, the following addressed to the Prince:]

In the next few days I will respectfully send YOUR ILLUSTRIOUS

AND SERENE HIGHNESS some new trios,[5] and I most humbly commend myself to your high favour and grace,

YOUR ILLUSTRIOUS AND SERENE HIGHNESS'

most humble

Joseph Haydn.

Eisenstadt, 22nd December 1768.

[Another hand has noted, on the cover of the file, the letter's date and a
short summary of its contents in Latin.]

[1]FRANTZ NIGST, violinist in the band from 1760 to 1772. When he was
engaged in 1760, his contract read *inter alia*: " . . . Must attend the church
choir, and make himself useful in the *Tafelmusique*, and in copying music."
Pohl II, 372.

[2]See p. 5. In the copy to Prince Esterházy, Haydn writes "Dietzl".

[3]KARL FRANZ, a member of the band from 1763 to 1776, was also an excellent baryton player. See Pohl I, 267.

[4]JOHANN MAY, a member of the band from 1765 to 1772 (Pohl II, 373).

[5]Baryton trios. We cannot identify exactly which ones are referred to.

[TO PRINCE NICOLAUS ESTERHÁZY. *German*]

[Autumn, 1770]

Serene Highness and Noble Prince of the Holy Roman Empire,
Gracious and dread Lord!

In order to purchase my house, I had to borrow 400 Gulden in
cash some years ago, and now this capital has been recalled. Since I
do not have the sum, I wanted to take out another loan in this
amount (on which I would pay interest) to repay the debt. But I
could not find any creditors here in Eisenstadt, and inasmuch as I
have to repay this loan soon, I would humbly ask Your Highness
graciously to allow me to have these 400 Gulden, against a receipt
from the cashier's office, whereby the 50 Gulden I receive quarterly
from that source (of which the first payment is due to me by the end
of January 1771) would be withheld until such time as the whole debt
is repaid. I most humbly commend myself to your favour and
grace,

Your Serene Highness'

most humble

Josephus Haydn.

[Another hand has noted on the cover of the file a short summary of the
letter's contents (in German), and a third hand has added the following
note: "Vide resolu[tion]em Parts. Miscit. D. Fol. 5", referring to a
parallel file. Haydn's request was granted.]

CONTRACT BETWEEN ZACHARIUS POHL[1] AND XAVIER MARTEAU[2]
IN HAYDN'S PRESENCE. *German*]
*Contractum inter Zachariam Pohl et Xaverium Marteau
Musicos vi cuius hic ob laesum Musici Pohl oculum ad respondas
in curam habitans expensas senet obligat.*

This day on the date and year recorded below is herewith set
down and agreed the following settlement and contract between the
Princely Esterházy oboist, Zacharias Pohl, and the Princely Esterházy bass-player, Xavier Marteau, because of the scandalous brawl
between them which occurred on the 23rd of the previous month of
June in the Esterházy Castle Tavern, whereby Zacharias Pohl lost his
right eye; to wit:—

Whereas, according to the statements of both parties and various
witnesses, it may be surmised that Xavier Marteau did not pur-
posely intend to inflict this damage with his ring on the eye of
Zacharias Pohl, but on the other hand, Zacharias Pohl is not entirely
guiltless, both parties have therefore agreed, in the presence of
Herr Kappelmeister Hayden [*sic*], to the following settlement: that
Xavier Marteau shall recompense Zacharias Pohl for the costs of the
cure and trip arising from the above-mentioned damage, in the
amount of forty-nine Gulden 13 Kreutzer, within six months, at the
rate of 8 Gulden 17⅙ Kr. per month, of which the first 8 Fl. 17⅙ Kr.
are to be paid on the first of January 1772; but Zacharias Pohl,
because of the indemnification here given him as a result of the
damage to his eye, shall not and can not demand anything at any
time from Xavier Marteau.

As witness thereto both parties have set their hands and their
customary seals.

Eisenstadt, the 21st of December 1771.

> L.s. Zacharias Pohl,
> > *hochfürstlicher Hautboist.*
> L.s. Xavier Marteau,
> > *hochfürstlicher Bassetist.*
> In my presence: Josephus Haydn,
> > *Hochfürstlicher Capellmeister* L.s.

[1]POHL was engaged in 1769 and remained in the band until his death, in 1781.
[2]FRANZ XAVIER MARTEAU (*recte*: Hammer) was a 'cellist and double-bass
player in the band from 1771 to 1778. He was also a composer.

[To Anton Scheffstoss, "Secretaire" and Chief Bookkeeper
of the Esterházy administration. *German*]

†

Eisenstadt, 9th January 1772.

Nobly born and highly respected *Monsieur* Scheffstoss,
    You have my grateful thanks for all your kind efforts on behalf of
my wishes, the fulfilment of which is the result of your intercession
for me. I would have thanked you long ago and acknowledged my
indebtedness, if I were not, and had not been, prevented by illness.
Dearest Monsieur Scheffstoss, please also help Marteau[1] through
your kindness to get the 6 cords of wood, 30 lbs. of candles, and
30 Gulden lodging money which should be his, and which His Highness promised me to give him; the mistake in this case lies in his
contract, according to which he is to receive the same allowance as
Lidl,[2] although even in Lidl's contract there is no mention of the
30 lbs. of candles (which, I assure you on my honour, His Highness
agreed to grant him). Apart from this please present my respectful
compliments to your wife and the Weigl[3] family (to whom I shall
write shortly), and to all other good friends. And I remain, with all
respect, noble Sir,

Your obedient servant,
Josephus Haydn.

[On the cover of the file, in another hand: "circa melioratione in Salarii
Musicae Marton exoperans".][4]

[1]See p. 14.
[2]Andreas Lidl, a baryton (and presumably 'cello) player, was a member of
the band from 1769 to 1774.
[3]See p. 8.
[4]In the *Prothocoll über verschiedene hochfürstl. Commissiones, Decretationes,
Intimata und andere Buchhaltereys Verordungenen de Anno 1734 [et seq.]* (Esterházy Archives, fasc. 2488, No. 776), we learn that Haydn's request was
quickly granted: "Resolution of His Serene Highness, dated Vienna, 14th
January 1772, according to which the bass player Marton [*sic*] is to be
granted annually six cords of firewood, 30 lbs. of candles and 30 Fl.
lodging money. . . ."

[To Prince Nicolaus Esterházy. *German*]
[Apparently an archive copy in a copyist's hand]
[March 1773]

Most Serene and Noble Prince of the Holy Roman Empire,
Gracious and dread Lord!
    Your Highness intimated to me, through His Highness' secretary

Schefstoss[1] [*sic*.] that you would be minded graciously and generously to provide a year's salary to me and to those chamber musicians
who entered the service of Your Serene Highness' brother[2] (provided
that each of us would submit a petition to that effect to Your
Highness).

May I therefore ask, in profound submissiveness, that Your
Highness confirm, in your infinite kindness, your willingness to
grant us this exceptionally gracious mark of esteem. For this, I shall
offer you at all times my most faithful services, and I recommend
myself to your serene favour and grace.

Your Serene Highness'
most humble
Joseph Hayden [*sic*]
Capell-Meister

[Address:] To His Serene and Noble Highness, Prince of the Holy
Roman Empire, Lord and Sire, Nicolaum Esterházy von Galantha,
Knight of the Golden Fleece, Privy Councillor in actual service of
His Imperial and Royal Majesty, General Field Marshal of the
Imperial and Royal Aristocratic Guards, Captain &c. &c. My
gracious Prince and Sire: this humble request is submitted *ut intus* by
CapellMster Haydn.

> [On the same sheet containing the above address is the following autograph
> note by Prince Esterházy: "If there is no counter-claim, the suppliant should
> be paid one year's salary according to the contract then in force, minus ten
> percent inheritance tax; this sum is to be paid out by our Chief Cashier's
> Office, but the sum for the inheritance tax is to be delivered to Doctor
> Sonleithner[3] after securing the necessary receipt. Vienna, 1st April 1773.
> Nicolaus Fürst Esterhazy m.p."]
> [1]*Recte*: Scheffstoss; see also p. 8.
> [2]PRINCE PAUL ANTON, who had died on 18th March 1762, at the age of fifty.
> [3]CHRISTOPH SONNLEITHNER (1734–1786), lawyer and also composer (his
> symphonies were passed off as Haydn's), who managed the Prince's legal
> affairs in Vienna.

[HAYDN'S RECEIPT TO THE ESTERHÁZY CASHIER FOR MONEYS RECEIVED
AS A RESULT OF THE ABOVE PETITION. *German*]

†

I, the undersigned, herewith acknowledge to have received
correctly and in cash from Herr Züsser, receiver-general of the
Princely Cashier's Office, the sum of 400 Fl. (in words: Gulden four

hundred), which according to a decree issued by His Serene Highness has been bequeathed to me as *qua* staff officer under the pro-
visions of the last will and testament of his late lamented Highness
Prince Antony Esterházy; and I acknowledge further that I cannot
make any other claim whatever on the Princely house.
Eisenstadt Castle, the 29th of April 1773.

Josephus Haydn [m.]pria
Capell Meister

[TO PRINCE NICOLAUS ESTERHÁZY. *German*]

[*c.* 18th March 1774][1]

Most Serene and Noble Prince of the Holy Roman Empire,
Gracious Prince and Lord!

Inasmuch as Your Serene Highness has ordered a month's salary
to be docked from the musicians Marteau,[2] Specht,[3] and Chorus,[4] I
humbly beg to remind Your Serene Highness graciously to remember how in Vienna recently, I myself asked and kindly received permission of Your Highness for Marteau to absent himself for a few
days. The reason why he remained a little longer is that he copied
some new concerti there, and also had to have his violoncello re-
paired. Concerning Chorus, there was not enough time to inform
Your Highness in advance of the fact that he had the chance to go
there [to Vienna] with Dr. Bertrand (who prescribed a change of air
for him on account of his constant ill health) for nothing, at no cost;
and it fell to me to give him permission to go. As far as Specht goes,
it so happened that his mother-in-law suddenly fell ill in Neustat. I
allowed him to go there just during the three days when he would
not miss any of the church services. For this reason I submit my
humble and obedient petition to Your Serene Highness, to refrain
from insisting on this financial punishment; we ask for such a mark
of graciousness in the most profound submissiveness.

Your Serene Highness'
humble and obedient servant,
Haydn.

[1]The date of this letter can be estimated accurately by examining the related
correspondence in the files of the Acta Musicalia (Esterházy Archives). On
15th March 1774, Prince Esterházy writes to Rahier, asking him at once to
"summon the Capellmeister and all the musicians to [him], so
that [he] can see for [himself], and report immediately to me, whom of the

musicians are absent, and how long they have been absent". (Acta Musicalia, 1370). On 16th March, Esterházy writes again, meanwhile having received Rahier's report, and orders a month's salary to be docked from "Cristien Specht, Xavier Marteau, Carl Corus, and Joseph Oliva". (Oliva's case seems to have cleared itself up at once, since his name is not mentioned in Haydn's letter). Esterházy then adds, rather amusingly: "But you must see that neither the *Capellmeister* Haydn nor the other musicians notice anything, and you must act as if nothing had happened." Of course Haydn got wind of what had occurred, and immediately protested on behalf of the three unfortunates.

²See p. 14.
³CHRISTIAN SPECHT, a viola player and bass singer, was a member of the Esterházy band from 1768 to 1790. It was also his responsibility to tune the harpsichords and wind up the special clocks (*Kunstuhren*): see Pohl II, 373.
⁴CARL CHORUS, an oboe player, was engaged in 1771 and left five years later.

[CONTENTS OF A LETTER FROM HAYDN TO PRINCE NICOLAUS ESTERHÁZY. *German*]

[Estoras], [March] 1776.¹

Haydn informs the Prince that Count Erdödy,² "because of his satisfaction with the pupil he entrusted to me", has given him two horses and a carriage. But as he is not capable of supporting the horses, he asks the Prince "in his serene graciousness to grant him hay and oats". [Pohl II, 23.]

¹Pohl does not give the exact date. However, the *Prothocoll . . . de Anno 1734* (see *supra*), No. 1091, includes the following note, the contents of which show that the Prince granted Haydn's request, and the date of which indicates that Haydn's letter must have been written sometime during March: "Resolution of His Serene Highness d[e] d[ato] Esterház, 29th March 1776, according to which *Cappelmeister* [sic] Haydn is to be issued the necessary fodder for 2 horses."
²A famous aristocratic family with whom Haydn was friendly. He dedicated his Quartets of Op. 76 to Count Joseph. Here it is undoubtedly Count Ladislaus of Pressburg who is meant, and I suggest that the pupil is none other than Pleyel, Erdödy's protégé, whom the Count sent to Haydn as a pupil in composition about this time (see Pohl II, 102).
³The Prince granted Haydn the necessary fodder, which was henceforth added to his yearly salary (Pohl II, 23).

[AUTOBIOGRAPHICAL SKETCH; TO MADEMOISELLE LEONORE.¹ *German*]

Estoras, 6th July 1776.

Mademoiselle!

You will not take it amiss if I hand you a hotchpotch of all sorts of

II Vienna seen from the Schlag–Brücke. Engraving by Johann Ziegler, 1780 (Artaria & Co., Vienna).

III Der Stock am Eisen Platz in Vienna; in the background, St. Stephen's Cathedral. Engraving by Carl Schütz, 1779: our version shows changes made on the plate to bring it up to date (c. 1805) (Artaria & Co., Vienna).

things as an answer to your request: to describe such things properly takes time, and that I don't have; for this reason, I do not dare write to Mons. Zoller personally, and therefore ask forgiveness.

I send you only a rough draft, for neither pride, nor fame, but solely the great kindness and marked satisfaction that so learned a national institution has shown towards my previous compositions, have induced me to comply with their demand.

I was born on the last day of March 1733,[2] in the market town of Rohrau, Lower Austria, near Prugg on the Leythä.[3] My late father was a wheelwright by profession, and served Count Harrach,[4] a great lover of music by nature. He [my father] played the harp without knowing a note of music, and as a boy of 5, I correctly sang all his simple little pieces: this induced my father to entrust me to the care of my relative, the schoolmaster in Haimburg,[5] in order that I might learn the rudiments of music and the other juvenile acquirements. Almighty God (to Whom alone I owe the most profound gratitude) endowed me, especially in music, with such proficiency that even in my 6th year I was able to sing some masses in the choir-loft, and to play a little on the harpsichord and violin.

When I was 7, the late *Capellmeister* von Reutter[6] passed through Haimburg and quite accidentally heard my weak but pleasant voice. He forthwith took me to the choir house [of St. Stephen's Cathedral in Vienna] where, apart from my studies, I learnt the art of singing, the harpsichord, and the violin, from very good masters. Until my 18th year I sang soprano with great success, not only at St. Stephen's but also at the Court. Finally I lost my voice, and then had to eke out a wretched existence for eight whole years, by teaching young pupils (many geniuses are ruined by their having to earn their daily bread, because they have no time to study): I experienced this, too, and would have never learnt what little I did, had I not, in my zeal for composition, composed well into the night; I wrote diligently, but not quite correctly, until at last I had the good fortune to learn the true fundamentals of composition from the celebrated Herr Porpora[7] (who was at that time in Vienna): finally, by the recommendation of the late Herr von Fürnberg[8] (from whom I received many marks of favour), I was engaged as *Directeur* at Herr Count von Morzin's,[9] and from there as *Capellmeister* of His Highness the Prince [Esterházy], in whose service I wish to live and die.

Inter alia the following compositions of mine have received the most approbation:

J.H.–D

The operas	*Le Pescatrice* [1769: perf. 1770] *L'incontro improvizo* [*sic*] [1775] *L'infedeltà delusa,* performed in the presence of Her Imperial and Royal Majesty [Maria Theresia, in 1773].[10]

The oratorio   *Il Ritorno di Tobia,* performed in Vienna [in 1775]

The *Stabat Mater* [1767], about which I received (through a good friend) a testimonial of our great composer Hasse,[11] containing quite undeserved eulogiums. I shall treasure this testimonial all my life, as if it were gold; not for its contents, but for the sake of so admirable a man.

In the chamber-musical style I have been fortunate enough to please almost all nations except the Berliners; this is shown by the public newspapers and letters adressed to me. I only wonder that the Berlin gentlemen, who are otherwise so reasonable, preserve no medium in their criticism of my music, for in one weekly paper they praise me to the skies, whilst in another they dash me sixty fathoms deep into the earth, and this without explaining why; I know very well why: because they are incapable of performing some of my works, and are too conceited to take the trouble to understand them properly, and for other reasons which, with God's help, I will answer in good time. *Herr Capellmeister* von Dittersdorf,[12] in Silesia, wrote to me recently and asked me to defend myself against their hard words, but I answered that one swallow doesn't make the Summer; and that perhaps one of these days some unprejudiced person would stop their tongues, as happened to them once before when they accused me of monotony. Despite this, they try very hard to get all my works, as Herr Baron von Sviten,[13] the Imperial and Royal Ambassador at Berlin, told me only last winter, when he was in Vienna: but enough of this.

Dear *Mademoiselle* Leonore: You will be good enough to give this present letter, and my compliments, to Mons. Zoller for his consideration: my highest ambition is only that all the world regard me as the honest man I am.

I offer all my praises to Almighty God, for I owe them to Him alone: my sole wish is to offend neither my neighbour, nor my gracious Prince, nor above all our merciful God.

Meanwhile I remain, *Mademoiselle,* with high esteem,

Your most sincere friend and servant

Josephus Haydn [m.p.] ria

[1]MADEMOISELLE LEONORE was later the wife of Prince Esterházy's *Wirth-schaftsrath* (economic adviser) and *Güterdirector* (estates' director), Lechner. Haydn was requested to write this sketch for a publication entitled "Das gelehrte Oesterreich", in which it appeared in volume I, 3rd *Stück*, p. 309(1776). The editor, Ignaz de Luca, seems to have applied for it in a very roundabout manner to a "Mons. Zoller" (see beginning of the letter), possibly an official in the Prince's service, who in turn asked "Mademoiselle Leonore". See Pohl I, 75 and II, 381.

[2]*Recte*: 1732.

[3]*Recte* (or rather in modern German orthography): Bruck-an-der-Leitha.

[4]The family owned a winter palace in Vienna (still extant—opposite the Schottenkirche) and a castle in Rohrau. Haydn remained devoted to the family throughout his life. In 1793, Harrach erected a monument to Haydn in his castle gardens at Rohrau—a gesture which naturally delighted the composer.

[5]*Recte*: Hainburg (on the Danube). The school rector, Johann Mathias Frankh, who was then still alive, died in 1783, shortly before his 75th birthday. See Pohl I, 23.

[6]GEORG KARL, Sen. (1708–1772).

[7]NICOLÒ PORPORA (1685–1766), an Italian composer whose vocal music, in particular, was much admired at that time.

[8]Haydn's first quartets were written about 1757 in Fürnberg's Summer Castle at Weinzierl, near the Monastery of Melk (Lower Austria). See Fritz Dworschak, "Joseph Haydn und Karl Joseph Weber von Fürnberg" (*Unsere Heimat*, 1932).

[9]Haydn was engaged in 1759: Morzin's castle was in Lukaveč (Bohemia).

[10]This clause ("performed . . .") is written in the autograph to the right of *L'incontro improviso*; I have placed it here in its correct position.

[11]See *supra*, p. 8.

[12]CARL DITTERS VON DITTERSDORF (1739–1799), one of Haydn's oldest friends, was a celebrated and prolific composer.

[13]GOTTFRIED VAN SWIETEN. This diplomat and patron of music was to play a decisive rôle in Haydn's later life, as the translator and arranger of the libretti of the *Seven Words* (choral version), *Creation* and *Seasons*. See also pp. 151, 162, 193 *passim*.

[TO SEITZ, AN OFFICIAL IN THE ESTERHÁZY ADMINISTRATION. *German*] *Monsieur* Seitz!

You are herewith requested please to issue to Herr Svoboda[1] on presentation of the enclosed receipt two bundles of E-strings. I remain, *Monsieur*,

Your obedient

Estoras, 1 June 1777. Josephus Haydn [mp]ria.

Capell Meister

[1]Not in the list of musicians; he was probably a valet or servant. His autograph signature on the same document reads "Joseph Swoboda".

[To Thaddäus Huber, Secretary of the "Tonkünstler-Societät" (Society of Musicians) in Vienna. *German*]

Estoras, 4th February 1779.

Nobly born,
Most highly respected Sir!

It was with considerable astonishment that I read through your letter of 18th January 1779,[1] and also the declaration appended to the end thereof (which I am supposed to sign and return), in default of which I am threatened with the immediate cancellation of my admission—THOUGH THIS IS ALREADY AN ACCOMPLISHED FACT; for the fact that the worthy Society admits me only under the proviso that I shall compose oratorios, cantatas, choruses, symphonies, *etc.*, as they require, flatly contradicts the circumstances of the session wherein my admission was considered. In the presence of *Herr Kapellmeister* von Bonno,[2] Herr von Starzer,[3] and the other honourable men, I directly protested against such a binding and obligatory declaration, for the following obvious reason: to satisfy a demand of this extraordinary kind would require two or three months every year, and therefore I should be unable to fulfil the duties required by my gracious Prince and Lord. But provided a clause reading "if time and circumstances permit me" were added, I agreed gladly to sign this declaration with all the demands enumerated above. Whereupon this my proposal was unanimously accepted, and my admission approved. In order to validate my admission, I was ordered to deposit on the spot the sum of 368 fl. 10 kr., in the presence of the assembled company, for it was particularly explained to me that as soon as the money was deposited, my admission would become valid. I deposited the money, and was thereupon admitted WITHOUT any such declaration.—I was congratulated.—I expressed, in all humility, many thanks for my admission. Of course, in matters of this kind, the whole affair should have been entered into the protocol by the duly authorized notary, and a declaration of this admission as an accomplished fact presented to the newly admitted member; but a worthy Society has not yet seen fit to do so in my case. Moreover:—

This clause, with the so-called DISCREET demands, depends in my opinion wholly on the fancy, or the envy, of some of the members; in time it might depend largely on those who have the least possible insight into the art of composition, for they could judge as DISCREET that which is INDISCREET (for instance, a whole oratorio instead of a few symphonies). I should be forced to compose the most DISCREET oratorios *in plurali* as a result of the INDISCRETION which they consider their right; and if not, the majority of the *vota*—purely out of DISCRETION, of course—would roar for my suspension *sine jure* (just as is now threatened). Why? Perhaps because I, freely and without any gain to myself, have provided the worthy Society with many good services and useful advantages? Perhaps because I am a "foreigner"?[4] In my case, the "foreign" means only that my person is of no use to the aborigines [*Inwärtigen*]: through my works I'm quite aboriginal enough, and if not the composer, oh well, his children are there in almost every concert and provide many nice advantages.

Now, my good friend! I am a man of too much sensitivity to permit me to live constantly in the fear of being quashed: the fine arts, and such a wonderful science as that of composition allow no gyves on their handicraft: the heart and soul must be free if they are to serve the widows[5] and collect profits. One more thing:—

This generous provision of 300 fl. I regard as a well deserved reparation for the 1000 fl. which the Society made on my *Ritorno di Tobia*, especially written for them free of charge. God the all-wise Provider of us all will also protect me and my wife, through my most gracious Prince and Lord, especially since I am convinced, that even the least of persons in the Princely Esterházy house has received an adequate pension. Therefore, on the 15th inst., Herr von Kleinrath, Princely Esterházy Inspector, will appear in my name, and to him a worthy Society will repay my 368 fl. 10 kr. in cash.

For my part, however, despite such a crude and threatening treatment, I shall "if time and circumstances so permit" compose various new pieces for the widows at no cost. I remain, Sir, with due respect,

Your obedient servant,
Josephus Haydn, m.p.
Kapell-Meister.

[1]The circumstances of this letter are briefly explained as follows. In 1775, Haydn had written an oratorio, *Il Ritorno di Tobia*, which was performed at one of the benefit concerts of the "Tonkünstler-Societät", a Viennese Society formed to provide pensions for the widows of composers. Most of Vienna's finest musicians belonged to the Society, and Haydn naturally wished to join. In the session of 18th November 1778 Haydn's petition was considered, and in view of his previous services to the Society, "but mainly because of the services he is to perform in future (he is to submit a declaration to that effect)", his petition was approved. The Society added the clause that "the demands for services to be rendered as per the enclosed

declaration shall never be indiscreet", and this clause with the use of the word "indiscreet" seems to have infuriated Haydn (with some justification). The real point, however, was that most of Haydn's bitterest enemies were members of the Society—a fact which the "foreigner" (*i.e.* non-resident of Vienna) felt very strongly. But because he was a non-resident, he would have been required to pay a reduced entrance fee (see end of the letter). See p. 150 for the happy end of this unfortunate episode. See Pohl, I, 84.

[2]GIUSEPPE BONNO (1710–1788) was Court *Kapellmeister* in Vienna.

[3]JOSEPH STARZER (1726–1787) was a well-known composer of the time; his ballets were especially highly thought of. Burney heard him play first violin (together with Carlos d'Ordoñez, Count Brühl and Weigl) in some Haydn quartets, given at the English Ambassador's house in Vienna. See *The Present State of Music in Germany, etc.*, London 1773, I, p. 290.

[4]"Auswärtiger", *i.e.* a non-resident of Vienna.

[5]Of the composers—it was for their benefit that the Society existed.

[To ARTARIA & CO., VIENNA. *German*]

Estoras, 31st January 1780.

Nobly born Gentlemen!

I send you herewith the 6th pianoforte Sonata,[1] because it is the longest and most difficult: I will certainly deliver the 5th in the next few days; meanwhile I remain, in the greatest haste, *Messieurs*,

Your most obedient servant,

Josephus Haydn [m.] pria.

[No address. Artaria's clerk notes: "Esterhase 31 Jan. 1780".]

[1]Artaria's first Haydn publication was six pianoforte Sonatas dedicated to the *Demoiselles* Francisca and Marianna von Auenbrugger, op. 30 (Nos. 35–39 and 20 of the chronological list). These two talented ladies, both excellent pianists, were the daughters of the well-known physician and scholar, Leopold von Auenbrugger, from Graz. The Sonatas were published in April, 1780 (pl. no. 7).

[To ARTARIA & CO., VIENNA. *German*]

Estoras, 8th February 1780.

Nobly born Gentlemen!

I send you herewith the 5th and last Sonata, and I would ask you to send me all 6 once more for correction; in any event, I hope to gain some honour by this work, at least with the judicious public; criticism of the works will be levelled only by those who are jealous (and there are many); should they have a good sale, this will encourage me to further efforts in the future, and to serve you diligently at all times in preference to all others. I remain, *Messieurs*,

> Your wholly obedient servant,
> Josephus Haydn
> *Capellmeister.*

[To Artaria & Co., Vienna. *German*]

Estoras, 25th February 1780.

Most highly respected Gentlemen!

I send you herewith the corrected proofs of all 6 Sonatas, and ask you to study them as carefully as possible: those numbers marked in red are the most urgent of all. The approval of the *Demoiselles* von Auenbrugger is most important to me, for their way of playing and genuine insight into music equal those of the greatest masters. Both deserve to be known throughout Europe through the public newspapers.

Incidentally, I consider it necessary, in order to forestall the criticisms of any witlings, to print on the reverse side of the title page the following sentence, here underlined:

Avertissement

Among these 6 Sonatas there are two single movements in which the same subject occurs through several bars: the author has done this intentionally, to show different methods of treatment.[1]

For of course I could have chosen a hundred other ideas instead of this one; but so that the whole *opus* will not be exposed to blame on account of this one intentional detail (which the critics and especially my enemies might interpret wrongly), I think that this *avertissement* or something like it must be appended, otherwise the sale might be hindered thereby. I submit the point in question to the judicious decision of the two *Demoiselles* Auenbrugger, whose hands I respectfully kiss. Please send one of the six copies you promised me to Herr Zach von Hartenstein[2] through the Royal Bavarian post-office, but the other 5 are to be addressed to Estoras.

I hope soon to receive an answer to the above point, and have the honour to be, most respectfully,

> Your most obedient servant.
> Joseph Haydn

[No address]

[1]Artaria did include an "Avertimento" which reads as follows: "Tra queste sei Sonate vi si trovano due Pezzi che cominciano con alcune battute

dell'istesso sentimento, cioè l'Allegro scherzando della Sonata No. II, e l'Allegro con brio della Sonata No. V. L'Autore previene averlo fatto a bella posta, cangiando però in ogn'una di esse la Continuazione del Sentimento medesimo."

[2]*Das Österreichische Adelslexikon,* Vienna 1822 (edited by F. G. Nägeli von Mühlfeld) lists two Austrian aristocrats under the name of Zach von Hartenstein: Johann Franz (raised to the nobility in 1764) and Joseph (raised to the nobility in 1756). Both are listed as "Postoffizier", *i.e.* officials in the Postal Department. The *Hof- und Staats-Schematismus,* Vienna 1785, p. 5, lists only "Franz Zach von Hartenstein, k.k. Oberst Hof- Postamtsverwalter Adjunkt".

[To Artaria & Co., Vienna. *German*]

Estoras, 20th March [1780].

Most highly respected Sir!

Everything that you write to me meets with my entire approval; I only regret one thing, that I cannot have the honour of dedicating these Sonatas to the *Demoiselles* von Auenbrugger myself.[1] I remain, with all due respect, Sir,

Your obedient servant
Josephus Haydn

[Address:] Monsieur
    Monsieur Artaria et Compag
    press: a
            Vienne.

[Artaria's clerk notes: "Haydn/ Esterhas 20th March/ 1780".]

[1]Many eighteenth-century dedications were made by the publisher rather than the composer.

[To Artaria & Co., Vienna. *German*]

Estoras, 29th March 1780.

Messieurs!

I received in the past day or two a letter from Herr Humel,[1] Royal Prussian Musical and Commercial Advisor, in which among other things I read with astonishment that my Sonatas have been sent to Berlin some time ago. Please therefore don't forget completely about my five copies. I remain, *Messieurs*, very respectfully,

Your most obedient servant,
Joseph Haydn.

[1]J. J. Hummel, the famous music publisher of Amsterdam and, later, Berlin.

[TO AN UNIDENTIFIED OFFICIAL OF PRINCE ESTERHÁZY'S
ADMINISTRATION. *German*]

Nobly born,
Gracious Sir!
  On the order of His Serene Highness, Your Grace should instruct
the administrator of Forchtenstein Castle[1] or the inspector-general
of ordnance there to send at the earliest possible opportunity a pair of
good military kettledrums [*Feld Paucken*] (such as are kept in the
arsenal there) to Estoras: to this end one should, in my humble
opinion, request the Forchtenstein schoolmaster and the *Pater Regens
Chori* of the *Serviten* Order to give their expert opinion as to the
best and most useful instruments. I remain, most respectfully,

Your Grace's
Obedient servant,
Josephus Haydn
CapellMeister.

Estoras, 7th November 1780

[1]Forchtenstein Castle, an ancient fortress belonging to the Esterházy family,
in the province of Burgenland. The castle stood good service in the second
Turkish invasion of 1683. A photograph of Forchtenstein may be found
on the jacket of Nowak's *Haydn* (Vienna, 1950). The *Serviten* Monastery
still owns some contemporary MSS. of Haydn's works (*Missa Sti. Joannis
de Deo*, etc.); and some scraps of instrumental music I found there recently
(1958)—*e.g.*, part of Haydn's Symphony No. 35, the reverse sheet of which
was used to copy a piece of church music—suggest that the collection must
have been much more extensive at one time.

[TO ARTARIA & CO., VIENNA. *German*]

Estoras, 27th May 1781.

Nobly born,
Most highly respected Sir!
  I am most obliged to you for the 4 copies, so beautifully engraved.[1] Concerning the *Lieder*,[2] I have completed 14 of the same
with all possible diligence, and the number would have been completed long ago if I had had the texts of them; I cannot quite understand why *Herr Hofrath* von Greiner[3] does not return them to me,
since at one time they were in my hands. I only wanted his opinion
as to the expression contained therein, and sent them to him *via*
Herr Walther, the organ-builder; but now I receive no answer from
either of them. If you would be good enough to try to press the

matter with Herr Walther, I should be most obliged to you, for I assure you that these *Lieder* perhaps surpass all my previous ones in variety, naturalness, and ease of vocal execution. I rather doubt, however, that you will take them, for in the first place I ask 30 ducats, secondly 6 copies, and thirdly the following short dedication, to be placed on the title page:

Collection of German Lieder
for the pianoforte,
dedicated
as a mark of special homage
to
Mademoiselle Clair
by
Mr. Joseph Haydn
Chapel Master to Prince Esterházy.

Between ourselves, this *Mademoiselle* is the darling of my Prince. You will certainly see for yourself what an impression such things make! If you agree to these points, I shall not fail to complete the others one after the other. These *Lieder* however, must appear first on Elizabeth Day, for this is the name-day of the fair lady.

Now something from Paris. Monsieur Le Gros,[4] *Directeur* of the Concert Spirituel, wrote me the most flattering things about my *Stabat Mater*,[5] which was performed there four times with the greatest applause; the gentlemen asked permission to have it engraved. They made me an offer to engrave all my future works on the most favourable terms for myself, and were most surprised that I was so singularly successful in my vocal compositions; but I wasn't at all surprised, for they have not yet heard anything. If they only could hear my operetta *L'isola disabitata*[6] and my most recent opera, *La fedeltà premiata*,[7] I assure you that no such work has been heard in Paris up to now, nor perhaps in Vienna either; my misfortune is that I live in the country.

I enclose Herr Boccherini's letter:[8] please present my respectful compliments to him. No one here can tell me where this place Arenas is. It cannot be far from Madrid, however; please let me know about this, for I want to write Herr Boccherini myself.

I remain most respectfully,

Your most obedient servant,
Joseph Haydn.

P.S. Many people are delighted with my portrait.[9] Return the oil-portrait to me in the same case.

[1]Of the *Sei Divertimenti Concertanti* (fl., 2 horns, str.) Op. 31, published in April (pl. no. 7). See illustration IV.

[2]Artaria accepted the *Lieder*, which they published in two sets: the first in December 1781, the second two years later. Concerning the dedication, see *infra*, p. 34 (35).

[3]FRANZ VON GREINER, a well-known music-lover in Vienna. His daughter, Caroline Pichler, wrote memoirs which are a useful source of information about contemporary Vienna. Mozart, Haydn, Salieri, Paisiello and Cimarosa were all friends of the house. See Artaria-Botstiber, p. 12.

[4]JOSEPH LE GROS (1739–1793) was a singer in the Paris Opéra. In 1777, he assumed the directorship of the Concert Spirituel. See Pohl II, 175.

[5]See p. 20.

[6]Performed at the Esterháza Theatre on the Prince's name-day, 6th December 1779.

[7]Performed at the Esterháza Theatre in the Autumn of 1780.

[8]Boccherini wrote to Artaria from Arenas in February 1781 as follows: ". . . Spero mi faranno un favore, che io stimerò moltis[mo] ed è che se alcuno di lor Sig[ri] (come è probabile) conoscesse il Sigr. Giuseppe Haidn [*sic*], scrittore da me, e da tutti aprezzato al Maggior segno, gli offra i miei rispetti, dicendoli che sono uno de i suoi più appassionati stimatori, e ammiratori insieme del suo Genio, e Musicali componimenti dei quali qui si fà tutto quel apprezzo, che in rigor di Giustizia si maritano . . . ." (Artaria-Botstiber, p. 11; Pohl II, 180, n. 6.)

[9]Artaria published a series of portraits (engravings) of well-known persons, musical and otherwise. In June 1781, Haydn's portrait, painted and engraved by J. E. Mansfeld, was announced. Although Haydn was pleased with it (it is the earliest picture of Haydn which we can date with certainty), the engraving is not a good likeness; at best one can describe it as "flattering". See Illustration V.

[To ARTARIA & CO., VIENNA. *German*]

Estoras, 23rd June 1781.

Nobly born,
Most highly respected Sir!

I received with the greatest pleasure the oil-portrait together with the twelve copies you enclosed of the beautifully engraved portrait. My gracious Prince, however, was even more delighted, for as soon as his attention was drawn to it, he immediately asked me to give him one. Since these 12 copies are not enough, I would ask you, good Sir, to send me another six at my expense. You can subtract the sum from my fee for the *Lieder*, six of which I shall send you in a few weeks.

Fifteen are now finished, but among them is one[1] which the strict censorship may perhaps not allow; it is one of those which you yourself gave me, and you shall have the words of it in a few days. I should be sorry about this, for I have composed a remarkably good air to it. To this day I have not received the other *Lieder* from Herr von Greiner; they are certainly lost. You would therefore oblige me if you would procure a dozen others from Herr von Greiner, but only good ones and varied, so that I may have a choice: for it often happens that a certain poem has a real antipathy to the composer, or the composer to the poem.

Moreover, I agree to the stipulated price of one ducat a piece, but no one should know anything about this. Also I do not want any money until all the proofs have been passed. I am still in doubt about the dedication: *i.e.*, whether I should dedicate it to her [*Mademoiselle* Clair] or to someone else. But enough—I reserve this right, and 12 free copies.

As soon as I come to Vienna, will you be kind enough, good Sir, to present me to the worthy Herr von Mansfeld?

Meanwhile I thank you for the copies [of the music][2] and the other portraits and remain, Sir, most respectfully,

Your obedient servant,
Joseph Haydn.

[No address: Artaria's clerk notes: "Haydn/ Esterhaz 13 June 1781/ ans. 5th July".]

[1] The twelfth, "Die zu späte Ankunft der Mutter", in which the daughter cries to the mother: "It has happened, so you might as well go away again."
[2] Probably either the Sonatas op. 30 and/or the Divertimenti Op. 31: see *supra*.

[To Artaria & Co., Vienna. *German*]
Estoras, 20th July 1781.

Nobly born,
Most highly respected Sir!

I send you herewith the first 12 *Lieder*, and will endeavour to send you the second dozen, good Sir, as soon as possible: some of them are written twice over, in case my handwriting should not always be entirely legible, but I would prefer that you engrave them from my autograph.

In the third *Lied*, please note that following the completed text, at the bottom, the words "N.B." must be engraved in just the same way as I have indicated below the text.

You will find the words of the 4th, 8th and 9th *Lieder* in Friebert's[1] *Lieder*, as published by Herr von Kurzböck,[2] but in case you cannot get them, I shall send them to you. These 3 *Lieder* have been set to music by *Capellmeister* Hofmann,[3] but between ourselves, miserably; and just because this braggart thinks that he alone has ascended the heights of Mount Parnassus, and tries to disgrace me every time with a certain high society, I have composed these very three *Lieder* just to show this would-be high society the difference: *Sed hoc inter nos.*

You will find the texts of the 10th and 12th Lieder among those you sent me, and I enclose herewith the texts. Under No. 12 you will find the text of which I recently expressed some doubt as to the censorship.

Those notes which I have marked in red should be engraved in very small type; They appear in only very few of the *Lieder* and are indicated by a "NB" in front of each line.

Above all I ask you to engrave the musical signs as I have written them: for instance, you will find the following: ᴡ, ∾, *tr*, ᴧ⌣ and likewise the *da capo* sign ꜱꜱ such as appears in every *Lied*. Please return the printed *Lied* which I have attached to No. 7.

I pray you especially, good Sir, not to let anyone copy, sing, or in any way alter these *Lieder* before publication, because when they are ready, I shall sing them myself in the critical houses. By his presence and through the proper execution, the master must maintain his rights: these are only songs, but they are not the street songs of Hofmann, wherein neither ideas, expression nor, much less, melody appear.

You once again make me your debtor for the portraits you sent; but do they sell? I'm curious. In any event the frame-makers and guilders have profited by those you sent to me.

When you have an opportunity, please send back the cardboard cover in which the *Lieder* were packed: such material is not to be had here.

Meanwhile I remain, most respectfully,

Your most obedient servant,
Joseph Haydn.

[No address; Artaria's clerk notes: "Haydn / Esterhaz 20th July 1781/ans.20th Sept."]

[1]Karl Friberth, a member of the Esterházy opera troupe: see *supra*, p. 3.
[2]Joseph von Kurzböck, a Viennese publisher who had issued six pianoforte Sonatas (Nos. 21-26 of the chronological list) for Haydn in 1774.

[3]LEOPOLD HOFMANN (1738–1793), Chapel Master of St. Stephen's Cathedral in Vienna, was a prolific composer of both secular and sacred music. His early compositions, which circulated as far as Paris and Leipzig in 1760 and 1761, are fully as talented as Haydn's of that period, though (like so many promising composers in Vienna) he did not develop beyond a certain point. Several dozen of his works were circulated in MS. and printed under Haydn's name.

[TO ARTARIA & CO., VIENNA. *German*]
Estoras, 18th October 1781.

Sir,

In great haste I inform you that next Monday I shall send you the proofs together with 6 new *Lieder*. Some small matters, and the 6 new Quartets[1] which must be ready in 3 weeks, kept me from the *Lieder*; but I shall deliver them in 14 days at the latest. I would like— if it is possible to have them quickly—to receive three new, gentle *Lieder* texts, because almost all the others are of a lusty character. The content of these can be melancholy, too: so that I have shadow and light, just as in the first twelve.

Your most obedient servant,
Joseph Haydn.

Please send me some more of my portraits.

[Address:] Monsieur
Monsieur Artaria et Compag. press:
Kupferstecher Comp.
à
Vienne.

[Artaria's clerk notes: "Haydn. 1781 —/Esterhaz 18th Oct./ (rec'd) 22nd ditto / (ans.) 23rd ditto".]

[1]The Quartets are those known as Op. 33 (from Artaria's numbering).

[TO J. C. LAVATER, ZÜRICH.[1] *German*]
[Only the signature autograph]

Most learned Sir and
Dearest Friend!

I love and happily read your works. As one reads, hears and relates, I am not without adroitness myself, since my name (as it were) is known and highly appreciated in every country. Therefore I take the liberty of asking you to do a small favour for me. Since I know that there are in Zürch [*sic*] and Winterthur many gentlemen amateurs and great connoisseurs and patrons of music, I shall not conceal from you the fact that I am issuing, by subscription, for the price of 6 ducats, a work, consisting of 6 Quartets[2] for 2 violins, viola and violoncello *concertante,* correctly copied, and WRITTEN IN IN A NEW AND SPECIAL WAY (FOR I HAVEN'T COMPOSED ANY FOR 10 YEARS). I did not want to fail to offer these to the great patrons of music and the amateur gentlemen. Subscribers who live abroad will receive them before I print the works. Please don't take it amiss that I bother you with this request; if I should be fortunate enough to receive an answer containing your approval, I would most appreciate it, and remain,

Most learned Sir,
Your ever obedient
Josephus Haydn m.pr.
Fürst Estorhazischer
Capell Meister

Vienna, 3rd December 1781.
To be delivered to Prince Esterhazy's house. In Vienna.

[1]JOHANN CASPAR LAVATER (1741–1801), a well-known Swiss writer, was one of the most talented and curious figures of the German-speaking *Sturm und Drang* literary movement. He was also a master of the silhouette and developed the science of physiognomy.
[2]Op. 33.

[TO PRINCE KRAFFT ERNST OETTINGEN-WALLERSTEIN,[1]
WALLERSTEIN CASTLE (BAVARIA). *German*]
[Only the end, from "humble . . ." to "*Capell Meister*"
autograph]
Most Serene Highness,
Gracious Prince and Dread Lord!

As a great patron and connoisseur of music, I take the liberty of humbly offering Your Serene Highness my brand new *à quadro* [Quartets[2]] for 2 violins, viola [and] violoncello concertante correctly copied, at a subscription price of 6 ducats. They are written in a new and special way, for I have not composed any for 10 years. The noble subscribers who live abroad will receive their copies before I issue them here. I beg for your favour, and a gracious acceptance of your offer, and remain ever, in profound respect,

Your Serene Highness'
humble and obedient
Josephus Haydn,
Fürst Estorhazischer Capell Meister.

Vienna, 3rd December [1781][3]
[Address:] To be delivered to Prince Esterhazy's house in Vienna.

[1]PRINCE KRAFT ERNST OETTINGEN-WALLERSTEIN, one of Southern Germany's most ardent patrons of music, maintained a band of virtuoso musicians, including the composer Rosetti (for some years *Kapellmeister*). In the following years the Prince became more and more enamoured of Haydn's music: see correspondence up to 1789.
[2]Op. 33.
[3]The year is missing, but see St. George's answer of 18th February 1782.

[To ARTARIA & CO., VIENNA. *German*]

Estoras, 4th January 1782.

Monsieur!

To my astonishment I read in the Vienna *Diario* that you intend to publish my Quartets[1] in 4 weeks; I wish you had shown sufficient consideration for me to delay the announcement till I had left Vienna: such a proceeding places me in a most dishonourable position and is very damaging; it is a most usurious step on your part. At least you could have waited with the announcement until the whole *opus* was completed, for I have not yet satisfied all my subscribers: Mons. Hummel[2] also wanted to be a subscriber, but I did not want to behave so shabbily, and I did not want to send them to Berlin wholly out of regard for our friendship and further transactions; and by God! you have damaged me to the extent of more than 50 ducats, since I have not yet satisfied many of the subscribers, and cannot possibly send copies to many of those living abroad: this step must cause the cessation of all further transactions between us.

I would only ask you to send a copy of the *Lieder*, bound in red taffeta, to Herr von Liebe[3] and an ordinary copy to my brother-in-law, Keller,[4] and three copies to me. You can substract the sum from the second dozen. Meanwhile I remain, respectfully

Your obedient servant,
Joseph Haydn.

[No address; Artaria's clerk notes: "Haydn/Esterhasj 4th Jan/1782/
ans. 14th ditto".]

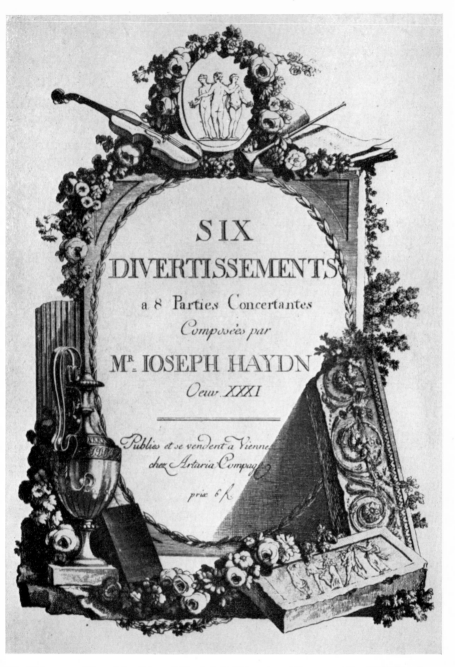

SIX

DIVERTISSEMENTS

a 8 Parties Concertantes

Composées par

Mr. IOSEPH HAYDN

Oeuv. XXXI

Publiés et se vendent a Vienne,
chez Artaria Compag.

prix 6 f.

IV Title page of Artaria's edition of Haydn's *Sei Divertimenti Concertanti* Op. XXXI (see letter of 27th May 1781).

V Haydn. Engraving by J. E. Mansfeld, 1781 (Artaria & Co., Vienna): see letters of 27th May and 23rd June 1781.

[1]Op. 33.
[2]See p. 26.
[3]The songs were dedicated to Francisca, daughter of ANTON LIEBE VON KREUTZNER, who was to receive the copy bound in red taffeta. Kreutzner ordered, also in 1782, a new solemn Mass from Haydn for performance in the pilgrimage church at Mariazell (the *Missa Cellensis* in C, called the "Mariazellermesse").
[4]JOSEPH KELLER, whose son later boarded with Haydn's old friend, Anton Stoll, at Baden. See p. 171.

[TO ARTARIA & CO., VIENNA. *German*]
Estoras, 20th January 1782.

Nobly born,
Most highly respected Sir!
  I must apologize for having written my last letter to you in the heat of anger, and I hope that nevertheless we shall remain good friends. There is no doubt that I gave you the Quartets so that you could engrave them, but it never entered my head that you would put it right into the newspapers.
  Well, it happened that way; another time both of us will be more cautious. I shall send you the *Lieder* with the next mail. I thank you for those you sent[1] and remain, most respectfully,
                    Your most obedient servant,
                    Joseph Haydn.

[Address:] Monsieur
      Monsieur Artaria et Compag
      press:
                à
            Vienne
[Artaria's clerk notes: "Haydn 1782/Esterhasi 20th Jan./rec'd 23rd
                    ditto/answered: (not filled in)".]

[1]See last paragraph of previous letter.

[TO ARTARIA & CO., VIENNA. *German*]
Estoras, 15th February 1782.

Nobly born,
Most highly respected Sir!
  Herr Breunig,[1] with whom I am engaged in a most unpleasant correspondence, and to whom I sent a copy of the passage in your

J.H.–E

last letter concerning the quartets of my composition which he offered you, has sent me the enclosed disgusting letter with the most impertinent threat that I should immediately forward this letter to you for his satisfaction; otherwise Herr Breunig must believe I am a liar. You will therefore have to defend not only me but also yourselves: but the further away from Herr Breunig you can put me, the more satisfactory will be your service to me. I remain, Sir, most respectfully,

Your wholly obedient servant,
Josephus Haydn.

P.S. About the songs, please have a little patience for a short time. I would like to see at least one single copy of my Quartets.

[No address; Artaria's clerk notes: "Haydn / Esterhazy 15. feb: 782".]

[1]CONRAD BREUNIG, a composer from Mainz, whose "6 Duetti per due Violini" Artaria had issued in 1776, offered Haydn's Quartets (Op. 33), obviously pirated from one of the advance subscription copies in MS. Artaria very decently refused to accept them.

[To HAYDN FROM ST. GEORGE, PRIVY COUNCILLOR AND CASHIER TO THE COURT OF PRINCE OETTINGEN-WALLERSTEIN.] [*Draft in German*]
Monsieur,
    Since I received neither an answer to my letter which I sent to you as early as 24th December, nor anything of the music we expected, my gracious Prince has instructed me to ask you for it once again: I do so herewith, and would ask you to be good enough to send whatever you have ready of the new *à quadro*[1] to His Serene Highness, at this address, but to inform me thereof, so that I can see that payment is made to you without delay. In expecting this, I have the honour to be, Sir, with every expression of my esteem . . .

S.

Wallerstein, 18th February 1782.

[1]Op. 33: see Haydn's letter to the Prince of 3rd December 1781.

[To ARTARIA & CO., VIENNA. *German*]
Estoras, 16th August 1782.

Nobly born,
Most highly respected Sir!
    Many thanks for the Cantata[1] you sent, which is very neatly engraved; as to the Overture of my new opera[2] (which isn't composed

yet), I cannot let you have this Overture before the first performance, but if you would like two others from my operas that no one—not a living soul—owns, you can have them at 5 ducats apiece. I promise, by the way, to make up half-a-dozen for you. Next week I shall send you 4 new *Lieder*. Meanwhile I remain, most respectfully,

Your most obedient servant,
Joseph Haydn.

[Address:]   Monsieur
> Monsieur Artaria et Compag
> press:
>> à
>> Vienne.

[1]"Come il cuore mi palpita", issued in score (pl. No. 29).
[2]*Orlando Paladino*. Artaria accepted the offer, and the set grew from two to five and then six, as the next letters show.

[TO ARTARIA & CO., VIENNA. German]
[c. 25th August 1782]

Nobly born,
Most highly respected Sir!

On the very day that I received your kind letter of the 2nd ult., I had the misfortune to injure my left foot by a fall so severely that I have not been able to leave the house up to now, and have had to live on a strict diet: this explains why my answer to you, which is long overdue, was delayed.

I foresaw the consequences of my bringing Herr Hummel[1] into the business of the Quartets just as easily as you will see, in the future, the unfortunate consequences entailed on me; for among many other people, Herr Baron van Sviten[2] gave me distinctly to understand that in future I should dedicate my compositions directly to the public. I hope you will see that this state of affairs is due to your over-hasty announcement, and that this very precipitation obliged me to offer my Quartets all over the place.

I send you herewith the enclosed[3] letter, and only regret that I cannot at present write to Herr Boccherini in my own hand, but when occasion offers, please present my devoted respects to him.

Many thanks for the copies[4] you sent me. As to the pianoforte Sonatas with violin [*i.e.*, trios], you will have to be patient a long time; for I have to compose a new Italian opera, and the Grand Duke and Duchess and perhaps His Majesty the Emperor will be coming here for it.[5]

Your defence against Breunig is excellently done. He received it recently against a signed receipt. Meanwhile I remain, Sir, most respectfully,

Your most obedient servant,
Josephus Haydn, m.pria.

[No address; Artaria's clerk notes: "Haydn 1782/Esterhaze dto. /rec'd. 27th August".]

[1]Haydn had obviously sold the Quartets to Hummel, who announced them in May 1782.
[2]*Recte*: Swieten. See pp. 20, etc.
[3]The original is not clear. Nohl reads "beide" (both), but Pohl's MS. copy suggests "beilig[ende]" (enclosed), and Professor Bartha, who examined the autograph for me in Budapest, is inclined to agree with Pohl's reading.
[4]Of the Quartets, Op. 33 (See P.S. in letter of 15th February).
[5]The opera was to be *Orlando Paladino*. The planned visit of the Russian Grand Duke Paul, with his wife, Maria Feodorowna (*née* Princess of Württemberg), did not materialize; but Haydn had won the Grand Duchess' heart the previous winter, when he had participated in a concert given in Vienna before the Emperor and the Grand Ducal pair on Christmas Day, 1781. She subsequently took a few music lessons with Haydn. See her letter to Haydn of 15th February 1805.

[To ARTARIA & CO., VIENNA. *German*]
Estoras, 29th September 1782.

Nobly born,
Most highly respected Sir!

At last I can send you the five Symphonies [Overtures] you wanted, neatly and correctly written and also well constructed; I rehearsed them myself with my orchestra; I assure you that you will make a considerable profit by their publication, for their brevity will make the engraving very cheap. I would ask you to put the 25 ducats (N.B.: full weight) into a little box, seal it up, and wrap or sew it in an oil-cloth cover, and write nothing on it except *à Mons. Haydn*; for I don't want anyone in my house here to know of my transactions. You can deliver the box to the Prince's porter,[1] and just tell him that it contains some money, and then I shall get it safely from the porter. In any event, you can get a receipt from the porter, which says that he has safely received the box.

The 5 *Lieder* are also herewith enclosed: you must engrave them

in the order in which I have numbered them. I shall try to complete
the remainder as soon as possible and remain, meanwhile,

Your wholly obedient servant,

Josephus Haydn.

[No address; Artaria's clerk notes: "Haydn 1782/Estoras 29th Sept.
/received 3rd Oct."]

[1]HERR ROSENBAUM, whose name appears on the envelopes of later letters.

[TO ARTARIA & CO., VIENNA. *German*]

Estoras, 20th October 1782.

Nobly born,
Most highly respected Sir!

I cannot understand why you did not receive my last letter fourteen days ago, in which I reported that when I was last in Vienna, I
had made an agreement myself with your partner[1] for five ducats for
each piece, to which *Mon.* Artaria[2] willingly agreed. I also wrote that
instead of *Sinfonie* you were to put *Overture*;[3] so this resolves your
doubts. I have been very annoyed at the delay, for I could have had
40 ducats from another publisher for those 5 pieces, and you make
such a fuss about something from which (considering how short the
pieces are) you will derive a thirty-fold profit. Your partner has long
since had the sixth piece. So finish the affair and send me either my
music or my money, and with this I remain, most respectfully,

Your most obedient servant,

Joseph Haydn.

[Address:]   Monsieur
    Monsieur Artaria et Com
            à
        VIENNE

[Artaria's clerk notes: "Haydn 1782/Estoras 20 October/ rec'd 22
ditto/ans.23 ditto".]

[1]Probably either Tranquillo Mollo or Giovanni Cappi.
[2]One of the young Artaria nephews, Carlo or Francesco.
[3]Despite Haydn's request, the works appeared as "Sei Sinfonie a gran
orchestra opera XXXXV"; they include overtures from his earlier operas
Lo speziale (1768), *L'incontro improvviso* (1775), *La vera costanza* (1776?),
L'isola disabitata (1779), the oratorio *Il ritorno di Tobia* (1774, perf. in 1775)
and one unidentified piece, probably the Overture to *L'infedeltà delusa*
(1773).

[To ARTARIA & CO., VIENNA. *German*]

Estoras, 27th January 1783.

Nobly born,

Most respected and honoured Sir!

You will certainly receive the *Lieder* together with the Symphonies[1] by the end of this month, through our palace superintendant [*Haus Hof Meister*] or *via* the Hussars: don't be angry at me, because upon my return home I caught a severe catarrh and had to stay in bed a fortnight.

I remain, most respectfully,

Your ever obedient servant,
Joseph Haydn.

[Address:]   Monsieur
Monsieur Artaria & Compagn
à
Vienne

[Artaria's clerk notes: "Haydn 1783/Esterhaz 27th January / rec'd 30th ditto/ ans'd 11th February".]

[1]Previously I thought that the Symphonies must be Nos. 76–78 (see *The Symphonies of Joseph Haydn*, p. 388, n.48); I now consider that Haydn was referring to the proofs of the *Sei Sinfonie* (see *supra*).

[To ARTARIA & CO., VIENNA. *German*]

Nobly born,

Most highly respected Sir!

Next Monday you will receive the Symphony (full of mistakes)[1] and also some *Lieder*.

I cannot understand what you write me about the trios of Count von Durazzo;[2] it's just the other way round: I never received from him, but the Count did receive from me a thematic list, and only yesterday I sent his nephew a catalogue. Possibly the letter and the catalogues went astray: would you please therefore let me have the exact details on the next post-day, for I value Count Durazzo's house above all others. Meanwhile I remain, Sir, respectfully,

Your most obedient servant,
Joseph Haydn.

Estoras, 20th March 1783.

[Address:]   Monsieur
Monsieur de Artaria et Compagne
à
Vienne.

[1]Symphony No. 69 in C, written about 1778. Haydn subsequently dedicated it to the Austrian *Feldmarschall* Laudon (or Loudon). Artaria published only a piano arrangement, which Haydn either made or looked through.
[2]JOHANN JACOB, COUNT DURAZZO, formerly Director of the Vienna Stadttheater nächst dem Kärnthnerthor, was appointed Austrian Ambassador to Venice in 1764.

[TO ARTARIA & CO., VIENNA. *German*]
Estoras, 8th April 1783.

Nobly born,
Most highly respected Sir!

I send you herewith the Symphony,[1] Sir, which was so full of mistakes that the fellow who wrote it ought to have his paw [*Bratze*] chopped off. The last or 4th movement is not practicable for the pianoforte, and I don't think it necessary to include it in print: the word "Laudon" will contribute more to the sale than any ten finales. My continued unhappy condition, that is, the present necessity to operate a polypus on my nose, made it impossible for me to work up to now. You must therefore have patience about the *Lieder* for another week, or at most a fortnight, until my enfeebled head, with God's help, regains its former vigour. Please have the goodness to present my respects to Count Durazzo,[2] and tell him that I cannot remember the themes of the trios nor can I recall having received them. I searched carefully all through my music and papers, and could find no trace of them; if it please the Count, however, I shall send him a catalogue of all my trios. I await the favour of your reply and remain, Sir, most respectfully,

Your wholly obedient servant,
Joseph Haydn.

P.S. Many thanks for the copies
you sent me.[3]

[Address:] Monsieur
Monsieur Artaria et Compag
à
Vienne

[1]See previous letter.
[2]See previous letter
[3]Possibly of the *Sei Sinfonie*, which had appeared that winter (see *supra*).

[TO ARTARIA & CO., VIENNA. *German*]

Estoras, 18th June 1783.

Nobly born,
Most highly respected Sir!

I send you herewith the Laudon Symphony, for which the violin part is not at all necessary and may be therefore omitted entirely. Please send me either the music or the first strophe of each of the 2nd part of the *Lieder*, so that I can complete the missing ones. Many thanks for the pianoforte Sonatas by Clementi,[1] they are very beautiful; if the author is in Vienna, please present my compliments to him when opportunity offers. I remain, Sir, most respectfully,

Your wholly obedient servant,
Joseph Haydn.

P.S. As to the pianoforte Sonatas with violin and bass, you must still be patient, for I am just now composing a new *opera seria*.[2]

[Address:]   Monsieur
Monsieur Artaria et Compag
à
Vienne.

[Artaria's clerk notes: "Haydn 1783./Esterhaz 18th June/ rec'd 20th and/ans'd 18th July."]

[1]Probably Artaria's edition of Op. 7 and/or Op. 9 (pl. nos. 32 and 36).
[2]*Armida*, first performed at the Esterháza Theatre in February 1784.

[TO BOYER, MUSIC PUBLISHER IN PARIS. *German*]

Nobly born,
Most highly respected Sir!

I did not receive your esteemed favour of 2nd June until my return yesterday, and noted your requests with much pleasure; I doubt, however, whether I can satisfy your wants, for the following reasons. First, I am not allowed, according to the terms of my contract with my Prince, to send any of my own autographs abroad, because he retains these himself. I could of course make two scores of a work, but I don't have the time and don't really see any adequate reason for doing so. For if a piece is neatly and correctly copied [in parts], it is able the more quickly to be engraved. Secondly, you must rely on my word of honour, and not believe in a scrap of paper. Last year I composed 3 beautiful, elegant and by no means over-lengthy Symphonies,[1] scored for 2 violins, viola, basso, 2 horns, 2 oboes,

1 flute and 1 bassoon[2]—but they are all very easy, and without too much *concertante* . . . .

[Summary of the rest of the contents:][3]

I wanted to produce them in England, but the journey did not materialize. I now offer you these Symphonies, and inquire after the best terms, for I am confident that these three pieces will enjoy tremendous sale. I am

[from the autograph:]

Your obedient servant,

Josephus Haydn [m.p.] ria.

Estoras, 15th July 1783.

[Address:]   Monsieur Boyer
        au Magazin de Musique
                  Paris

[1]Symphonies Nos. 76–78 (E flat, B flat, C minor). The Viennese firm of Torricella issued them in July 1784; an announcement in the *Wiener Zeitung* specifies that Haydn himself corrected them. He also sold them to Forster in London, where they appeared in 1784. Boyer, too, purchased the Symphonies and published them as Op. 37.

[2]There are in fact two bassoon parts.

[3]Summary from Martin Breslauer (London), Cat. No. 71 (1950) item 39, written in the third person.

[TO ARTARIA & CO., VIENNA. *German*]

Estoras, 3rd February 1784

Nobly born,

Most highly respected Sir!

I shall send you the missing *Lieder* next Friday or Saturday; I would only ask you to let me know the key of the final printed *Lied*, and how its text begins, so that I can decide the keys of the ones to follow. Meanwhile I remain, Sir, most respectfully,

Your wholly obedient servant,

Joseph Haydn.

N.O. Please present my compliments to the Bavarian house[1] and Herr von Hoffmann.

N.B. I have mislaid among my papers the print of the *Lieder* you sent me long ago, and cannot find it any more.

[Address:]   Monsieur
        Monsieur
        Artaria et Compag
                  à
              VIENNE

Herr Rosenbaum[2] is asked to expedite this.
[Artaria's clerk notes: "Haydn—1784/ Esterhatz 3 febr[i] / rec'd—
6th/ ans'd 6th."]

[1]It is not clear what is meant by the "Bavarian house".
[2]Prince Esterházy's porter.

[To HAYDN from HEINRICH, PRINCE OF PRUSSIA.[1] *German*]
I thank you for the Quartets[2] which were sent to me, and which give me
much pleasure. Please accept the enclosed trifle[3] as a token of my particular satisfaction. I remain, with sincere esteem,

Your ever well-disposed[4]
Heinrich.

Berlin, 4th February 1784.

[1]HEINRICH, PRINCE OF PRUSSIA, brother of the King, Friedrich II.
[2]Op. 33, to which the Prince probably subscribed directly from Haydn.
[3]A gold medal and the Prince's portrait (Dies, p. 70).
[4]"Ihr wohlaffectionirter".

[To ARTARIA & CO., VIENNA. *German*]

Estoras, 1st March 1784.

Dearest and best friend!

The day after tomorrow, this coming Wednesday, you shall
certainly receive the *Lieder*. Yesterday my *Armida*[1] was performed
for the 2nd time with general applause. I am told that this is my best
work up to now. I ask *Fräulein* Nanet Peyer,[2] whom I embrace a
thousand times, to forgive my mistake; she may rest assured that not
I, but the press of work, is responsible for it. Meanwhile I remain,
most respectfully,

Your wholly obedient servant,
Haydn.

In haste
[Address:]   Monsieur
          Monsieur d'Artaria
                    a
               Vienne
Herr Rosenbaum is asked to expedite this at once.

[1]Haydn's new opera (see also, p. 46).
[2]NANETTE PEYER (see also letter of 5th May 1786) was *Kammermädchen* to
Count Apponyi at Pressburg.

[To ARTARIA & CO., VIENNA. *German*]

Estoras, 5th April 1784.

Nobly born,

Most highly respected Sir!

Although I have always received more than 100 ducats for my quartets[1] by subscription, and although Herr Willmann[2] also promised to give me this sum, I agree to your offer of 300 fl. with the following stipulations; first that you are patient until July, though all six should be finished by then; secondly, I demand either 12 copies or my choice of the dedication. If this proposal is agreeable to you, I shall await your draft of a contract: those quartets which I am at present working on, and of which half are finished, are very short and consist of three pieces only; they are intended for Spain.[3] On the next post-day I shall send you an article, *i.e.*, an analysis of my Cantata[4] which you engraved, and which has been a great success. Professor Kramer[5] from Kiel sent it to me together with a letter.

Farewell, meanwhile: I am pressed for time.

Your most obedient servant,
Joseph Haydn.

[Envelope:]   Monsieur

Monsieur d'Artaria et Comp

à

Vienne.

[1]Op. 50 ("Prussian"), which did not, however appear till December 1787 (see *infra*).

[2]Probably MAXIMILIAN WILLMANN, 'cellist in the service of Prince Grassalkovics and not, as in Hoboken (p. 408n.), Johann Ignaz, the violinist, who was later leader in the Theater an der Wien under Count Palffy's patronage.

[3]It is doubtful if Haydn really completed his set: the single quartet, Op. 42 (autograph: 1785) may belong to it.

[4]"Ah, come il cuore".

[5]*Recte*: C. F. Cramer, who wrote the forty-two page analysis himself. It was published the year before, in Cramer's *Magazin der Musik*.

[To ARTARIA & CO., VIENNA. *German*]

Estoras, 8th April 1784

Nobly born,

Most highly respected Sir!

In my last letter I forgot to ask you to have someone deliver a copy of the new *Lieder* in my name to Fräulein von Liebe.[1] She now lives in the Leopoldstadt.[2] The Prince's porter will be able to tell you where. More on next Wednesday.

Josephus Haydn [m.] pria.

Please could you get for me the German book on composition, in 4to format, by *Capellmeister* Fux, entitled *Gradus ad Parnassum*. I would be much obliged to you.

N.B.: Herr von Liebe lives at No. 10.

[Address:]   Monsieur
          Monsieur d'Artaria
                    à
                    VIENNE

[Artaria's clerk notes: "Haydn 1784/Esterhaz 8. Apr./ rec'd the 10th ditto/ ans'd the 29th ditto".]

[1]FRANCISCA LIEBE VON KREUTZNER, to whom both sets of the *Lieder* were dedicated: see *supra*, p. 35.
[2]A suburb of Vienna, now the 2nd District.

[TO ARTARIA & CO., VIENNA. *German*]
Estoras, 18th May 1784.

Mon tres chere Amy!

As to the Quartets,[1] the agreement remains; as to the extract[2] from my *Armida*, I cannot yet say for certain, because I would like to show it to the world in its entirety. I am grateful to you for Cramer's *Magazin*[3] and am your debtor for it. I would ask you only to send to me at my expense 2 copies of the last *Lieder*, and also of the first.

Meanwhile I remain, as always,

Your wholly obedient servant,
Haydn.

[Address:]   Monsieur
          Monsieur d'Artaria
                    a   [Artaria's clerk writes: "Haydn—
                    Vienne.   1784/ Esterhaz 18th May/ rec'd
                              20th".]

[1]Op. 50.
[2]"Auszug": Haydn may mean here "Piano-vocal score", in which case "in Ihrer ganzen gestalt" would mean "in full score" rather than "in its entirety."
[3] See also letter of 5th April. Artaria must have sent a new number.

[To NADERMANN, MUSIC PUBLISHER IN PARIS.[1] *German*]
Nobly born,
Most highly respected Sir!

Since you, good Sir, accepted three of my Symphonies last year, once again I offer you three brand new Symphonies,[2] very diligently composed and neatly and correctly copied, for the price of 15 ducats; I would deliver them by the end of November. If, good Sir, you accept this offer, I shall devote my energies to delivering to you at the first opportunity the pianoforte piece which you asked for in your last letter. In the hope of receiving the favour of an early reply I am, with the most sincere esteem, Sir,

Your wholly obedient servant
Josephus Haydn.

Estoras, 25th October 1784.

[1]This letter was published for the first time in 1838 (*Neue Zeitschrift für Musik*: see Sources). The man who discovered it, C. A. Mangold, reports that he found it in a bundle of old music, and that it is addressed to Nadermann, who—as Mangold does not mention—became Boyer's successor a few years later. Mangold does not, however, give the actual address and it is possible that none was included on the letter. Either Nadermann was a partner in Boyer's business earlier than we knew, or else the letter is really addressed to Boyer. Perhaps the bundle of music had belonged formerly to the Nadermann music business, and Mangold was not aware that Nadermann was Boyer's successor (and thus that the letter may have been addressed to Boyer). The connection between this letter and that to Boyer of 15th July 1783 is, however, obvious. In conclusion it should be said that (1) Boyer really bought Symphonies Nos. 76–78 and issued them; (2) that he did not buy Nos. 79–81; (3) Nadermann issued neither.
[2]Symphonies Nos. 79–81, which Haydn also sold to Torricella (see next letter), and (except No. 79) to Forster.

[To ARTARIA & CO., VIENNA. *German*]
Estoras, 20th November 1784.

Dearest friend!

Don't be angry at me that I cannot fulfil any of your wants just now; the 3rd Symphony[1] is now ready, but you cannot have it before my arrival in Vienna because of some small profit which I shall try to make on all three. The main difficulty in everything is the long sojourn of my Prince in Estoras, even though he doesn't have much to amuse him, since half of the theatre is sick or away. So you can imagine what trouble I constantly have to amuse His Highness.

You will therefore be good enough to be patient until I have the

pleasure of seeing you personally. Meanwhile I remain, with profound esteem,

> Your most sincere friend and servant,
> Joseph Haydn [m.] pria.

My respectful compliments to the Bavarian house.

[Address:]   Monsieur
            Monsieur d'Artaria
                    a
                VIENNE

[Artarias clerk writes: "Haydn / Esterhaz 20th Nov./1784".]

[1]Nos. 81, 80 and 79 (in that order) were published as Op. 38, 39 and 40
in March 1785. Haydn sold them to the Viennese publisher Torricella who,
after having engraved the first one (No. 81), ceded the rights of all three to
Artaria, who then issued them. Torricella was obviously in straightened
financial circumstances at this time, and shortly afterwards went bankrupt;
Artaria subsequently acquired most of Torricella's plates, which were sold
by public auction.

[TO FRANZ PHILIPP VON WEBER, *Hofsecretaire* AND MASTER OF
CEREMONIES AT THE MASONIC LODGE "ZUR WAHREN EINTRACHT",
VIENNA[1]. *German*]
[Only the signature autograph]

Nobly born,
Most highly respected *Herr Hoff Secretaire*,

The highly advantageous impression which Freemasonry has
made on me has long awakened in my breast the sincerest wish to
become a member of the Order, with its humanitarian and wise
principles. I turn to you, Sir, with the most urgent request that you
have the great kindness to intervene on my behalf with the Lodge of
the Order, in order to implement this my petition, as indicated
above.

I have the honour to remain, with profound esteem,

> Your obedient servant,
> Josephus Haydn,
> *CapellMeister* to Prince Esterházy.

Vienna, the 29th of the Christmas Month
1784.

[1]Haydn, like Mozart (who was an ardent freemason) was attracted to the
"humanitarian and wise principles" of Freemasonry, and applied for
membership. His sponsors were Count Anton Georg Apponyi of Pressburg

(see pp. 52f.), von Weber to whom the letter is addressed, and Heinrich Joseph Walter von Aland, "Privy Councillor [*Geheimer Rat*] to the *Kurfürst* of Trier and Accredited Minister to the Archiepiscopal Court of Passau at the Imperial and Royal Court in Vienna". On 10th January 1785, through Weber's motion, Haydn was proposed to the Lodge officially, on 24th January he was voted in "by unanimous and delighted consent" and his official initiation took place on the 28th. Mozart attended that meeting, but Haydn was prevented from coming, and his initiation had to be postponed until 11th February. Unlike Mozart, however, Haydn seems to have been disappointed by what he found, and never attended another meeting, though his name appears on the rolls until 1787, when it was removed entirely. See O. E. Deutsch, "Haydn bleibt Lehrling", *Neue Freie Presse*, 14 March 1933, p. 6.

[TO COUNT ANTON GEORG APPONYI, VIENNA[1] *German*]
[Extracts]

Estoras, 2nd February 1785

. . . . Just yesterday I received a letter from my future sponsor Herr von Weber, saying that they had anxiously awaited me last Friday [28th January], when I should have been admitted (and to which event I look forward with great longing); but since I did not receive the letter of invitation in time, because of an oversight by our Hussars, they have postponed the occasion till next Friday [4th February.] Oh, if it were only Friday!—so that I could have the inexpressible Joy of being among a circle of such worthy men . . . .

[Pohl II, 208]

[1]COUNT APPONYI had his principal palace at Pressburg but seems to have spent at least part of each winter in Vienna. The circumstances of this letter are explained in the notes to the previous letter, of 29th December 1784.

[TO HAYDN FROM W. A. MOZART[1]. *Italian, in the "Tu" form*]
To my dear friend Haydn:

A father, having resolved to send his sons into the great world, finds it advisable to entrust them to the protection and guidance of a highly celebrated man, the more so since this man, by a stroke of luck, is his best friend.—Here, then, celebrated man and my dearest friend, are my six sons.—Truly, they are the fruit of a long and laborious effort, but the hope, strengthened by several of my friends, that this effort would, at least in some small measure, be rewarded, encourages and comforts me that one day, these children may be a source of consolation to me.—You yourself, dearest friend, during your last sojourn in this capital,[2] expressed to me your satisfaction with these works.—This, your approval, encourages me more than anything else, and thus I entrust them to your care, and hope that they are not wholly unworthy of your favour.—Do but receive them kindly, and be their father, guide, and friend! From this moment I cede to you all my rights over them: I pray you to be indulgent to their mistakes, which a father's partial eye may have overlooked, and despite this, to cloak them in the mantle of your generosity which they value so highly. From the bottom of my heart I am, dearest friend,

Your most sincere friend,
W. A. Mozart.

Vienna, 1st September 1785.

[1]Written as a dedication to Artaria's edition of Mozart's Six String Quartets Op. X (K. 387, 421, 428, 458, 464, 465).

[2]LEOPOLD MOZART, when visiting Wolfgang in his house in the Schüler-strasse (still extant), writes to his daughter on 16th February 1785: "Saturday evening Herr JOSEPH HAYDN and the two Baron Tindis were here; the new Quartets were played, but only the 3 NEW ones which he [Wolfgang] has added to the 3 we already have—they are a little easier but excellently written. Herr Haydn said to me: 'I TELL BEFORE GOD AND AS AN HONEST MAN, THAT YOUR SON IS THE GREATEST COMPOSER I KNOW, PERSONALLY OR BY REPUTATION, HE HAS TASTE AND APART FROM THAT THE GREATEST POSSIBLE KNOWLEDGE OF COMPOSITION.'" The autograph of this letter is in private possession in New York City; Professor O. E. Deutsch kindly showed me a photograph.

[TO ARTARIA & CO., VIENNA. *German*]

Estoras, 26th November 1785.

Dearest friend!

Please let me know, by the Monday dispatch of the Princely Hussars, if my Sonatas[1] are already engraved, and when you intend to give them to the Countess Witzey;[2] the reason why I would very much like to know is that, before my departure, which will be in a fortnight at the latest, I want to pay a visit to the Countess at her estate; I only waited for the first proofs of the Sonatas, in order to correct them, for there is a mistake that needs to be set right. There-fore please write me once more on next Monday. I would also ask you to send me a copy of the last *Lieder* on this occasion; I shall pay for it with thanks. I am, most respectfully.

Your wholly obedient servant,
Haydn.

[Address:]   Monsieur
      Monsieur d'Artaria et
      Compag
              à
                    Vienne.
Please expedite.

Salomon

VI   J. P. Salomon. Pencil sketch with touches of reddish crayon by George Dance, 1794.
From the editor's collection.

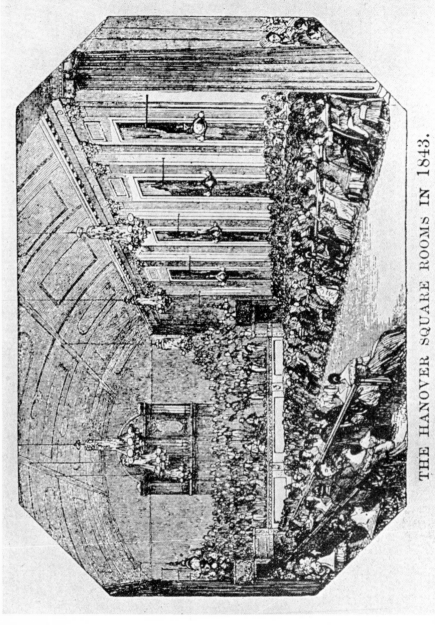

THE HANOVER SQUARE ROOMS IN 1843.

VII Interior of Hanover Square Rooms, 1843, from Charles Knight's *London* (reproduced from Terry's *John Christian Bach* by kind permission of Oxford University Press)

[Artaria's clerk notes: "Haydn/ Esterhass 26th Nov. 1785/ answered 6th Dec."]

> [1]Pianoforte Trios Nos. 6–8 of the chronological list, which Artaria published as Op. 40 the following Spring.
> [2]MARIANNE WITZEY (or Witzay), *née* Countess Grassalkovics de Gydrak, to whom Artaria dedicated these three Trios. Haydn was befriended by the Grassalkovics family, at whose palace in Pressburg he had conducted the music for a splendid ball, given on 16th November 1772 (Pohl II, 52).

[TO ARTARIA & CO., VIENNA. *German*]

Estoras, 10th December 1785.

Mon tres cher Amy!

Day before yesterday I received the pianoforte Sonatas,[1] and was greatly astounded to have to see such bad engraving, and so many glaring errors in all the parts, especially in the pianoforte part. I was at first so furious that I wanted to return the money to you and send the score of the Sonatas instantly to Herr Hummel[2] in Berlin; for the sections which are occasionally illegible, and the passages omitted or badly spaced, will bring little honour to me and little profit to you. Everyone who buys them will curse the engraver and have to stop playing, especially on page 8, and on the first page of the 3rd Divertimento,[3] page 15, where the [   ] marked in red are especially badly laid out, and this really seems to be the result of complete torpidity. I would rather pay for two new plates out of my own pocket than to see such confusion.

Even a professional would have to study before disentangling this passage, and then where would the dilletante be? Four notes are missing on page 18, and in the last line the engraver was too lazy to write out the whole of the bass part: such abbreviations[4] and signs are all very well in the viola part of symphonies, but not in pianoforte parts. Moreover, most of the natural signs ♮ are so small, and occasionally so close to the note, that you can barely see them: one such case is found on page 18, at the end of the uppermost stave. There are prodigiously many wrong notes and omitted notes. On pages 6 and 8 most of the following signs ∾ are wrongly placed, for they ought not to be put directly over the note but over the neighbouring dot, in this way: (page 6, bar 4). All the way through, the dots ought to be further away from the notes, so that the sign ∾ comes directly over the dot. And on this very page, in the second stave, you should put instead of the sign *tr*: the following: ⋎, for the first one, as the engraver has done it, means a trill, whilst mine is a half mordent.[5] If, therefore, the Herr Engraver doesn't know signs of this sort, he should inform himself by studying the masters, and not follow his own stupid ideas. In the 2nd Sonata he even forgot the tempo at the beginning, where the clef is. A whole bar is missing in the violin part, too. I spent the whole of yesterday and half of today in correcting, and yet I have only glanced over them.

Now, my good friend, see to it that everything is corrected, for otherwise little honour will accrue to either of us. By the way, I hope to see you personally and am, meanwhile, most respectfully,

Your wholly obedient servant,
Joseph Haydn.

[1]Trios, see previous letter.
[2]HUMMEL, the celebrated music publisher, whose name often occurs in these letters.
[3]Divertimento, another name for Sonata (*i.e.* Trio).
[4]"Schlender", literally "lounger", "dawdler". Probably the engraver put // or "col basso", as Haydn would have written it in the score. Since Artaria published parts, the abbreviations would be meaningless.
[5]I have recently examined the autograph of the second Trio, in D, No. 7 of the chronological list; it is owned by Thomas Odling, Esq., London. Haydn even took the trouble to put the three principal ornaments, *tr*, ∞ and ⋎ —all by themselves—in the bottom right-hand corner of the first page which is, apart from the title, *etc.*, blank.

[To NANETTE PEYER, PRESSBURG.[1] *German*]
Estoras, 5th May 1786.
Dearest Nanette!
I cannot tell you how happy I am that I shall be seeing you soon. Would you kindly ask His Grace the Count[2] if he would be good enough to send his carriage for me on this coming Thursday the 11th inst. as far as Fraunkürchen,[3] where I shall arrive on Friday the 12th at 9 o'clock at the latest, having left Estoras at 5 in the morning with my own horses. I would then go on to Pressburg with the Count's carriage and arrive there between 1 and 2. I must tell you in advance, however, that I can't stay there more than 24 hours. Hoping to embrace you soon, I am, with the greatest esteem,

Your most obedient servant,
Joseph Haydn.

P.S. I respectfully kiss the hands
of the Count and Countess.
[On the outside is the following note in another hand: "dt. 5 et
accept 7ᵗ. May 1786 / Jos Hayden (*sic*)".]

[1]See p. 44.
[2]Apponyi.
[3]Frauenkirchen, a pilgrimage town in Burgenland, about midway between
Esterháza and Pressburg.

[CONTRACT WITH WILLIAM FORSTER, LONDON. *French*]
[Only the signature in Haydn's hand]
[1786: the exact date is not known]
D[1]

I acknowledge to have received of *Monsieur* Guillaum Forster,
merchant and music publisher, domiciled in the Strand at London,
the sum of seventy pounds Sterling for 20[2] Symphonies, Sonatas,
and other pieces of music composed by me, as enumerated below,
the beginnings of which are as follows:

No. 1 a Symphony for various instruments which begins thus[3]:

[6 Divertimenti] for 2 *Flûtes traversieres* and Violoncello, which
begin as follows[4]:

First Set of three Sonatas for the Harpsichord, with Accompaniment of a Violin [and Violoncello][5]:

Second Set of three different Sonatas for the Harpsichord, with Accompaniment of a Violin [and Violoncello][6]:

And I certify and declare to the whole world that I sold the said Symphonies, Sonatas and other pieces to said *Monsieur* Guillaum Forster, and that I sent him the manuscripts on the following dates, *viz.*:

The six Sonatas for two *Flûtes traversieres* and Violoncello on 31st May 1784.

The Symphonies listed above as Nos. 1 and 2 through *Monsieur le General* de Jermingham[7] on 19th June 1784.

The Symphonies Nos. 4, 5 and 6 together with the afore-mentioned First Set of 3 Sonatas for the Harpsichord on 25th October 1784.

The Symphonies listed above as Nos. 7, 8 and 9 on 8th November 1784.

And the afore-mentioned Second Set of 3 Sonatas for the Harpsichord on 28th October 1785.

I further certify and declare that he has paid me the price we agreed upon, and that this sum of seventy pounds Sterling has been paid to me in full by letters of exchange on Vienna which he sent me for this purpose (with the exception of the fee for the two Symphonies Nos. 1 and 2, which fee was paid on my behalf to *Monsieur le General* de Jermingham[7], then in London).

And I further certify and declare that the said Guillaum Forster is the sole proprietor of the said works, that I sold them to him as such, and that I cede and transfer to him all my rights and covenants thereto. In witness of which I have set my signature to this document at Esterhaz, this [not filled in] 1786.

Giuseppe Haydn [m.p.]ria, *Maestro*
di capella di S: Alt: S: il principe
Estorhazy.

[1]This "D", which may mean "Document", was probably added when the paper was used as evidence against Longman and Broderip. On the reverse side of this contract is a note, "Haydns subjects", and "D/Forster agt Longman & ant—This Paper Writing was shewn to Jos. Haydn at the time of his exam". in this Court before [me?] Ja Eyre". This curious note refers to the suit between the two London publishers which must have taken place in 1791 or 1792, when Haydn was in England. Longman had imported the Artaria prints of the very pieces which Haydn had sold to Forster under exclusive contract. No more details of this suit are known. See letter of 28th February 1788 and the correspondence with Artaria of this period.
[2]The figure "o" is almost illegible.
[3]Symphonies 74, 70, 76, 77, 78, 81, Overture to *Armida*, Symphony 80.
[4]These six Divertimenti are partly based on pieces from Haydn's earlier (1777) opera, *Il mondo della luna*.

[5]Trios Nos. 3–5 of the chronological list. The first two are actually by Haydn's pupil Pleyel.
[6]Trios Nos. 9, 2 and 10 of the chronological list.
[7]GENERAL GERMINGHAM, English Ambassador to the Court of Vienna. See also letter of 28th February 1788. It was he who provided the connection between Forster and Haydn.

[TO ARTARIA & CO., VIENNA. *German*]

Estoras, 11th February 1787.
Mon tres cher Amy!

This is to report that I have arranged 4 of the Sonatas[1] as quartets, and have completed them; you will receive the whole work this coming Friday. Meanwhile you can give the first violin part[2] of the first four Sonatas to the engraver, just as it stands, because there was no need to change anything. You will receive the Quartet[3] a week from tomorrow. Please don't forget my portraits.[4] Should you not find any safe and convenient opportunity in the Esterházy mansion, please send them next Monday by the diligence to the following address in Oedenburg:

A Monsieur

Mons. Baumgartner, Princely Esterházy House-Master

a

Oedenburg

from whom I shall have them collected by my own carriage. In any event you can dispatch it under my name, or inform the conductor about it verbally.

Meanwhile I am, most respectfully,

Your most obedient servant,

Joseph Haydn.

[Address:]   Monsieur

Monsieur d'Artaria et Comp.

a

Vienne.

[1]The Oratorio, *The Seven Words of the Saviour on the Cross*, written for Cadiz in 1785, and consisting of seven "Sonatas", an Introduction and a Finale ("The Earthquake"). It was scored for full orchestra.
[2]Of the orchestral version, which Artaria also issued.
[3]One of Op. 50, which Artaria was preparing to publish.
[4]See *supra*, p. 29.

[To Artaria & Co., Vienna. *German*]
                                        Estoras, 14th February 1787.

Mon tres cher Amy!

I enclose herewith all four altered parts,[1] and hope that the copyist will understand me well, and especially that he will do all the parts in the right order, that is, as proper quartets. If there should arise any doubt about certain passages, the copyist should let me know about them at once, so that I can help him in time. All 4 parts, that is, each Sonata in which there are changes, must be written out anew.

As soon as proofs of the Sonatas (both as quartets and for full band) can be made, please send me the first copy, so that I can correct it. The content[2] of the Sonatas expressed in music is also enclosed herewith, and it must be printed in the quartet version as well.

The Quartet[3] will follow soon. The opera rehearsals here detain me. Meanwhile I am, most respectfully,

                                        Your most obedient servant,
                                        Joseph Haydn.

P.S. Please buy 7 copies of the enclosed sheet of "Bemerkungen und Errinerungen" at Herr von Tratnern[4] and send them to me here. I shall pay for it with thanks.

[No address; Artaria's clerk notes: "Joseph Haydn 1787/Esterhatz 14. February /ans'd 17 ditto."]

[1] Of the *Seven Words* (see previous letter). Obviously Haydn took the four principal string parts of the orchestral version and adapted them to make the quartets.
[2] Haydn means the actual words of the Saviour (see letter of 8th April 1787), which were prefaced to each Sonata.
[3] From Op. 50.
[4] A Viennese bookseller and publisher; *recte*: (Johann Thomas) Trattnern.

[To Artaria & Co., Vienna. *German*]
                                        Estoras, 27th February 1787.

Mon tres cher Amy!

Many thanks for the portraits you sent me, which arrived safely the day before yesterday; please have the kindness to let me know what I owe you for the frames.

But now, my dear friend, as to the letter from Paris that you sent me,[1] I must frankly tell you that after due consideration, I cannot agree to it, for the following reasons: first, because by so doing I would terribly offend the gentlemen from Cadiz, who after all are responsible for my having written the Sonatas, and who paid me for them; secondly, the French gentlemen would be even more offended if I accepted payment for a work which was to be published in three weeks, from which work you, my good friend, certainly stand to derive the greatest possible profit, the more so since it can be sold as a whole as well as in quartet form.

Another thing: yesterday I received a letter from Herr von Jacoby,[2] Royal Prussian Minister, in which he wrote the following: WHAT ARE THE CIRCUMSTANCES OF SOME PIECES OF YOURS WHICH HERR ARTARIA INTENDS TO SEND TO THE KING AT BERLIN? I WOULD LIKE TO HAVE AN EXPLANATION FROM YOURSELF, AND THEREFORE BEG YOU TO GIVE ME ONE.

I hope that you do not perhaps intend to dedicate these Sonatas[3] to His Majesty, either as quartets or for full band, because that would be contrary to all common sense; but I believe that you must mean the new Quartets, which I highly approve of, if this is what you intend to do.

Please let me know about this, to allay my suspicions; I wouldn't want you thereby to disgust me altogether, for I have always been your sincere friend and will remain so.

Your most obedient servant,
Joseph Haydn.

[Address:]   Monsieur
Monsieur d'Artaria
et Compagnie
a
Vienne.

[Artaria's clerk notes: "Haydn 1787./ Esterhatz 27 February"]

[1]From the Concert Spirituel, who must have offered to print the work or perform it from MS. parts.
[2]KONSTANTIN VON JACOBI (JACOBY), Prussian Minister to the Court at Vienna, was also on good terms with the Mozarts. See Leopold's letter of 21st February 1785 (Deutsch-Paumgartner, *Leopold Mozarts Briefe an seine Tochter*, Salzburg 1936, p. 72).
[3]The *Seven Words*.

[TO ARTARIA & CO., VIENNA. German]
Estoras, 7th March 1787.
Dearest friend!
   I have no objections to any of the negotiations you propose to

undertake because of the Sonatas,[1] but motives of policy prevent my agreeing to the letter from the *Concert Spirituel*.[2] If you wish to make an offer in your name, I shall be quite satisfied. I approve of your holding back the engraving, and quite see the substantial and advantageous profits you will thereby gain. I am sincerely delighted for your sake, for I know that you will not be stingy with me on other occasions. Herr von Jacobi [*sic*] only wanted to know what work it was that you intended to dedicate to the King of Prussia, and I wrote to him that I believed it would be quartets.

I send you herewith the first movement of the 3rd Quartet;[3] you will receive the others one of the next days. I am pressed for time.

> Your wholly obedient servant,
> Joseph Haydn.

[No address.]

[1]The *Seven Words*.
[2]See previous letter.
[3]From Op. 50.

[To WILLIAM FORSTER, LONDON. *German*]
Estoras, 8th April 1787.

Monsieur!

After a long silence I must at last enquire after your health, and at the same time report that the following new works may be had of me, *viz*.: 6 elegant Symphonies;[1] a big pianoforte Concerto;[2] 3 small pianoforte Divertimenti for beginners, with violins and bass[3]; a Sonata for pianoforte alone.[4]

A brand new work, consisting of purely instrumental music divided in 7 Sonatas, each Sonata lasting 7 or 8 minutes, together with an opening Introduction and concluding with a *Terremoto*, or Earthquake. These Sonatas are written around, and composed according to, the Words which Christ our Saviour spoke on the Cross, and are entitled the *Seven Words*.

The first Word: Pater, dimitte illis, quia nesciunt, quid faciunt.
The 2nd — hodie mecum eris in Paradiso.
The 3rd — Mulier, Ecce filius tuus.
The 4th — Deus meus, Deus meus, ut dereliquisti me?
The 5th — Sitio.
The 6th — Consumatum est.
The 7th — In manus tuas commendo Spiritum meum.

The conclusion follows immediately afterwards, *i.e.*, The Earth-quake.

Each Sonata, or rather each setting of the text, is expressed only by instrumental music, but in such a way that it creates the most profound impression even on the most inexperienced listener. The whole work lasts a little more than one hour, but there is a bit of a pause after each Sonata so that one can contemplate the following text. As far as the copying goes, all the Sonatas together require a little more space than one of my symphonies, and the whole work would take about 37 sheets. Item: I have, moreover, 3 brand new and charming Notturni[5] with violin *obligato*—but not at all difficult —flute, violoncello, 2 violins ripieno, 2 hunting horns, viola and contrabasso. If you want anything of all these works, please be good enough to let me know at your earliest convenience, and also the fee you propose to give me. The 7 Sonatas are already copied, neatly and clearly, on small-sized music paper for mailing [*klein(es) Post Papier*]. Hoping for an answer I am, with esteem,

Your wholly obedient servant,
Joseph Haydn.

Please answer in French.

I hope to see you personally at the end of the year, but since I haven't heard from Herr Cramer[6] up to now, I shall accept an engagement to go to Naples this Winter.[7] But I am much obliged to you for your kind offer to put me up.

[Envelope:]　　To Mr. Will. Forster, Musical-Instrument-Maker
　　　　　　　to the Prince of Wales, N. 348, Strand.

[The letter is written on 3 pp.; the 4th is blank: no envelope is bound in with the letter at present, but Pohl (H in L, p. 356) quotes the above address: perhaps at that time the envelope was still extant.]

[1]The six "Paris" Symphonies (Nos. 82–87), written in 1785 and 1786 for the *Concert de la Loge Olympique.*
[2]The famous D major Concerto, known as "Op. 37", Hoboken XVIII: 11.
[3]Probably earlier works: Haydn wrote numerous Divertimenti and Concertini for this combination of instruments, mostly about 1760.
[4]Possibly the piano Sonata No. 48 in C.
[5]This description is not clear: Haydn may refer to the Divertimenti which Artaria had issued as Op. XXXI (Hoboken X, 12, 3, 5, 1, 4, 2) for flute, two violins, viola, bass and two horns; or (and this seems more likely) he may mean arrangements of some of the Concerti for 2 lyrae (a kind of hurdy-gurdy), 2 violins, 2 violas, 'cello (bass) and 2 horns which Haydn had composed for Ferdinand IV, King of Naples, in 1786.
[6]WILHELM CRAMER, born in Mannheim, came to London and made a considerable reputation for himself as leader, solo violinist and impresario.

He almost succeeded in persuading Haydn to come to London at this time.
⁷The afore-mentioned Concerti had evidently so delighted Ferdinand that
he had invited Haydn to come to Naples.

[TO HAYDN FROM FRIEDRICH WILHELM II, KING OF PRUSSIA. *German*]
  His Majesty, King of Prussia, &c., &c. is sensible of the mark of respect which
Herr Kapellmeister Haydn, in sending him six new Symphonies¹, again wishes to
show to His Serene Majesty. They have especially pleased him, and there is no
doubt that His Highness has always appreciated *Herr Kapellmeister* Haydn's works,
and will appreciate them at all times. To provide concrete assurance of the same,
he sends him the enclosed ring as a mark of His Highness' satisfaction and of the
favour in which he holds him.

F. Wilhelm.

Potsdam, 21st April 1787.

¹The "Paris" Symphonies (Nos. 82–87). For some curious reason Dies,
and every later biography, substituted the word "Quartets" for "Symphonies", and it was Hoboken who first discovered the correct text, as printed
in the *Wiener Zeitung* on 6th June 1787; see Hoboken, p. 408.

[TO ARTARIA & CO., VIENNA. *German*]
Estoras, 26th April 1787.

Dearest friend!
  Thank you many times for the unexpected 12 ducats—a proof of
your friendship, mine, and your efforts on my behalf. I hope to earn
the same often by my diligence, especially if, as a true friend and
honest man, you will candidly tell me who it was that offered you
my new Symphonies;¹ I swear to you on my honour not to say a
word about it; but as such a theft can be disastrous to me in the
future, and might thereafter cause damage to you, too, your con-
science should dictate to you to tell me the truth of the matter, so
that I can discover this dangerous embezzlement in time: I assure you
that I shall be eternally grateful to you. I therefore await with distress
a speedy reply, and then I shall explain further about the Symphonies. I am, most respectfully,

Your most obedient servant,
Joseph Haydn.

[No address: Artaria's clerk notes: "Haydn from Esterhaz/ 26 Apl
1787/ ans'd 27 ditto".]

¹The "Paris" Symphonies (Nos. 82–87). As the next letter shows, Artaria
must have been offered other symphonies, already known.

[To Artaria & Co., Vienna. *German*]

Estoras, 2nd May 1787.

Nobly born,

Most highly respected Sir!

I was most delighted to hear of the falsehood concerning my Symphonies. I daily expect a letter from Paris: as soon as I receive the permission, you alone shall have the right to them. I enclose a letter from Wallerstein.[1] I would like to know, one day, who this Ludwig is,[2] but there's no hurry about it. In the next mail you will hear of a present which I received quite unexpectedly from a great man.[3] Meanwhile I am, most respectfully,

Your wholly obedient servant,

Joseph Haydn.

P.S. A young Viennese composer by the name of Joseph Eybler[4] has composed 3 pianoforte Sonatas, not at all badly written, and has asked me to recommend them to you for engraving and publication. The young man is very promising, plays the pianoforte well, and knows a great deal about composition. If you wish to examine these works further, in order to guard yourself against loss, you can discuss the details with him personally. He lives on the Hoher Markt in the Juden Gässl in the Lagenhof No. 500, 2nd floor, at Herr Höbert's, silvermaster.

[No address]

[1]From someone in the service of Prince Oettingen-Wallerstein, with whom Haydn was in contact (see *supra*, p. 33 and *infra*, p. 74).
[2]The man who offered Artaria some of Haydn's symphonies (see previous letter).
[3]The ring from Friedrich Wilhelm II (see *supra*, p. 61).
[4]Joseph Eybler (1765–1846) was later Court *Kapellmeister* in Vienna. See also next letter.

[To Joseph Eybler, Vienna. *German*]

Estoras, 2nd May 1787.

Well born,

Most highly respected Sir!

I never received your first letter. The second, however—which is not dated—, I read with pleasure, and have sent a letter in today's mail to Herr Artaria, suggesting to him as warmly as possible (for you certainly deserve it) that he agree with your wish. In case you do not hear about this from Herr Artaria, be good enough to go and see him personally, and then he will discuss the details with you. I consider it my obligation to serve you in any way I can, and am, with great esteem,

Your most obedient servant,
Josephus Haydn [m.p] ria.

[No address on the other side of the sheet.]

[To ARTARIA & CO., VIENNA. *German*]
Estoras, 19th May 1787.

Most worthy friend!

This is to inform you that I have already finished the 4th Quartet,[1] and will certainly send it next Friday. Now here is something important I have to tell you: you know that I received a beautiful ring from His Majesty, the King of Prussia. I feel deeply in His Majesty's debt because of this present, and for my part I can think of no better and more fitting way to show my thankfulness to His Majesty (and also in the eyes of the whole world) than by dedicating these 6 Quartets to him; but you won't be satisfied with that, because you will want to dedicate the works yourself, and to someone else. But to make amends for this loss, I promise to give you other pieces free of charge. Let me know what you have to say to this. Perhaps we can both be satisfied. In haste,

Your most obedient
Joseph Haydn.

[Address:]   Monsieur
            Monsieur d'Artaria et
            Compag
                   à
                Vienne.

[Artaria's clerk notes: "Haydn, Giuseppe/ Esterhase/ 19 Mag /87".]

[1]From Op. 50.

[To ARTARIA & CO., VIENNA. *German*]
Estoras, 10th June 1787.

Dearest friend!

Since I shall complete the 5th Quartet this week, I assure you that you shall receive both Quartets in good order by a week from to-morrow, and finally the 6th in a short time.

I read in the paper today that my *Seven Words* is already at the engraver's. Please send me only one single copy. I understand that we shall soon have the honour of seeing you here: this would give me great pleasure.

Meanwhile I remain, most respectfully,

Your wholly obedient servant,
Josephus Haydn.

[TO ARTARIA & CO., VIENNA. *German*]

Nobly born,
Most highly respected Sir!

I have revised and corrected the *Seven Words*, not only for full band but also for quartet and piano score; but I cannot send it today with the Hussars because the parcel is too large, and so I shall send you everything, together with the 4th and 5th Quartets,[1] on Sunday at the latest, with the widowed Princess von Liechtenstein,[2] or Count von Lamberg.[3] I am sorry that the Berliners have anticipated you, but you are to blame for it yourself, for they did not receive it from me.[4] As for the dedication of the Quartets to His Majesty, the King of Prussia, I should prefer that you have it drawn up yourself by some intelligent person in Vienna, but brief and to the point. The Minister, Herr von Jacoby,[5] could assist you best of all. You can ask him in my name, too, and I shall write to the worthy gentleman myself this coming Thursday.

Meanwhile you can announce the Quartets on your own subscription.

If you want to have the first 3 Symphonies[6] from me, please let me know. Meanwhile I am, most respectfully,

Your wholly obedient servant,
Joseph Haydn.

Estoras, 21st June 1787

[No address; Artaria's clerk notes: "Haydn Giuseppe/ die Esterhazi/ 21st June 87 / ans'd 5th July".]

[1]From Op. 50.

[2]PRINCESS VON LIECHTENSTEIN, apparently the wife of Joseph Wenzel (1696–1772), the celebrated general and statesman.

[3]COUNT VON LAMBERG, Prince Esterhàzy's nephew.

[4]It is not quite clear to which work (or works) Haydn refers. The passage may refer to Hummel's first set of the Paris Symphonies, which he brought out in the same month (December 1787) as did Artaria; it seems unlikely, however, that Hummel would have announced the works half a year before

he issued them. The *Seven Words* cannot be meant either, because Hummel's
edition of that work did not appear until after Artaria's.
[5]See *supra*, p. 58.
[6]Of the "Paris" set: see letter of 2nd August 1787. Artaria published them
in sets of three each, as Op. 51 and 52.

[TO ARTARIA & CO., VIENNA. *German*]
Estoras, 23rd June 1787.

Dearest friend!

I send you the proofs of the *Seven Words* in all 3 forms.[1] *Inter alia*
I compliment you on the piano score, which is very good and has
been prepared with the greatest care. I should be happy if you could
place the word "Fr—lim"[2] of the 3rd Sonata in the first violin part
of the version for full band, just as I have indicated it in the quartet
version. I enclose the fourth Quartet,[3] you will quite certainly
receive the 5th this coming week.

I am, as always,
Your most obedient servant,
Haydn.

N.B. The last movement, *il Terremoto*, is not engraved in the viola
part at all.
[No address: Artaria's clerk notes: "Haydn Giuseppe/ Esterhaze
23rd June/ 87/ ans'd 5th July".]

[1]See previous letters.
[2]It is unclear what Haydn means here: the Words which preface the third
Sonata are "Mulier, Ecce filius tuus", nor does "Fr——lim" stand for these
words in French or German.
[3]From Op. 50.

[TO WILLIAM FORSTER, LONDON. *French*]
Monsieur!

I enclose the music composed after the Seven Last Words which
Jesus Christ spoke on the Cross; I leave it to your judgement to send
me what you think I deserve for it.

I hope perhaps to have the pleasure of seeing you this Winter;
meanwhile I am, *Monsieur*, respectfully,
Your most humble and obedient servant,
Joseph Haydn [m.p.] ria.

Estoras, 28th June 1787.

[No address on the letter (it was sent with the Oratorio in one parcel); the blank reverse side contains the date of arrival in London: "July 16th/p".]

[To Artaria & Co., Vienna. *German*]

Estoras, 12th July 1787.

Well born,
Most highly respected Sir!

I send you herewith the 6th Quartet.[1] Lack of time prevented my having the 5th copied up to now, but I have composed it meanwhile. I would have gladly sent you the Quartet version of the *Seven Words*, but there was no opportunity yet; I hope, however, to find one soon.

I shall bring you the Symphonies[2] myself after St. Anne's Day.[3] Meanwhile I am, most respectfully,

Your most obedient servant,
Joseph Haydn.

[No address; Artaria's clerk notes: "Haydn Giuseppe/ Esterhaze 12th July/87".]

[1]From Op. 50.
[2]The first of the "Paris" Symphonies.
[3]July 26.

[To John Gallini,[1] London. *Italian*]

Estoras, 19th July 1787.

. . . I acknowledge to have received your letter dated the 26th of last June and then, when I thought to have heard of your offers, you request once more to know my terms. So I tell you this: that I promise and commit myself to write a new opera and to assist at your concerts in Hanover Square, and my final demand for this is £500 stirling [*sic*] and a free benefit concert. And in giving me that sum within a limited time, I shall be entirely at your service during the contract. If, on the other hand, you can agree with Mr. Cramer[2] and his Associates that between you the sum of £500 shall be made up, I will write a new opera for you, assist at your concerts in Hanover Square, and I will compose for Mr. Cramer and his Associates six pieces of instrumental music, and in that case, each of you must give

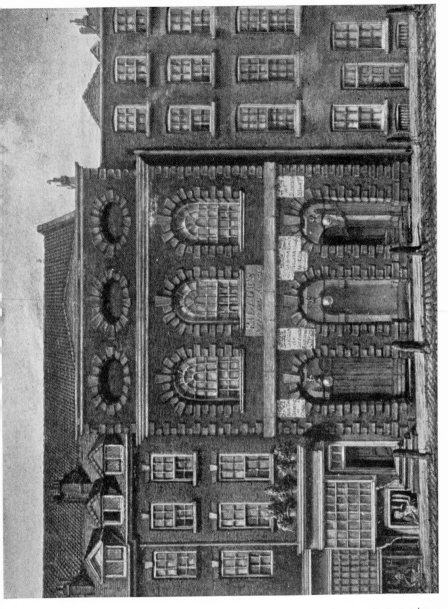

VIII The King's Theatre, Haymarket, 1783, from the print by William Capon (reproduced from Terry's *John Christian Bach* by kind permission of Oxford University Press).

OPERA HOUSE or KINGS THEATRE in the HAY-MARKET.

An Inside View of the Opera House.

IX   The King's Theatre, Haymarket, interior, reproduced with kind permission of the Royal College of Music, London.

me a free benefit; so that if you choose to have me alone, I ask £ 500 and only one free benefit. If, on the other hand, with Cramer &c., the same sum of £ 500 and two benefits, *i.e.* one from you and another from Mr. Cramer and his Associates. If you come to an agreement with each other for this sum, I am ready to comply with your request, and as soon as it is settled, I oblige myself by these presents to execute the commission, and give you authority to announce my arrival in the public newspapers. I desire nothing more at present than the pleasure of knowing you personally, as I have hitherto by reputation, and look forward to putting my modest talents at your disposal. . . .

Giuseppe Haydn.

[From the English translation in Sotheby, Wilkinson & Hodge's Catalogue No. 569, of 1905.]

[1]GALLINI, impresario and director of the Italian opera, later commissioned Haydn to write *L'anima del filosolo*, in 1791 (see *infra*, pp. 115*f*., 126).
[2]WILHELM CRAMER, see *supra*, p. 60.

[TO GEORG ANTON KREUSSER,[1] *Kapellmeister* TO THE *Kurfürst von Mainz. German*]

Estoras, 28th July 1787.

Nobly born,
Most highly respected Sir,

I take the liberty of asking you to be good enough to deliver in my humble name the two Symphonies[2] herewith enclosed to your gracious Prince and Serene Highness; and as he recently wanted to know the costs of all the music I sent him up to now, I beg to inform His Highness that the copying charges were 50 gulden, and for my underserving self I humbly suggest one hundred Taler. If this demand should seem in any way exorbitant to your most gracious Prince, I won't demand a Kreutzer.[3] I deem myself fortunate to enjoy the privilege of having His Highness condescend to listen to my humble efforts.

I commend these two Symphonies to your profound insight; and with the hopes that they will be performed in a manner commensurate with the same, I am, Sir, with profound respect,

Your wholly obedient servant,
Josephus Haydn [m.] pria.

[No envelope extant]

J.H.–G

[1]KREUSSER was a well-known composer; his Symphonies and other works were widely circulated in manuscript and printed editions (*e.g.* Hummel). Adolf Sandberger, who first published the letter (see Sources), thought the letter might have been addressed to Johann Michael Schmid (or Schmidt), but he was a very old man in 1787 (if in fact he was still alive), and Kreusser was undoubtedly the recipient.

[2]Either two of the "Paris" Symphonies (Sandberger's and Larsen's opinion) or Symphonies Nos. 88 and 89 (1787) (Hoboken's opinion). In view of the fact that Haydn was offering the "Paris" Symphonies to many publishers and individuals at this time, I consider Sandberger's and Larsen's suggestion the more plausible of the two.

[3]*I.e.,* "I won't demand a farthing."

[TO ARTARIA & CO., VIENNA. *German*]

Estoras, 2nd August 1787.

Well born,
Most highly respected Sir!

Last time I forgot to indicate the order of the Symphonies,[1] which should be engraved as follows: the Symphony in A Number 1, in Bb No 2, in g [minor] No. 3, in Eb No. 4, in D No. 5, in C No. 6.

You can print the first 3 in 3 months, as you have promised, but if at all possible I would ask you to wait a little with the last 3.

You must tell the person to whom you will give the Symphonies for copying emphatically not to pass them on.

Now may I ask you, if it is possible, to have the piano score of the *Seven Words* copied for one of my special friends; I promise you on my honour that you will not suffer the least damage because of it. I shall pay for the copying at once. Please send me the portraits of Morichelli and Salieri.[2] Meanwhile I remain, most respectfully,

Your most obedient servant,
Jos: Haydn.

[Address:]   Monsieur
          Monsieur d'Artaria et
          Compag.
               à
          Vienne.

[Artaria's clerk notes: "Haydn Giuseppe/ Esterhaze 2 Agt/87".]

[1]The "Paris" Symphonies. Artaria's order is possibly the order in which they were written, *i.e.* 87, 85, 83, 84, 86, 82; 87 and 83 are dated 1785 on the autographs, 84, 86 and 82, 1786; the complete MS. of 85 has not survived.

[2]The famous soprano, ANNA MORICHELLI, who later sang in Haydn's benefit

concert (see p. 306) and the Court *Kapellmeister* Antonio Salieri (1750–1825), both of whose portraits (engraved, as had been Haydn's, by Mansfeld) Artaria had published.

[To William Forster, London. *French*]

Monsieur,

I hope that you will have received my last letter [28th June], and the music of the *Seven Words*. I would like to inform you that I have composed six Quartets and six Symphonies,[1] which I have not yet given to anyone. If you would like them, be good enough to let me know it at your earliest convenience. I will give you all twelve pieces for twenty-five guineas. I am, with all possible esteem,

Your most humble servant,
Joseph Haydn.

Estoras, 8th August 1787.

[Address:] [postal stamp "Au[g] 25", the date of arrival in London]

To Mr Forster Musical
Instrument-Macker, to the
Prince of Wales.
Nro 346 [*sic*]   a
in the Strand

London.

[1]Quartets Op. 50 and the "Paris" Symphonies. Forster took them both.

[To Artaria & Co., Vienna. *German*]

Estoras, 16th September 1787.

Nobly born,
Most highly respected Sir!

Because no safe opportunity presented itself, I could not send the enclosed Quartet[1] before. Now, thank God! I am glad that I finished them at last.

Please send the proofs of the first [Quartets] of the series for correction as soon as possible.

I am, most respectfully,

Your wholly obedient servant,
Joseph Haydn [m.] pria.

[No address]

[1]The fifth of Op. 50.

[TO WILLIAM FORSTER, LONDON. *French*]

Monsieur!

I received your letter with much pleasure. I would inform
you that I have received five guineas from *Mons. le General* Jermingham,[1] but you must see yourself that for music such as that of the
Seven Words I deserve more; you could give me at least five guineas
more.[2] Meanwhile I send you the six Quartets,[3] for which you will
be kind enough to send me twenty guineas as soon as possible, as
stipulated in the contract. I shall not fail to send you the six Symphon-
nies[4] at the first opportunity. I await the favour of your early reply,
and remain with all possible esteem, *Monsieur*,

Your most humble and obedient servant

Joseph Haydn [m.p.] ria.

Estoras, 20th September 1787.

[No address, since the letter was sent with the Quartets in a parcel; on the other
side of the sheet, Forster or one of his clerks has written: "with Haydn's 4tos
[quartettos] Op. 44", the Op. No. under which Forster published them.]

[1] See *supra*, p. 55 (56).

[2] Forster seems to have paid Haydn the additional five guineas; in the firm's
account book is the note: "July 1787. Recd of Haydn M.S.S. of the Cruci-
fixion published with title of 'Passion'. Ten guineas was paid for this instrumental piece; and the Postage cost fifteen Shillings" (Sandys and Forster,
The History of the Violin, London 1864, p. 310).

[3] Op. 50. Forster made Haydn sign a contract. The following interesting
letter from Charles Jermingham throws some light on the negotiations:
"Sir/I received Your favour 21 ins.t & send here inclosed a letter for Mr
Giuseppe Hayden to whom I have written very circumstantially & inclosed
to him a procuration which he is to gett drawn up either in French, German,
or Latin, & authenticated by two wittnesses & a publick notary, which
gives it full force in all Countries; you may depend on it that what I have
sent to Mr. Hayden is to the full as strong as the letter of Attorney you sent
me in which theres nothing but a repetition of words. If you receive from
Hayden a letter for me send it to Lady Jerminghams in Grovener [*sic*]
square she will take care I get it[.] when Hayden has sent you his procuration
to print his musick lett me know it and am Sir Your most obedt humble
servt Charles Jermingham. Cawsey August 24th 1787."

[4] The "Paris" Symphonies.

[TO ARTARIA & CO., VIENNA. *German*]

Estoras, 7th October 1787.

Mon tres cher amy,

I shall send you the Quartets,[1] at the very first opportunity, and
I shall be playing through them today; I cannot send them in the
mail bag. I was astonished at your penultimate letter concerning the

theft of the Quartets.[2] I assure you on my honour that they were not copied by my copyist,[3] who is a most honest fellow, whereas your copyist is a rascal, for he offered mine 8 gold ducats this Winter if he would give him the *Seven Words*. I am sorry not to be in Vienna myself so as to have him arrested: My plan would be to make Herr Lausch appear before Herr von Augusti, the mayor, and make him confess from whom he received the Quartets. Herr von Augusti is an old friend of mine and will certainly help you in this matter, as he did once before in just such an affair. Although you have everything copied on your own premises, you may be swindled all the same, because the rascals put a piece of paper *a parte* under the music, and thus by degrees they secretly copy the part they have in front of them. I am sorry that this misfortune happened to you. In future I shall take the precaution of sending my own copyist up to you. I am, most respectfully,

Your wholly obedient servant,
Haydn.

[Address:]   Monsieur
                    Monsieur d'Artaria et
                    Compag
                              a
                         Vienne.

[Artaria's clerk notes: "Haydn Giuseppe/ Esterhaze 7th Oct/ 1787 ans'd 25th Oct."]

[1]The proofs of Op. 50.
[2]L. LAUSCH, a well-known Viennese music copyist who sold MS. copies of the newest works of Haydn, Mozart, *etc.*, seems to have bribed someone to get the Quartets (Op. 50) which Artaria was in the process of publishing. Apparently Artaria felt that the sale of these copies, even though in MS., was detrimental to his business. In a letter to Artaria of 18th August 1788, Haydn's old friend Dittersdorf (see *supra*, p. 21) offers some new quartets, and adds in a P.S. "I must add that no one has the quartets (not like the Hayden Quartets you printed, which not only the Prince here, but various other people had bought long before in MS. copies, on subscription, for 6 ♯ [ducats]) . . ." (Artaria–Botstiber, p. 43).
[3]Probably Johann or Joseph Elssler Jr.

[TO ARTARIA & CO., VIENNA. *German*]
Estoras, 22nd November 1787.

Nobly born,
Most highly respected Sir!

I regret that it was not till today that I had a safe opportunity by which I could return to you the corrected Quartets and Symphonies.[1]

Concerning the lie of Herr Bartolozzi, or rather the true cavalier of Verona,[2] I don't know whether I should laugh or be angry, since I am grateful to the Lord when I am able to complete my works once in my handwriting; these are boastful and wild imaginings, and such falsifications attempt to belittle my credit. In the end I won't publish anything at all. Meanwhile I am, Sir, most respectfully,

Your wholly obedient servant,
Josephus Haydn.

[Address:]   Monsieur
          Monsieur Artaria et
          Compag.
                    à
                    Vienne.
Together with a parcel of music
[Artaria's clerk notes: "Haydn di / Esterhaze 2(*recte*:22) Nov./ 1787".]

[1]Op. 50 and the "Paris" Symphonies.
[2]Probably GAETANO BARTOLOZZI, the well-known artist and engraver, who lived in London and with whom Haydn later became friends. See also p. 265. The clause "des sicheren Cavaliers aus Verona" may be a paraphrase of some play or *Singspiel* (a translation of Shakespeare's *Two Gentlemen of Verona*?). Bartolozzi must have informed Artaria of Forster's forthcoming edition of the new Quartets (see next letter), and said that Haydn had sent a second autograph to London. Forster had received parts, of course.

[TO ARTARIA & CO., VIENNA. *German*]

Estoras, 27th November 1787.

Nobly born,
Most highly respected Sir!

You will forgive me, good Sir, that I have been unable to answer you sooner, for want of a good opportunity. You want me to give you a certificate [*Attest*] for the 6 Quartets: I enclose it herewith. It is not true, however, that I gave a separate certificate to Herr Forster, giving him the sole rights to these works; but it is true that I sent one to him after the Quartets had already been engraved. It's your own fault, because you could have sent the Quartets to Herr Langmann[1] 3 months ago, and at the same time given him the sole rights. But your having held them back derives from your own great selfishness:

no one can blame me for attempting to secure some profit for myself, after the pieces have been engraved: for I am not properly recompensed for my works, and have a greater right to get this profit than the other dealers. Therefore you will see that the contracts between us are more carefully drawn up, and I that I am sufficiently remunerated. If you lose GENERALLY because of this, however, I shall find a way to compensate you in another way. Meanwhile I remain, with the greatest esteem, Sir,

Your most obedient servant,
Joseph Haydn.

[Artaria's clerk notes: "Haydn Giuseppe / Esterhaze 27th Nov. /1787".]

[1]LONGMAN & BRODERIP, Artaria's London associates, later published many of Haydn's late pianoforte trios, *etc.*

[To FRANZ ROTH (ROTT),[1] *Oberverpflegs-Verwalter,* PRAGUE. *German*]
December 1787.[2]

. . . . You ask me for an *opera buffa.* Most willingly, if you want to have one of my vocal compositions for yourself alone. But if you intend to produce it on the stage at Prague, in that case I cannot comply with your wish, because all my operas are far too closely connected with our personal circle (Esterház, in Hungary), and moreover they would not produce the proper effect, which I calculated in accordance with the locality. It would be quite another matter if I were to have the great good fortune to compose a brand new libretto for your theatre. But even then I should be risking a good deal, for scarcely any man can brook comparison with the great Mozart.

If I could only impress on the soul of every friend of music, and on high personages in particular, how inimitable are Mozart's works, how profound, how musically intelligent, how extraordinarily sensitive! (for this is how I understand them, how I feel them)—why then the nations would vie with each other to possess such a jewel within their frontiers. Prague should hold him fast—but should reward him, too; for without this, the history of great geniuses is sad indeed, and gives but little encouragement to posterity to further exertions; and unfortunately this is why so many promising intellects fall by the wayside. It enrages me to think that this incomparable

Mozart is not yet engaged by some imperial or royal court! Forgive me if I lose my head: but I love the man so dearly. I am, &c.

Joseph Hayden [sic].

N.S. My respectful compliments to the Prague Orchestra and all the virtuosi there.

[1]Roth (or more probably Rott, as in Dlabacz) held concerts several times a year in his house in Prague. See Schönfeld, *Jahrbuch der Tonkunst für Wien und Prag*, 1796, p. 140; Dlabacz, *Künstler-Lexicon für Böhmen*, Prague 1815, II, 597.
[2]The letter, first printed in Niemetschek's *Mozart* (Prague 1798, pp. 51*f*.) and later that year in the *Allgemeine Musikalische Zeitung*, is not dated more exactly. The autograph has not survived.

[To Ferdinand Müller von Müllegg,[1] Vienna. *German*]

Estoras, 3rd February 1788.

Nobly born,
Most highly respected Herr von Müller!

The appreciation which His Highness the Prince von Oettingen has shown for my modest compositions is of the greatest possible value to me, and I only regret that at present I cannot have the great pleasure of writing the 3 Symphonies that are demanded, because I now have to compose 6 Notturni for His Majesty the King of Naples[2] and a new opera[3] for my gracious Prince. But when these works are finished, I shall make every effort to compose the 3 Symphonies, for which I do not presume to set a price, but beg to leave this entirely to the discretion of His Most Serene Highness the Prince. For the oratorio,[4] which I recently improved by adding two new choruses, I beg to ask 16 ducats, five of which I must pay the copyist. Should I be fortunate enough to receive the gracious approval of some of these proposals, I shall then await further commands. Meanwhile I am, Sir, in profound submission,

Your most obedient servant,
Joseph Haydn.

[1]Ferdinand Müller von und zu Müllegg (*c.* 1758–1824) was an ardent amateur musician and, among other things, Prince Oettingen-Wallerstein's Court Agent in Vienna. On 16th January the Prince had written to von Müller concerning the oratorio and 3 new Symphonies, which (said the Prince) "no one should own except me". See letter of *c.* 17th October 1789. This and the following notes are based largely on Diemand, 'Joseph Haydn und der Wallersteiner Hof' (*Zeitschrift des historischen Vereins für Schwaben und Neuburg*, Band 45 [1920–1922], pp. 31*ff*.).

[2]FERDINAND IV. Haydn delivered the Notturni in 1790, when Ferdinand was visiting his royal relatives in Vienna.
[3]This is possibly a white lie, because Haydn wrote his last opera for the Prince in 1784 (*Armida*).
[4]The oratorio was *Il ritorno di Tobia* (1774–1775): the score is still preserved in the Oettingen-Wallerstein Archives, Harburg Castle.

[To ARTARIA & Co., VIENNA. *German*]
Nobly born,
Most highly respected Sir!
   Please don't take it amiss that through lack of time I couldn't write to you myself recently[1] about the Oratorio. Should the Oratorio be copied already (which I trust is the case), please give it to our porter, from whom I shall receive it safely. Send him the bill for the copying costs at the same time, which I shall repay at the first available opportunity. By the way, I am very much obliged to you for the excellent cheese you sent me, and also for the sausages, for which I am your debtor; But I shall not fail to return the obligation, when an opportunity offers.
   Please also send me C. P. Emanuel Bach's last two pianoforte works.[2] Meanwhile I remain, Sir, most respectfully,
                          Your most obedient servant,
                              Joseph Haydn.
Estoras, 16th February 1788.
[Address:]   Monsieur
            Monsieur d'Artaria et Compag
                      a
                          Vienne.
         Please expedite.

[1]Haydn got his brother, Johann, who was a tenor in the Esterházy choir, to write. The letter (Stadtbibiliothek, Vienna, cat. 69610) reads: "Nobly born and highly respected Sir, At the request of my brother, *Cappell Meister* Haydn, I take the liberty of asking you to send me the *Seven Words* for the pianoforte, in his arrangement; you should give it, marked with my address, to Herr Rosenbaum, Prince Esterházy's porter. My brother will see to the payment, and he has permitted me in the future to ask in his name for those pieces which I require. He will confirm this when he pays you his next visit. Hoping to receive the piece soon, I remain, Sir, &c. Johann Haydn. Eisenstadt, 9th December 1787."
[2]C.P.E. Bach, who died in December 1788, published only one work with

Artaria: Six Sonatas for Harpsichord (pl. no. 181). Haydn, however, probably referred to the recent German editions of the 5th and 6th collections of
Clavier-Sonaten (1785 and 1787—Wotquenne 59 and 61), or the *Sechs
neue Sonatinen*, 1787 (Wotquenne 63).

[TO WILLIAM FORSTER, LONDON. *German*]
                                        Estoras, 28th February 1788.
My very dear *Mons*: Forster!
   Don't be angry at me that you have disagreeableness with Herr
Langmann.[1] I shall make it up to you another time. It's not my fault
but the usurious practices of Herr Artaria. This much I can promise
you: that as long as I live neither Artaria nor Langmann shall have
anything from me, directly or indirectly. I am too honest and
straightforward to want to hurt your feelings or to damage you. But
you certainly must realize that whoever wants to have the exclusive
rights for 6 new pieces of mine must pay more than 20 guineas. In
fact I have recently signed a contract with someone who pays me
100 and more guineas for each 6 works. I shall write you more about
this another time. Meanwhile I am, with great respect,
                                   Your wholly obedient servant,
                                          Joseph Haydn.
[Address:] [postal stamp "M[a]r 15", the date of arrival in London]
                     To Mr Forster Musical
               Instrument-Macker to the Prince
               of Wales. N^ro 348 in the Strand.
                                a
                            London.
   [1] *Recte*: Longman (& Broderip): see *supra*.

[TO ARTARIA & CO., VIENNA. *German*]
                                        Estoras, 22nd May 1788.
Dearest friend!
   I would be unjust and ungrateful if I were to throw away your
friendship so boorishly. I shall never forget that you gave me preference over many, though I well know that I occasionally deserved
it more than the others; as soon as my present affairs are completed,
you shall have some of my works, as before. If you were to write me
before your departure, so that I could answer it in time, I should be

pleased for a number of reasons. My time is too short today. I am, as always, most respectfully,

Your wholly obedient servant,
Josephus Haydn.

[To Artaria & Co., Vienna. *German*]

Estoras, 10th August 1788.

Well born,
Most highly respected Sir!

My manifold affairs have prevented me from writing my long-overdue answer to your last letter. I repeat that it will always be a pleasure to supply you with my works. Since I am now in a position where I need a little money, I propose to write for you, by the end of December, either 3 new Quartets or 3 new pianoforte Sonatas with accompaniment of a violin and violoncello. I would ask you, for your part, to send me an *a conto* of 25 gold ducats next Wednesday by our outgoing Hussars. You can leave the letter and the money with our porter Wednesday morning. Meanwhile the present letter should serve as your security. You shall have the receipt on the coming Monday. Of course it is understood that I shall then complete the other 3 Quartets, or pianoforte Sonatas, so that the edition will comprise half-a-dozen, as usual. NB.—For 6 Quartets the previous sum of one hundred ducats, for 6 pianoforte Sonatas 300 fl. In the hope of a favourable answer, I am Sir, most respectfully,

Your most obedient servant,
Josephus Haydn.

[Address:]   Monsieur

Monsieur d'Artaria et Compag
à
Vienne.

[To Artaria & Co., Vienna. *German*]

Estoras, 17th August 1788.

Well born,
Most highly respected Sir!

Many thanks for the 25 ducats which you sent me. The zeal I shall bestow on the 3 pianoforte Sonatas[1] with accompaniment of a violin and violoncello which you want, shall be a guarantee of my wish to retain your friendship in the future. Meanwhile I am, Sir, most respectfully,

Your most obedient servant,
Josephus Haydn.

[1]Nos. 11–13 of the chronological list: Artaria published them in July 1789 as Op. 57 (pl. no. 239).

[To Artaria & Co., Vienna. *German*]
Estoras, 29th August 1788.

[No copy available: the only known reference to this letter occurs in a Parisian antiquarian bookseller's catalogue of 1887.]

[To Artaria & Co., Vienna. *German*]
Estoras, 22nd September 1788.

Monsieur
et mon tres cher Amy!

   A few days ago I was told that you, my dear Sir, were supposed to have purchased from Herr Tost[1] my very newest 6 Quartets and 2 new Symphonies. Since I would like to know, for various reasons, if this is true or not, I would ask you to let me know on the next post-day. I remain, Sir, most respectfully,

Your most obedient servant,
Joseph Haydn.

[Address:]   Monsieur
Monsieur d'Artaria et compag:

a

Vienne.

[1]Johann Tost, violinist in the Esterházy band, who went on a journey to Paris about this time, taking with him the 6 Quartets Op. 54 and 55, and two new Symphonies, Nos. 88 and 89. Tost, when he returned to Vienna in 1789 or 1790, married a rich wife and became a well-known merchant (*Grosshandlungs-Gremialist*) and patron of chamber music. Both Haydn and Mozart wrote some of their loveliest works for him. See Larsen, p. 114 n. 56, and Hoboken's address in *Das Archiv für Photogramme* (brochure published by the Österreichische Nationalbibliothek, Vienna 1958, pp. 37*f*.), for the most recent research on the subject.

[TO ARTARIA & CO., VIENNA. *German*]

Estoras, 26th October 1788.

Well born,

Most highly respected Sir!

    In order to compose your 3 pianoforte Sonatas particularly well, I had to buy a new fortepiano. Now since no doubt you have long since realized that scholars are sometimes short of money—and that is my situation at present—I should like to ask you, Sir, if you would be kind enough to pay 31 gold ducats to the organ and instrument-maker Wenzl Schanz, who lives on the Leimgruben at the Blauen Schif[f] N$^{o.}$ 22; which 31 ducats I shall repay to you, with thanks, by the end of January of the coming year 1789. To convince you that I shall keep my word, I have enclosed a small promissary note which I have recalled today. But should you have any doubts of my integrity, I shall send you on the next post-day a bond for a thousand Gulden signed by my Prince himself. I don't like to be in debt to tradesmen, and—thank God!—I am free of such burdens; but since great people keep me waiting so long for payment, things have come to a standstill. Meanwhile this letter should be your security, and shall be valid in any court. I will pay off the interest in cash.[1] Confident that you will not refuse my request I wrote to the organ-builder, who will quite certainly come to get his money.

    Please excuse this liberty: it is bestowed on a man who is grateful, and will ever remain

Your most obedient servant,

Joseph Haydn

Capell Meister.

P.S. I shall have the pleasure of seeing you in Vienna towards the end of December.

[Address:]   Monsieur

Monsieur d'Artaria et

Compag.

à

Vienne.

[Artaria's clerk notes: "Heydn [*sic*] Giuseppe/Esterhaze 26th Oct/ 1788/ ans'd 30th ditto".]

---

[1]Haydn writes "mit Notten ersetzen", which may mean either "in [bank] notes", *i.e.* cash, or "with music".

[To Artaria & Co., Vienna. *German*]

Estoras, 16th November 1788.

Well born,
Most highly respected Sir!

Many thanks for the correct payment which you made in my name to Herr Schanz. I shall keep my word punctually, not only as to the repayment but also as to the 3 new Sonatas, of which one and one-half are already completed. Meanwhile I remain, respectfully,

Your most obedient servant,
Joseph Haydn.

[Address "as always"—note on Pohl's MS. copy, the earliest preserved source.]

[To Artaria & Co., Vienna. *German*]

Estoras, 8th March 1789.

Well born,
Most highly respected Sir!

The abrupt decision of my Prince to leave Vienna, which he hates, caused my hasty departure for Estoras, and prevented my being able to take leave of the greater number of my friends; I hope that you, too, will therefore forgive me. On the day of my departure I was seized with such a violent catarrh that for three whole weeks I was of no use to anyone, but now—thank God!—I feel better. I promise to send the 3rd Sonata[1] in a week, and enclose herewith the two signatures you requested. As to the other works—some of which I have finished—I shall inform you another time. Meanwhile I am, dear Sir, most respectfully,

Your most obedient servant,
Josephus Haydn.

[No address; Artaria's clerk notes: "Heydn Giuseppe/Esterhaze 8. Marzo/1789".]

[1]The last of the three pianoforte Trios: see *supra*, p. 77 (78).

[To Johann Traeg,[1] Vienna. *German*]

Estoras, 8th March 1789.

Well born,
Most highly respected Sir!

This is to inform you that the new pianoforte Sonata which Herr

Breitkopf requested[2] shall be finished by the coming week. You will therefore be good enough to let me know to whom I should address the sonata, and who shall pay me the 10 ducats upon delivery of the same. I hope to receive a satisfactory reply and am, most respectfully,

Your most obedient servant,
Josephus Haydn [m.p] ria.
Capell Meister von
Fürst Esterhazy.

P.S.: You need only leave your letter at the porter's in the Prince's mansion; a carriage leaves almost daily.

[Address:]

Dem Wohl Edlen Herrn Johann
Traeg Musicalien Händler zu
zustellen.[3]
auf den Hohen Marck[t] in
N^ro 423 in   Wienn.
4^tn Stock

[1]JOHANN TRAEG, one of Vienna's busiest copyists, later became a music publisher.
[2]CHRISTOPH GOTTLOB BREITKOPF had made a journey to Austria in the autumn of 1786, and had intended to visit Haydn in Esterháza; the composer happened to come to Vienna in December, however, and Breitkopf met him there. On 10 January 1789, Breitkopf wrote a letter to Haydn. The letter no longer exists, but we can quote a summary of it (Hase, pp. 3*f*.) Breitkopf writes that "he would like to have a new pianoforte Sonata, one which has never before been printed, to include in a collection of various pieces of music which he [Breitkopf] is putting together. As a recommendation for the whole undertaking, he would like to have an original composition by Haydn, even if it is only one movement. Haydn can choose his own fee, and the Sonata must be in his hands by March at the latest, because he intends to start the publication in that month . . . He asks if Haydn would not do him the honour of giving his firm other compositions, and if so, would [Haydn] not write six pianoforte Sonatas; he can choose his own fee for these works, too." Haydn chose the Sonata No. 48 in C which, however, he could not send until 5th April (see letter, *infra*). The Sonata was published as the first number of "Musikalischer Pot-Pourri". In all these dealings, Traeg acted as the go-between.
[3]"To be delivered to . . ." &c.

[TO JOSEPH EYBLER,[1] VIENNA. *German*]
Estoras, 22nd March 1789.

Dearest *Mons.* Eybler!
Thank you so much for all your good wishes: I return them all to

you with my whole heart. I was pleased to hear of the good reception of your Symphony and regret that I could not be there as an eye- and ear-witness, but I hope to hear it in Vienna. Now, my dear friend, I would ask you to write 3 new Dance Minuets for me, but including a Trio with each one. I shall tell you the reason for my request myself, by and by; meanwhile I can only say that these 3 Minuets are intended for one of my best friends, and that you must not give them to anyone else beforehand, much less have them per- formed. *Sed hoc inter nos.*

You can tell Herr Humel[2] that 2 of my Symphonies, which I composed for Herr Tost,[3] will soon appear in print. The other two, however, will not appear for a few years. Please excuse this hasty note, but this is the 10th letter I have to mail. Meanwhile I am, most respectfully,

Your most sincere friend and servant,
Jos: Haydn.

Please send my affectionate greetings[4] to the 2 great men, Mozart and Albrechtsberger.[5]

[Address:]   Monsieur
    Monsieur Joseph Eybler
      Maitre de la Musique
    in der Kohlmesser
    gasse N^r: 668 im   a
    2^{tn} Stock   Vienne.

[1]See *supra*, p. 62.
[2]Hummel, the Berlin music publisher.
[3] Symphonies Nos. 88 and 89: see *supra*, p. 78.
[4]"Küssen Sie stat meiner".
[5]JOHANN GEORG ALBRECHTSBERGER (1736–1809), a well-known composer and theorist; especially esteemed for his knowledge of counterpoint. He was one of Haydn's oldest friends, and had played 'cello in the quartet parties at Schloss Weinzierl, where Haydn first performed his early string Quartets.

[TO ARTARIA & CO., VIENNA. German]
Estoras, 29th March 1789.

Mon très cher amy!

I send you herewith the 3rd Sonata,[1] which I have rewritten with variations, to suit your taste. Please hurry the engraving of all 3 as best you can, because many people are anxiously awaiting the publication. In my leisure hours I have completed a new *Capriccio*[2] for the pianoforte which, from its taste, singularity and careful execution cannot but fail to be received with approbation from professional and non-professional alike. It's only one piece, rather long, but not all too difficult; since I always give you the preference in my works, I now offer it to you for 24 ducats: the price is rather high, but I assure you a profit on it; since in any case I am your debtor, you can deduct the sum from the debt. In awaiting your opinion, I remain, most respectfully,

Your most obedient servant,
Joseph Haydn.

[Address:]   Monsieur
Monsieur d'Artaria et
Compag
With a roll of music
Vienne.

[Artaria's clerk notes: "Heydn Giuseppe / Esterhaze 29.Marzo/1789/ ans'd 2 Apl.".]

[1]Pianoforte Trio (see *supra*, p. 77 (78).
[2]The *Fantasia* in C, which Artaria published as Op. 58 (pl. No. 250) in September; an advance copy was sent to Haydn two months earlier (see letter of 5th July 1789).

[To CHRISTOPH GOTTLOB BREITKOPF, LEIPZIG. *German*]
Estoras, 5th April 1789.

Well born,
Most highly respected Sir!

Through Herr Traeg[1] I am sending you the new pianoforte Sonata, fully hoping that it will meet with the musical world's approbation. I have received the 10 # [ducats] in good order, for which I thank you. As for the other demands in your letter, I cannot accomodate you because I am simply overloaded with work. I would only ask for a clean engraving, and that you send me a few copies. Meanwhile I remain, most respectfully,

Your most obedient servant,
Joseph Haydn.

I would ask you at your convenience to send me a few English engravings, but beautiful ones, for I am a great admirer of them; I shall repay you gratefully by something of my work.

J.H.–H

[1]See the commentary on Haydn's letter to Traeg of 8th March,1789. The passage in the present letter concerning "the other demands" may be explained as follows: we have seen that Breitkopf wanted Haydn to write six new Sonatas. Haydn seems to have told Traeg that he would do so, and that the price would be 60 ducats; if pianoforte Trios, his price would be 80 ducats, but this time he would give them to Breitkopf for only 70. Breitkopf thereupon announced the six pianoforte Sonatas in February 1789 on a subscription basis, and wrote to Haydn in March reminding him of the works. As it happened, the response to the subscription was not very promising, and Breitkopf subsequently (June 1789) asked Haydn to send two rather than six Sonatas, which would be included in further numbers of the "Pot-Pourri". But nothing came of this new plan, either. (Hase, pp. 4*ff.*)

[To JEAN-GEORGES SIEBER, PARIS. *German*]

Estoras, 5th April 1789.

Monsieur!

I am very surprised not to have received a letter from you, because (as Herr Tost[1] wrote to me a long time ago) you are supposed to have purchased 4 Symphonies and 6 pianoforte Sonatas for one hundred Louis d'or: as far as I am concerned, I regret being bound to Herr Tost for the 4 Symphonies, because he still owes me 300 f [Gulden] for the 4 pieces. If you will take over this debt of 300 f, I guarantee to compose these four Symphonies for you; but Herr Tost has no rights at all to the six pianoforte Sonatas, and has thus swindled you; you can claim your damages in Vienna. Now I would ask you to tell me candidly just how, and in what fashion, Herr Tost behaved in Paris. Did he have an *Amour* there? And did he also sell you the 6 Quartets, and for what sum? Please let me know all this as soon as possible. Meanwhile I remain, most respectfully,

Your wholly obedient servant,

Josephus Haydn.

[Address:]   Monsieur Sieber

Marchand de la Musique,

Paris.

[1]With this letter the *affaire* Tost, to which Haydn had previously referred in a letter to Artaria (see *supra*, p. 78), becomes even more mysterious. Tost had with him Symphonies Nos. 88, 89 and six Quartets (known as Op. 54 and 55). Haydn never denied Tost's rights to these works, and obviously expected Tost to sell them, as the end of the present letter shows. But how the two Symphonies suddenly became four is most unclear. Perhaps Haydn intended to write two more for Tost. (See also the passing reference to the four works in the letter of 22nd March, *supra*.) In 1788 and 1789, Haydn

did in fact compose three new Symphonies (Nos. 90–92), but he dedicated them to the Comte d'Ogny in Paris, and they were patently intended for the *Concert de la Loge Olympique,* for which he had written the "Paris" Symphonies. The *affaire* Tost is further complicated by the fact that Tost seems to have sold Sieber a Gyrowetz Symphony under Haydn's name (Symphony in G: see Larsen, p. 115 and Landon, p. 3). The six Sonatas are possibly Nos. 33, 34 and 43 together with 40–42; three, however, may have been Nos. 44–46, earlier works which Artaria issued as Op. 54 about this time.

[TO ARTARIA & CO., VIENNA. *German*]
                                    Estoras, 6th April 1789.

Well born,
Most highly respected Sir!
    I enclose the two security receipts which you asked for, and also the *Capriccio*,[1] with the solemn promise that no other soul shall receive it from my hands. I am sorry that the work involved does not allow me to reduce the price of 24 ducats by a single Kreutzer. I would ask you only that the Sonatas[2] and the *Capriccio* be neatly and legibly engraved.
    Please expedite at once the enclosed letter to Herr Sieber,[3] the Parisian publisher: it concerns his best interests.
    Meanwhile I remain, most respectfully,
                                    Your most obedient servant,
                                        Joseph Haydn.
Please answer in the German language.
[Address:]   Monsieur
                Monsieur d'Artaria et
            Compag   à
Please expedite.   Vienne.
[Artaria's clerk notes: "Heydn Giuseppe / Esterhaze 6 April/1789/ (ans'd) 18th June".]

[1]The *Fantasia* in C: see *supra*, p. 83.
[2]The piano Trios: see *supra*, p. 77 (78).
[3]The previous letter (5th April).

[TO HAYDN FROM MARIA ANNA GENZINGER. *German*]
                        † † †
Most respected Herr v. Hayden,
    With your kind permission, I take the liberty of sending you a pianoforte arrangement of the beautiful Andante from your so admirable composition. I

made this arrangement from the score quite by myself, without the least help from my teacher; please be good enough to correct any mistakes you may find in it. I hope that you are enjoying perfect health, and I wish for nothing more than to see you soon again in Vienna, so that I may demonstrate still further the esteem in which I hold you. I remain, in true friendship,

Your obedient servant,
Maria Anna *Noble v.* Gennzinger
née Noble v. Kayser.

My husband and children also
ask me to send you their
kindest regards.
Vienna, 10th June 1789.

[TO MARIA ANNA VON GENZINGER, VIENNA. *German*]
Nobly born and gracious Lady!

In all my previous correspondence, nothing delighted me more than the surprise of seeing such a lovely handwriting, and reading so many kind expressions; but even more I admired the enclosure—the excellent arrangement of the Adagio, which is correct enough to be engraved by any publisher. I would like to know only whether Your Grace arranged the Adagio from the score, or whether you took the amazing trouble of first putting it into score from the parts and only then arranging it for the pianoforte; if the latter, such an attention would be too flattering to me, for I really don't deserve it.

Best and kindest Frau v. Gennsinger! [*sic*] I only await a hint from you as to how and in what fashion I can possibly be of service to Your Grace. Meanwhile I return the Adagio, and very much hope to receive from Your Grace some demands on my modest talents; I am, with sincere esteem and respect,

Your Grace's
most obedient servant,
Josephus Haydn [m.p] ria.

Estoras, 14th June 1789.
N.S. Please present my respectful compliments
to your husband.

[TO ARTARIA & CO., VIENNA. *German*]

Estoras, 5th July 1789.

Well born,
Most highly respected Sir!
Thank you very much for the 3 Sonatas and the *Fantasia*[1] which

you sent to me; I only regret that, here and there, some mistakes have crept in, which can no longer be corrected, because the works are already circulated and on sale. It is always painful for me that not a single work of mine that you have published is free from errors. Formerly you always sent me the first copy, before publication, and you acted wisely; I could not use the single copies of the Sonatas you sent me as samples, because I didn't want to soil them and was also afraid of having to do without them for such a long time, or perhaps of losing them altogether, which is always irritating to an author. As to my debt of 39 fl., I ask you to be patient a little longer; I have hopes of collecting a debt of seven years' standing from the Arch-duke of Milan, and would then gratefully repay you in cash. Mean-while please be good enough to send me 3 copies of the Sonatas, 3 of the Fantasia, likewise a copy of the Seven Words in piano score, and a copy of the new Quartets.[2]

Now I would like to know the truth about something: that is, from whom you procured the 2 new Symphonies[3] which you recently announced—whether you purchased them from Herr Tost or whether you got them already engraved from Herr Sieber in Paris. If you purchased them from Herr Tost, I beg you to furnish me at once with an a parte written assurance of the fact, because I am told that Herr Tost pretends I sold these 2 Symphonies to you and thereby caused him a great loss.

Hoping for a speedy reply I am, Sir, most respectfully,

Your most obedient servant,

Josephus Haydn.

[No address]

[1]See supra, p. 87.
[2]Op. 50.
[3]Nos. 88 and 89.

[To Jean-Georges Sieber, Paris. German]

Estoras, 27th July 1789.

Monsieur!

[Contents of the first part of the letter:]

[Haydn discusses publication of the four Symphonies (see letter of 5th April 1789) and two Sonatas (probably pianoforte Trios), and describes his correspondence with Artaria on the subject. He agrees][1]

to compose [the Symphonies], and this present letter should serve to protect your interests in any court. On the other hand, I beg you to convince Herr Tost as well, and in order to deprive him of all his other claims to these 4 Symphonies, please send me your authentic signature of contract so that my interests are protected. Thus you are protected for your part, and I am for mine, while Herr Tost will be reduced to silence for ever. I hope to receive the favour of an early reply. Meanwhile I am, most respectfully,

Your most obedient servant,
Josephus Haydn.

[1]Summary from Maggs Brothers' Catalogue No. 320 (1914), item 328.

[To Jean-Georges Sieber, Paris. *German*]
Estoras, 28th August 1789.

Monsieur!
[Abbreviated translation][1]
Since I am now quite certain that the four Symphonies which I am to compose are for you, I shall make every possible effort to furnish them as soon as possible, and will send them one after another as they are completed. You need have no doubts as to the care I shall take, for I never forget either my honour or my reputation. N.B. I want one of the four Symphonies to be entitled the "National" Symphony. . . .
[Address:]   Monsieur Sieber
Marchand de la Musique très Renommé
a
Paris.

[1]The original letter is unavailable at present. See Sources.

[To Prince Nicolaus Esterházy. *German*]
[Esterháza, beginning of October 1789]
Most Serene Highness and Noble Prince of the Holy Roman Empire, Gracious and dread Lord!
The undersigned, together with all the members of the Princely band, make the following humble request to your illustrious and Serene Highness: that Your Highness graciously allow them to receive the value of their summer uniforms in cash, as was the case in previous years, instead of receiving the actual uniforms; for they

are all in possession of several brand new summer uniforms which they have saved. Commending ourselves in profound submissiveness,

Your Illustrious and Serene Highness'
humble and obedient servant,
Joseph Hayden, *Kapellmeister*.[1]

[The file contains the following note as an answer:]

On the 10th inst., His Highness granted the suppliants' request that they be paid cash instead of the new summer uniforms which would have had to have been made, the payment to take place at the time the uniforms would have been delivered, *viz.*: the *Herr Capellmeister* one hundred and fifty Gulden, and the other musicians seventy-five Gulden each.

Datum ex Commissione Celsissimi Principatus Esterháziani Kismartonii 12-Octobris 1789.

Paulus Ötvös *Praeses*
Franciscus Gáll mp. *Act.*

[1]The whole letter is a copy written by a Princely clerk.

[To FERDINAND MÜLLER VON MÜLLEGG, VIENNA. *German*]

Estoras [*c.* 17th October 1789[1]].

Nobly born,
Most highly respected Herr von Müller!

At last I can deliver to you, Sir, the 3 Symphonies for His Serene Highness, the most gracious Prince Oettingen von Wallerstein. I beg you sincerely to forgive the delayed delivery, but you, Sir, must see for yourself how difficult it is (when one serves a master who even at an advanced age has an insatiable appetite for music) to keep one's word. I intended day after day to satisfy the most kind Prince von Wallerstein, but my many daily duties prevented me against my will from doing so. A week from today, at the latest, I shall take the liberty of sending 12 brand new Dance Minuets with 12 Trios for this wonderful celebration.[2]

Now I would humbly ask you to tell the Princely *Kapellmeister* there that these 3 Symphonies, because of their many particular effects, should be rehearsed at least once, carefully and with special concentration, before they are performed.

Meanwhile I am, Sir, most respectfully,

Your most obedient servant,
Josephus Haydn.

[1]On 21st October von Müller writes to the Prince that he "will send to His Highness the 3 requested Symphonies, which the composer Herr Josef Haydn finally, and after repeated requests, delivered; I shall place it on the

next mail-coach." Haydn's undated letter must have been written shortly before. The Symphonies are Nos. 90–92, and the copies are still extant in the Oettingen-Wallerstein Archives at Harburg Castle. Haydn actually wrote the works for the Comte d'Ogny in Paris: see *supra* p. 85n.
²Prince Krafft Ernst's (second) marriage celebrations.

[To Haydn from Maria Anna von Genzinger. *German*]
Vienna, 29th October 1789.

† † †

Most respected Herr v. Hayden,
I hope that you will have safely received my letter of 15th September together with the 1st movement of the Symphony (the Andante of which I sent you some month ago), and now here is the last movement, too, which I have arranged for the pianoforte as best I could; I only hope that it pleases you, and I entreat you to correct at your leisure any mistakes that you may find—a service which I shall always accept from you, dear Herr v. Hayden, with the utmost gratitude. Please be good enough to let me know whether you received my letter of 15th September together with the movement, and if it suits your taste, which would delight me; for I am very uneasy and concerned whether you have received them safely, or if perhaps it has not met with your approval. I hope you enjoy the best of health, which I would be very happy to hear, and commending myself to your further friendship and remembrance, I remain your devoted friend and servant,

Maria Anna *Noble v.* Gennzinger
née Noble v. Kayser

My husband also sends you his compliments.

[To Maria Anna von Genzinger, Vienna. *German*]
Nobly born and gracious Lady!
I beg your forgiveness a million times for the long delay in returning your laborious and admirable work: when my apartments were cleaned, which occurred just after receiving the first movement, my copyist mislaid it among the mass of other music, and just recently I was fortunate enough to find it in an old opera score. Dearest and best Frau von Gennziger! [*sic*] Don't be angry at a man who values you above everything else; I should be inconsolable if this delay was responsible for my losing even a fraction of your favour (of which I am so proud).
These two movements are fully as admirably arranged as the first. I do admire the trouble and patience which Your Grace spends on my modest talents, and on the other hand I assure you that, in my frequent depressed moods, nothing cheers me so much as the flattering conviction that your memories of me are pleasant; for which

favour I kiss your hands a thousand times and remain, with sincere esteem,

Your Grace's
most obedient servant,

Estoras, 7th November 1789.   Joseph Haydn [m.p.] ria.

P.S. My respectful compliments to your husband and the whole family. I shall soon claim permission to wait on you.

[To Haydn from Maria Anna Genzinger. *German*]
Vienna, 12th November 1789.

† † †

Most respected Herr v. Hayden,
   I am quite incapable of expressing adequately the pleasure I felt on reading your kind letter of the 9th [*sic*]. How well am I rewarded for my pains when I see your satisfaction! I would wish nothing more ardently than to have more time (which my many household affairs do not allow), for then I would certainly devote many hours to music, my most agreeable and favourite of occupations. You must not take it amiss, dear Herr v. Haydn, that I bother you once again with a letter (but I could not miss the chance of informing you of the safe arrival of your letter): I look forward with the greatest pleasure to the happy day when I shall see you in Vienna. I commend myself to your further friendship and remembrance, and remain as always

Your most devoted friend and servant,
[no signature].

My husband and children also send you their compliments. The bearer of this letter is a jeweller here, his name is Siebert and he's a trustworthy man.

[To Artaria & Co., Vienna. *German*]
Estoras, 15th November 1789.

Well born,
Most highly respected Sir!
   Since you have often shown me various kindnesses, and since I really am your debtor, you may be assured that at all times you shall have the preference for my works. I have various new pieces which I shall tell you about when—and this will be soon—I arrive in Vienna. Last week Mr. Bland, an Englishman, was here to see me and wanted to purchase various pieces from me; but on your account he did not receive a single note.[1] Hoping to see you soon, I am, Sir, most respectfully,

Your wholly obedient servant,
Josephus Haydn.

[Address:]   Monsieur
        Monsieur Artaria et Compag.
                    à
                Vienne.

[1]This is, of course, not true. John Bland, a well-known London music publisher, supposedly took with him the autographs of the "Razor" Quartet (from Op. 55) and the Cantata *Arianna a Naxos*. See note to the letter of 11th January 1790.

[To MARIA ANNA VON GENZINGER, VIENNA. *German*]
                    Estoras, 18th November 1789.
Nobly born and gracious Lady!
    The letter which I received through the jeweller Sibert gave me still another proof of your excellent heart, for Your Grace, instead of rebuking me for my recent remissness, gave me renewed proof of your friendship, and this, combined with such great indulgence, kindness and special attention, quite astonished me; in return I kiss Your Grace's hands a thousand times. If my modest talents enable me, even in small measure, to return so many compliments, I venture to offer you a little musical vegetable pot; indeed, I do not find too much that is fragrant in this *pot-pourri*, but perhaps the publisher may rectify this fault in future editions.[1] If the arrangement of the Symphony in it is yours, Oh! then I shall be doubly pleased with the publisher; if not, I dare to ask Your Grace to have one of the Symphonies you arranged copied at your leisure and sent to me, when I shall then deliver it forthwith to the publisher at Leipzig to be engraved.
    I am happy to have found an opportunity which, I trust, will lead to few more delightful lines from you. Meanwhile I am, in lifelong respect,
                            Your Grace's
                            sincere friend and obedient
                            servant,
                                Josephus Haydn [m.p] ria.
My sincere compliments to your husband
and the whole family.

[1]Breitkopf's "Musikalischer Pot-Pourri", the first volume of which included Haydn's piano Sonata No. 48 and a pianoforte arrangement of Symphony No. 79 in F. See also above, p. 83 (84).

[TO FERDINAND MÜLLER VON MÜLLEGG, VIENNA. *German*]

Nobly born,

Most highly respected Herr von Müller!

According to our arrangement, I should have sent scores of the Symphonies[1] and not copies of the parts. But because I suffered almost all Summer from the most terrible pains in my eyes, I was unfortunately quite incapable of writing a clean score, and thus was forced to have these 3 illegible Symphonies (of which the enclosed, the best of the three, can serve as a sample) copied in my room by one of my composition pupils, and then to have the parts made by several copyists (so that the works would not be stolen). Any connoisseur can judge from the enclosed illegible score what the others are like; this time it is not my fault, for since my youth I have been accustomed to write very neat scores. If, however, there are any wrong notes in the Symphonies I sent, I would ask the *Concertmeister* there to inform me of them at once in a letter, so that I can send him the exact corrections. Therefore I would ask His Serene Highness the Prince humbly to excuse me: but if His Highness nevertheless insists on the scores, I shall of course dutifully deliver them (but it will be very hard for me, because I am still not free of the pains in my eyes). The most gracious Prince's approbation of these 3 Symphonies is a source of great encouragement to me, and will remain so to the last days of my life. I would like to have a portrait of His Highness, but only a silhouette, for I am a great collector of leading personalities.

My dear Herr Müller (our long-standing acquaintance makes me bold enough to suggest this form of address), you will be kind enough to excuse me to the gracious Prince, on account of the true reasons given above.

I remain, noble Sir, with every esteem,

Your most obedient servant,

Esterhaz, 29th November 1789.   Joseph Haydn.

I did not receive your letter till yesterday, because it was addressed to Eisenstadt instead of to Esterhaz.

[1]Nos. 90–92 (see the previous correspondence with von Müller). The Prince seems to have objected to Haydn's having sent parts rather than the scores. Haydn's answer at first satisfied the Prince, for he asks von Müller ". . . to write to Haiden [*sic*] and ask him if he can take it upon himself to write 3 new Symphonies and bring them here in score . . .". Haydn apparently had no time for this new commission, although the Prince repeatedly asked von Müller about it. Subsequently the Prince seems to have heard that he was by no means the sole owner of Nos. 90–92 (the autographs of which,

beautifully written, Haydn dedicated to the Comte d'Ogny in Paris). On 9th December 1789, von Müller tries to convince the Prince of Haydn's innocence; in fact von Kees, whom the Prince suspected as having the Symphonies, did own them (the copies are now in the Thurn und Taxis Library at Regensburg). Von Müller writes: "He [Haydn] wrote 3 new Parthyen [Symphonies] some time ago and published them, too, and these will be the ones that Herr von Kees owns, for I am convinced that he [Haydn] will not give the works he wrote specially for you to anyone else, as is stipulated." The "3 new Parthyen" von Müller refers to are probably Symphonies from the Paris set, though he may mean Nos. 76–78 or 79–81. Concerning von Kees, a famous Viennese patron of music, see Landon, pp. 36*ff*.

[TO ARTARIA & CO., VIENNA. *German*]
[Vienna] From my home,
11th January 1790.

Nobly born,
Most highly respected Sir!

I had hoped, in vain, to see you here day before yesterday morning, so that I could show you various pieces of music; but you won't have been able to come because of your many affairs. This is to inform you that this very day I received a letter from *Mon.* Bland in London, wherein he asks me for pianoforte Sonatas with accompaniment of a violin and violoncello.[1] But this time I give you the preference and so I herewith inform you that you can have the first Sonata from me any time, the 2nd in a fortnight, and the third by the end of carnival time—each, as usual, for 10 ducats. Will you be good enough to let me have your decision by tomorrow morning?— A couple of lines will do. But in order to cancel my debt to you, you must also accept the 12 new and most splendid Minuets with 12 Trios, for 12 ducats.[2] Hoping to receive the favour of your reply, I am, Sir, most respectfully,

Your wholly obedient servant,
Josephus Haydn.

[Address:]   Monsieur
Monsieur d'Artaria
et Compag.

a

Son Logis.
[Artaria's clerk notes: "Haydn Giuseppe / di qui"]

[1]It is not quite clear which three Trios are meant here: either No. 14 in

A flat, and Nos. 15 and 16 (with flute instead of violin), or Nos. 15–17 (the latter also with flute). In view of the fact that Artaria published Nos. 14–16 in 1790, but No. 17 two years later, it would seem that this letter refers to the former three. Haydn sold Nos. 15–17 to Bland, but not No. 14, which he later asked Genzinger to send him to London (see p. 123). Bland published the Trios with the following note: "This & the Two following Trios were wrote at the particular request of the Publisher when he was with Mr. Haydn in Novr. last [1789] . . . J. Bland thinks this sufficient notice to other Publishers not to pirate the same." Bland must have received the first work (No. 16) early in 1790, the second (No. 15) about June—he entered it at Stationers' Hall on June 28th—and the third (No. 17) probably on 12th July: an envelope large enough to contain a Trio, addressed in Haydn's hand to Bland, and containing someone's (Bland's?) note "Haydn 12 July 90", has been discovered recently; the owners, J. A. Stargardt of Marburg/Lahn, kindly permitted me to examine this envelope. See also Hoboken, p. 701. Artaria accepted Haydn's offer, and Haydn signed a a receipt in two (or three?) almost identical copies, dated Vienna, 13th January 1790. He received 35 Gulden for the Trios, and Artaria was to be the sole owner.
[2]Artaria did not publish these Dances.

[To Maria Anna Genzinger, Vienna. *German*]
Dear, kind Frau von Gennzinger!
   This is to tell your Grace that all the arrangements for the little quartet party we agreed to have this coming Friday are completed. Herr von Häring[1] considered himself fortunate to be able to assist me on this occasion, the more so when I told him of the attention and all the other kind favours I had received from Your Grace. Now I hope only to receive a small measure of approbation. Your Grace shouldn't forget to invite the Pater Professor.[2]
   Meanwhile I kiss your hands and am, most respectfully,
                                Your Grace's
                                sincere and most obedient servant,
                                Josephus Haydn.
[Vienna] From my home, 23rd January 1790.
[Address:]   Madame
             Madame de Gennzinger
             Noble de Kayser
                    a
                 Son Logis.

[1]Johann Baptist von Häring (or possibly Herring), a Viennese banker whose violin playing was highly esteemed. See Nohl, p. 112.
[2]Probably from the neighbouring *Schotten* (Scottish) Monastery.

[To Maria Anna von Genzinger, Vienna. *German*]
Noble and kindest Frau von Gennzinger!

I was most flattered to receive yesterday Your Grace's most recent invitation that I should spend the evening with you today, but painful as it is, I must tell you that I cannot even thank you personally for all the kind favours I have received from you; I regret this very much, and from the bottom of my heart I wish you, not only tonight but for ever and ever, the most agreeable and happy of gatherings. Mine are over—tomorrow I return to dreary solitude. May God only grant me good health, but I fear the contrary, for I am far from well today. God bless your Grace—your dear husband —and all your sweet children. I kiss your hands once more and am as always, now and my whole life

Your Grace's
obedient servant,
Joseph Haydn.

[Vienna] From my home, 3rd February 1790.
[Address:]   Madame
      Madame Noble de
      Gennzinger Noble de
      Kayser

a

Son Logis.

[To Maria Anna von Genzinger, Vienna. *German*]
Nobly born,
Most highly respected and kindest Frau von Gennzinger,

Well, here I sit in my wilderness—forsaken—like a poor waif— almost without any human society—melancholy—full of the memories of past glorious days—yes! past alas!—and who knows when these days shall return again? Those wonderful parties? Where the whole circle is one heart, one soul—all these beautiful musical evenings—which can only be remembered, and not described— where are all these enthusiastic moments?—all gone—and gone for a long time. Your Grace mustn't be surprised that I haven't written up to now to thank you. I found everything at home in confusion, and for 3 days I didn't know if I was *Capell*-master or *Capell*-servant. Nothing could console me, my whole house was in confusion, my pianoforte which I usually love so much was perverse and disobedient, it irritated rather than calmed me, I could only sleep very little, even my dreams persecuted me; and then, just when I was happily dreaming that I was listening to the opera, *Le nozze di Figaro*,[1] that horrible North wind woke me and almost blew my nightcap off my head; I lost 20 lbs. in weight in 3 days, for the good Viennese food I had in me disappeared on the journey; alas! alas! I thought to myself as I was eating in the mess here, instead of that delicious slice of beef, a chunk of a cow 50 years old; instead of a ragout with little dumplings, an old sheep with carrots; instead of a Bohemian pheasant, a leathery joint; instead of those fine and delicate oranges, a *Dschabl* or so-called *gross Sallat* [*sic*]; instead of pastry, dry apple-fritters and hazelnuts—and that's what I have to eat. Alas! alas! I thought to myself, if I could only have a little bit of what I couldn't eat up in Vienna. —Here in Estoras no one asks me: Would you like some chocolate, with milk or without? Will you take some coffee, black, or with cream? What may I offer you, my dear Haydn? Would you like a vanilla or a pine-apple ice? If I only had a good piece of Parmesan cheese, especially in Lent, so that I could more easily swallow those black dumplings and noodles; just today I told our porter here to send me a couple of pounds.

Forgive me, kindest and most gracious lady, for filling the very first letter with such stupid nonsense, and for killing time with such a wretched scrawl, but you must forgive a man whom the Viennese terribly spoiled. I am gradually getting used to country life, however, and yesterday I studied for the first time, and quite Haydnish, too. Your Grace will certainly have been more industrious than I. The pleasing Adagio from the Quartet has, I hope, by now received its true expression from your fair fingers. My good friend *Fräulein* Peperl[2] will (I hope) be reminded of her teacher by singing the Cantata[3] frequently; she should remember to have a distinct articulation and a correct vocal production, for it would be a crime if so beautiful a voice were to remain hidden in her breast; so therefore I ask her to smile frequently, lest I be disappointed in her. Likewise I advise *Mons.* Francois[2] to cultivate his musical talents; even when he sings in his dressing-gown, he does very nicely. I shall often send him some new things to encourage him. Meanwhile I again kiss your hands for all your kind favours, and am, as always, most respectfully,

Your Grace's
most sincere and wholly obedient servant,
Josephus Haydn.

Estoras, 9th February 1790.

N.S. Please present my respectful compliments to Your Grace's husband, and also my compliments to *Mons.* Hofmeister Junior, to *Fräulein* Nanette and the whole Hacker family.[4]

[1]Mozart's opera was revived in August 1789. But *Figaro* was in Haydn's head for another reason too: he was intending to perform it at the Esterháza Court Theatre. Recently the bills for copying, *etc.* have come to light in the Esterházy Archives, Budapest (now National Museum). The first reference is a *Nota* "Datu ex comissione Celsissimi Principatus Esterhaziani Kismartonii [Eisenstadt] 7 January 1789", in which a number of scores were bought for the Princely Theatre. Haydn countersigned the receipt, which includes "Score Le Nozze di Figaro . . . 30 [Gulden]" and "vocal parts for the above-mentioned operas . . . 30 [Gulden]." The bill for the scenery has also been found, as well as the whole orchestral material: Pietro Travaglia, the stage designer for the Esterházy Theatre, submitted his bill for *Figaro* on 8th August 1789, but most of the parts are dated "1790"; the performance probably took place during the 1790 season.
[2]PEPERL (JOSEPHA) and FRANÇOIS (FRANZ), then sixteen and fifteen, the eldest children of Maria Anna.
[3]*Arianna a Naxos* (see next letter).
[4]Hofmeister was the family tutor in foreign languages (see letter of 13th May); Fräulein Nanette is Maria Anna de Jerlischek or Gerlischek (see *infra*, p. 133), who apparently became Prince Nicolaus' housekeeper after the death of the Princess Esterházy (25th February); she later married Johann Tost, who has figured in these pages so often (Hoboken p. 775). Anna Maria's mother was *née* Hackher zu Hart, an old Austrian aristocratic family.

[TO MARIA ANNA VON GENZINGER, VIENNA. *German*]
                                        Estoras, 14th March, 1790.
Nobly born,
Most esteemed and kindest Frau von Gennzinger!

I ask Your Grace's forgiveness a million times for having so long delayed the answer to your kind 2 letters. This is not negligence (a sin from which Heaven will preserve me as long as I live) but is because of the many things I have to do for my most gracious Prince in his present melancholy condition. The death of his wife[1] so crushed the Prince that we had to use every means in our power to pull His Highness out of this depression, and thus the first 3 days I arranged enlarged chamber music every evening with no singing; but the poor Prince, during the concert of the first evening, became so depressed when he heard my Favourite Adagio in D that we had quite a time to brighten his mood with the other pieces.

On the 4th day we had an opera, on the 5th a comedy [play], and then our theatre daily as usual. Meanwhile I ordered them to prepare the old opera *L'amor Artigiano* by Gasman,[2] because the Prince had said to me recently that he would like to see it: I wrote 3 new arias for it,[3] which I shall be sending Your Grace shortly, not because of their beauty but to show Your Grace how diligent I am. Your Grace shall receive the promised Symphony[4] during the month of April, but in time so that it can be produced at the Kees Concert.[5]

Meanwhile I respectfully kiss Your Grace's hands for the Zwieback you sent me, which however I did not receive till last Tuesday; but it came at just the right moment, for I had just eaten up the last of the previous lot. I am delighted that my favourite *Arianna* [Cantata] is well received at the Schottenhof,[6] but I do recommend *Fräulein* Peperl to articulate the words clearly, especially the passage "chi tanto amai". I take the liberty of sending you my best wishes for your approaching name-day,[7] and ask you at the same time to retain me in your favour, and to consider me on every occasion as your own, though unworthy, teacher.

I also take the liberty of informing you that the language teacher can come here any day, his journey will be paid for here, and he can travel either by the diligence or by some other carriage, the schedules of which may be found daily in the Madschakerhof.[8]

I shall return the box for the Zwieback to Your Grace at the first opportunity.

Since I am sure that Your Grace takes an interest in all my doings (far more, in fact, than I deserve), I should like to tell Your Grace that last week I received a present of a charming gold snuff-box, weighing the value of 34 ducats, from Prince Oetting von Wallerstein,[9] together with an invitation to pay him a visit at his expense sometime this year; His Highness is specially desirous of making my personal acquaintance (a pleasant encouragement for my drooping spirits). Whether I shall make up my mind to go is another question.

Do please forgive this hasty letter; I am, with every possible esteem, as always

Your Grace's
sincere and obedient servant,
Josephus Haydn.

N.S.   My respectful compliments to Your Grace's
husband and the whole Hacker family.

I have just lost my faithful and
honest coachman; he died on
the 25th of last month.

[1]MARIA ELISABETH, *née* COUNTESS WEISSEN WOLF, died on 25th February.

[2]FLORIAN LEOPOLD GASSMANN (1723–1774), whose *L'amor Artigiano* was first produced at the Burgtheater in Vienna in 1767 (Gustav Donath, 'Florian Leopold Gassmann als Opernkomponist', *Studien zur Musikwissenschaft* Heft II [1914], p. 50).

[3]At least one of these "insertion arias" has survived: "Da che penso a maritiarmi" (for tenor, E flat).

[4]Haydn did not then compose this Symphony, though he later refers to it. Perhaps it turned into one of the Salomon Symphonies (No. 93?): see letter of 2nd March 1792.

[5]See *supra*, p. 94.

[6]The Schottenhof, still extant, is the group of buildings in one part of which the Genzinger family lived: it is next to the Schottenkirche.

[7]Haydn must have confused the date, because the Virgin Mary's Ascension (and Maria Anna's name-day) occur on 15th August (see letter of that day, *infra*).

[8]A Viennese tavern, connected with the Monastery of Göttweig.

[9]For Symphonies Nos. 90–92; see the previous correspondence with von Müller. On 9th February, von Müller wrote to the Prince: ". . . je lui ai écrit, pourqu'il m'assigne une personne, à qui je pouvais confier la Tabattière d'or avec les 50 Ducats, affin qu'ils lui parviennent . . . et lui ai proposé de faire un tour à Wallerstein aux frais de Votre Altesse, qui souhaiteroit faire la connoissance personelle . . ." (L. Schiedermair, 'Die Blütezeit der Öttingen-Wallerstein'schen Hofkapelle', *Recueil de la Société Internationale de Musique*, 9ième Année, Livr. 1, Oct.-Dec. 1907, p. 106.

[To MARIA ANNA VON GENZINGER, VIENNA. *German*]
Estoras, 13th May 1790.

Nobly born,
Gracious and kindest Frau von Gennzinger!

I was astonished to see from your kind letter that Your Grace did not receive my last letter, in which I mentioned that our landlord had engaged a French teacher, who came by chance to Estoras, and so I at once made my excuses not only to Your Grace but also to Herr Hofmeister.[1] My dear benefactress, this is not the first time that some of my letters, and also those of many others, have gone astray, inasmuch as our letter-bag, on its way to Oedenburg, is always opened by the house-master there (in order to put the letters into it), as a result of which mistakes and other disagreeable occurrences have often arisen: for greater security in the future, however, and to put a stop to this disgraceful curiosity, henceforth I shall enclose all my letters in an extra envelope addressed to our porter, Herr Pointner. This occurence makes me the more unhappy because Your

Grace might blame me for my negligence, from which Heaven defend me! Anyway, these curious people, male or female, cannot have discovered anything improper in this last letter, or in any of the others either. And now, my dear benefactress, when shall I have the inexpressible happiness of seeing Your Grace in Estoras? Since business doesn't permit me to go to Vienna, I console myself with the thought that I shall quite surely kiss your hands here this summer. In which flattering thought, meanwhile, I am, most respectfully,

Your Grace's
most sincere and obedient servant,
Josephus Haydn [m.p] ria.

My respectful compliments to
Your Grace's husband and the whole family.

¹See *supra*, p. 98.

[TO MARIA ANNA VON GENZINGER, VIENNA. *German*]
Estoras, 30th May 1790.

Nobly born,
Most highly esteemed and kindest Frau von Gennzinger!

I was just at Oedenburg when I received your last welcome letter, whence I had gone to enquire about the lost letter: the house-master there swore by all that is holy that he had seen no letter in my hand-writing at that time, and so this letter must have gone astray in Estoras. Be that as it may, this curiosity can do me no harm, much less Your Grace, for the whole contents of the letter were partly about my opera, *La vera costanza*, which was performed at the new theatre in the Landstrasse,¹ and partly about the French teacher who was to have come to Estoras. Your Grace need have no fear, therefore, either about the past or about the future, for my friendship and the esteem in which I hold Your Grace (tender as they are) will never be reprehensible, because I always have in mind my respect for Your Grace's profound virtue, which not only I, but all who know Your Grace, must admire. Therefore I beg Your Grace not to be frightened away from consoling me occasionally by your pleasant letters, for they comfort me in my wilderness, and are highly necessary for my heart, which is so often deeply hurt. Oh! If only I could be with Your Grace for a quarter of an hour, to pour forth all my troubles to you, and to hear all your comforting words. I have to put up with many annoyances from the Court here which, however, I must accept in silence. The only consolation left to me is that I am—thank God!—well, and eagerly disposed to work; I am only sorry that despite this eagerness, Your Grace has had to wait so long for the promised Symphony, but this time it's simply bare necessity which is responsible, arising from my circumstances here and the present rise in the cost of living. Your Grace therefore mustn't be angry at your Haydn who, often as his Prince absents himself from Estoras, cannot go to Vienna even for 24 hours; it's scarcely credible, and yet the refusal is always couched in such polite terms, so polite in fact that I just don't have the heart to insist on receiving the permission. Oh well! As God pleases! This time will also pass away, and the day come when I shall have the inexpressible pleasure of sitting beside Your Grace at the pianoforte, hearing Mozart's masterpieces, and kissing your hands for so many wonderful things. With this hope, I am,

> Your Grace's
> most sincere and humble servant,
> Josephus Haydn.

My respectful compliments to Your Grace's
husband and the whole family, likewise to
the Hackers and the P. Professor.

[1]Written in 1776 for Vienna, where intrigue prevented its being given; the first performance took place in Esterháza in the Spring of 1779. The theatre in the Landstrasse—then a suburb of Vienna (now the 3rd District) —had been opened in 1790. See Gustav Gugitz, *Alt-Wiener Thespiskarren*, Vienna 1925, pp. 235-237, 382f.

[To Maria Anna von Genzinger, Vienna. *German*]
Estoras, 6th June 1790.

Nobly born,
Most estemed and kindest Frau von Gennzinger!

I am terribly sorry that Your Grace was so long in receiving my last letter, but the previous week none of the Hussars was dispatched from Estoras, so it's not my fault that the letter reached you so late.

Between ourselves! I must inform Your Grace that our *Mademoiselle* Nanette[1] has commissioned me to compose a new pianoforte Sonata for you, but which no one else can own. I esteem myself fortunate to have received such a command. I shall deliver the Sonata to Your Grace in a fortnight at the latest. This *Mademoiselle* Nanette promised to pay me for the work, but you can easily imagine that I shall refuse it now or any other time: the best reward for me will always be to hear that I have in some measure received your approbation. Meanwhile I am, most respectfully,

Your Grace's
most obedient servant,
Jos: Haydn.

[1]NANETTE was (Maria) ANNA DE JERLISCHECK: see *supra*, p. 98. The Sonata was to be No. 49 in E flat, and Haydn began it on the 1st of June (the autograph is now in the Vienna Stadtbibliothek).

[To FRIEDRICH JAKOB VAN DER NÜLL,[1] VIENNA. *German*]
Estoras, 7th June 1790.

Nobly born,
Most highly respected Sir!

One of my pupils, by the name of Magnus, a poor but well-educated and well-bred young man from Livonia, to whom I give composition lessons free of charge because of his extraordinary diligence, has at last, through my insistent intervention, received a cheque from his father in the amount of [not filled in]. No one hereabouts can or will accept this cheque, and since I have long been convinced of your inborn love for your fellow men, I come to you with the humble request, please, if at all possible, to help the poor young man in this instance. Our porter, Herr Pointner, who is a trustworthy man, will deliver this cheque to you, good Sir, and you can entrust him with the money without any risk at all.

Hoping that you will fulfil my wish to encourage this poor young man in his industry, I am, Sir, with all possible esteem,

Your wholly obedient and humble servant,
Joseph Haydn.

N.S. My respectful compliments to all the gentlemen who live in the Häring[2] house; as for the ladies, I respectfully kiss their hands with all the musical tenderness which I have been capable of expressing throughout my life.

[1]FRIEDRICH JAKOB VAN DER NÜLL, a wholesale merchant and a partner in the firm of Ignaz von Schwab; Haydn usually refers to him as "von" rather than "van" der Nüll. His house was on the Michaelerplatz. See Caroline Pichler, *Denkwürdigkeiten aus meinem Leben*, a new edition (E. K. Blümml), Munich 1914, I, pp. 545*f*. Van der Nüll was a passionate admirer and "amateur" of music; he subscribed to Haydn's *Creation*, for example. See also letter of 25th March 1796.

[2]HÄRING (Herring), probably the banker and amateur violinist mentioned in the letter of 23rd January 1790.

[CERTIFICATE FOR JOSEPH EYBLER. *German*]
[Only the place, date, signature & title in Haydn's hand]

I the undersigned cannot fail to give the bearer of these lines, Herr JOSEPH EYBLER, the certificate which he humbly requested of me, and which should wholly reflect his outstanding talents and the diligence he has hitherto shown in the field of music. He possesses not only all the musical and theoretical knowledge necessary to pass with distinction the most difficult examination of any musical judge; but as a practical musician he is a highly respectable pianoforte player and violinist, and as such can win the approval of any connoisseur. In view of the former, he can fill the post of a *Kapellmeister* with distinction, and in view of the latter, he can be a useful member of any chamber music concert.

As far as his knowledge of COMPOSITION is concerned, I think that I can give no higher recommendation than if I say that he is a pupil of the justly celebrated Herr Albrechtsberger.[1] Equipped with all these abilities, he lacks nothing more than a generous Prince who will give him the position wherein he can further develop and demonstrate his talents, in which capacity the undersigned hopes soon to be able to congratulate him.

Josephus Haydn [m.] pria,
Fürst: Esterhazischer
Capell Meister.

Esterhaz, 8th June 1790.

[1]See *supra*, p. 82. Mozart also wrote a letter of recommendation for Eybler (30 May 1790).

[TO MARIA ANNA VON GENZINGER, VIENNA. *German*]
Estoras, 20th June 1790.

Nobly born,
Most esteemed and kindest Frau von Gennzinger!

I have taken the liberty of sending Your Grace a brand new pianoforte Sonata with accompaniment of a flute or violin, not as anything remarkable, but simply a trifle to amuse you in moments of utmost boredom.[1] I would only ask you to have it copied as soon as possible and then to send it back to me. The day before yesterday

I delivered the new Sonata[2] to *Mademoiselle* Nanette, my patroness;
I had hoped that she would express a wish to hear me play this
Sonata, but up to now I have not received any such order, and for
this reason I also do not know whether Your Grace will receive this
Sonata in today's mail or not. This Sonata is in E flat, brand new,
and was written especially for Your Grace to be hers forever, but it
is a curious coincidence that the last movement is the very same
Minuet and Trio which Your Grace asked me for in your last letter.
This Sonata was destined for Your Grace a year ago, and only the
Adagio is quite new, and I especially recommend this movement to
your attention, for it contains many things which I shall analyze for
Your Grace when the time comes; it is rather difficult but full of
feeling. It's a pity, however, that Your Grace has not one of Schantz's[3]
fortepianos, for Your Grace could then produce twice the effect.

N. B. *Mademoiselle* Nanette must know nothing of the fact that
this Sonata was already half completed, for otherwise she might get
the wrong impression of me, and this might be very disadvantageous
for me, since I must be very careful not to lose her favour. Meanwhile I consider myself fortunate to be at least the means of provid-
ing her with some amusement; especially since the sacrifice is made
for your sake, dearest Frau von Gennzinger. Oh! how I do wish that
I could only play this Sonata to you a few times; I could then recon-
cile my staying for a while in this wilderness. I have so much to say
to Your Grace, and so many things to tell you about which are
destined for Your Grace alone and no one else: but what cannot be
now will, I hope to God, come to pass this Winter; almost half the
time has already elapsed. Meanwhile I console myself patiently, and
am content that I have the inestimable privilege of subscribing myself
Your Grace's

most sincere and obedient friend
and servant,

Josephus Haydn [m.p] ria.

My respectful compliments to your
husband and all the family. I kiss
Your Grace 1000 times—on the hands.

[1] A pianoforte Trio: from the presence of the flute we can deduce that it was
either Trio No. 15, 16 or 17; if it was really "brand new", it was probably
No. 17, which Haydn seems to have sent to Bland at this time. See also
supra, p. 95.
[2] Pianoforte Sonata No. 49: see *supra*, p. 103.
[3] WENZEL SCHANZ: see also letters of 26th October and 16th November
1788.

Estoras, 27th June 1790.

Nobly born,

Highly esteemed and kindest Frau von Genzinger!

Your Grace will certainly have received the new pianoforte Sonata, but if not, you will perhaps receive it along with my letter. 3 days ago I had to play this Sonata at *Mademoiselle* Nanette's in the presence of my gracious Prince. At first I rather doubted, because of its difficulty, whether I would receive any applause, but was soon convinced of the contrary, inasmuch as I was given a gold tobacco-box as a present from [her] own hand. Now I only hope that Your Grace will be satisfied with it, so that I may earn the increased approval of my benefactress; and for this reason I would ask Your Grace to tell her, if not personally, then at least through your husband, that I could not conceal my delight at her generosity, the more so since I am sure that Your Grace shares my pleasure at all the benefits conferred on me. It's only a pity that Your Grace doesn't own a Schantz fortepiano, on which everything is better expressed. I thought that Your Grace might turn over your still tolerable piano to *Fräulein* Peperl, and buy a new one for yourself. Your beautiful hands and their facility of execution deserve this and much more. I know I ought to have composed this Sonata in accordance with the capabilities of your piano, but I found this impossible because I was no longer accustomed to it.

Again I find that I am forced to remain here. Your Grace can imagine how much I lose by having to do so. It really is sad always to be a slave, but Providence wills it so. I'm a poor creature! Always plagued by hard work, very few hours of recreation, and friends? What am I saying? One true one? There aren't any true friends any more—one lady friend? Oh yes! There might be one. But she's far away from me. Oh well! I have my thoughts. God bless you, and may you never forget me! Meanwhile I kiss Your Grace's hands 1000 times, and am as always, most respectfully,

Your Grace's

sincere and most obedient servant,
Josephus Haydn.

My respectful compliments to your husband
and all the family.

Please forgive my bad handwriting today: I am suffering a little from pains in my eyes.

1761

1799

1804

X   Three autograph receipts of the years 1761, 1799 and 1804 (the first two in the Esterházy Archives, Budapest; the third in the British Museum).

XI   Letter to Anton Scheffstoss of 20th March 1768 (Esterházy Archives, Budapest).

Krinn zu verkaufen, mir alle Freytag nachmittag bey denen
Fr. Miseric: die Ehre unsers gnädigsten Fürstens durch produc-
cirung meiner Chor zu befördern, mouchtey ubmuls wurden
Cuer in Ehren Stand einbraten: Vom H: Durchlaucht befohlen,
wolte resodele del die Friheit meinem meeham Hinabzusenden:
Liebster Mons: Schleßstoff bitte um beschleinigung meines verzeichnus
Der ich mit aller Veneration verbleibe

Eueur Wohl Edlen

Gehorsamster diener
Josephus Haydn mpria

P.S. Mein Compliment an alle Messieurs.
Die Austrockener Divertimenten werde
H: Durchl: diese wochen gewiss einhändigen.

XII   Verso of letter on facing page.

XIII   Letter to Prince Nicolaus Esterházy of 22nd December 1768 (Esterházy Archive, Budapest): Detail from the first page.

XIV   Letter to Anton Scheffstoss of 22nd December 1768, quoting the letter of the same date to the Prince and asking if it meets with Scheffstoss's approval: Detail from the first page (Esterházy Archives, Budapest).

XV Receipt to Esterházy Administration, "Schloss Eisenstadt", 29th April 1773 (Esterházy Archives, Budapest).

XVI Letter to an official in the Esterházy Administration, 7th November 1780 (Esterházy Archives, Budapest).

XVII Letter to William Forster, London, of 28th June 1787 (British Museum).

XVIII Letter to Artaria & Co., Vienna, of 17th August 1788 (British Museum).

XIX Address (*above*) and letter (*at left*) to Luigia Polzelli of 13th December 1791 (Harvard College Library).

XX Second page of a letter from Pietro Polzelli to his mother, Luigia (22nd October 1792), with a postscript in Haydn's hand. (From a facsimile in the *Musical Quarterly* of April 1932: the original has disappeared.)

XXI Letter to Prince Nicolaus II Esterházy of 6th July 1804: the text and date in Johann Elssler's hand, the signature autograph (Esterházy Archives, Budapest).

I acknowledge to have received of Mr George Thomson Esqr of ye City of
Edinburgh in Scotland by the hands of Mess? Fries & Comp. par order
of Mess? Thos Coutts & Comp. of London Fifty ducats for composing
Rittornelles & Accompaniments for the Piano forte etc. to twelve Welsh
& Scottish Airs, and I declare these, in addition to the 158 which I
before composed for the said G: Thomson to be his sole property.—
Given under my hand at Vienna the 18th of December 1803.

Dr Haydn mpria

XXII Receipt to George Thomson, Edinburgh, of 18th December 1803 (British Museum).

ai 6 d'Aprile.
804.

225

Stimatissimo Signor mio.

Ho l'onore di mandarvi dodici Arie e le ultime due
che ho ricevuto poco fa, con la solita speranza
che daranno l'istesso piacere come le altre, ed
in poco tempo riceverete anche il fine:
fra tanto mi raccomando alla vostra amicizia
e bacciando le mani alla vostra cara e graziosa
figlia per la sua bella lettera sono con tutta la
Stima e venerazione
            Vostro Sincerissimo D amfs? Serva
                    Giuseppe Haydn

mi darò tutta la pena di procurarvi mio piccolo
ritratto.

XXIII Letter to George Thomson, Edinburgh, of 6th April 1804 (British Museum).

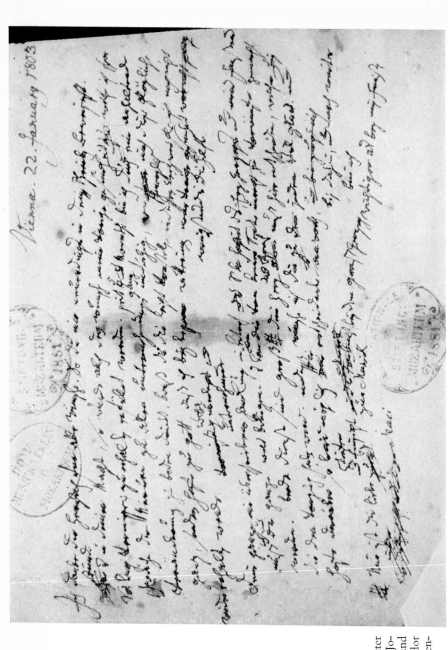

XXIV Draft of a letter to Haydn's brother, Johann Michael, of 22nd January 1803 (Sándor Wolf Museum, Eisenstadt).

XXV Address (*left*) in Johann Elssler's hand with Haydn's seal "JH", and letter (*above*) to J. N. Hummel, Eisenstadt, 28th September 1804 (Frau Margarete Hummel, Florence).

a

Monsieur

Monsieur 𝒟 Artaria

& Comp.

Stimati Signori Artaria

Spero che per questi dodici pezzi Di Musica il vecchio Haydn avrà meritato un piccolo regalo. vostro Sincero amico e .

Dr Haydn

al 17.^t Agost. 1805

XXVI   Address (*at top*) in Johann Elssler's hand with Haydn's seal "JH", and letter to Artaria & Co. of 17th August 1805 (the "1805" in another [Johann Elssler's?] hand). (From facsimile in Artaria–Botstiber: the original has disappeared.) The address is written on the back of the letter.

[To Maria Anna von Genzinger, Vienna. *German*]
Estoras, 4th July 1790.

Nobly born,
Kindest Frau von Genzinger!

I have just received your letter, and this very moment the mail goes out. I am simply delighted that my Prince intends to give Your Grace a new fortepiano, all the more so since I am in some measure responsible for it: I constantly implored *Mademoiselle* Nanette to persuade your husband to buy one for Your Grace, and now the purchase depends entirely on Your Grace and simply consists in Your Grace choosing one to fit your touch and suit your fancy. It is quite true that my friend Herr Walther[1] is very celebrated, and that every year I receive the greatest civility from that gentleman, but between ourselves, and speaking frankly, sometimes there is not more than one instrument in ten which you could really describe as good, and apart from that they are very expensive. I know Herr von Nikl's fortepiano: it's excellent, but too heavy for Your Grace's hand, and one can't play everything on it with the necessary delicacy. Therefore I should like Your Grace to try one made by Herr Schanz, his fortepianos are particularly light in touch and the mechanism very agreeable. A good fortepiano is absolutely necessary for Your Grace, and my Sonata will gain double its effect by it.

Meanwhile I kiss Your Grace's hands for exercising the caution I suggested with regard to *Mademoiselle* Nanette. It's a pity that the little gold box she gave me, and had used herself, is so tarnished, but perhaps I can have it polished up in Vienna. As yet I haven't received any order to buy a fortepiano. I fear that they will deliver one to Your Grace's house, which will be beautiful outside but will have a stiff action within. Your husband should refer them to me, and say that I consider Herr Schanz at present to be the best pianoforte maker; I shall then arrange everything else. In great haste I am

Your Grace's
most obedient servant,
Jos: Haydn.

[1]Anton Walther (Walter), a Viennese pianoforte manufacturer whose instruments were particular favourites of Mozart's.

[To Haydn from Maria Anna von Genzinger. *German*]
Vienna, 11th July 1790.

† † †

Most respected Herr v. Haydn,
I duly received your letter of 4th July, and leave it entirely to you to choose

me an excellent fortepiano, for *Mademoiselle* [Nanette], as soon as she arrives here, will give you the commission to purchase one in the Prince's name. I am also quite willing (since you think it best) to purchase one from Herr Schanz, but I would prefer that you try it out yourself before I take it, because I don't really know enough about it and might perhaps choose one that is not really good.

I like the Sonata very much, but there is one thing which I wish could be changed (if by so doing it does not detract from the beauty of the piece), and that is the passage in the second part of the Adagio, where the hands cross over; I am not used to this and thus find it hard to do, and so please let me know how this could be altered.

I shall return the other Sonata [Trio] in a few days, it too is very beautiful. But I should like to ask one thing, and that is about the Symphony you promised me, which you agreed you would write just for me and no one else, and to which I look forward so very much: I hope that it hasn't been displaced by the Sonata. I know I shouldn't bother you any more, especially since you have just gone to such pains for me, but the great pleasure I have in all your delightful compositions will not allow it to be otherwise.

By the way, I hope that you are well; as for myself, I have not yet quite recovered from my catarrh, and the day before yesterday I began taking a cure of soda water with milk; I hope, God willing, that I shall soon feel its good effects. I must close now, and remain with much veneration,

Your sincere friend,
Maria Ana [*sic*] Noble *v*. Gennzinger,
née Noble v. Kayser.
My family all send you their best wishes.

[TO JOSEPH ZÜSSER, RECEIVER-GENERAL OF THE PRINCELY
CASHIER'S OFFICE, EISENSTADT. *German*]
Esterház, 31st July 1790.

Well born,
Most highly respected Herr Züsser!

I do not doubt that you have long since received, through Herr Kaufmann,[1] the commission concerning a newly engaged female singer by the name of Melo,[2] who will get a yearly salary of 1000 Fl. beginning on 1st July, but who did not receive her monthly wage along with the money sent here. Therefore please give her monthly wage to the bearer of this letter, our chief-baker-mistress [*Frau Beckermeisterin*]. With my compliments to your family I am, most respectfully,

Your most obedient servant,
Joseph Haydn.

[Address:]   Monsieur de Züsser Receveur
              general de S: Altesse Monseig[neur]
              le Prince Esterházy
                        à
                   Eisenstadt.
[In the hand of the chief baker-mistress: "Received 83 Gulden
A.M.Tauber"]

¹KAUFMANN was Princely Secretary ("Hochfürstl. Esterházischer Sekretär").
²THERESIA MELO.

[TO MARIA ANNA VON GENZINGER, VIENNA. *German*]
                              [Estoras 15th August 1790]¹
Nobly born,
Kindest Frau von Gennzinger!
    It would have been my duty to have written to you last week in
answer to Your Grace's letter, but I had been thinking of this day for
a long time, and had gone to all sorts of pains to think out just how
and what I was to wish for Your Grace today; and thus a week went
past and now, when my wishes should have taken some form, my
small intellect comes to a standstill and (ashamed of itself) doesn't
know what to say at all. Why? Because I could not fulfil those musical
hopes which Your Grace certainly had the right to expect today
at her own home. If only Your Grace knew and could see how
troubled my heart is about this, you would certainly feel pity and
indulgence for me: the poor, long expected Symphony has haunted
my imagination ever since it was commissioned, but (unfortunately)
the pressure of urgent business has hitherto prevented its being born.
The hope, however, of your kindly lenity towards me for this delay,
and the happier time, now approaching, when my promise can be
more easily fulfilled, will help soon to make my wish reality. Among
all the many hundred congratulations you will have received yesterday and today, mine will perhaps appear to be an insignificant inter-
loper: I say perhaps, because it would be vain of me to think that
Your Grace couldn't find anything better to wish for. So you see,
kindest and most gracious lady, that I cannot wish you anything at
all on your name-day, because my wishes are too feeble and therefore unproductive! I—now I must wish something too, for myself:
your kind indulgence, your continuing friendship and your goodness which is so important to me; this is what I most want. If you

still have room for one more wish, then mine should change and become identical with your own, for I am sure that none other remains, except that I always wish to be allowed to subscribe myself

Your Grace's

most sincere friend and servant,

Josephus Haydn [m.p] ria.

My respectful compliments to your husband
and the whole family.
On the day after tomorrow I expect an answer about the fortepiano; Your Grace shall then receive the alteration in the Adagio.

[1]The letter, though undated, was obviously written on Maria Anna's name-day, 15th August (the Virgin Mary's Ascension Day).

[To Artaria & Co., Vienna. *German*]
I the undersigned promise and swear to deliver the 6 new *Variazioni*[1] for the pianoforte to Herr Artaria one week from today. Vienna, 22nd November 1790.

Joseph Haydn

Capellmeister.

[1]Artaria, hearing of Haydn's imminent journey to London, must have feared that he would not find the time to finish the *Variazioni*, for which Artaria had presumably contracted and paid. The above receipt exists in two autograph copies, with minor differences (the second one has an abbreviated date and no "Capellmeister"). The Variations (Hoboken XVII: 5) appeared early in 1791.

[To Maria Anna von Genzinger, Vienna. *German*]
Calais, 31st December 1790.

Nobly born,
Most highly respected Frau von Gennzinger!
The recent bad weather and the continual downpour of rain were responsible for my having just arrived (as I write this letter to you) at Calais this evening. Tomorrow morning at 7 we cross the sea to London. I promised Your Grace to write from Brussels, but I could not stay there more than an hour. I am well, thank God! though I am somewhat thinner, owing to fatigue, irregular sleep, and eating and drinking so many different things. In a few days I shall describe my journey in more detail to Your Grace, but I must beg you to

excuse me today. I hope to God that Your Grace, your husband and the whole family are well. I am, most respectfully,

Your Grace's

most obedient servant,

Jos: Haydn.

[Address:]   Madame
        Madame Noble de Gennzinger
            née Noble de Kayser
                à
                Vienne.

[TO MARIA ANNA VON GENZINGER, VIENNA. *German*]
London, 8th January 1791.

Nobly born,
Gracious Lady!

I hope that you will have received my last letter from Calais. I should have written you immediately after my arrival in London, but I wanted to wait a few days so as to be able to write about several things at once. So I can tell you that on the 1st inst., New Year's Day, after attending early mass, I boarded the ship at 7:30 a.m. and at 5 in the afternoon I arrived, thank God! safe and sound in Dower [*sic*]. At the beginning, for the first 4 whole hours, we had almost no wind, and the ship went so slowly that in these 4 hours we didn't go further than one single English mile, and there are 24 between Calais and Dower. Our ship's captain, in an evil temper, said that if the wind did not change, we should have to spend the whole night at sea. Fortunately, however, towards 11:30 o'clock a wind arose and blew so favourably that by 4 o'clock we covered 22 miles. Since the tide, which had just begun to ebb, prevented our large vessel from reaching the pier, 2 smaller ships came out to meet us as we were still fairly far out at sea, and into these we and our luggage were transferred, and thus at last, though exposed to a medium gale, we landed safely. The large vessel stood out to sea five hours longer, till the tide turned and it could finally dock. Some of the passengers were afraid to board the little boats and stayed on board, but I followed the example of the greater number. I remained on deck during the whole passage, so as to gaze my fill at that mighty monster, the ocean. So long as it was calm, I wasn't afraid at all, but towards the end, when the wind grew stronger and stronger, and I saw the monstrous high waves rushing at us, I became a little frightened, and a little indisposed, too. But I overcame it all and arrived safely, without vomiting, on shore. Most of the passengers were ill, and looked like ghosts, but since I went on to London, I didn't feel the effects of the journey right away; but then I needed 2 days to recover. Now, however, I am fresh and well again, and occupied in looking at this endlessly huge city of London, whose various beauties and marvels quite astonished me. I immediately paid the necessary calls, such as to the Neapolitan Ambassador and to our own; both called on me in return 2 days later, and 4 days ago I lunched with the former—N.B. at 6 o'clock in the evening, as is the custom here.

My arrival caused a great sensation throughout the whole city, and I went the round of all the newspapers for 3 successive days. Everyone wants to know me. I had to dine out 6 times up to now, and if I wanted, I could dine out every day; but first I must consider my health, and 2nd my work. Except for the nobility, I admit no callers till 2 o'clock in the afternoon, and 4 o'clock I dine at home with *Mon*. Salomon. I have nice and comfortable, but expensive, lodgings. My landlord is Italian, and also a cook, and serves me 4 very respectable meals; we each pay 1 fl. 30 kr. a day excluding wine and beer, but everything is terribly expensive here. Yesterday I was invited to a grand amateur concert,[1] but I arrived a bit late, and when I showed my ticket they wouldn't let me in but led me to an antichamber, where I had to wait till the piece which was then being played in the hall was over. Then they opened the door, and I was conducted, on the arm of the *entrepreneur*, up the centre of the hall to the front of the orchestra, amid universal applause, and there I was stared at and greeted by a great number of English compliments. I was assured that such honours had not been conferred on anyone for 50 years. After the concert I was taken to a handsome adjoining room, where a table for 200 persons, with many places set, was prepared for all the amateurs; I was supposed to be seated at the head of the table, but since I had dined out on that day and had eaten more than usual, I declined this honour, with the excuse that I was not feeling very well, but despite this I had to drink the harmonious health, in Burgundy, of all the gentlemen present; they all returned the toast, and then allowed me to be taken home. All this, my gracious lady, was very flattering to me, and yet I wished I could fly for a time to Vienna, to have more quiet in which to work, for the noise that the common people make as they sell their wares in the street is intolerable. At present I am working on symphonies,[2] because the libretto of the opera[3] is not yet decided on, but in order to have more quiet I shall have to rent a room far from the centre of town. I would gladly write you in more detail, but I am afraid of missing the mail-coach. Meanwhile I am, with kindest regards to your husband, *Fräulein* Pepi and all the others, most respectfully,

Your Grace's
most sincere and obedient servant,
Joseph Haydn.

Now I have a request to make of Your Grace. I don't know whether I left the Symphony in E flat,[4] which Your Grace returned to me, in my apartments at home, or whether it has been stolen from me *en route*. I missed it yesterday and need it urgently, and so I beg you to get it from my kind friend, Herr von Kees, and to copy it in your own home on small-sized paper for mailing, and send it here in the mail as soon as possible. Should Herr von Kees hesitate about this, which I don't think likely, Your Grace can always send him this letter. My address is as follows:

À Mo[ns]:
Mon: Haydn
N[ro] 18 great Pulteney Street.

[1]The Academy of Ancient Music, given at Freemasons Hall; Salomon was the leader, and Michael Kelly and Nancy Storace sang. Dr. Arnold was the conductor.
[2]Nos. 96 and 95 (probably in that order).
[3]*L'anima del filosofo*—see next letter.
[4]No. 91, as yet unknown in England.

[To PRINCE ANTON ESTERHÁZY, VIENNA. *German*]
Most noble Prince of the Holy Roman Empire!

I report respectfully that, despite unpleasant weather and a great many bad roads throughout the whole trip, I arrived in London this 2nd of January, happy and in good health. My arrival created a great stir, and forced me to take larger quarters that same evening: I received so many calls that I shall hardly be able to repay them in 6 weeks. Both the ambassadors, *i.e.* Prince Castelcicala of Naples[1] and Herr Baron von Stadion;[2] and I had the pleasure of lunching with both of them at 6 o'clock in the evening. The new opera libretto which I am to compose is entitled *Orfeo*, in 5 acts,[3] but I shall not receive it for a few days. It is supposed to be entirely different from that of Gluck. The *prima donna* is called Madame Lops[4] from

Munich—she is a pupil of the famous Mignotti.[5] *Seconda donna* is Madam Capelletti.[6] *Primo homo* [*sic*] is the celebrated Davide.[7] The opera contains only 3 persons, *viz.* Madam Lops, Davide, and a castrato, who is not supposed to be very special.[8] Incidentally, the opera is supposed to contain many choruses, ballets and a lot of big changes of scenery: the first opera, *Pirro* by Paisiello, will be given in a fortnight. The concerts will begin next month on the 11th of February, and I shall dutifully write Your Highness more about that later. Meanwhile I remain,

Your Serene Highness'
submissive and obedient
Joseph Haydn [m.p.] ria.

London, 8th January 1791.
I take the liberty of respectfully kissing the hands of the loveliest Princess, Your Highness' most charming wife, and also the Princess Marie and Her Highness' husband.[9] My address is, unofficially,

N^{ro} 18 Great Pulteneÿ Street
Golden Square
London

[1]FERDINAND IV, KING OF NAPLES and the TWIN SICILIES, had given this recommendation to Haydn personally; the King was in Vienna for the triple marriage of the Crown Prince Francis of Naples with the Archduchess Marie Clementine, and Ferdinand's two daughters, the Princess Marie Therese and Ludovika Louise, with the Archduke Francis (later Emperor Francis II of Austria) and Ferdinand, Grand Duke of Tuscany; the ceremony took place on 19th September. Haydn saw the King a few days before he left for London (on 15th December); see also *supra*, p. 74.

[2]The letter of recommendation from Prince Kaunitz to Count Stadion, dated 13th December 1790, has survived; it is printed in its entirety in Pohl III, 15 (with a wrong date).

[3]*L'anima del filosofo*, the text by Da Ponte's arch-enemy, Carlo Francesco Badini. Haydn completed four acts, which means either that the opera is unfinished (which an examination of the music suggests is doubtful) or poet and composer merged five acts into four. Because of an operatic squabble, Haydn's *Orfeo* was not given. See also *infra*.

[4]ROSA LOPS, "a good and finished singer; she has every accomplishment but youth and beauty" (*Morning Chronicle* of February 1791: see Pohl, H. in L. p. 125).

[5]REGINA MINGOTTI, a Neapolitan, was then seventy. She accompanied her pupil, Lops, to London.

[6]THERESA POGGI CAPPELLETTI was also engaged to sing at the Haydn-Salomon Concerts. See Landon, pp. 441f.

[7]GIACOMO DAVIDDE sang at the Haydn-Salomon Concerts and was a brilliant success. Haydn wrote a concert aria for him which is unfortunately lost. See Landon, pp. 441-459, 461-463 and Pohl H. in L. *etc.*

⁸The principal characters in Haydn's opera are Orfeo (tenor, Davidde), Euridice (soprano, Lops), the Genio (castrato)—she sings only one brilliant and difficult aria—and a high baritone part, Creonte.

⁹It is difficult, in view of the many Marie's and Marie Therese's in the Esterházy family, to know just whom Haydn means, but the most likely choice would seem to be the Princess Maria Josepha Hermenegild, youngest daughter of Prince Franz Joseph von Liechtenstein, who was the wife of Prince Nicolaus II Esterházy, Haydn's last patron. Haydn was very attached to the Princess; while in London the second time he dedicated three pianoforte Trios (Nos. 21–23) to her.

[To Luigia Polzelli, Vienna. *Italian, "Tu" form*]
London, 14th March 1791.

Most esteemed Polzelli,

I am very sorry for you in your present circumstances, and I hope that your poor husband will die at any moment; you did well to put him in the hospital, to keep him alive. I hope that my Pietro feels better; please tell him to pay better attention to his health and to obey his mother. Dear Polzelli, you will receive one hundred florins [Gulden] from *Mons.* Pierre, the steward-in-waiting to the Prince. As soon as I have given my benefit concert, I shall send you some more. I have written to *Mons.* Pierre that your sister¹ has sent the money, because I don't want him to know that it comes from me. Your sister told me that she will send you something herself. I haven't seen her for some time, because I have a lot to do, with all the concerts and opera, and I am persecuted the whole time by the subscription concerts. Up to now our opera has not yet opened, and since the King won't give the licence, *Signor* Gallini² intends to open it as if it were a subscription concert, for if he doesn't, he stands to lose twenty thousand pounds Sterling. I shan't lose anything, because the bankers Fries in Vienna have already received my money. My opera, entitled *L'anima del filosofo,* will be staged at the end of May; I have already completed the Second Act, but there are five acts, of which the last are very short. In order to show the public his theatre, his opera and his ballet, *Signor* Gallini has had the clever idea of arranging, one evening a few days ago, a dress rehearsal in such a manner as if it were the real opening night; he distributed four thousand tickets, and more than five thousand came. The opera, entitled *Pyhro* [*Pirro*], by Paisiello, was very successful. Only our *prima donna* is a silly goose, and I shan't use her in my opera. The ballet was simply magnificent. We now await a yes or a no from the

King, and if our theatre is opened, the other theatre, that is, our rivals, will have to close their doors, because the castrato and the *prima donna* are too old, and their opera didn't please anyone. At the first concert of Mr. Salomon I created a furor with a new Symphony,[3] and they had to repeat the Adagio: this had never before occurred in London. Imagine what it means to hear such a thing from an Englishman's lips! Write soon, dear Polzelli, and think of me. I am, and will always be,

Your most sincere friend,
Giuseppe Haydn.

[Address:]   Madame Polzelli à Vienna
             im Starnbergischen Freyhaus auf der Wieden N^{ro} 161
[Polzelli added the following note in pencil: "He will die—an enemy has followed Haydn to London to overthrow him".]

[1]Luigia's sister Cristina Negri, was a soprano in the Italian opera.
[2]Director of the Opera; see also p. 67.
[3]Symphony No. 96 in D, in all probability the first Symphony Haydn performed at the Salomon Concerts (March 11th).

[AN OPEN LETTER TO MR. HAYWARD,[1] OXFORD. *English*]

[London, *c.* 25th May 1791]

Whereas at the Request of Mr. Jung, an Acquaintance of mine from Vienna, I faithfully promised to play the Harpsichord at Mr. Hayward's Benefit Concert, the 18th, Instant (*which Day I had appointed myself*), but was prevented from coming on Account of a Rehearsal at the Opera House, which lasted from Two till Half-past Four on that Day, I take the Liberty by this Paper to express the greatest Sorrow for not having been able to stand to my Promise. As the University of Oxford, whose great Reputation I heard abroad, is too great an Object for me not to see before I leave England, I shall take the earliest Opportunity of paying it a Visit, and hope at the same time to make a personal apology to those Ladies and Gentlemen who were kind enough to honour Mr. Hayward with their Company.

Joseph Haydn.

[1]Hayward was one of Oxford's leading musicians; his Benefit Concert took place on 18th May, and the following week several London newspapers printed a report from Oxford, in which Haydn's absence was "bitterly and justly complained of". Hayward himself published a letter of protest on 21st May. Haydn's letter of apology was published in *Jackson's Oxford Journal* of 28th May, which suggests that he wrote it two or three days previously.

[To LUIGIA POLZELLI, VIENNA. *Italian, "Tu" form*]

London, 4th August 1791.

Dear Polzelli!

I hope that you will have received my last letter through Count Fries and also the hundred florins [Gulden] which I transferred to you. I would like to do more, but at present I cannot. As far as your husband is concerned, I tell you that Providence has done well to liberate you from this heavy yoke, and for him, too, it is better to be in another world than to remain useless in this one. The poor man has suffered enough. Dear Polzelli, perhaps, perhaps the time will come, which we both so often dreamt of, when four eyes shall be closed.[1] Two are closed, but the other two—enough of all this, it shall be as God wills. Meanwhile, pay attention to your health, I beg of you, and write me very soon, because for quite some time now I have had days of depression without really knowing why, and your letters cheer me, even when they are sad. Good bye, dear Polzelli, the mail won't wait any longer. I kiss your family and remain always

Your most sincere

Haydn.

[Address:]   Madame Polzelli Virtuosa di Musica à

Vienna en Autriche

abzugeben im Starnbergischen Freyhaus auf der Wieden N$^{ro.}$ 161 [This last sentence is crossed out and the postman has written "nicht auf der Wieden"; Polzelli had already left, but obviously the letter was forwarded and she did receive it.]

[1]The sentence refers to Frau Haydn and Sig. Polzelli.

[To MARIA ANNA VON GENZINGER, VIENNA. *German*]

Nobly born and gracious Lady!

I have received no reply as yet to my 2nd letter of 3rd July, which I entrusted to a composer here, Herr Diettenhofer, together with the pianoforte arrangement of a little Andante from one of my new Symphonies,[1] to give to Your Grace; nor have I any answer either about the Symphony in E flat[2] which I asked for; and so I cannot wait any longer to enquire after Your Grace's health, and that of your husband and all your dear family. Could it be that the odious proverb, "Out of sight, out of mind", is true everywhere? Oh no! either urgent affairs, or the loss of my letter and the Symphony, are responsible. I feel sure that Herr von Keess [*sic*] is quite willing to send the Symphony I asked for, because he said so in his letter to me; but since both of us will have to bear this loss, we shall have to leave it to Providence. I flatter myself that I shall receive a short answer to this. Now, my dear good gracious lady, how is your fortepiano? Is a Haydnish thought brought to mind, now and then, by your fair hand? Does my dear *Fräulein* Pepi sometimes sing poor *Ariadne*? Oh yes! I can hear it even here, especially during the last two months, when I have been living in the country, amid the loveliest scenery, with a banker's[3] family where the atmosphere is like that of the Gennzinger family, and where I live as if I were in a monastery. I am all right, thank the good Lord! except for my usual rheumatism; I work hard, and when in the early mornings I walk in the woods, alone, with my English grammar, I think of my Creator, my family, and all the friends I have left behind—and of these you are the ones I most value. Of course I had hoped to have the pleasure of seeing you sooner, but my circumstances—in short, fate—will have it that I remain in London another 8 or 10 months. Oh, my dear gracious lady! how sweet this bit of freedom really is! I had a kind Prince, but sometimes I was forced to be dependent on base souls. I often sighed for release, and now I have it in some measure. I appreciate the good sides of all this, too, though my mind is burdened with far more work. The realization that I am no bond-servant makes ample amends for all my toils. But, dear though this liberty is to me, I should like to enter Prince Esterházy's service again when I return, if only for the sake of my family. I doubt whether this will be possible, however, for in his letter my Prince strongly objects to my staying away for so long, and absolutely demands my speedy return; but I can't comply with this, owing to a new contract which I have just made here. And now, unfortunately, I expect my dismissal, whereby I hope that God will give me the strength to make up for this loss, at least partly, by my industry. Meanwhile I console myself by the hope of hearing something soon from Your Grace. You shall receive my promised new Symphony in two months, but in order to inspire me with good ideas, I beg Your Grace to write, and to write a long letter, too, to one who is ever

Your Grace's

most sincere friend and obedient

servant,

Jos: Haydn.

London, 17th September 1791.

My respectful compliments to Herr von Gennzinger and the whole family. Please forgive my taking the liberty of enclosing a letter to Herr von Keess, but I didn't have his address.

¹No. 95 in C minor (as subsequent correspondence shows), JOSEPH DIETTEN-HOFER was a Viennese composer who had lived for some time in England: see also letter of 20th December 1791.
²No. 91, see *supra* and *infra*.
³NATHANIEL BRASSEY, whose house, Roxford, was about a mile from the village of Hertingfordbury in Hertfordshire. See also London Notebooks, p. 271.

[TO MARIA ANNA VON GENZINGER, VIENNA. *German*]
London, 13th October 1791.

Nobly born and gracious Lady!

I take the liberty of making the urgent request that you advance 150 fl. for a short time to my wife, but only on the condition that Your Grace doesn't imagine that since my departure I have become a bad manager. No, my dear gracious lady, God has been kind to me. There are 3 circumstances to blame. First, that since my departure I have repaid my Prince the 450 fl. he advanced me for the journey; secondly, I cannot demand any interest from my bank bonds, because the bonds are in the strong-box which I entrusted to Your Grace's care, and moreover I can't remember their names or numbers and therefore couldn't write a receipt; thirdly, I cannot get at the 5883 fl. which I recently deposited, 1000 in my Prince's hands and the rest at the Count von Fries's, especially since it is English money. Your Grace can see, therefore, that I am still a good manager. This leads me to hope that Your Grace will not refuse my present request, to lend my wife 150 fl. This letter shall be Your Grace's security, and shall be valid in any court. I shall repay the interest with a thousand thanks on my return. Meanwhile I am, most respectfully, with my kindest regards to your husband, *Fräulein* Pepi and all the others,

Your Grace's
most obedient servant,
Jos: Haydn [m.p] ria.

Since I cannot remember the little opening Adagio at the beginning of the Symphony in E flat,¹ I take the liberty of noting the ensuing Allegro:

p:

Shall I be so fortunate as to receive this Symphony by the end of January 1792? Oh yes, I flatter myself that I shall! But how strangely things sometimes come to pass: I think that Your Grace will have received my letter on the very day that I was reading your cruel reproach that Haydn was capable of forgetting his friend and bene-factress. Oh! how often I wish that I could be with you at the piano even for a quarter of an hour, and then to have some good German soup for lunch. Well, we can't have everything in this world! May God grant me good health; I've enjoyed it up to now, and I hope that through my good conduct the Almighty will continue to grant it to me. I was very pleased to hear that Your Grace is well. May Providence long watch over you! By the way, I hope to see Your Grace in the course of 6 months: I shall have many things to tell you. [Original language:] Adieu. Good Night—it is time to go to bed. Auf deutsch—gute nacht, es ist zeit zu bette zu gehen, [German:] it's 11: 30. One more thing: to ensure the safety of the money, Herr Hamburger,[2] a very good friend of mine, a man of tall stature, who is my wife's landlord, will bring you this letter himself; and you can safely entrust him with the money; but just the same you should get a receipt from him, and from my wife.

Inter alia Herr von Keess writes me that he would like to know my circumstances here in London, because there are various rumours about me in Vienna. From my youth on, I have been exposed to envy, and so I am not surprised that people attempt wholly to crush my modest talents; but the Almighty is my support. My wife writes me, but I don't believe it, that Mozart speaks very ill of me. I forgive him. There is no doubt that many people in London are also envious of me, and I know almost all of them. Most of them are Italians. But they cannot harm me, for my credit with the common people has been firmly established for a long time. Apart from the professors,[3] I am respected and loved by everyone. As for my remu-neration, Mozart can enquire of Count Fries for information, with whom I deposited £ 500, and of my Prince, who has 1000 Gulden, that makes nearly 6000 fl. in all. I thank my Creator daily for this boon, and I flatter myself that I can take home a few thousand more, notwithstanding the fact that I have many expenses, and notwith-standing the costs of the journey. Now I won't bother Your Grace any more. Isn't this handwriting appalling?

How is Pater——[4]? My compliments to him.

[1]No. 91.

[2]JOHANN NEPOMUK HAMBURGER, an official ("Registrator") in the Lower

Austrian Government whose house was on the Wasserkunst-Bastei. It was
rebuilt in 1805 and occupied the place now known as the beginning of the
Seilerstätte. Karajan, pp. 15f. and Pohl II, 244, n. 8.
³Haydn probably means the rival Professional Concerts.
⁴Probably the Pater Professor (of the Schottenstift?) referred to in earlier
letters.

[To Maria Anna von Genzinger, Vienna. *German*]
                              London, 17th November 1791.
Nobly born and gracious lady!
In the greatest haste I beg you to deliver the accompanying
parcel, which I have addressed to you, to Herr von Keess, for it contains the two new Symphonies¹ I promised. I was waiting all this
time for a good opportunity, but could hear of none, and was
therefore obliged to send them by mail. Please tell Herr von Keess
that I ask him respectfully to have a rehearsal of both these Symphonies, because they are very delicate, especially the last movement
of that in D major, for which I recommend the softest *piano* and a
very quick *tempo*. I will write you in more detail in a few days. N.B.
I was forced to send both Symphonies to Your Grace, because I
don't know Herr von Keess' address. I kiss Your Grace's hands, and
with kind regards to your husband and family, I am
                              Your most obedient servant,
                                        Haydn.
I have just returned from the country today. I have been staying
with a Lord for the past fortnight, 100 miles from London.²
[Address:]   Madame
            Madame Anne Noble de
                Gennzinger Noble de Kayser.
in schotten Hof, auf   à
der Haupt Stiege   Vienne
    im 2ᵗⁿ Stock   an autriche.

¹Nos. 96 in D major and 95 in C minor. Kees entered them in his catalogue
of Haydn Symphonies as "NB. arrived from London".
²Sir Patrick Blake: see London Notebooks *infra*, p. 272.

[To Luigia Polzella, Bologna. *Italian, "Tu" form*]
                              London, 13th December 1791
Dear Polzelli!
You gave me quite a shock with you last letter, because I thought

my letter had gone astray, and also the money with it. I was so upset that I couldn't sleep for three days, until I received your second letter. I hope that you will never again entertain such cruel suspicions of me, for I esteem and love you as I did on the very first day. I am very sorry for you, and it pains me terribly that I can't do more for you. But be patient, perhaps the day will come when I can show you how much I love you. Write soon, and let me know how your lodgings are, how you are, and if you arrived safely with your two dear sons. Tell Pietro to be obedient and to study hard; if he doesn't, I shan't take him with me. Your sister sends you a thousand kisses; she is still in a most unhappy state: the poor thing now lives in a room, separated from her husband, with whom she is still on bad terms. She will send you a little something. Dear Polzelli, I can't write more today. More another time.

    Meanwhile I am your most sincere

                                Giuseppe Haydn.

[Address:]   Madame
    Madame Loise Polzelli,
    Virtuosa di Musica
            a
                Bologna.

[TO MARIA ANNA VON GENZINGER, VIENNA. *German*]

                        London, 20th December 1791.

Nobly born and gracious Lady!

    I was very surprised that you did not get my letter at the same time as the 2 Symphonies,[1] for I posted them myself here and gave them every instruction. My mistake was that I didn't enclose the letter in the parcel. That is what generally happens, gracious lady, to those who have too much head work. But I do hope that you will receive the letter somewhat later; if not, I should explain that both Symphonies were destined for Herr von Keess, but with the stipulation that after Herr von Keess had copied them, the scores were to be delivered to Your Grace, so that Your Grace could make a pianoforte arrangement of them, if you felt so disposed. As for the Symphony intended for Your Grace, I shall deliver it by the end of February at the latest. I am sorry to have had to address this large package to Your Grace, but I didn't have Herr von Keess' address;

Herr von Keess will of course refund you the postage costs and, I hope, give you 7 ducats *a parte*. Now may I respectfully ask Your Grace to use this money and have the Symphony in E flat,[2] which I ask for so often, and of which I sent you the *incipit* recently, copied on small-sized paper for mailing, and sent to me by mail as soon as possible; for it may be half a year before a courier is dispatched from Vienna, and I need the Symphony very urgently. Further I must bother Your Grace once again; this time it is the last pianoforte Sonata in A flat[3]—that is, with 4♭ signs—with accompaniment of a violin and violoncello, and one other piece, the Fantasia in C [for pianoforte] unaccompanied; please buy these at Herr Artaria's, and have them, too, copied on small-sized paper for mailing and sent here by mail, because these works are not yet engraved in London. Your Grace, however, must be clever enough not to mention a word of this to Herr Artaria, for otherwise he will anticipate the sale here. Your Grace should subtract the costs from the 7 ducats. To come back to the aforesaid 2 Symphonies, I must tell Your Grace that I sent the pianoforte arrangement of Andante of that in C minor through Herr Diettenhofer. It is reported, however, that Herr Diettenhofer[4] either died *en route* or must have met with an accident, and so you can make the pianoforte arrangements yourself, if you are so disposed. The principal part of the letter I entrusted to Herr Diettenhofer described the conferment of the doctor's degree on me at Oxford, and all the honours I received there.[5] I must take this opportunity of informing Your Grace that 3 weeks ago I was invited by the Prince of Wales to visit his brother, the Duke of York, at the latter's country seat. The Prince presented me to the Duchess, the daughter of the King of Prussia, who received me very graciously and said many flattering things. She is the most delightful lady in the world, is very intelligent, plays the pianoforte and sings very nicely. I had to stay there 2 days, because a slight indisposition prevented her attending the concert on the first day. On the 2nd day, however, she remained continually at my side from 10 o'clock in the evening, when the music began, to 2 o'clock in the morning. Nothing but Haydn was played. I conducted the symphonies from the pianoforte, and the sweet little thing sat beside me on my left and hummed all the pieces from memory, for she had heard them so often in Berlin. The Prince of Wales sat on my right side and played with us on his violoncello, quite tolerably. I had to sing, too. The Prince of Wales is having my portrait painted just now, and the picture is to hang in his room.[6] The Prince of Wales is the most handsome man on God's earth; he has an extraordinary love of music and a lot of feeling, but not much money. *Nota bene*, this is between ourselves. I am more pleased by his kindness than by any financial gain. On the third day the Duke of York sent me two stages with his own span, since I couldn't catch the mail-coach.

Now, gracious lady, I would like to take you to task a little, for believing that I prefer the city of London to Vienna, and that I find the sojourn here more agreeable than that in my fatherland. I don't hate London, but I would not be capable of spending the rest of my life there, even if I could amass millions. I shall tell Your Grace the reason when I see you. I look forward tremendously to going home and to embracing all my good friends. I only regret that the great Mozart will not be among them, if it is really true, which I trust it is not, that he has died. Posterity will not see such a talent again in 100 years! I am delighted that Your Grace and your family are well. I have enjoyed excellent health up to now, thank God! but a week ago I got an attack of English rheumatism which was so severe that sometimes I had to cry aloud. I hope soon to get rid of it, however, inasmuch as I have adopted the usual custom here of wrapping myself in flannel from head to foot. I must ask you to excuse the fact that my handwriting is so poor today. In the hope of being consoled by a letter, and with every esteem for yourself and my respectful compliments to your husband, dear *Fräulein* Pepi, and all the others, I am

Your Grace's
most obedient servant,
Joseph Haydn.

Please convey my respects to Herr von Kreybich.[7]

[1] Nos. 96 and 95: see *supra*.

[2] No. 91: see *supra* and *infra*.

[3] No. 14: it was performed by the young JOHANN NEPOMUK HUMMEL (1778–1837), Salomon and Menel at the eighth Haydn-Salomon Concert of the 1792 season (20th April), and engraved shortly afterwards by Longman and Broderip. Concerning Hummel, see also *infra*, p. 234. From 1804 to 1811 he was Prince Esterházy's *Kapellmeister*. He had been a pupil of Mozart, and was later a popular composer, and—as a pianist—a rival of Beethoven.

[4] Diettenhofer did not die *en route*, for Gerber (*Neues historisch-biographisches Lexikon der Tonkünstler*, Leipzig, 1812, I, p. 891) reports that he was still active in London in 1799.

[5] Haydn had received an honorary degree (Mus.Doc.) at Oxford on 8th July.

[6] The portrait was by JOHN HOPPNER (1758–1810), who had been Court

Painter to the Prince of Wales from 1789. Haydn's portrait now hangs in Buckingham Palace; it is reproduced in colour in Geiringer's *Haydn* (1932).
[7]FRANZ KREIBICH (1728–1797), Court Director of Chamber Music under Joseph II, was formerly one of Haydn's (and Mozart's) bitterest enemies.

[EXTRACTS FROM A LETTER TO JOHANN MICHAEL PUCHBERG, VIENNA. *German*]

London, January 1792.

. . . . For some time I was beside myself about his [Mozart's] death, and I could not believe that Providence would so soon claim the life of such an indispensable man. I only regret that before his death he could not convince the English, who walk in darkness in this respect, of his greatness—a subject about which I have been sermonizing to them every single day . . . . You will be good enough, my kind friend, to send me a catalogue of those pieces which are not yet known here, and I shall make every possible effort to promote such works for the widow's benefit; I wrote the poor woman three weeks ago, and told her that when her favourite son reaches the necessary age, I shall give him composition lessons to the very best of my ability, and at no cost, so that he can, to some extent, fill his father's position. . . .

[1]JOHANN MICHAEL PUCHBERG, the Viennese banker, was one of Mozart's friends. Puchberg and Haydn attended the rehearsals of *Così fan tutte* in 1790, the only two friends Mozart invited. This letter was first printed in Nottebohm's *Mozartiana* (1880), without the exact date and including only the passages pertaining to Mozart. The autograph has probably disappeared forever.

[TO LUIGIA POLZELLI, PIACENZA. *Italian, "Tu" form*]

London, 14th January 1792.

My dearest Polzelli! This very moment I received your letter, and hasten to answer it. I am relieved that you are in good health, and that you have found a position in a little theatre; not so much because of the payment but to have the experience. I wish you every possible success, in particular a good rôle and a good teacher, who takes the same pains with you as did your Haydn. You write that you would like to send your dear Pietro to me; do so, for I shall embrace him with all my heart; he is always welcome, and I shall treat him as if he were my own son. I shall take him with me to Vienna. I shall remain in London until the middle of June, not longer, because my Prince and many other circumstances make it imperative that I return home. Nevertheless I shall try, if possible, to go to Italy, in order to see my dear Polzelli, but meanwhile you can send your Pietro to me here in London; he will always be either with me or with your sister, who is now alone and who has been separated quite some time now from her husband, that beast. She is unhappy, as you were, and I am very sorry for her. I see her but rarely, for I have a lot to do, especially now, when the Professional Concert has had my pupil Pleyel[1] brought over, to face me as a rival; but I'm not afraid, because last year I made a great impression on the English and hope therefore to win their approval this year, too. My opera was not given, because *Sig.* Gallini[2] didn't receive the licence from the King, and never will; to tell you the truth, the Italian opera has no success at all now, and by a stroke of bad luck, the Pantheon Theatre burned down just this very day, two hours after midnight. Your sister had been engaged in the last piece;[3] I am sorry for all of them.

I am quite well, but am almost always in an "English humour", that is, depressed, and perhaps I shall never again regain the good humour that I used to have when I was with you. Oh! my dear Polzelli: you are always in my heart, and I shall never, never forget you. I shall do my very best to see you, if not this year, then certainly the next, along with your son. I hope that you won't forget me, and that you will write me if you get married again, for I would like to know the name of him who is fortunate enough to have you. Actually I ought to be a little annoyed with you, because many people wrote me from Vienna that you had said the worst possible things about me, but God bless you, I forgive you everything, for I know you said it in love. Do preserve your good name, I beg you, and think from time to time about your Haydn, who esteems you and loves you tenderly, and will always be faithful to you. Write me, too, if you have seen and spoken with anyone who was formerly in Prince Esterházy's service. Good bye, my dear, that's all for this evening: it's late.

Today I went to see your dear sister, to ask her if she would be able to put up Pietro in her house. He will be received with the greatest pleasure; he can sleep there and have his meals there, too, since I always eat out and am invited out every day; but Pietro can come every day to me for his lessons—I live only a little way from your sister's. I give your sister a bit of money, because I am very sorry for her; she is not exactly poor, but she has to be very economical. I shall clothe your son well, and do everything for him. I don't want you to have any expense on his account; he shall have everything he needs. I shall certainly leave for Vienna in the middle of June, but I shall take the route *via* Holland, Leipzig and Berlin (in order to see the King of Prussia); my Petruccio[4] will always be with me. I hope, however, that up to now he has been an obedient son to his dear mother, but if he hasn't been, I don't want him, and you must write me the truth. I don't want to have an ungrateful boy, for then I would be capable of sending him away at a moment's notice. Your sister embraces you and kisses you thousands and thousands of times. Write me often, dear Polzelli, and remember that I shall be always your faithful

Haydn.

My compliments to *Signor* Negri.[5]

Dear Polzelli, *Signor* Hauder, who is Prince Esterházy's Master of the Horse, and a rascal, wrote to me that you had sold his harpsichord. I cannot recall that you ever had any other harpsichord than mine. See how they torment me on your account! My wife, that devilish beast, wrote me so many things that I was forced to answer her that I would never go home the rest of my life; and from that moment she was much more sensible. Take good care of this letter.

[Address:]   Madame
v [ON] LONDON Madame Aloise Polzelli née
       Moreschi.   Virtuosa di Musica
                      à
                   Piacenza
     al Theatro
     di Piacenza   en Italie.

[1]IGNAZ PLEYEL (1757–1831), Haydn's pupil (see *supra*, p. 18), was later *Maître de Chapelle* in Strasbourg. In his time a famous composer, he later retired to Paris (after being arrested and almost guillotined) and became a successful music publisher, in which capacity Haydn wrote to him several times. See *infra*, letters of 4th May 1801 and 6th December 1802.
[2]See *supra*, p. 67.
[3]Guglielmi's *La pastorella nobile*: see the London Notebooks, p. 266.
[4]The Italian diminutive for Pietro.
[5]SIGNOR NEGRI, probably the singer who had been a member of the Esterházy opera company from 1782–1784: he had sung Rodomonte in Haydn's *Orlando Paladino* (1782).

[To Maria Anna von Genzinger, Vienna. *German*]

London, 17th January 1792.

Nobly born,

Kindest and most gracious Lady!

I ask your forgiveness a thousand times. I own and bemoan that I should not be so remiss in fulfilling my promise, but if Your Grace could only see how I am tormented, here in London, by having to attend all sorts of private concerts, which cause me great loss of time; and by the vast amount of work which has been heaped on my shoulders, you would, my gracious Lady, have the greatest pity on me. I never in my life wrote so much in one year as I have here during this past one, but now I am almost completely exhausted, and it will do me good to be able to rest a little when I return home. At present I am working for Salomon's concerts, and I am making every effort to do my best, because our rivals, the Professional Concert, have had my pupil Pleyel from Strassburg come here to conduct their concerts. So now a bloody harmonious war will commence between master and pupil. The newspapers are all full of it, but it seems to me that there will soon be an armistice, because my reputation is so firmly established here. Pleyel behaved so modestly towards me upon his arrival that he won my affection again. We are very often together, and this does him credit, for he knows how to appreciate his father. We shall share our laurels equally and each go home satisfied.

On the 14th inst., the Professional Concert met with a great misfortune, inasmuch as the new theatre, built only last year—it is called The Pantheon—burned down at 2 o'clock in the morning. The fire was started deliberately. The damage is estimated at more than £ 100,000 Sterling. So at the moment there is no Italian theatre in London. Now, my angelic[1] and gracious lady, I am going to upbraid you a little, too. How often have I repeated my request that you send me by mail the Symphony in E flat,[2] of which I once sent you the *incipit*, copied on small-sized paper for mailing. I have sighed for it a long time now, and if I don't get it by the end of next month I shall lose 20 guiness. The copy which Herr von Keess has made for me may not arrive in London for 3 [months], or 3 years, because it may be that long before a courier is dispatched. I also asked Herr Von Keess in the enclosed letter to take the responsibility for the whole matter, and if he couldn't, I ventured to transfer the commission once more to Your Grace, because I flattered myself that you would certainly fulfil my urgent request. I further asked Herr von Keess to repay to Your Grace the money expended on his behalf, in order that you have no expenses.[3] Now, kindest and best Frau von Gennzinger, I beg you once more to see to this matter, for you will be rendering me the greatest possible service: I shall explain the reason for all this when we meet, when I shall respectfully kiss your fair hands a thousand times, and repay my debt with gratitude. The celebration[4] you describe in honour of my modest talents touched me very much; but not quite as much as if Your Grace had been completely satisfied by it. Perhaps I can supply this imperfection by another Symphony which I shall be sending Your Grace shortly; I say perhaps, because I, or rather my brain, is indeed exhausted. Providence alone supply that which my waning powers cannot. I pray to Him daily, for without His assistance I should be a poor creature indeed! And now, my unique and gracious lady, I trust and pray for your indulgence. Oh yes! I can see you quite clearly in front of me, and I can hear you say: "Well, this time I shall forgive you, you wretched Haydn, but—but!" No, no, henceforth I shall perform my duties far better. I must close now, by saying that as always I hold you in the greatest possible esteem, and shall ever be

My most gracious Frau von Gennzinger's
most obedient servant,
Joseph Haydn.

My respectful compliments to your
husband and all the others.
Please forgive the fact that I always take
the liberty of enclosing the letters to
Kees, but I don't have his address.

[1]"Englische", a play on words: "English" and "angelic" (= "englische", as for example in "der Englische Gruss").

[2]No. 91: see *supra* and *infra*.

[3]Haydn refers to the package containing Symphonies Nos. 96 and 95, for which Maria Anna would have paid the postage upon its arrival.

[4]A description of this "Grand Concert", at which Symphonies Nos. 95 and 96 were played, was printed in the London *Public Advertiser*: see Landon, p. 472. Presumably the concert was arranged by von Kees.

[To Maria Anna von Genzinger, Vienna. *German*]
London, 2nd February 1792.
Nobly born,
Most esteemed Frau von Gennzinger!
Today, 1st [!] February, I received your kind letter together with

the Fantasia and the Sonata *a tre*.[1] But I was rather saddened, on opening the parcel, because I had hoped and believed that the Symphony in E flat[2] for which I have so long and patiently waited would be included. Gracious lady! I beg you urgently to have it copied at once on small-sized paper for mailing and then to send it to me immediately; I shall be only too happy to pay for all the expenses incurred, for God only knows when the Symphonies will arrive here from Brussels.[3] I cannot dispense with this work without great loss. Please forgive me, kindest and most gracious lady, for bothering you so often with this matter; I shall appreciate it very much. I am so burdened with work at present that I simply cannot write to Herr von Keess, and therefore I beg you to apply to him for the said Symphony, and to present my respectful compliments to him. Meanwhile I remain, with kind respects,

Your Grace's

most obedient servant,

[no signature.]

My respects to your husband, the
dear children, and von Kreubich.[4]
Your Grace shall receive a good portion
of the sewing needles.[5]

[Address:]   Madame
          Madame Anna Noble de
          Gennzinger née noble de Kayser
                    a
im Schotten Hof auf   Vienne
     der Haupt Stiege.   en autriche.

[1]See *supra*, p. 123.
[2]No. 91: see *supra* and *infra*.
[3]Kees had sent off the parts, which had apparently got as far as Brussels. See letter of 2nd March 1792.
[4]Kreibich: see *supra*, p. 125.
[5]See London Notebooks, *infra*, p. 251.

[To JOHANN JOSEPH DUSSEK[1] (CZASLAU, BOHEMIA). *German*]
My dear Friend!
I thank you with all my heart that you also remembered me in your last letter to your son. I return the compliment with interest,

and consider myself fortunate to be able to assure you that you have, in your son, a most honourable and polished man who is a distinguished musician.

I love him just as dearly as I do you, and he well deserves it. If you give him a father's blessing, he will continue to be happy, which—because of his great talents—I heartily wish him to be.

With every respect, I am

> Your most sincere friend,
> Joseph Haydn.

London, 26th February 1792.

[1]JOHANN JOSEPH DUSSEK (or Dussik) was a well-known musician in his day, and was organist at Czaslau. His son, JOHANN LUDWIG (LADISLAUS) (1761–1812) was a brilliant pianist and a talented composer; he appeared in many of the Haydn-Salomon concerts. His wife, Sophia Corri, also sang in Haydn's programmes. Later they formed the firm of Corri, Dussek & Co., with which some of Haydn's new works appeared. (See J. W. Davison's article on Dussek in Grove's *Dictionary,* 1st ed. (1879) I, pp. 473–477, where (p. 474) this letter was first printed.)

[To MARIA ANNA VON GENZINGER, VIENNA. *German*]
                              London, 2nd March 1792.

Nobly born and gracious Lady!

Yesterday evening I received your welcome letter and the Symphony[1] I had asked for; I respectfully kiss Your Grace's hands for the prompt and careful delivery. Six days before I had in fact received it through Herr von Keess from Brussels, but the score was much more useful, for I have to change many things for the English public.[2] I only regret that I must bother Your Grace so often with my commissions, the more so since at present I cannot show you how grateful I am. I must confess and admit to Your Grace that this causes me great embarrassment and that there are days in which I am terribly sad; especially because at present I cannot send Your Grace the Symphony[3] which is dedicated to you, for the following reasons: first, because I intend to alter the last movement of it, and to improve it, since it is too weak compared with the first. I was convinced of this myself, and so was the public, when it was played the first time last Friday; notwithstanding which, it made the most profound impression on the audience. The second reason is that I really dread the risk of its falling into other hands. I was not a little shocked to hear the unpleasant news of the Sonata.[4] By God! I would rather have lost 25 ducats than to hear of this theft, and no one except my own copyist can have done it. Nevertheless I hope to God to be able to replace the loss, once again through Madam Tost, for I certainly don't want to incur any reproaches from her. Your Grace must therefore be indulgent towards me until the end of July, when I can have the pleasure of delivering personally not only the Sonata but also the Symphony; *nota bene*, I shall give you the Symphony myself, but the Sonata through Madam Tost. Moreover, I cannot deliver the promised Symphonies[5] to Herr von Kees either, for here too there is a want of faithful copyists. If I had the time I would copy them myself, but there isn't a day, not a single day, in which I am free from work, and I shall thank the dear Lord when I can leave London—the sooner the better. My labours have been augmented by the arrival of my pupil Pleyel, whom the Professional Concert have brought here. He arrived here with a lot of new compositions, but they had been composed long ago; he therefore promised to present a new work every evening. As soon as I saw this, I realized at once that a lot of people were dead set against me, and so I announced publicly that I would likewise produce 12 different new pieces. In order to keep my word, and to support poor Salomon, I must be the victim and work the whole time. But I really do feel it. My eyes suffer the most, and I have many sleepless nights, though with God's help I shall overcome it all. The people of the Professional Concert wanted to put a spoke in my wheel, because I would not go over to them; but the public is just. I enjoyed a great deal of success last year, but still more this year. Pleyel's presumption is sharply criticized, but I love him just the same. I always go to his concerts, and am the first to applaud him. I am delighted that Your Grace and the family are well. Please give my kind respects to all of them. The time is drawing near when I must put my trunks in order. Oh! how happy I shall be to see Your Grace again, to show you how much I missed you and to show the esteem in which, gracious lady, you will ever be held by

Your most obedient servant,
Jos: Haydn.

I hasten to ask Your Grace to present my respectful compliments to Herr von Keess, and to tell him that the press of affairs does not give me time to write, and to explain to him that, for the above reasons, I cannot send him the new Symphonies. I shall have the honour of conducting them at his coming Christmas Concert.

[Address:]   Madame
                    Madame Anna Noble de
            Gennzinger, née Noble de Kayser
                                à
                            Vienne
im Schotten Hof.   en autriche.

[1]No. 91.

[2]Haydn's revision has not, unfortunately, survived, though the score Maria Anna sent him is probably the "score on small-sized paper for mailing" of an E flat Symphony listed in Haydn's musical legacy. Presumably Haydn would have added trumpets and kettledrums, and possibly a second flute part.

[3]This passage is not quite clear. On 2nd March, Symphony No. 98 was first performed, and the first and last movements encored. "Last Friday", however, Symphony No. 93 had been performed, not for the first but for the second time (see Landon, p. 480). Obviously No. 93 is the work to which Haydn, rather inaccurately, refers. It is not known if the version of the finale we play today is the revised one, or if Haydn ever found the time to "improve it".

[4]The Sonata referred to is probably No. 49, which Haydn had delivered to Madam Tost when she was still Anna de Jerlischeck (see *supra*, p. 98). Meanwhile Artaria had printed the Sonata—it had been announced in August 1791—and presumably "Mademoiselle Nanette", or rather Madam Tost, had objected to Maria Anna. Haydn obviously suspected Johann Elssler, who by that time had become Haydn's personal copyist, of having stolen the work and sold it to Artaria. The new Sonata which Haydn intended to deliver, again "via Madam Tost", is perhaps the piano Trio in G major (Hoboken XV: 32) which has hitherto been wrongly regarded as a violin Sonata. (Haydn refers to it in his London Catalogue—see *infra*, p. 309—as a Sonata, as he usually describes his piano trios.) Hoboken's catalogue, pp. 717f. and 774f., needs correcting in this respect.

[5]Some of the new Salomon Symphonies (Haydn had already sent Nos. 95 and 96 to von Kees): perhaps Nos. 93, 94 and 98.

[TO PRINCE ANTON ESTERHÁZY, (EISENSTADT?). *German*]
Most Serene Prince of the Holy Roman Empire,
Gracious Lord and Sire!

Since I must leave England in a short time, I hasten to place my entire faithful services in all matters—as far as I shall be able to fulfil them—at Your Serene Highness' disposal. Our concerts will be finished at the end of June, after which I shall begin the journey home without delay, in order to serve my most gracious Prince and Lord again. I am, in humble submission,

Your Serene Highness'
Most humble Joseph Haydn, m.p.,
Capellmeister.

London, 10th April 1792.

[TO MARIA ANNA VON GENZINGER, VIENNA. *German*]
London, 24th April 1792.

Nobly born and gracious lady!

Yesterday evening I was delighted to receive your last letter of 5th April, with the enclosed newspaper cutting in which the Viennese are informed of my poor talents. I must admit that this little choral piece,[1] my first attempt at the English language, has earned me considerable credit as a composer of vocal music with the English. It is only a pity that I could not compose more such pieces during my present stay here, but we couldn't have any boy choristers on the days our concerts were held, because they had already been engaged for a year past to sing at other concerts, of which there is a great number. Despite great opposition and the musical enemies who are so much against me—all of whom, together with my pupil Pleyel, tried their very hardest to crush me, especially this Winter—I have gained (thank God!) the upper hand. But I must admit that with all this work I am quite exhausted and wearied, and look forward longingly to the peace which will soon be mine. I kiss Your Grace's hands for your kind solicitude about my person, and just as Your Grace advises, I do not intend to go to Paris at present; but there are other reasons too, which I shall explain to Your Grace when I see you. I am expecting my Prince, to whom I wrote recently, to tell me where I am to go. It may be that he summons me to Frankfurt,[2] but if not, I shall go (*entre nous*) *via* Holland to Berlin, to the King of Prussia, and from there to Leipzig, Dresden, Prague and—at last!—to Vienna, where I shall embrace all my friends. Meanwhile I remain, most respectfully, my kindest

Frau von Gennzinger's
most obedient servant,
Joseph Haydn.

My kind regards to your husband, *Fräulein* Pepi and all the others, no less to Her von KREUBICH[3] "I am so gl- gl- glad" that he has the pleasure of enjoying your friendship. N.B. I hope to be able to kiss Your Grace's hands at the end of July. Please forgive my not making an envelope today, but there isn't time.

[Address:]

VON LONDON

Madame
Madame Anna Noble de
Gennzinger née Noble de Kayser.

à

Vienne

IM SCHOTTEN HOF.   en autriche.

[1] *The Storm: Madrigal*, a work for soli, chorus and orchestra, first performed at the Haydn-Salomon concert of 24th February 1792.
[2] For the Coronation of the Emperor Francis II.
[3] Kreibich: see *supra*, p. 125.

[OPEN LETTER TO CHARLES CLAGGET, LONDON. *English*]

[London, April 1792[1]]

To Mr. *Clagget*, musical Museum, Greek street, Soho.—Sir! I called at your house, during your absence, and examined your improvements on the Pianoforte, and Harpsichords, and I found you had made them perfect instruments. I therefore, in justice to your invention, cannot forbear giving you my full approbation, as by this means you have rendered one of the finest instruments ever invented, perfect, and therefore the fittest to conduct any musical performance, and to accompany the human voice. I wish you to make this known through such channels as may appear to be most advantageous to you. I am etc. Josephus Haydn.

[1] This letter appeared in *The Morning Herald* on 27th April 1792.

[TO LUIGIA POLZELLI, BOLOGNA. *Italian, "Tu" form*]

London, 22nd May 1792.

Dear Polzelli,

I received your letter and saw from it that at any rate you are well again. You write that I should get you an engagement at a theatre; I assure you that there is no chance of that in London now, for they don't know whether there will be any Italian opera here next year.

The English are not too fond of Italian opera, because they don't understand the language; but I shall do my very best to get something for you when I return to Vienna. I shall send you the money for Pietro very soon, as I promised, and shall let you know the day of my departure from London. The ENGLISH WANT ME TO STAY HERE, BUT THIS IS IMPOSSIBLE AT PRESENT, BECAUSE IT'S ABSOLUTELY ESSENTIAL FOR ME TO GO HOME, in order to put my affairs in proper order; I left all my things in Esterháza. My Prince wants me to come to the Coronation at Frankfurt. I shall go there, for I have to take this route home anyway. I shall very soon be sending a trunk with various things for Pietro, and some clothes for you from your sister. Meanwhile farewell; in the hope that God will allow me to see you and embrace you, I am, as always, your faithful

                              Giuseppe Haydn.

[Address:]   Madame
          Madame Loise Polzelli
          Virtuosa di Musica

                              a
     Ferma in Posta   BOLOGNA
                         en Italie.

[To LUIGIA POLZELLI, BOLOGNA. *Italian, "Tu" form*]
                         London, 13th June 1792.
My dear Polzelli!

I received your letter with the false news about my wife: in fact she is not quite well, but with her usual sicknesses she may, if she pulls through, outlive me by many years. Well, we shall have to leave her fate to Providence. I SHALL LEAVE LONDON AT THE END OF THIS MONTH, and shall write you from Frankfurt. Yesterday I heard that my Prince will go there as Bohemian Ambassador and will arrive on the 25th of this month, together with his musicians. I think, therefore, that I shall have to stay with him for a time. Enough, I shall write you soon, to tell you when your Pietro should leave. Yesterday I purchased a little trunk in which to put the things that we bought together, your sister and I. Pietruccio[1] can then use this same trunk when he leaves Bologna. My dear Polzelli, I hope to see you next year, and to tell you about all the things that have happened to me since I left you; and I hope, as God is my witness,

always to be the same to you as I have been. I love you and will
always be your faithful

Giuseppe Haydn.

I send your sons many kisses.

My compliments to your dear sister.[2]

[1]See *supra*, p. 127.
[2]We know nothing of this second sister, who apparently lived in Bologna.

[To Maria Anna von Genzinger, Vienna. German]

Gracious Lady!

Since Herr von Keess has invited me for lunch today, I shall have
the opportunity to give his wife the knitting-needles I promised her.
If, therefore, Your Grace would be good enough to have some sent
over, I shall be able to fulfil my promise, for which I kiss Your
Grace's hands and remain, respectfully,

Your wholly obedient servant,
Joseph Haydn.

[Vienna] From my home, 4th August 1792.
[Address:]   Madame
Madame de Gennzinger

a

Son Logis.

[Pietro Polzelli to Luigia Polzelli (Bologna) with a postscript by
Haydn.] [Italian: Pietro in "Lei" form, Haydn in the "Tu"]

[Vienna] 22nd October [1792.]

Dearest Mother!

I beg you to forgive me for not being able immediately to answer the letter of
2nd October you sent to me. The reason is that I had kept on hoping to be able
to include a little something with it. Dear Mother, I have spoken to *il Sig^r Maestro*
Häyde [*sic*] and begged him many times on your account, dearest Mother, but he
cannot do more than he has done already. Through Sig: Valentino Pertoja[1] of
Venice whom you know well from Esterháza, and who is at present here in
Vienna on business, *il Sig^r Maestro* Häyden [*sic*] sends you twenty-six florins
[Gulden] and 30 xr [Kreutzer] together with this present letter. He says to tell you
that he cannot send more at present, because he is incapable of doing so: he has
many expenses on my behalf, and also for his own household. Dearest Mother, I
must inform you that I shall leave Cristina's[2] house today, since *il Sigre Maes.*
Haydn has found a place for me in his own home, so as to have more time to be
able to teach me everything. I must further inform you that through the kindness

of *Sig*^{re} *Maestro* Haydn I have found a house where I can earn something: it is at the home of the Countess Weissenwolf,³ where I teach her own daughter how to play the harpsichord. Thus I hope to be able to help a little, and I shall never fail to do my very best. I am, as always,

Your most obedient son,
Pietro Polcelli [*sic*]

The 22nd of October
    1792.

[HAYDN'S POSTSCRIPT]

Dear Polzelli, Your son has been very well received by my wife, and I hope this situation will continue. Pietro must teach the Countess Weissenwolf's daughter, and he asked me of his own accord to send all the money he earns to his dear mother. I am mortified not to be able to send you any more than these twenty-six florins at present, but I have many expenses. Farewell. I am your most sincere Giuseppe Haydn.

¹PERTOJA or BERTOJA, violoncellist in the Esterházy band from 1780 to 1788.
²We do not know who this "Cristina" was; probably a relative.
³PRINCE NICOLAUS I had been married to *Freiin* Maria Elisabeth von Weissenwolf (d. 1790—see *supra*, p. 100); his second son, Count Nikolaus, had married Countess Maria Anna von Weissenwolf in August 1777, for which occasion Haydn had written *Il mondo della luna.*

[TO MARIA ANNA VON GENZINGER, VIENNA. *German*]

Gracious Lady!

Apart from wishing you Good Morning, this is to ask you to give the bearer of this letter the final big Aria in F minor from my opera,¹ because I must have it copied for my Princess. I will bring it back to you myself in 2 days at the latest. Today I take the liberty of inviting myself for lunch, when I shall have the opportunity of kissing Your Grace's hands in return. Meanwhile I am, as always,

Y[our] G[race's]
most obedient servant,
Joseph Haydn.

[Vienna]   From my home, 13th November 1792.
[Address:]   Madame
Madame Noble de Gennzinger
a
Son Logis.

¹Orfeo's aria in the second act of *L'anima del filosofo.*

[RECEIPT TO ARTARIA & CO., VIENNA. *German*]
[Only the signature autograph]

> 15 Kreutzer
> stamp

　　　　　　　For the sum of twenty-four ducats I, the undersigned, herewith cede to Messrs. Artaria Comp. here in Vienna all
the rights to the Minuets and German Dances[1] which I composed for
the benefit of the Artists' Widows Society here, and which were
performed at the Redoutensaal Ball on 25th November of this past
year. I promise to give the afore-mentioned Minuets and German
Dances to no one else, and acknowledge to have received this day
the correct sum of twenty-four ducats in cash. Vienna, 7th December 1792.

　　　　　　　　　　　　　Attested:
　　　　　　　　　　　　　　　Josephus Haydn.

For 24 ducat pieces

[Artaria's clerk notes: "Haydn / 108 Gulden /1792".]

[1]The works are Hoboken IX: 11 & 12. Haydn probably wrote them in
England; see Landon, p. 563. Artaria published only an arrangement for two
violins and bass.

[To LUIGIA POLZELLI, BOLOGNA. *Italian.* *"Tu" form*]
　　　　　　　　　　　Eisenstadt, 20th June 1793.
Dear Polzelli!
　　I hope that you will have received the two hundred florins [Gul-
den] which I sent *via* Sig. Buchberg,[1] and perhaps also the other
hundred, a total of 300 florins; I wish I were able to send more, but
my income is not large enough to permit it. I beg you to be patient
with a man who up to now has done more than he really could.
Remember what I have given and sent to you; why, it's scarcely a
year ago that I gave you six hundred florins! Remember how much
your son costs me, and how much he will cost me until such a day as
he is able to earn his own daily bread. Remember that I cannot work
so hard as I have been able to do in the years past, for I am getting
old and my memory is gradually getting less reliable. Remember,
finally, that for this and many other reasons I cannot earn any more
than I do, and that I don't have any other salary except the pension of

my Prince Nicolaus Esterházy (God rest his soul), and that this
pension is barely sufficient to keep body and soul together, particularly in these critical times. Your son received the watch from *Sig.*
Molton, who however didn't want to give it to him, and made up
all sorts of reasons, excuses and lies for not doing so; I had to go to
him myself in order to get it. This man is a terrible liar! He told me
to my face that he had sent you the 25 florins I had given him four
months ago; and he boasted in front of me how much he had done
for you, and how he was ready at any time to have you come to
Vienna and marry him; you can imagine just what I thought of you!
But I am studying this man carefully, to ascertain his true character,
and I am getting to know him better and better: tomorrow he is
leaving for Poland with his Princess, but he won't slip through *my*
fingers with those twenty-five florins! At present I am alone with
your son in Eisenstadt, and I shall stay here for a little while to get
some fresh air and have a little rest. You will receive a letter from
your son along with mine; he is in good health, and kisses your
hand for the watch. I shall stay in Vienna until the end of September,
and then I intend to take a trip with your son, and perhaps—perhaps
—to go to England again for a year; but that depends mainly on
whether the battleground changes; if it doesn't, I shall go somewhere
else, and perhaps—perhaps—I shall see you in Naples. My wife is still
sick most of the time, and is always in a foul humour, but I don't
really care any more—after all, this woe will pass away one day.
Apart from this, I am much relieved that you, for your part, are a
little more relieved about your dear sister.[2] God bless you and keep
you in good health! I shall see to it that you receive what little I can
offer you, but now you really must be patient for a while, because I
have other onerous debts; I can tell you that I have almost nothing
for all my pains, and live more for others than for myself. I hope to
have an answer before you leave for Naples. I kiss you, and am your
most sincere

Guiseppe Haydn.

[Address:]   Madame
                 Madame Loise Polzelli
                 Virtuosa di Musica
                        in
Ferma in posta.   Bologna
                                en Italie.

[1]Michael Puchberg: see *supra*, p. 125.
[2]Probably CRISTINA NEGRI in London: see *supra*, p. 116.

[TO THE VIENNA CITY MAGISTRACY. *German*]
[Copy in an unknown hand in the Vienna City files]
To the worthy Magistracy of the Imperial and Royal capital city of Vienna:

The undersigned is thinking of slightly enlarging his house, which is situated at No. 71, Kleine Stein-gasse near Gumpendorf, in the territory of the Windmühl property, and therefore comes under the Registry of Landed Property pertaining to your worthy Magistracy. Ground-plan A, attached, shows said enlargement, whereby another storey would be added to the original building. Since your exalted consent is required beforehand, the undersigned begs you to grant it to him; in support of his request, he would point out that:

1mo In this projected construction, good materials would be employed, but altogether it would be planned in accordance with the rules established by the Board of Works, and would contribute to improving the general looks of the street. He hopes therefore that his plan will be approved, the more so because

2do By enlarging the building, an increase of tax-money would accrue to the most exalted *orario*.

Vienna, 14th August 1793.
Franz Heiden [*sic*] *Fürstl. Esterhazis.*
Capellmeister and Property Owner in
the Kleine Steingasse No. 71.

[HAYDN TO MAXIMILIAN FRANZ, THE ELECTOR OF COLOGNE, BONN.
German]
[Only signature & title autograph]
Serene Electoral Highness!

I humbly take the liberty of sending Your Serene Electoral Highness some musical works, *viz.*, a Quintet, an eight-part Parthie, an oboe Concerto, Variations for the fortepiano, and a Fugue,[1] compositions of my dear pupil Beethoven, with whose care I have been graciously entrusted. I flatter myself that these pieces, which I may recommend as evidence of his assiduity over and above his actual studies, may be graciously accepted by Your Serene Electoral Highness. Connoisseurs and non-connoisseurs must candidly admit, from these present pieces, that Beethoven will in time fill the position of one of Europe's greatest composers, and I shall be proud to be able to speak of myself as his teacher; I only wish that he might remain with me a little while longer.

While we are on the subject of Beethoven, Your Serene Electoral Highness will perhaps permit me to say a few words concerning his financial status. 100 #² were allotted to him during the past year. Your Serene Electoral Highness is no doubt yourself convinced that this sum was insufficient, and not even enough to live from; undoubtedly Your Highness also had his own reasons for choosing to send him into the great world with such a paltry sum. Under these circumstances, and to prevent him from falling into the hands of usurers, I have in part gone bail for him and in part lent him money myself, with the result that he owes me 500 fl., of which not a Kreutzer³ was spent unnecessarily; which sum I would ask you to send to him here. And since the interest on borrowed money grows continually, and is very tedious for an artist like Beethoven anyway, I think that if Your Serene Electoral Highness were to send him 1000 fl. for the coming year, Your Highness would earn his eternal gratitude, and at the same time relieve him of all his distress: for the teachers which are absolutely essential for him, and the display which is necessary if he is to gain admission into numerous salons, reduce this sum to such an extent that only the bare minimum remains. As for the extravagance which one fears will tempt any young man who goes into the great world, I think I can answer for that to Your Serene Electoral Highness: for a hundred circumstances have confirmed me in my opinion that he is capable of sacrificing everything quite unconstrainedly for his art. In view of so many tempting occasions, this is most remarkable, and gives every security to Your Serene Electoral Highness—in view of the gracious kindness that we expect—that Your Highness will not be wasting any of your grace on usurers as far as Beethoven is concerned. In the hope that Your Serene Electoral Highness will continue his further patronage of my dear pupil by graciously acceding to this my request, I am, with profound respect,

Your Serene Electoral Highness'
most humble and obedient
Joseph Haydn
Capell Meister von Fürst Nicolas Esterházy

Vienna, 23rd November 1793.
[The envelope also includes a short letter from Beethoven.]

¹The compositions referred to in this letter have been more or less satisfactorily identified (see Kinsky-Halm, *etc.*) with the exception of the oboe Concerto, which is believed to be lost. I should like to make the tentative suggestion that the oboe Concerto in C, originally found under "Anony-

mous" in Zittau (Haydn's name was apparently added later), may be
Beethoven's lost work.
[2]= 100 ducats, or 450 Gulden, not 500 (as in the Elector's answer).
[3]= "Not a farthing".

[TO HAYDN FROM MAXIMILIAN FRANZ, THE ELECTOR OF COLOGNE.
German]
[Draft in a secretary's hand, corrected in the Elector's hand].[1]
Nomine Serenissimi.
To Prince Esterházy's *Kapellmeister* [*sic*] in Vienna. d. d. Bonn the 23rd of
December 1793 [in a third hand: "Exped. sequenti."].
   I received the music of the young Beethoven which you sent me, together with
your letter. Since, however, with the exception of the Fugue, he composed and
performed this music here in Bonn long before he undertook his second journey to
Vienna, I cannot see that it indicates any evidence of his progress.
   Concerning the money which was hitherto available for his subsistence in
Vienna, it is true that this consists only of 500 fl.; but apart from these 500 fl., his
salary here of 400 fl. has been paid to him the whole time, so that he will always
receive 900 fl. annually. Therefore I do not see at all why his financial circumstances
should be as reduced as you have indicated to me.
   I am wondering if he would not do better to begin his return journey here, in
order that he may once again take up his post in my service: for I very much
doubt whether he will have made any important progress in composition and
taste during his present sojourn, and I fear that he will only bring back debts from
his journey, just as he did from his first trip to Vienna.

[1]The original letter, dictated to a secretary, is still more unfriendly: for
example, in the last paragraph, the Elector had written: "for I very much
doubt if he can have learnt anything from you. . ."

[TO JOSEPH WEIGL,[1] JR. VIENNA. *German*]
Dearest Godson!
   When I took you in my arms after your birth, and had the
pleasure of becoming your godfather, I implored Omnipotent
Providence to endow you with the highest degree of musical talent.
My fervent request has been heard:—It has been a long time since I
felt such enthusiasm for any music as for your *La Principessa d'Amalfi*[2]
yesterday: it is full of ideas, it has grandeur, it is expressive; in short
—a masterpiece. I heartily participated in the well-deserved applause
with which it was received. Continue, my dearest godson, to write
in this genuine style, so that you may once again convince the
foreigners of that which a German can accomplish. Meanwhile, keep

a place in your memory for an old fellow like myself. I love you affectionately and am, dearest Weigl,

Your bosom-friend and servant,
Joseph Haydn.

[Vienna] From my home, 11th January 1794.

¹The son of the Joseph Weigl who had been 'cellist in the Esterházy band: see *supra.*, p. 8. Haydn left for England eight days after having written this letter.
²Performed at the Burgtheater.

[To (John?) Parke,¹ London. English]

[London, 22nd October 1794²]

I am much obliged to you for the two so charming Prints, I tack me the liberty to Send for the Mistris Park a little Sonat, and to come to Her next Friday or Saturday between 1 and 2 o'clock. I am

Your most obedient Sᵗ
Haydn

[Address:]   Mʳ Park
          Piccadilly Nʳ 32.

¹There were two Parke brothers, both oboists: the elder, John, was a member of the Prince of Wales' private band, while the younger, William, was oboist at Covent Garden and later wrote his celebrated *Musical Memoirs*. Haydn had a close connection with the whole family. The Mistress Parke —she was twenty-one at this point—was John's daughter, and often sang at the Haydn-Salomon concerts; Haydn "presided" at her benefit concert in 1794 (Landon, p. 525). Presumably the letter was addressed to John, where "Mistris Park" would have been living. The two prints mentioned are listed under No. 46 of the catalogue of Haydn's legacy. See Pohl, *Haydn in London*, pp. 40f.
²Undated; but at the bottom of the letter is the following note: "22 Oct. 1794" followed by "The celebrated Musician, Dʳ. Haydn." (the latter in another handwriting).

[To Thomas Holcroft,¹ London. English]

[London, 1794 or 1795²]

Dear Sir!
    I tack me the liberty to Send you the Canon, and the 2 Songs and if is possible, I self will come to you to day, o[r] to morrow. I was

oblieged to tack a Medicine to Day, perhaps I see you this Evening.
I am

       Sir with the greatest Respect

           Your

           Oblig Ser^v

           Haydn[3]

[Address:] M^r. Holcroft[4]

[1]THOMAS HOLCROFT, the well-known dramatist (1745–1809), translated Haydn's German Lied, "Eine sehr gewöhnliche Geschichte" (B. & H. Gesamtausgabe, Ser. XX/I, No. 4), into English. Perhaps this is one of the "2 Songs" mentioned in the letter. The Canon may be "Thy Voice, O Harmony, is Divine" (written for the Oxford Faculty in 1791), or possibly one of the "Ten Commandments" which Haydn wrote for the Saxon Ambassador in London, Count von Brühl.

[2]I suggest that this undated letter was written in 1794 or 1795, rather than during the first London visit, when Haydn had spoken practically no English at all.

[3]Under the signature is the following, in another hand: "The immortal/ 'The Shakespeare of/Music' J. H. 1805" followed by an asterisk and an explanation that these additions are in the handwriting of [Thomas] Holcroft.

[4]Under Haydn's words is the following, in another hand: "communicated by Mrs Monoft [Holcroft?] 1st 8–1800 to me lelio [?]" and in a third hand: "the handwriting of HAYDN".

[TO CHARLES BURNEY (CHELSEA?). *Italian*]

         [During the second(?) London
               sojourn][1]

Most esteemed *Sig*^r Dr Burney,

I beg you to send me a copy of that canzonetta, because I can recall neither the melody nor the text of it. I shall not fail to be at your disposal in the future, Sir, and remain, with every esteem,

           Your most obedient servant,

           Haydn.

[1]This letter is obviously the kind delivered by messenger: therefore it was written during one of the London visits. The mention of a canzonetta suggests that the song Haydn wanted was part of "Dr. Haydn's VI Original Canzonettas . . . Printed for the Author, & Sold by him at No. 1 Bury Street, St. James's—at Messrs. Corri Dussek & Co. . . .", published in 1794, or part of the "Second Sett of Dr. Haydn's VI Original Canzonettas". In other words, the letter—if (as I assume) it refers to the English Canzonettas—must have been written in 1794 or 1795 and not in 1791 or 1792.

[AGREEMENT WITH JOHANN PETER SALOMON, LONDON. *German*]
[Only the signature autograph]

The undersigned herewith testifies that, according to the agreement signed this day between myself and Herr Johan [*sic*] Peter Salomon, the afore-mentioned Herr Salomon shall have the exclusive rights pertaining to the following specified Overtures[1] which I composed for his concerts; and that I hereby renounce any further claims whatever on him, now or at any other time. The afore-mentioned Overtures have the following *incipits*:

Executed at London this 13th of August 1795.

Joseph Haydn [m.p] ria.

[1]Overtures, the English term then generally applied to symphonies; the six Symphonies listed are those composed for the first London trip, in 1791 and 1792, as follows: No. 96, No. 98, No. 95, No. 93, No. 93, No. 97, No. 94; they are not in chronological order, which would be: Nos. 96, 95, 93, 94, 98, 97. It is curious that Salomon did not make Haydn sign the agreement for the second set until the following February.

[AGREEMENT WITH JOHANN PETER SALOMON, LONDON. *German*]

Vienna, 27th February 1796.

I, the undersigned, testify and declare that Herr Salomon shall be in perpetuity the sole owner and proprietor of my last six Symphonies, of which 3 are of the year 1794, and the last 3 of the year 1795,[1] and promise on my honour to make no other but personal use of them.

Josephus Haydn [m.p] ria.

[1]Haydn refers to the dates when the works were first performed, not necessarily when they were composed (*e.g.* No. 99 was written in 1793). The last six London Symphonies are Nos. 99–104.

[To Friedrich Jakob van der Nüll,[1] Vienna. *German*]
A. T.
My good Herr von der Nüll!
    I herewith take the liberty of asking you respectfully if you would
be good enough to lend me, just on the strength of my pock-marked
face, one hundred Gulden in bank notes, to be repaid after 6 weeks.
My signature below is your guarantee, so help me God, and so help
me that it is also an honour to be, my dear Herr v. der Nüll, most
respectfully,

Your most sincere and obedient servant,
Jos. Haydn.

[Vienna] 25th March 1796.
[Address:]   Monsieur
                Monsieur Von der Nüll.

[1]See *supra*, p. 103.

[To the Commissioners of Parliament.[1] *English*]
Vienna, ye 15th Aprill 1796.
    I empower herwith M^r. Squire to receive for me from the H^ble
Comissioners One hundred Pounds due to me by His Royal High-
ness the Prince of Walis and acknowledge hereby the receipt of that
Sum in full of all demands.

Doctor Haydn [mp] ria.

[1]Haydn never received any fee for his numerous appearances before the
Prince of Wales (see London Notebooks, *infra*, pp. 305), and upon the
advice of his friends, the composer finally decided to send a bill to Parliament, which was promptly paid.

[To Christoph Gottlob Breitkopf, Leipzig[1]. *German*]
Vienna, 16th April 1796.
[Breitkopf's clerk notes: "rec'd the 21st".]

Nobly born,
Most highly respected Sir!
    I must apologize a thousand times for not having answered all
your letters. Please do not be angry at a man who will never be
ungrateful. If you will be patient a little longer, I shall send you the
J.H.—M

money and the music, and this as surely as I am, Sir, most respectfully,

Your devoted and indebted servant,
Jos: Haydn.

[Address:] Dem Wohl Edl gebohrnen Herrn
        Breitkopf Music Verleger zu
        zustellen.   [Breitkopf's clerk notes above the
           Leipzig.   address: "1796/16 Ap / 21 / (blank
                        space for date of answer)" and to
                        the right "Wien / Haydn."]

[1]CHRISTOPH GOTTLOB BREITKOPF (1750–1800) was the son of Johann
Gottlob Immanuel, who had visited Haydn in 1786. The money Haydn
owed the firm was probably for the English engravings he had ordered
(see letter of 5th April 1789). The promised music was, as the next letter
shows, the pianoforte Trio in E flat (No. 30, 1795), which Breitkopf published as Op. 88.

[To CHRISTOPH GOTTLOB BREITKOPF, LEIPZIG. *German*]

Vienna, 9th November 1796.
[Breitkopf's clerk notes: "rec'd 10th Dec."]

Nobly born,
Most highly respected Sir!
    The bearer of this letter, Herr Wägl[1] from Vienna, will at last
give you the promised pianoforte Sonata together with 15 f. in
bank notes: meanwhile I thank you once again and am, Sir, most
respectfully,

Your obliging and obedient servant,
Jos: Haydn
Fürstl. Esterhazyscher Capell Meister.

[Address:]

von Vienne
Monsieur
Monsieur de Breitkopf
Leipzig.

[Breitkopf's clerk notes: "1796 / 9 Nov. /(rec'd) 10 Dec. / (ans'd)
2 Jan 97." To the right: "Wien / Haÿdn".]

[1]Probably JOSEPH WEIGL JR. (see *supra*, pp. 8, 143*f.*). In Hase, *Joseph Haydn
und Breitkopf & Härtel*, p. 6, the date of this letter is wrongly given as 1795,
and Breitkopf's answer as 2nd January 1796, which has caused great confusion in subsequent Haydn literature (see Larsen, Hoboken, *etc.*).

[To Prince Esterházy's Administrator]
[End of 1796 or beginning of 1797[1]]
[From an old copy]

Nobly born,
Highly respected Administrator!

From the letter addressed to me and the enclosure of the worthy
Privy Economic Administration of His Serene Highness Prince
Esterházy, I saw that I am more or less CONDEMNED to pay the debt
of Luegmayer,[2] who because of INSOLVENCY is not able to do so.
Why? Because I am thought to possess the necessary MEANS: I wish
to God it were so! But I SWEAR by the Kyrie eleison which I am at
this moment supposed to compose for my FOURTH Prince, that since
the death of my SECOND Prince—God rest his soul!—I have fallen
into the SAME STATE OF INSOLVENCY as that of Luegmayer, but with
the difference that he has fallen from his horse to the back of an ass,
whilst I have managed to remain on the horse, but without saddle
or harness.[3]

I therefore beg the worthy Privy Economic Administration of His
Highness to wait at LEAST till I have finished the Dona nobis pacem,
and until the Prince's house-master Luegmayer shall begin to receive
the salary rightly due to him from his most gracious Prince, instead
of drawing it, as he has hitherto done, from the SMALL salary of
Capellmeister Haydn (who has been 36 years in the Princely service).
For nothing is sadder or more dissonant than when one SERVANT
pays another SERVANT, in this case the *Capellmeister* having to pay the
house-master. If I should, perhaps today or tomorrow, be placed in
a BETTER position, either as a result of my own merits or by the
voluntary impulse of my most gracious Prince (FOR FLATTER AND
BEG I WILL NOT), of course I shall not fail to comply with the above
demand.

I am, Sir, with every respect,

Your most obliging servant,
Fran[z] J: Haydn
Doctor of Oxford and Princely Esterházy
Capellmeister.

[1]The passage, "36 years in the Princely service", would place the date in
the year 1797. Two Masses were written (or rather begun) in 1796, the
Missa in tempore belli (dated "Eisenstadt 1796") and the *Missa Sti. Bernardi
de Offida* (1796, probably begun in Vienna), and no mass was composed in
1797. It seems probable, therefore, that the letter was written at the end of
1796, in which year the "Kyrie eleision" of both Masses were begun.
[2]JOSEPH ALOIS LUEGMAYER was married to Haydn's niece, Anna Katharina

(daughter of Haydn's sister, Anna Maria Fröhlich of Rohrau). Luegmayer was often a source of embarrassment and frustration to Haydn, who gave him large sums of money over a long period of time: see also letter of 10th June 1798 and Haydn's Will.
[3]This robust simile has its basis in the difference in horsemanship between Don Quixote and Sancho Panza.

[To Haydn from Antonio Salieri and Paul Wrani(t)zky, on behalf of the *Tonkünstler-Societät*, Vienna.[1] *German*]
To Herr Joseph Hayden, *Capellmeister* to His Serene Highness Prince Esterházy.
Most esteemed *Herr Capellmeister!*
You must and should rightly be accustomed to hearing the praises of your own unattainable services to music, and accustomed to being admired for your inexhaustible creative mind, for you have won the most fervent and justified approbation of entire nations.
The Society for the Promotion of Musicians' Widows and Orphans—for which you, worthy Sir, have so often earned considerable sums through your admirable compositions—will therefore forgo all eulogies; it now has the honour of thanking you for all the kindnesses you have shown it in the past, and assures you of its boundless admiration. As a small token of its gratitude, it sends you a free ticket of admission for all future concerts of the Society; you need only show this ticket when you enter, retaining it for further use. Please do not in any way consider this act to be a kind of small recompense,[2] but rather the wish to show you our kindest and best intentions, and to assure you of the gratitude, but also of the eternal obligation which will always be owed you by

The Society for the Promotion of Musicians'
Widows and Orphans.

Ex concluso Sessionis
dat. 20. January 1797   Paul Wranizky,
Anton Salieri.   *pro tempore* Secretary.

[1]Antonio salieri (1750–1825). The two brothers, Anton and Paul Wranizky (or Wranitzky), were amongst Vienna's leading musicians and composers. Anton (1761–1819) was a violinist and was *Kapellmeister* to Prince Lobkowitz; Paul (1756–1808), also a violinist, studied with Haydn, was one of the moving figures in the *Tonkünstler-Societät*, and was leader of the Court Theatre Orchestra in the Burgtheater. His opera *Oberon* (Vienna, 1789) is generally cited as his outstanding work.
[2]For the appalling way in which they had treated Haydn in 1779, see pp. 22ff. Wranizky was in large measure responsible, not only for this letter, but also for making the Society admit Haydn as a member without charging him any entrance fee. In the session of 20th January, Wranizky hoped that the Society's "previous conduct would be forever erased from my memory, and from Haydn's too, if that is possible." (Pohl, *Denkschrift*, p. 23). Haydn was then elected in December 1797, and made *Assessor senior* for life. His performances of the *Seven Words*, *Creation* and *Seasons* made the Society a huge fortune.

[To Franz Count Saurau, Vienna. *German*]

[Vienna, 28th January (?) 1797[1]]

Excellence!

Such a surprise and such mark of favour, especially as regards the portrait of my dear monarch, I never before received in acknowledgement of my unworthy talents. I thank Your Excellency with all my heart, and am ready at all times to serve Your Excellency. I shall deliver the proof by 11 o'clock. I am, in profound respect,

Your Excellency's

Most humble and obedient servant,

Jos. Haydn.

[1]This conjectured dating is based on the content of the letter, which concerns the Austrian national hymn, "Gott erhalte". In 1820, Count Saurau, then President of the Lower Austrian Government (later Minister of the Interior), gave this letter, together with an accompanying note concerning the hymn, to Count Moritz Dietrichstein; otherwise we should not have known to whom it was written. Here is a brief summary of the origin of "Gott erhalte". Inspired by "God save the King", Haydn wanted to write something similar for his country, and asked Baron van Swieten, who had just written the text for the choral version of the *Seven Words*, for his advice. Swieten in turn asked Saurau, who had the poet Lorenz Leopold Haschka prepare the words, which Haydn then set to music. On 28th January, Count Saurau gave his "imprimatur" to the final proofs, and the new hymn was then performed at the Burgtheater on 12th February, in the Emperor's presence. This letter must have been written *on* 28th January—or perhaps the day before—because Haydn speaks of the "Abdruck" (*i.e.* proof); if it were printed, he would have said "Exemplair" (copy). Presumably Haydn gave his "imprimatur" for the musical part, "deliver[ed] the proof by 11 o'clock" to Saurau, who then gave the order to print. See Pohl III, 115*ff.* The "mark of favour" was a snuff-box, containing the Emperor's portrait, and a substantial sum of money (Pohl III, 118).

[To Herr Kürchner, Prince Esterházy's *Valet de chambre*, Oedenburg. *German*]

Vienna, 1st June 1798.

Dearest Friend!

I would ask you to be good enough to advance my niece Luegmayer[1] 25 fl. (though she really doesn't deserve it); you shall be repaid this sum at the earliest possible moment by the Chief Cashier Stessel, whom I have already informed about the matter. For this kindness I shall wait on your dear daughter, when I arrive in

Eisenstadt, with a new pianoforte Sonata. Meanwhile I am, with my
kind regards to your wife, most respectfully,

Your most obedient servant,
Joseph Haydn.

[Address:]   Monsieur
    Monsieur de Kürchner Valet
    d Chambre de S: Alt Monseig le
    Prince Nicolaus Esterházy
in fürst Esterhazisch[en]   a OEDENBURG
Hauss.   en Hongern.

[1]Anna Katharina: see *supra*, p. 149.

[To C. F. FREDENHEIM, PRESIDENT OF THE ROYAL SWEDISH
ACADEMY OF MUSIC IN STOCKHOLM. *German*]

[End of April 1799[1]]

Nobly born,
Most highly respected Sir!

I cannot express adequately in words the surprise and delight
which I felt, and will always feel, upon receiving, through the
Councillor of Legation Herr von Silverstolpe, the diploma wherein
I am graciously nominated a member of your worthy Royal
Swedish Academy of Music. I only regret that at present my
advanced age and weakened powers do not permit me to repay this
great honour. If, however, PROVIDENCE should grant me a few more
years of the necessary musical strength, I shall try to compose a
small remembrance for your worthy Society; meanwhile I take the
liberty of conveying my respectful thanks to the President C. F. von
Fredenheim, and to the whole worthy Society, and am, Sir, most
respectfully,

Your obedient servant,
J: H:

[1]C.-G. Stellan Mörner's excellent book, *Johan Wikmanson und die Brüder
Silverstolpe*, Stockholm 1952, provides us with the necessary background to
the above letter. In May 1796, F. S. Silverstolpe was sent to Vienna as
Councillor of Legation, and as a passionate music-lover, soon made Haydn's
personal acquaintance. At Silverstolpe's instigation, Albrechtsberger, Salieri
and Haydn were made honorary members of the Academy. The diplomas
arrived in April 1799, and on the 10th Silverstolpe writes that he will
deliver the diplomas that week (Mörner, p. 339). Having announced the

matter in the Viennese papers, Silverstolpe then writes to the Academy's
Secretary, Pehr Frigel, thanks him for his own (Silverstolpe's) nomination,
and encloses letters by the three Viennese composers (Mörner, p. 341). Since
Silverstolpe's letter is dated 22nd May, Haydn must have received the
diploma and thanked the Academy between 10th April and 22nd May;
Haydn always answered such things punctually, and we may assume that
the above letter was written about the end of April.

[TO JOHANN PETER SALOMON, LONDON. *German*]
Vienna, 18th May 1799.

Dearest Friend!

The bearer of this letter is Herr von Sonleithner,[1] a distinguished
young man of great wit, whose character you, with your great insight, will be able to judge far better and more accurately than I am
able to do. His musical project is one of the most interesting, but I
fear that without the help and counsel of many people he will not be
able to realize it. He has asked me to recommend someone in London
who was honest and well-informed, and I therefore took the liberty
of suggesting you, my dear friend. If you are able to assist him in his
project, you will be of great service to the world. Apart from this
I am, with every esteem, dearest friend,

Your sincere friend and servant,
Jos: Haydn [m.p] ria.

[Address:]

M^r. Salomon.

N^{ro} 34,
Clipstone Street,   London,
    Fitzroy Squarre [*sic*]

---

[1]JOSEPH SONNLEITHNER'S project was a kind of *Denkmäler der Tonkunst*—
a history of music in score, *i.e.* a representative selection of masterpieces
from all schools and all periods. Haydn obviously thought the idea a
magnificent one, but doubted Sonnleithner's ability to execute it, for a
few days later Georg August Griesinger (Breitkopf & Härtel's "middle-
man" between Haydn and the Leipzig firm) writes (25th May) that Haydn
"considers this plan to be a swindle and is sure that nothing will come of it"
(Pohl III, 139). Nothing did. Sonnleithner (1766–1835) was an official in
the Ministry of War, a writer, and a member of an illustrious family. He
was later one of Schubert's admirers and friends. (See O. E. Deutsch,
Schubert: Die Erinnerungen seiner Freunde, Leipzig 1957, p. 3 *passim*.) His
father has been mentioned above (see p. 16).

[To Christoph Gottlob Breitkopf, Leipzig. *German*]

Vienna, 12th June 1799.

Dearest Friend!

I am really very much ashamed to have to offend a man who has written so often[1] and honoured me with so many marks of esteem (which I do not deserve), by answering him at this late date; it is not negligence on my part but the vast amount of BUSINESS which is responsible, and the older I get, the more business I have to transact daily. I only regret that on account of my growing age and (unfortunately) the decrease of my mental powers, I am able to dispatch but the smallest part of it. Every day the world pays me compliments on the fire of my recent works, but no one will believe the strain and effort it costs me to produce them: there are some days in which my enfeebled memory and the unstrung state of my nerves crush me to the earth to such an extent that I fall prey to the worst sort of depression, and thus am quite incapable of finding even a single idea for many days thereafter; until at last Providence revives me, and I can again sit down at the pianoforte and begin to scratch away again. Enough of this!

Yesterday Herr Griesinger[2] brought me the 2nd, 3rd and 4th volumes of our immortal Mozart, together with the musical periodical.[3] Please let me know how much I owe you for them, and to whom I should give the money here in Vienna.

The publication of both these things does you great credit. I WOULD ONLY WISH, AND HOPE, THAT THE CRITICS DO NOT DEAL TOO SEVERELY WITH MY CREATION: THEY MIGHT PERHAPS OBJECT A LITTLE TO THE MUSICAL ORTHOGRAPHY OF CERTAIN PASSAGES, AND POSSIBLY SOME OTHER MINOR POINTS ELSEWHERE; BUT THE TRUE CONNOISSEUR WILL SEE THE REASONS FOR THEM AS READILY AS I DO, AND WILL PUSH ASIDE THIS STUMBLING-BLOCK. NULLA REGOLA S[ENZA] E[CCEZIONE]. N.B.: AS FOR THE TATTERED SECTION IN THE DUET OF THE "CREATION", YOU WILL FIND IT ENTIRELY DIFFERENT IN THE EDITION FROM THAT WHICH HERR TRAEG HAD THE TWOPENNY KRAMER[4] PREPARE FOR HIM: but all this UNDERLINED INTER NOS.

Apart from all this, I shall be very happy to serve you in any possible way. Meanwhile, my dear friend, I remain, with every esteem,

Your obliging and obedient servant,
Joseph Haydn [m.p] ria.

[Letter enclosed a full score of the *Creation* and also a letter from

Griesinger to Breitkopf & Härtel; therefore no address; Breitkopf's clerk notes: "V 99/ 12 Juny/ (rec'd) 3 July / Wien / J. Haydn".]

[1]Breitkopf & Härtel wrote to Haydn in the Summer of 1798, and asked him to contribute to the newly-established periodical, the *Allgemeine Musikalische Zeitung*. Haydn did not answer, and Breitkopf wrote him again in April 1799. See Hase, p. 8.

[2]See Introduction and *supra*, p. 153.

[3]The Mozart volumes were part of the *Oeuvres complettes*; the periodical is the *Allgemeine Musikalische Zeitung*. When Griesinger brought him the Mozart volumes, which were to serve as a model for the proposed *Oeuvres complettes* of Haydn, he "looked through them several times and said: really fine, really fine; Mozart and I appreciated each other very much, and he too used to call me his Papa." (Griesinger's report to Breitkopf of 12th June 1799; Hase, p. 21.)

[4]The *Allgemeine Musikalische Zeitung* had printed the Duet, "Der thauende Morgen", as a "Beilage" to the periodical: they had used the text printed by the Viennese publisher Traeg (see also *supra*, p. 81), which was, however, very faulty. This "10-Kreutzer" Kramer, as it turned out, had copied the Duet from memory, after having heard a few performances of the work. Traeg issued the Duet, separately, in March 1799. See Alexander Weinmann, "Verzeichnis der Musikalien des Verlages Johann Traeg in Wien" (*Studien zur Musikwissenschaft* XXIII, 1956, p. 147) and Hase, p. 10.

[ANNOUNCEMENT FOR SUBSCRIPTION TO THE *Creation* IN THE *Allgemeine Musikalische Zeitung. German*]

The success which my Oratorio, *The Creation*, has been fortunate enough to enjoy here, and the wish expressed in the 16th number of the [*Allgemeine*] *Musikalische Zeitung* that its dissemination would not, as was often the case previously, be left to those abroad, have moved me to arrange for its distribution myself.

Thus the work is to appear in three of four months, neatly and correctly engraved and printed on good paper, with German and English texts; and in full score, so that, on the one hand, the public may have the work in its entirety, and so that the connoisseur may see it *in toto* and thus better judge it; while on the other, it will be easier to prepare the parts, should one wish to perform the work anywhere.

The price of the Oratorio, which will consist of some 300 pages, is to be 3 ducats, or 13 Fl. 30 Kr. in Viennese currency; and although payment does not need to be made until delivery, I wish nevertheless that those who contemplate its purchase would inform me provisionally thereof, and give me their names, in order that they may appear in the subscription list at the front of the score.

The actual appearance of the Oratorio in print—every copy will be signed—will be announced by a special notice, when the time comes.

Vienna, 15th June 1799.

> Joseph Haydn,
> Doctor of Music, *Kapellmeister*
> in the Service of His Highness
> the Prince Esterházy, and Mem-
> ber of the Royal Swedish Mus-
> ical Academy.

In Vienna, Vorstadt Gumpendorf, untere Steingasse, Nr. 73.

[To a Friend in England, possibly Christoph Papendiek[1].
German]

Nobly born,
Most esteemed Friend!

You will certainly be surprised to receive this letter, after we have been separated for so long, but since I was convinced of your cordial friendship for me from the very first moment of our acquaintance, and since I know you are a truly good and generous man, I now take the liberty of asking you to read the following; you will then be able to decide whether you are in a position to help me.

Last year I composed a German Oratorio called the *Creation*, which has met with exceptional approval by everyone. This approval moved me to publish this Oratorio in full score, with German and English text; the score, which should be ready in 4 or at the most 5 months, will be correctly engraved, and printed on the finest paper, at a subscription price of £1 10 shillings, which sum, however, does not need to be paid until delivery. The subscription offer is made in advance so that the subscribers' names can be included in the score. The publication will be so arranged that those living abroad will be sent their copies 3 or 4 weeks earlier; I shall pay the consignment charges myself. Now my most ardent wish is to enjoy the royal favour of having Her gracious Majesty the Queen of England condescend to subscribe to this work (N.B. without making a deposit): the presence of her name in the printed list of subscribers will convince the world that during my sojourn in London I enjoyed the royal favour of having displayed my small talents to the royal court by playing there. In the hope that you will heed my request, and at the proper moment yourself persuade Her Majesty the Queen (before whom I prostrate myself), I am, my most esteemed friend, most respectfully,

Your most obedient friend and servant,
Joseph Haydn [m.p] ria.

Vienna, 25th June 1799.
If I should be fortunate enough to receive an answer, please address the letter to me in Vienna.
P. S. My respectful compliments to your wife.

[1]CHRISTOPH PAPENDIEK, a flautist, taught music to the Royal Family. His wife, Charlotte, was Assistant Keeper of the Wardrobe to Queen Charlotte, and wrote some delightful memoirs (see Landon, pp. 446f. for her description of the first Salomon concert). Of all Haydn's English friends, none stood closer to the Royal Family, and I think it very likely that this letter was addressed to Papendiek. At any rate, almost the whole Royal Family subscribed, including the King.

[TO AN UNKNOWN FRIEND.[1] *German*]

Vienna, 5th July 1799.

Dearest Friend!
I sent you the Mass with today's mail-coach. The costs for copying it were 11 f. 56 xr. and the carrying charges 1 f. 34 xr. If you should ever have a similar wish in the future, you have only to command your servant,

Joseph Haydn.

[1]There are several possibilities: the first choice would be perhaps Anton Stoll, the *Regenschori* at Baden, who was Mozart's friend, and at whose house Frau Haydn later boarded. As music director of the Stadtpfarrkirche, Stoll often performed Haydn's late masses. If the *Nelson Mass* (1798) is the work referred to, the letter may be addressed to the *Regenschori* of Klosterneuburg Monastery near Vienna, where I discovered an authentic set of parts of the *Nelson Mass*, copied by Johann Elssler (Haydn's copyist). Klosterneuburg also owns a very early and important set of parts of the *Missa in tempore belli* (1796) which Haydn may have sent them.

[TO ARTARIA & CO., VIENNA. *German*]

Messieurs!
I am most grateful to you for the copies of the Quartets[1] you sent me, which are a great credit to me and—because of the legible engraving and the neat title page—to you.

Herr Count Joseph Erdödy wrote me many kind things, and thanked me for having made them available to the world at last. I hope that His Excellency will have received his copy by now. In a little while I will send the 5th Quartet in D major, and then the last in E flat.[2]

Meanwhile I remain, with respects to the whole firm,

Your most obedient servant,
Joseph Haydn [m.p.] ria.

Eisenstadt, 12th July 1799.
[Address:]   Monsieur
Monsieur Artaria et Compag:
a
Vienne.

[Artaria's clerk notes: "Haydn / Eisenstadt 12th July 1799./ rec'd 16th ditto/ ans'd 16th ditto".]

[1]Op. 76, composed in 1796 and dedicated to Count Erdödy. Artaria issued them in two sets of three, with Haydn's portrait on the title page, as Op. 75 and 76; they were announced (in the *Wiener Zeitung* of 17th July) with the proud words that "nothing which our house has ever published equals this edition" (Artaria-Botstiber, p. 73). The second set (the last three) were still in preparation, as the letter shows.
[2]The MSS. of Op. 76, Nos. 5 and 6 (Artaria's Op. 76, Nos. 2 and 3).

[TO HAYDN FROM PRINCE NICOLAUS II ESTERHÁZY. *German*]
Herr Kapellmeister Haydn:

I expect your written opinion concerning the enclosed petition[1] of the trumpeters Sebastian Bindter [*sic*][2], Michael Altmann, and Johann Pfann, who ask that an annual salary be granted them for their services in the choir loft and in other musical performances here; in particular, what kind of yearly contract could be established, taking into account the number of services in which they perform? And what would be the best wages they would otherwise get for each single performance?

By the way, I have instructed that their bill for 50 Fl. 15 xr. be paid to them.
Eisenstadt, 18th July 1799.

Exp.[3] Esterházy.

[1]The three trumpeters began this particular period of their service, according to an attached bill, on 30th September 1798: thus, they had played the three trumpet parts in Haydn's "Nelson Mass", which had been first performed in honour of the Princess Maria's Name Day that Autumn. The petition (Esterházy Archives, Acta Musicalia, Fasc. XXVI, 1855) is dated July 1799 and reads: "Last year, the undersigned made bold most humbly to ask Your Highness if, in your graciousness, you would grant us an annual salary; the suppliants, however, have not hitherto received any decision

regarding their humble petition, and thus take the liberty of presenting Your Highness the enclosed bill for 50 Fl. 15 xr. with the most humble request that Your Highness have the grace to instruct payment therefor to be made . . ."

[2]Bindter's name is usually spelled "Binder".

[3]"Exp." = "expedited for", *i.e.* actually sent. These late letters to Haydn are, of course, copies for the Princely files.

[To Prince Nicolaus II Esterházy. *German*]
[Eisenstadt, between the middle of
July and September 1799][1]

Inasmuch as, for some years now, the 3 trumpeters have been paid per performance, which amounted to an annual sum of 111 Fl., in my humble opinion it would be something of a saving to pay each of them a cash annual salary of 25 Fl. and two measures [*Metzen* = 6.88 litres] of corn: they, for their part, should be obliged to attend all the performances which are scheduled, in the church and otherwise.[2]

Joseph Haydn [m.p]ria,
Capell Meister.

[1]The date is uncertain. Its earliest date is 19th July (see above) and its latest 14th September, when the Prince decided to accept Haydn's proposal: Esterházy's letter to the Economic Administration, written in Eisenstadt, is preserved in the Acta Musicalia (Fasc. XXVI, 1854) of the Esterházy Archives. The letter ends with the request that the "*Kapellmeister* Haydn is to be reminded . . . " of the acceptance.

[2]German: "in der Kammer" ("and otherwise"), which of course means not only "in the chamber", *i.e.* for chamber music (wherein trumpets do not ordinarily play) but in symphonies, operas, *etc.* This fine distinction cannot, unfortunately, be rendered literally into English.

[To Artaria & Co., Vienna. *German*]
Messieurs!

I send you herewith the 5th Quartet, which you should arrange to have copied at the earliest opportunity; and as soon as you send it back to me, you shall have the last one. Please send me at the same time the names of the subscribers to date, so that I can enter them in my book.[1]

Meanwhile I am, most respectfully,
Your most obedient servant,
Jos: Haydn.

Eisenstadt, 20th July 1799.

[Address:]   Monsieur
                Monsieur Artaria et Compag:
                         a
                      Vienne.

[Artaria's clerk notes: "Haydn/Eisenstadt 20th July 1799/ received 23rd ditto/ answered 24th ditto."]

> [1]Haydn's booklet, listing the subscribers to the *Creation*, is still preserved in the Vienna Stadtbibliothek (cat. 99280) and is entitled: *Verzeichnüss der Praenumeranten über die Schöpfung*. It is an important source of addresses and names of Haydn's friends, and will be referred to several times *infra*.

[To FRANZ XAVER GLÖGGL,[1] LINZ. *German*]

Well born,
Most highly respected Sir!

You have done me an inestimable honour, Sir, by subscribing to the *Creation*, and it will be a pleasure to include your name in the subscribers' list; I am still more indebted to you for the important recommendation to my old and clever friend, the *Herr Abbé* von Stadler; all this inspires an old man to further energies. Thus as soon as the work is printed, I shall not fail to send you a copy by the diligence. Meanwhile I am, Sir, with my compliments to the *Herr Abbé*, most respectfully,

                         Your most obedient servant,
                              Joseph Haydn.
Vienna, 24th July 1799.
[Address:] An den Wohlgebohrn Herrn Franz Xaver Glöggl
                Stadt und Dom Capell Meister in Linz
                in Oberoesterreich.

> [1]GLÖGGL's father, JOHANN JOSEPH, was one of Haydn's ardent admirers; the Monastery of St. Florian owns Glöggl's copies of four Haydn Symphonies. FRANZ XAVER (1764–1839) was City and Cathedral Chapel-Master at Linz and, like his father, *Thurnermeister* there. He later gained a certain reputation as the author of various musical treatises. See *Musik in Geschichte und Gegenwart*, V, 296–298.

[To KARL FRIEDRICH MORITZ PAUL, COUNT VON BRÜHL,[1]
                WEIMAR. *German*]

Excellence!
Your Excellency has done me an inestimable honour and favour

by subscribing to the *Creation*, and inspired an old man to further
energies. Thus as soon as the work is printed, I shall not fail to send a
copy, and also one to the most charming Baroness von Loewenstern,
by the diligence. Meanwhile I am, in profound submission,

Your Excellency's
obedient servant,
Joseph Haydn [m.p.] ria.

Vienna, 10th August 1799.
[No name nor address extant]

[1]The mention of the Baroness Loewenstern helps us to identify the Count
von Brühl to whom this letter is supposedly written. Haydn's list of subscribers to the *Creation*, mentioned above, includes "Baronesse Loewenstern
von Weimar in Sachsen"; the young Count Brühl (1772–1837), nephew of
the infamous Saxon Minister under August III, Heinrich (1700–1763), was
in Weimar during the year 1799. (The next year he moved to Berlin, as
Kammerherr of Prince Heinrich of Prussia.) But despite the mention of the
Baroness von Loewenstern, it is just possible that Haydn wrote the letter to
another member of the family. The son of the Saxon Minister, as we have
seen (p. 24 *supra*), had been in Vienna and Burney had heard him play
viola in a Haydn quartet. See also Meyer's *Konversations-Lexikon*, 6th ed.
(1908), III, p. 492f. To complete this picture of confusing Count Brühls,
one should add that Haydn had written his canons. "The Ten Commandments", in London for Count Hans Moritz von Brühl, Saxon Minister to
the Court of St. James. Hans Moritz died in London in 1809, and it seems
doubtful if he would have ordered the *Creation* for Baroness Loewenstern in
Weimar. Haydn's invaluable subscription list does not help us in this case,
for it says only: "Graf Brühl königl. preussische Jagd Junker." See also letter
of 11 May 1800.

[To P. Cornelius Knoblich, Grissau Monastery near
Landeshut in Silesia. *German*]

Most worthy and Reverend Sir!

Your most worthy Abbot[1] has done me an inestimable honour
by subscribing to the *Creation*, and thus as soon as the work is
printed, I shall not fail to send a copy to Your Reverence by the
diligence.

Inasmuch as my present young Prince issued the moderate command four years ago that in my old age I must compose a new Mass
once a year, it will be indeed a pleasure to be able to send you one
of them; but you must only write me if, apart from trumpets and
kettledrums, you also have 2 oboes or clarinets, so that I can make

the proper choice—that is, if you do not find 12 fl. too expensive for the copying charges.[2]

Your Reverence has only half enjoyed The *Seven Words of Our Saviour*, because 3 years ago I added a new 4-part vocal music (without changing the instrumental parts). The text was written by a well-versed and musicianly canon at the Passau Cathedral,[3] and our great Baron von Swieten[4] corrected it; the effect of this work surpassed all expectation, and if I should ever travel to your part of the world before I die, I would take the liberty of performing it before your Abbot. But at present no one possesses it except our Monarch. Perhaps —— ——.

Write me (BETWEEN OURSELVES) the day and the month of your Abbot's birthday and name-day. Hoping to receive an answer, I am, most respectfully,

Your Reverence's
most obedient servant,
Joseph Haydn.

Vienna, 10th August 1799.
[Address:]   To the Worthy and Reverend Herr Cornelius Knoblich Music Director and Member of the Cistercian Monastery of Grissau bey Landeshutt [*sic*] in Silesia.

[1]JOHANNES LANGER (note in Haydn's *Creation* subscription book).
[2]The invaluable subscription book (see note 1) tells us which Mass Haydn sent them. His entry reads: "Knoblich from Grissau in Upper Silesia payed a copy of the *Creation* and the Mass in C" (*i.e.*, the *Missa in tempore belli* (1796).
[2]JOSEPH FRIBERTH, brother of Carl (see *supra*, p. 4), who made his vocal version in 1792. On his way back to Vienna in 1795, Haydn heard a performance of the Friberth arrangement in the Passau Cathedral, and thought he "could have written the vocal parts better". A year later, with van Swieten's collaboration, Haydn produced the vocal version, which was performed in Eisenstadt (textbook printed by Anna Klara Siess in Oedenburg) and in Vienna (textbook printed by Matthias Andreas Schmidt). See Sandberger's excellent article, 'Zur Entstehungsgeschichte von Haydns "Sieben Worte des Erlösers am Kreuze" ' (*Peters Jahrbuch* 1903).
[4]See *supra* (p. 151) and *infra* (p. 193 *passim*).

[TO ARTARIA & CO., VIENNA. *German*]

Messieurs!

I take the liberty of sending you the enclosed letter from Frankfurt, and would ask you to inform me how and in what way I should react to the request of these two gentlemen, Gayl and Hedler, since

I have never engaged in transactions of this kind. I realize that every publisher looks to his own interests in these matters, but I would like you to write me your frank opinion whether they ought to pay cash for every copy, or whether one pays the bill for each dozen sold with the 13th copy. I think, however, that neither the one nor the other applies here, because the application comes directly to me from abroad. I am convinced of this as a result of orders I have already received from Berlin, Danzig, Leipzig, Regenspurg [*sic*], and so forth. Nevertheless I should be glad of your opinion, and shall certainly be most grateful to you for all your trouble.

I should have delivered the Third Quartet[1] to you, but certain doubts hold me back from doing so: I have not yet received an answer as to the last three Quartets which I sent to London,[2] and I fear that if the gentlemen issue all 6 Quartets together and not divided—*i.e.*, if they have not yet announced them—your edition and announcement could appear earlier than that in London; though that is difficult to believe, for I sent the first 3 Quartets as early as 27th March and the last 3 on 15th June. If the publication in Vienna should be earlier than that in London (which I hope will not be the case), and if the gentlemen were to discover that you at once received the same 3 Quartets from me, I should lose £75 Sterling, which would be a serious matter. You must therefore take immediate action, *sub rosa*, to ascertain positively whether the first 3 are out, and likewise approximately when the last 3 will appear, so that I won't have a double fine imposed on me. I shall send you the Third Quartet shortly, but you must wait with the publication until we know that the 2nd set has been published in London. I rely on your integrity in this matter, and for my part I shall always be,

Messieurs,

Your most obedient servant,

[signature forgotten].

I would ask you to answer by return of mail; if at the same time you can let me have some of the names of the subscribers [to the *Creation*], I should be grateful.

Eisenstadt, 15th August 1799.

[Artaria's clerk notes: "Haydn/ Eisenstadt 15th August 1799/ received 16th ditto/ answered 16th ditto"./

---

[1]Op. 76, No. 6 (Artaria's Op. 76, No. 3).
[2]To Messrs. Longman, Clementi & Co., who issued them as Op. 76, Books 1 and 2. The first book, though announced as early as April, did not appear till June; the second book appeared nearly a year later.

J.H.–N

[To Haydn from Charles Burney. *English*]

Chelsea College, August 19, 1799.

My dear and much-honoured Friend!

The reverence with which I have always been impressed for your great talents, and respectable and amiable character, renders your remembrance of me extremely flattering. And I am the more pleased with the letter which you have honoured me, of July 15th as it has pointed out to me the means by which I may manifest my zeal in your service, as far as my small influence can extend. I shall, with great pleasure, mention your intention of publishing your oratorio *della Creazione del Mondo*; by subscription, to all my friends; but you alarm me very much by the short time you allow for solicitation. In winter it would be sufficient, but now (in Aug.) there is not a single patron of music in town. I have been in Hampshire myself for three weeks, and am now at home for two or three days only, on my way to Dover, where I shall remain for a month or six weeks, and where I shall see few of the persons whom I mean to stimulate to do themselves the honour of subscribing to your work. I wish it were possible to postpone the delivery of the book in England till next winter. The operas, oratorios, and concerts, public, and private, seldom begin in London till after Christmas, nor do the nobility and gentry return thither from the country till the meeting of Parliament about that time. Now, three months from the date of your letter, my dear Sir, will only throw your publication to the middle of October, the very time in the whole year when London is the most uninhabited by the lovers of field sports, as well as music.

I had the great pleasure of hearing your new *quartetti* (*opera* 76) well performed before I went out of town, and never received more pleasure from instrumental music: they are full of invention, fire, good taste, and new effects, and seem the production, not of a sublime genius who has written so much and so well already, but of one of highly-cultivated talents, who had expended none of his fire before. The Divine Hymn, written for your imperial master, in imitation of our loyal song, "God save great George our King", and set so admirably to music by yourself, I have translated and adapted to your melody, which is simple, grave, applicating, and pleasing. *La cadenza particolarmente mi pare nuova e squisitissima.* I have given our friend, Mr. Barthelemon,[1] a copy of my English translation to transmit to you, with my affectionate and best respects. It was from seeing in your letter to him, how well you wrote English, that I ventured to address you in my own language, for which my translation of your hymn will perhaps serve as an exercise; in comparing my version with the original, you will percieve that it is rather a paraphrase than a close translation; but the liberties I have taken were in consequence of the supposed treachery of some of his Imperial Majesty's generals and subjects, during the unfortunate campaign of Italy, of 1797, which the English all thought was the consequence, not of Bounaparte's heroism, but of Austrian and Italian treachery.

Let me intreat you, my dear Sir, to favour me with your opinion of my proposition for postponing the publication of your oratorio, at least in England, till March, or April, 1800. But whatever you determine, be assured of my zeal and ardent wishes for your success, being, with the highest respect and regard,

Dear Sir

your enthusiastic admirer and

affectionate Servant

Charles Burney.

[Address:]

    Al Celeberrimo
       Signore Giuseppe Haydn, in Vienna.

[1]F. H. Barthélemon, the violinist, to whom Haydn was very attached. See *infra*, p. 264.

[To Charles Burney, Chelsea. *Italian*]

Most esteemed and dearest *Sig^r Dottore!*

I regret extremely, my dear Sir, that you did not receive my letter dated 21st September [*sic*],[1] in which I had said that I could not wait too long with the subscription, as you, my dear Sir, were thinking of doing, in view of the fact that I have promised publicly to issue my *Creation* towards the end of September, or at the latest in the month of January 1800. Meanwhile I am very happy to be able to include in my list of subscribers all the names which you, my dear Sir, indicated in your kind letter, and to these I shall now add the name of Sir William Parson, and also the name of the Duke of Leed's son (I regret extremely the death of his amiable father). As soon as the printing of the *opus* is finished, I shall not fail to send all the copies immediately, and also a few extra ones besides.

It makes me very happy to be able to show to the world how I was, and still am, esteemed in England; I really don't deserve such a fine list of subscribers, but I hope that this work will meet with everyone's satisfaction, particularly when it is performed.

My dear and much-honoured Doctor! I cannot sufficiently express to you how very grateful I am for all your efforts on my behalf. God bless you for them! I shall always remember your good heart, and I only regret that I cannot be there personally to show you my gratitude: I do not find the words; but enough! He who knows YOUR GREAT TALENT also knows YOUR KIND NATURE: happy he who can boast of enjoying your dear friendship! As for myself, there remains only to say that I am, and shall always remain, with every regard and the highest respect,

            my dearest *Sig^r Dottore,*
            your most humble and devoted servant,
                Giuseppe Haydn [m.p] ria.

Vienna, 14th September 1799.

[1]Obviously Haydn wrote the wrong date: I suggest that he meant "2" instead of "21". Meanwhile Burney had written again, and had apparently

rounded up a goodly number of subscribers; he then followed it up with a second letter, adding the names of Sir William Parsons (*recte*), the conductor and specialist in old music who is also mentioned in the London Notebooks (see *infra*, p. 290), and the son of the Duke of Leeds (see *infra*, p. 251).

[To M. B. Veltmann, Osnabrück (Westphalia). *German*]
                                        Vienna, 21st September 1799.

Nobly born,
Most highly respected Sir!

I am most obliged to you for the honour you have shown me in subscribing to my *Creation*, and in your satisfaction of my poor talents; as soon as the work is printed, I shall send it to you through the music dealers Gayl and Hedler[1] in Frankfurt, and would ask you to inform them of this. Should you not find any banker in Osnabrick [*sic*] who is in correspondence with ours, please send me the money through the gentlemen I mentioned above. I should so much like to be able to admire not only the 4 great organs, but also you, who, I am told, are one of the greatest living players.

The best Roman gut strings are to be had of Herr Artaria here. Meanwhile I am, most respectfully,
                                        Your most obedient servant,
                                               Joseph Haydn.

[Address:]   Sʳ Wohlgebohrn
      Dem Herrn M. B. Veltmann Organist zu St. Marien und
                          Musikhändler
                                   in
                                        Osnabrick [*sic*]
                                   in Westphalen.

[1]See also *supra*, p. 162. Haydn delivered the work about October 1800. One of Artaria's receipts to Haydn for copies sold—the receipt is undated but must have been written sometime in October 1800—mentions "1 Es. spedito a Weltmann [*sic*] d'Osnabruck . . . . fl. 13.30" See Artaria-Botstiber, p. 83.

[To E. L. Gerber,[1] (Sondershausen?). *German*]
                          [Only extracts preserved]
                                        Vienna 23rd September 1799.
. . . . [Speaks of his new Oratorio, *The Seasons*.] Since this subject

cannot be as sublime as that of the *Creation*, comparison between the two will show a distinct difference. Despite this, and with the help of Providence, I shall press on, and when this new work is completed I shall retire, because of the weakened state of my nerves, in order to be able to complete my last work. This will consist of vocal quartets,[2] with accompaniment only of the pianoforte, based on German texts of our greatest poets; I have already composed thirteen such pieces, but have not yet performed any of them. . . ."

[1]ERNST LUDWIG GERBER (1746–1819), the famous German musical lexico-grapher, whose *Historisch-biographisches Lexikon der Tonkünstler* (Leipzig, 1790–1792) and *Neues historisch-biographisches Lexikon der Tonkünstler* (Leipzig, 1812–1814) are among the most important musico-biographical *lexica* ever written. The extract from this letter is taken from the second volume of this latter publication (see Sources).

[2]These choruses, of which Haydn was very proud, were later published by Breitkopf & Härtel.

[TO HAYDN FROM NIKOLAUS SIMROCK,[1] BONN. *German*]
                                                     Bonn, 30th September 1799.
To Herr *Kapellmeister* Haydn
          in Vienna.

It was not until today that I discovered you are publishing the score of your *Creation*. I herewith subscribe to 2 copies, which I would ask you to send to me at the following address: Herr Halm, postmaster in Sieburg, for Herr Simrock *via Frankfort am Mayn*. When the time comes I shall arrange payment through the music dealer Träg [Traeg][2]. I wish I could have engraved the work myself, for I would have made every effort to do justice to it.

[1]Haydn had visited the famous German music publisher on his way back from London in 1792. Simrock published the first edition of Symphonies Nos. 99, 102 and 104 as Op. 98, possibly under Salomon's licence. (When Simrock published the pianoforte trio arrangement of the last six London Symphonies, he announced them as the property of Mr. Salomon, "who has given me full rights to engrave, print and publish them." See Hoboken, 204.)

[2]The Viennese music dealer: see letter of 8th March 1789.

[TO CHRISTOPH GOTTLOB BREITKOPF, LEIPZIG. *German*]
Well born,
Most highly respected Sir!

The score of the *Creation* will not appear until the end of December, and so if you will let me have the names of your subscribers by

January, I shall be able to include them in the printed subscription list at the front of the score; perhaps no work has ever been published with as many different subscribers as this one.

You do me great honour by supporting my undertaking with such assiduity, and I shall be pleased to send you the copies you asked for: the subscription price will not be raised by a single farthing [Heller] after publication.

You shall receive one copy for the use of your concerts for the widows' benefit, and I shall send it to you by mail as soon as it comes off the press; I would like to be able to conduct it myself.

Since the *Creation* will be engraved and printed here in Vienna, I was obliged to give Herr Artaria the principal commission. But as far as the pianoforte arrangement is concerned, lack of time prevents me from doing this myself. Anyone is free to do it.

Apart from all this, I am much obliged to you for all your kind wishes and remain, as always, Sir, most respectfully,

Your most obedient servant,
Joseph Haydn.

Vienna, 1st November 1799.

[To The Baden City Magistracy. German]
[Only the signature autograph]

[Baden, 24th March 1800]

Worthy Magistracy,

Inasmuch as my wife, the late Maria Anna Haydn,[1] has deemed me residuary legatee under the terms of her last will and testament, dated 9th September 1799 and publ. on 22nd March 1800:

I would ask to be declared legatee *cum Beneficio Legis et Inventarij* under the terms of said will, and request this my statement of legacy to be noted *protho-collando*.

Joseph Haydn [m.] pria.

[On reverse side of sheet the following remarks by the Baden *Syndicatus*: "The original to be retained, and copies made upon request. Baaden [*sic*] 25th March 1800. In Baden City Mag. Joseph Grundtgeiger mp, *Synd* [*icatus*]. *Prato*: 24th March 1800. City Magistracy Baaden [*sic*] Joseph Hayden [*sic*] asks that this statement of legacy be accepted."]

---

[1]Haydn's wife had died at Baden on 20th March.

[To a Friend in Berlin.[1] *German*]

My most esteemed Friend!

I am most obliged to you for the 9 gold ducats you sent me (it is A RARITY for us Viennese to see gold coins)—I probably can't expect such from the Count von Brühl,[2] but meanwhile you might remind His Excellency, so that by degrees I can retrieve my large expenses.

The 3 copies of the piano score you asked for will be sent from here on this coming Wednesday. It's true about the 4 *Seasons*; just now I am working on the "Summer" and hope, despite the fact that I was very ill recently, that I can finish it by the end of the coming Winter. But if such a difficult task should not prove successful, every connoisseur of music will understand the reason why.

The retail price of the score of the *Creation* is the same as the subscription price. As often as you speak of our Naumann,[3] I envy you his friendship; perhaps I shall be able to see him before I die. Meanwhile I am, most respectfully,

Dearest Friend,
Your most sincere servant,
Jos. Haydn.

Vienna, 11th May 1800.

[No address; on the cover someone has written the date of arrival: "Praessent. Berlin/ den 23sten Mai".]

[1]Perhaps the music publisher J. J. Hummel, with whom Haydn had been in contact often before. The letter concerns payment for the *Creation*.
[2]See *supra*, letter of 10 August 1799.
[3]JOHANN GOTTLIEB NAUMANN (1741–1801). Haydn went all the way to Dresden on his return from England in 1795, to see Naumann, but found him away. See also letter to Naumann's widow of 22 September 1802.

[STATEMENT TO LUIGIA POLZELLI. *Italian*]

I, the undersigned, promise to *Signora* Loisa Polzelli (in case I should consider marrying again) to take no wife other than said Loisa Polzelli, and should I remain a widower, I promise said Polzelli to leave her, after my death, a pension for life of three hundred Gulden (in figures, 300 fl.) in Viennese currency. Valid before any judge, I herewith set my hand and seal,

Joseph Haydn
Maestro di Capella di S. Alt. il Principe
Esterhazy.

[Haydn's seal]

Vienna, 23rd May 1800.

[To Haydn from Joseph Michael Böheim,[1] Berlin. *German*]

Berlin, 16th June 1800.

[Contents:]

. . . . The writer, despite his profession as an actor, has run a music shop
for the past 12 years; the only things missing in his stock are the articles from
the Viennese publishers. Haydn should suggest someone with whom he
could procure Viennese music. Böheim asks for 12 copies of the *Creation* in
pianoforte arrangement, all his newest Quartets, *etc.* Mentions the first
performance of the *Creation* in Berlin, which took place on 7th May
1800. The King had ordered it to be performed for the benefit of Weber,[2]
music director at the *Schauspielhaus*; it was then performed twice again upon
special request, each time to a full house, and with enormous applause.
Böheim also wants good wind-band pieces and small symphonies, for these
are in great demand by amateur orchestras, whose forces are suited for
works of this kind. . . .

[1]An actor at the Royal National Theatre in Berlin. Haydn turned the letter
over to Artaria, which is why it was (is?) still preserved.
[2]Bernhard Anselm Weber (1766–1821).

[To Georg August Griesinger, Vienna. *German*]

1st July 1800.

[No copy available]

[It is just possible that this letter is in fact identical with that to Härtel of the
same date.]

[To Gottfried Christoph Härtel, Leipzig. *German*]

Vienna, 1st July 1800.

. . . . Please forgive an old and busy man who, instead of having
written the late-lamented Herr Breitkopf,[1] writes to you, his successor, at this late date to thank you for the precious ring.[2] Dearest
Friend! I shall never be unthankful, but I regret that at present I am
not capable of serving you with new pianoforte Sonatas. The
difficult task which I now have, to compose the *Seasons*, and my
weakened physical state do not permit me to work on two things at
once; but to show my gratitude, at least in some measure, I will, if it
is agreeable to you, send you the full score of the *Seven Words* in the
vocal version as soon as possible. You could then publish the work
with the vocal parts by Michaelmas, either in piano score, which is
already printed without the vocal parts, or in full score, as you see fit.
I do not doubt that it will have a good sale, for it is undoubtedly one

of my best works, and is not difficult to perform.³ Meanwhile I send you two little Duets,⁴ of which one is especially esteemed by the connoisseurs. As soon as the *Seasons* are finished, I shall serve you before everyone else, by writing a pianoforte Sonata. . . .

Between ourselves, I am really to be pitied that I entrusted my costly *Creation* to the sleepy Herr Artaria, the more so since I let them have the piano score, and some other small things, at no cost. Therefore I should be happy to come to some sort of an arrangement with you in the future, and meanwhile I should like to know, at your convenience, and after you have duly considered the matter, what you think about the entire production of the *Seasons*. . . .

¹Christoph Gottlob had died on 7th April 1800.
²Breitkopf & Härtel had sent Haydn a ring, as a small recompense for all his work on the *Oeuvres complettes*: the Leipzig firm had sent Haydn long lists of his earlier works, and Haydn had marked which were genuine and which not, and had dated the authentic ones in groups of ten years. Griesinger reports: "The honourable Father Haydn won't admit that you owed him anything, and he was ashamed and delighted with your courteous and generous gift. 'Tell Messrs. Breitkopf & Härtel [said Haydn] that they have touched my weak spot: I'm like a child, for presents of this sort are much more agreeable to me than large sums of money. . . ." ' (Hase, p. 20).
³Breitkopf were not at first very eager to publish the work, but then changed their minds. See Härtel's letter of 18th July.
⁴Two delightful Italian Duets, for soprano, tenor and pianoforte, which Haydn had written in 1796. The words are by Carlo Francesco Badini, who had written the libretto to *L'anima del filosofo* (London, 1791): of the two works, "Guarda qui, che lovedrai; senti qui, che il sentirai" (F major), and "Saper vorrei se m'ami" (G major), the first is perhaps the more beautiful. Breitkopf printed them, some years later, in *Cahier* 8 of the *Oeuvres complettes*.

[To ANTON STOLL,¹ BADEN. *German*]
Dearest Friend!
Frau von Keller, my sister-in-law, has asked me to send her kind regards to both of you, and to send you the 30 fl. which she has long owed you for the board of her little son;² I would only ask you to send a receipt for it at your convenience. I would also ask you to give the enclosed receipt for 59 fl. 6 kr., which I paid to the Lower Austrian Receiver-General's Office, and also the 9 Gulden which I am supposed to pay to the Baden Town Mortuary,³ to the City Receiver's Office, and to present my respectful compliments to that gentleman. Moreover, I shall not fail to send all the other receipts of

the heirs, as soon as they have been paid out in full. Meanwhile I hope that everyone is well, and am,

Dearest Friend,

Your most sincere servant,

Joseph Haydn.

Vienna, 7th July 1800.

[1]See *supra*, p. 157.
[2]His father was Joseph Keller.
[3]Bills connected with Frau Haydn's death.

[To Haydn from Gottfried Christoph Härtel, Leipzig. *German*]

Leipzig, 18th July 1800.

To Herr J. Haydn, Vienna.

Concerning your admirable music to the *Seven Words*, which every connoisseur considers a masterpiece, it is true that the instrumental version is already generally known, but my firm would nevertheless consider it an honour to publish this work in a correct score; for with the added vocal parts it will appear like a new work to its admirers, and will thus be the more interesting for them.

I presume that you would rather see it appear in score, and am therefore prepared to print it in its entirety, just as I receive it from you; I await only the manuscript so that I may begin with the publication. As far as my part of the transaction is concerned, this remains to be fulfiled, and I shall expect your terms. If, on the other hand, you should want me to make a proposal, I should have to admit, with a certain embarassment, that my offer would by no means approximate to the high value of this work; but perhaps I may ask if—in view of the fact that I cannot set too high a price on this work if it is to achieve the proper distribution and recognition—you would be willing to accept 50 ducats as a token of our good will in this matter.[1]

[Gottfried Christoph Härtel]

[1]Haydn accepted the sum because, as Griesinger reported, "he wants to return the many favours with at least one of his own." (Hase, pp. 42*f.*) Haydn later signed the foreword which Griesinger, using information which the composer had given him, drafted (March 1801).

[To Luigia Polzelli, Vienna (?). *Italian, "Tu" form*]

Eisenstadt, 2nd August 1800.

. . . . Up to now I have felt ill the whole time, and today is the first day that I am better; but in a little while I hope to be cured completely. . . . I shall answer your letter in a few days, and meanwhile I send you 15 fl. to pay the rent of your house. . . .

Your sincere and faithful friend,

Giuseppe Haydn.

[TO GEORG HELBIG,[1] VIENNA. *German*]
Eisenstadt, 3rd August 1800.

Well born and respected Sir!

Since at present my many affairs of business do not permit my going to Vienna myself, I would ask you to pay out to the bearer of this letter, my copyist, this small bill in the amount of 37 fl. 30 x [Kreutzer] which is made out to you. He will give you a receipt for it at once. I hope to have the opportunity of making your personal acquaintance and remain, meanwhile, with every esteem, Sir,

Your most obedient servant,
Jos: Haydn.

[Address:]   An den Wohl Edlen Herrn
Georg Helbig bürgerlichen Instrumenten Macher
in
Wienn.

[1]GEORG HELBIG a manufacturer of musical instruments. Almost nothing is known about him.

[TO ARTARIA & CO., VIENNA. *German*]
Eisenstadt, 11th August 1800.

Messieurs!

I would ask you please to read through the enclosed letter from Herr Schritter in Würzburg, and to send him the missing pages[1] as soon as possible. By the way, I would like to know the address of Herr Georg Helbig, *bürgerlicher*[2] instrument-maker, and if possible to deliver to him the enclosed letter[3] and a receipt for monies received in the amount of 37 fl. 30 kr., and to send the receipt down to me through our Princely porter, Mayer. As always I remain

Your most indebted servant
Joseph Haydn.

[1]An imperfect copy of the *Creation*.
[2]Literally: "bourgeois", *i.e.* not an "Imperial and Royal" instrument-maker.
[3]See the previous letter. Obviously Haydn's copyist, Johann Elssler, could not go to Vienna, and Haydn therefore asked Artaria to get the money instead.

[TO ARTARIA & CO., VIENNA. *German*]
Eisenstadt, 22nd August 1800.

Messieurs!

Yesterday I received a letter of 16th July from Herr Clementi in

London, in which I read to my surprise that the copies of my *Creation* had not arrived there. I would ask you urgently to ascertain the reason for the delay, for they were dispatched more than 3 months ago. Because of this delay, I am in danger of losing two thousand Gulden, because Herr Clementi has already published the work himself.

Please write if you really have not received any confirmation of its arrival there. Meanwhile I remain, *Messieurs,*

Your most obedient servant,
Jos. Haydn.

[Pohl notes on his MS. copy—the earliest preserved source—"Address as usual".]

[CERTIFICATE FOR JOHANN SPECH.[1] *German*]

I, the undersigned, acknowledge and certify that my pupil Herr Johan [*sic*] Spech, under my direction and supervision, has mastered advanced composition, and consequently everything which concerns the vocal and instrumental branches; I further certify that he has made sufficient progress therein to enable him to preside over any music school, not only as director but also as a teacher of pianoforte and organ. I herewith testify to this.

Eisenstadt, 28th August 1800
Joseph Haydn [m.p] ria,
Capell Meister to Prince Esterházy.

[1]JOHANN SPECH was born in Budapest in 1764, studied law and then, following the advice of his friend Count Leopold Nadasdy (with whom he is buried in the family vault at Oberlimbach [Felsö-Lerdya]), devoted himself entirely to music. After leaving Haydn, he went to Paris and studied for four years at the Conservatoire there. Upon his return to Hungary, he devoted himself to the reform of church music; he died in 1836. His great-great-grandson, *Studienprofessor* F. Boccali of Kempten in the Allgäu, now owns this letter, and kindly provided the above information.

[TO ARTARIA & CO., VIENNA. *German*]

Eisenstadt, 3rd September 1800.

Messieurs!

Forgive me for bothering you once again. From the enclosed letter of my pupil Pleyel,[1] you will see that I cannot, in such critical times, procure for him the passport he requires from the Foreign

Office [*Stadts Canzley*]—especially now, when the name-day[2] of my Princess renders it impossible for me to go to Vienna, not to speak of Dresden. But I want to oblige him about my portrait, and so I would ask you, gentlemen, to send to Dresden, in my name, a pull of the very good portrait[3] which I saw at your office last time, and which is perhaps published by now. He will copy and publish it in a reduced size with the Quartets.[4] I shall pay the costs at the earliest opportunity. In the hope of your complying with this request, I am, *Messieurs,* most respectfully,

Your most obedient servant,
Joseph Haydn.

P.S. Two days after I received your last letter, I heard from Herr Clementi that the first hundred copies had arrived in London at last.[5] N. B. If you are able and willing, Gentlemen, to go to the trouble of procuring that passport for Herr Pleyel from the Foreign Office, you will greatly oblige us both. I hope for a few lines about this. One more thing. My Princess, who has just arrived from Vienna, tells me that Mylady Hamilton[6] is coming to Eisenstadt on the 6th of this month, when she wishes to sing my Cantata *Ariadne a Naxos;*[7] but I don't own it, and would therefore ask you to procure it as soon as possible and sent it here to me.

[Address:]   Monsieur
Monsieur Artaria et Compag
a
VIENNE.

[Artaria's clerk notes: "Haydn / Eisenstadt 3rd Sept. 1800 / received 5th ditto / answered 5th ditto".]

[1]Pleyel had meanwhile become a successful Parisian publisher and a French citizen. The Parisians intended to perform the *Creation* in the Grand Opéra, and Pleyel was supposed to persuade Haydn to go to Paris and conduct the performance personally. From Hamburg he wrote to Artaria on 19th August (in French!), asking them to forward letters for Haydn and Pichl, and announcing his arrival in Vienna. He must have asked Haydn to get him a passport. But neither Haydn nor Artaria could procure it, and Pleyel only got as far as Dresden. (Artaria-Botstiber, pp. 81*f.*)
[2]8th September; the church service generally took place on the Sunday following, which, in the year 1800, was the 14th.
[3]Probably that engraved by J. Neidl after the Zitterer portrait: it is certainly not a "very good portrait".
[4]Pleyel was preparing a collected edition of Haydn's quartets in parts.
[5]See letter of 22nd August, *supra.*
[6]NELSON and LADY HAMILTON did come to Eisenstadt, and they later visited Haydn a second time, in Vienna. For the most accurate account of this visit,

see Brand, *Die Messen von Joseph Haydn*, pp. 313*ff*. See also O. E. Deutsch, 'Haydn und Nelson' (*Die Musik*, 1932).
[7]Artaria had published the Cantata in 1790.

[To Paul Wrani(t)zky,[1] Vienna. *German*]
                                    Eisenstadt, 3rd September 1800.
Dearest and most highly-honoured Friend!

Much as I have tried to help everyone all my life long, I can only very unwillingly give my consent to this performance, for a work of this kind is not at all suitable for the place.[2] With your own profound insight you will surely understand my refusal; nevertheless, one could surely help poor Neuherz[3] a little if all the musicians in Vienna were to combine forces to assist him. But since I cannot be present at this proposed benefit concert, I take the liberty of sending him the enclosed bank-note for ten f. [Gulden]. I kiss your wife's hands, and remain, my highly-honoured Friend, most respectfully,
                              Your most obedient servant,
                                    Joseph Haydn [m.p] ria.
[Address:]   Monsieur
             Monsieur Paul Wranitzky,
         Maitre de la Musique tres célèbre
                              a
                          Vienne
Enclosing 10 f.

[1]See *supra*, p. 150.
[2]Apparently Wranitzky suggested that one of Haydn's operas or oratorios be performed.
[3]Possibly Naucharz (Nohl's reading).

[To Artaria & Co., Vienna. *German*]
                                    Eisenstadt, 6th October 1800.
Messieur!

Please be good enough to send a copy of my *Creation* as soon as possible to M[r]. Silvester in London. The bearer of this letter, a servant [*Cammerdiener*] in the Princely house, will give you the address. You make me more and more your debtor by your diligent attention, for which I shall always remain
                              Your most obedient servant,
                                    Joseph Haydn.

[Underneath is the following address, written in pencil by another hand: "adressate a Noveletti e Bombardoni / per spedirle a Londra: / a Mʳ. Charles Silvester / Messenger / at Lord Grinvills [*sic*] office / London".]

[Address:] Monsieur
Monsieur Artaria et Compa[g]
à
Vienne.

[Artaria's clerk notes: "Haydn/Eisenstadt 6th Oct. 1800/received 8th ditto/answered O".]

[To ARTARIA & CO., VIENNA. *German*]
Eisenstadt, 16th October 1800.

Messieurs,

Yesterday I received the two enclosed letters, of which the small slip, presumably from the House of Arnstein, contains the instruction (as you will see for yourselves) to send a copy [of the *Creation*] to Danzig.[1] In case none has been sent there yet, please do send a copy, packed, with a statement of costs, to the specified office in the Herrngasse. At the same time I should like to know if in the meantime some more copies [of the *Creation*] have been printed or not, and if not, I would ask you once again to press the matter through Baron von Swieten, to whom I send my respects; for yesterday I received a letter from Dr. Burney in London, in which he asks for 40 copies more to be sent to him as soon as possible. In the hope that you will grant my request, I am, most respectfully,

Messieurs,
Your most obedient servant,
Jos: Haydn.

[Address:] Monsieur
Monsieur Artaria et Compag
à
Vienne.

[Artaria's copyist notes: "Haydn/Eisenstadt 16th Oct. 1800 / received the 17th inst./ answered O".]

[1]The letters were from one Johann Friedrich Wagner and are dated 1st July and 30th September. The autographs were formerly in possession of Artaria and Co. The Arnsteins directed a famous banking house with branches throughout Europe.

[TO PRINCE NICOLAUS II ESTERHÁZY. *German*]
[October or November 1800]
Since the petition of Gabriel Lendway[1] contains nothing but the complete truth, I can equally truthfully make the obedient request to Your Serene Highness that, in connection with the present enlargement of the orchestra, and since he is a very useful individual, he be engaged in YOUR SERENE HIGHNESS' SERVICE, at a yearly salary of 200 Fl. and the assurance, WHEN THE TIME COMES, of a lodging and SOME firewood; this is in accordance with the two oral resolutions which Your Highness gave me on 1st October 1800.
Joseph Haydn [m.p] ria,
Capell Meister

[1]GABRIEL LENDVAY or LENDWAY had been engaged as a horn player in 1787. In the Esterházy band of 1800 he appears in the list as "Supernumerarius Gabriel Lendvay". See Brand, *op. cit.*, p. 318.

[TO HAYDN FROM PRINCE NICOLAUS II ESTERHÁZY. *German*]
To *Herr Kapellmeister* Haydn:
Well born, Dear *Kapellmeister* von Haydn!
Inasmuch as frequent warnings to the violoncellist Maukert[1] have had so little effect that, against the standing orders, without my permission, and without informing you, he has ignored his duties and gone to Vienna, I wish you to remove him permanently from his post, and I also wish you to look for the best possible substitute for his job, concerning which I shall expect your proposal.
Eisenstadt, 10th December 1800.
Exp. Esterhazy.

[1]IGNAZ MAUKERT (in some lists he appears as "Mauker" or "Manker"), who had been in the band for several years.

[TO AUGUST HARTUNG, BRAUNSCHWEIG. *German*]
[*Contents*:]   [No date: *c.* 1800?[1]]

Haydn sends seven subscription copies [of the *Creation*] with a list of the subscribers.
[From R. Geering's Cat. 402: see Sources]

[1]The letter obviously deals with subscription copies of the *Creation*, and was probably written some time during the year 1800, or at the latest in 1801. August Hartung seems to have been a music dealer.

[To Haydn from Prince Nicolaus II Esterhazy. *German*]

To *Kapellmeister* Haydn:

Concerning the request of Major Mayern from Györ, I would not object to his receiving old but still useable wind instruments for use abroad by the *Insur-rections-Bataillon*, and I herewith instruct you to find a number of such instruments as soon as possible, and to suggest the best price to me beforehand; whereby, when the *Insurrections-Bataillon* is dissolved, the instruments could then be used again by my own band.

Vienna, 30th March 1801.   Exp. Esterházy.

[To Hyde & Clementi, London. *German*]

Sir!¹   Vienna, 28th April 1801.

Thank you for the hundred guineas which you sent to me, but I also hope to receive the rest of the money at your earliest convenience. For my part, I shall endeavour to serve you with 3 good pianoforte Sonatas by the end of the Summer.

You received through Herr Artaria and Comp. two hundred and twelve (IN FIGURES: 212) copies [of the *Creation*]. I should now like to inform you that the music of my *Four Seasons* has been received with the same undivided approbation as was the *Creation*; in fact some prefer it to the *Creation* because of its variety. The words have already been translated into English and French. In hopes of a speedy answer, I remain, with every esteem,

Your most obedient servant,

Joseph Haydn [m.p] ria.

[Address:]   [postal stamp, indicating date of arrival: "Foreign Office 1801, Ma[y] 19".]

Mr Hyde and Clementi.

N^ro 26.

Cheapside.   London.

¹The letter is probably addressed to Clementi personally. Together with Haydn's autograph, an old, possibly contemporary translation has been preserved; it is in rather curious English—to say the least—and inaccurate in details.

[To Ignaz Pleyel, Paris. *German, "Du" form*]

Vienna, 4th May 1801.

Dearest Pleyel,

I would very much like to know when your beautiful edition of my Quartets will appear, and whether or not you have received the copy of my *Creation* and also the portrait which Artaria sent to you.[1] Is it really true that one can buy the *Creation* in Paris, both the score and the pianoforte reduction? At the same time, please do tell me if it has been well received there, and whether there is any truth in the report that the entire orchestra has expressed a desire to offer me a gold medal. Please let me know about all these matters as soon as possible, because here in Vienna the whole thing is thought to be a wild exaggeration.

Last week they performed my new work, *The Four Seasons*, three times in front of the nobility, with an unparalleled success; in a few days it will be given for my benefit, either at the Theatre, or in the Large Redoutensaal.[2] We prefer performing the *Seasons* to the *Creation*, for it makes a pleasant change. It [the *Seasons*] has already been translated into French and English, after Tompson [*sic*], by our great Baron von Swieten. Everyone hopes for a speedy publication; but it will not appear for a little while, because I want to print the English and French words *a parte*, which will render the work easier to perform.

I send you my best regards, as always, and ask to be remembered to your wife. I am,

Dearest Pleyel,

Your most sincere friend,

Joseph Haydn.

P.S. My poor wife has been dead for a year now.

[Address:] Monsieur Pleyel,

Compositeur très-célèbre

à

Paris.

[1]See letter to Artaria of 3rd September 1800, *supra*.

[2]There were two "general" (*i.e.* public) rehearsals of the *Seasons*, followed by the first, semi-private performance at the Schwarzenberg Palace, on 24th April. On 24th May, Haydn conducted a performance at the Court, in which the Empress Marie Therese sang the soprano part (Haydn: "much taste and expression, but a weak voice"), and the first public performance took place in the Large Redoutensaal on 29th May. Nancy Storace was among the audience. Pohl III, pp. 178f.

[To HAYDN from the "FELIX MERITIS" SOCIETY,[1] AMSTERDAM, *Dutch*]

The Society of Merit, founded in Amsterdam under the motto "Felix Meritis", wishes happiness and prosperity for each and everyone. Its primary purpose is to further the general well-being of this country's inhabitants; by a knowledge of true merits, and by encouraging and practicing useful arts and sciences, it wishes to expand and increase this country's trade, its merchant marine, its agriculture, its factories, &c. Nothing can be more pleasing to the Society than to increase its membership by the constant addition of men of good will, capacity and ability.

To further this end, it has elected Joseph Haydn, Professor of Music, member of the Royal Swedish Academy of Music, and *Kapellmeister* in the actual service of H. H. Prince Esterházy, as an honorary foreign member of this Society, in the hope that said Joseph Haydn will assist them in their salutary intentions, and will live up to the flattering hopes they entertain of him.

As proof of his election, the majority of the members voted to send you the present open letter, signed by the commission appointed thereto, and affirmed by their seal.

Executed at Amsterdam this 4th of May 1801

Wagtendorp   Presiding Commissioner
Secretary   Jacques Breguet.

[1]The files of the "Felix Meritis" Society, of which photostatic copies were placed at my disposal, show that Haydn's membership was proposed and agreed to on 30th March. The Secretary, A. Buijn, then asked Haydn if he would accept the membership, and upon receiving an affirmative answer, he thanked Haydn (see 25th July 1801) and sent him the official diploma and the Society's statutes. Haydn's formal note of acceptance was then written on 18th October 1801 (see *infra*). Pohl III, p. 182 thus requires correction.

[To Haydn from the Commission of the "Felix Meritis" Society, Amsterdam, *Dutch*[1]]

The Commission chosen by the Philanthropic Society in Amsterdam, "Felix Meritis".

To Joseph Haydn, Teacher of Music, Member of the Royal Swedish Music Academy and *Kapellmeister* in the actual service of His Highness, Prince Esterhazy.

Amsterdam, 4th May 1801.

Since the Society which we have the honour of representing always directs its aim towards fulfilling its primary purpose, as explained in the accompanying open letter, it is therefore a pleasure for us to offer you, in said open letter, our honorary foreign membership. Your numerous merits, so very well known, vouch for the Society's inclination, and remove from it every doubt that you will accept its offer, thereby assisting its name and its philanthropy: to which end we commend ourselves and enclose a copy of our statutes.

We remain, respectfully,

Commissioners of the above Society, and in
its name and at its request:
Jacques Breguet,
M. Wagtendorp.

[1]A German translation of the year 1811 is included in the Esterházy Archives —see Sources.

[To Freiherr Max von Droste-Hülshoff,[1] Münster. *German*]
                                        Vienna, 20th May 1801.
Nobly born Freiherr von Droste,

   The general and undeserved success of my *Creation* so inspired my 69-year-old soul that I have dared to compose yet another one, the *Seasons*, after Tomson [*sic*]. People here are very satisfied with this work, the composition of which was exhausting. If I should receive as much success abroad, perhaps I shall undertake to write something more (if my physical powers are equal to the task). Then, when I am in Heaven, I shall thank my Almighty God for having given me His blessing, and shall remember all those to whom I could render some little pleasure. I remain, Sir, most respectfully,
                                        Your most obedient servant,
                                        Joseph Haydn [m.p] ria.

[Address:]   An
          Den Freiherrn Max: Von Droste
          zu Hülshoff Hochwohlgeboren,
                              zu
                              Münster
Lives near the   in Westphalen
Lambertii Church
there.

[1] The father of Annette Elisabeth, the celebrated German poetess (1797–1849).

          [To Haydn from Prince Nicolaus II Esterházy. *German*]
To *Kapellmeister* Haydn!

   Since I am not accustomed to receiving reports from anyone except from those who are directly responsible, through whom the material [*Verhandlungsgegenstände*] is passed to me for my information, I do not see how the report of *Claviermeister* Fuchs concerning the petition of the trumpeter Martin Zech from the *Insurrections-[Batallion]* could be sent to me; for Fuchs is not in a position to act as your substitute. I shall therefore expect the necessary information directly from yourself, and return herewith the files on the subject to you.
Eisenstadt, 2nd June 1801.

                                        Exp. Esterhazy.

          [To Georg August Griesinger, Vienna. *German*]
                                        Eisenstadt, 1st July 1801.
Well born,
Most highly respected Sir!

   I am really quite astonished to see how badly much of the *Seven*

Words was translated, and also astonished at the delay. My dear Friend, I cannot possibly make the corrections myself at present, because of my Prince,[1] and I cannot think of any other solution than that Herr Härtel should find someone in Leipzig who can make the necessary improvements. Meanwhile Herr Härtel should publish the work as soon as possible in German. I hope that neither you, dear Herr von Griesinger, nor Herr Hartl [*sic*] will be angry at me, and remain, Sir, most respectfully,

Your most obedient servant,
Joseph Haydn [m.p] ria.

[1]Haydn was about to compose the *Schöpfungsmesse*, his penultimate Mass, in B flat major, which was to be performed on the Princess' name-day in September. He began the score on 28th July.

[To GEORG AUGUST GRIESINGER, VIENNA. *German*]

Well born,
Most highly respected Sir!

I have never doubted Herr Härtel's trustworthiness and integrity, and as a proof of my opinion he shall have the preference over all the others, provided that he agrees with what I now propose. First, in order to rid me of Herr André[1] and his female negotiator in Vienna, and so as to lose no time, Herr Härtel or you, Sir, as his business representative, must write me that Herr Härtel (I having demanded 6000 fl. for the *Seasons*) is willing to pay me 5000 fl. to have the exclusive rights thereof; which sum Herr André will never be able to give, the less so since I demanded cash from him. BUT OF COURSE THE AGREEMENT BETWEEN US FOR 4500 FL. IN VIENNESE BANK-NOTES STANDS. Secondly, I ask for one thousand Gulden immediately upon signature of contract and delivery of the score, and the remaining 2500 fl.[2] within a period of 6 weeks following the Easter fair. On the other hand, I waive all further rights to the score and pianoforte reduction, except for two copies for my personal use; but Herr Härtel must agree to send 24 copies (which, however, will be paid for), as soon as the score shall have been printed, to the group of noblemen here,[3] either through me or through Herr Baron von Swieten. N.B.: This must take place a week or two before the official publication, but Herr Härtel can then publish both the score and the pianoforte reduction, as soon as this period of time expires. I shall not fail to correct said pianoforte reduction, but I cannot stop its being pirated in the Imperial and Royal States, since publication will take place abroad. Herr Härtel should not worry about this point, however, for our publishers here are quite incapable of undertaking anything of this size. At any rate, I hope that Herr Härtel will be satisfied with my proposal. I must add only one thing more: the autograph, like that of the *Creation* is to remain in the hands of Baron von Swieten, inasmuch as, after the Baron's death, both works, together with his own beautiful collection, will be left as mementos to the Imperial and Royal Library. Meanwhile I have had a clean, legible copy prepared in my house, under my own supervision, and have corrected it; this cost me 80 fl., but I do not require this sum to be repaid to me. I hope to have the favour of your early reply, and remain, Sir, with profound esteem,

Your obedient servant,
Joseph Haydn.

Eisenstadt, 3rd July 1801.

[1] The well-known music publisher, whose offices were at Offenbach on the Main.
[2] There is obviously a mistake here (Haydn's autograph is not available: see Sources): the "one thousand Gulden" and the "2500 fl. [Gulden]" do not add up to 4,500 Gulden. Haydn was probably paid 2,000 Gulden upon signature of contract.
[3] The group of noblemen who guaranteed the costs of the first performance and also Haydn's fee.

[To Georg August Griesinger, Vienna. German]

Well born,
Most highly respected Sir!

Two hours before I received the favour of you letter, containing the assurance that Herr Härtel had decided to pay me the sum of four-thousand-five-hundred Gulden for the *Seasons*, Herr Hofmeister[1] from Leipzig walked into my room and in all seriousness demanded the score of the *Seasons* from me; he agreed to pay cash at once, even if it cost five thousand Gulden. But I answered him that this very day I was expecting a letter from Herr Härtl [*sic*] with the assurance that Herr Härtel would pay me the five-thousand Gulden I demanded without hesitation. Scarcely a quarter of an hour after Herr Hofmeister had left my room, I received your letter, which I subsequently showed to Herr Hofmeister so that he could pass on its contents to the home office. At the same time I asked him to inform Madame N. N. von Offenbach[2] in Vienna that I had

actually sold the work to Herr Härtel, so that she will no longer
entertain any hope of getting it: in this way I got rid of both these
plagues at once. Therefore I await the contract, and as soon as that is
signed, I shall have my servant deliver the score to you, Sir. Meanwhile I remain, my dear Sir, most respectfully,

Your obedient servant,

Jos. Haydn.

Eisenstadt, 10th July 1801.

[1]In 1784, the composer FRANZ ANTON HOFFMEISTER (*recte*) had opened a
music-publishing business in Vienna. He subsequently published some
Haydn and a good deal of Mozart for the first time, and after various vicissi-
tudes sold most of his business to Artaria (1793) and then moved to Leipzig
where, with Ambrosius Kühnel, he formed the firm of "Hoffmeister und
Comp.", which later became the "Bureau de musique", and still later
C. F. Peters. Hoffmeister's Leipzig firm was about a year old at the time of
present letter. See Alexander Weinmann, 'Wiener Musikverleger und
Musikalienhändler von Mozarts Zeit bis gegen 1860' (*Festgabe der Akademie
der Wissenschaften, Band* 230, 4th *Abhandlung*, Vienna 1956).
[2]André's "female negotiator" mentioned in the previous letter.

[TO HAYDN FROM 142 FRENCH MUSICIANS, PARIS. French]

*De Paris, ce 1 Thermidor an 9 de la Ré-
publique Française.*

[20th July 1801]

The French artists, gathered together in the *Théâtre des arts* to perform that
immortal work, the *Creation of the World*, composed by the celebrated HAYDN,
are filled with a just admiration for his genius, and beg him to accept the hommage of their respect, of the enthusiasm which inspired them, and the medal[1]
which they have struck in his honour.

No year goes by in which a new product of this composer does not enchant
the artists, enlighten their minds, contribute to the progress of the art, widen the
immense spaces of harmony, and prove that its expanses are boundless if one
follows the luminous torch with which HAYDN has brilliantly illuminated the
present and which points the way to the future. But the imposing conception of
the ORATORIO even surpasses, if such a thing be possible, everything which this
wise composer has hitherto offered to an astonished Europe.

When in this work HAYDN imitates the FIRE OF HEAVEN, he seems to have por-
trayed himself, and thus persuades us all that his name will shine fully as long as
the stars whose rays he seems to have absorbed.

P. S. If we here admire the skill and the talent by means of which Citizen
GATTEAUX has so well reflected our intentions in the engraving of the medal we
offer to HAYDN, we must also pay tribute to the loftiness of his [Gatteaux's]
sentiments, for he has been content to receive for his efforts merely the glory which
is his today.

Rey, *chef de l'orchestre du théâtre des arts*. Segur le jeune. Auvray. Fr. Rousseau.
Xavier. Rey 3me. Saillar. [*etc., etc.*]

¹The large gold medal, N. *Gatteaux sculpsit*, was reproduced in the *Allgemeine Musikalische Zeitung*, 4. Jahrgang, 5. Stück. Haydn left it to Prince Esterházy (see Will of 1801, § 56).

[TO GEORG AUGUST GRIESINGER, VIENNA. *German*]

Well born,
Most highly respected Sir!

On the 18th¹ inst I duly received your kind letter together with the attached contract, and send you herewith the contract, which I find well drawn-up, and which I have signed. I cannot, however, allow the part of the public announcement which I have underlined, because no publisher should have reason to believe, or to suspect, that I have thrown away this large work, or have been obliged to give it away for a pittance, or that I shall receive some of the profits only in the course of time; for people might thus believe that our agreement concerning the 5 thousand Gulden, which I myself read to Herr Hofmeister from Leipzig, is not authentic. Therefore I wish you would omit this article altogether, and inform Herr Härtel about it while there is still time, for I don't want to lay myself open to criticism from all other publishers, and moreover Herr Baron von Sweiten would never approve of it; I wish I could ask his advice about the matter. Herr Härtel should not put the subscription price too high if he wants to protect himself against anyone pirating the work. Because of its 4 sections, the *Seasons* are a good deal longer than the *Creation*; the choruses have just as many vocal parts. Meanwhile I am, Sir, most respectfully,

Your most obedient servant,
Eisenstadt, 21st July 1801.   Jos. Haydn.

¹In Mandyczewski's copy, the only available source, "den 28ᵗⁿ dieses", which I presume should read "den 18ᵗⁿ". In Nohl, *Addenda*, p. LVI, "den 20ten".

[TO CHARLES OCKL, ST. JOHANN NEAR PLAN, BOHEMIA. *German*]
[Only the signature and title autograph]

Nobly born and most respected Sir!

I have duly received your two letters of the 29th May and 5th July with which you favoured me, and have noted their contents with pleasure. I was quite delighted to hear that my Oratorio was received by all the music-lovers in your district with the approbation which it has been fortunate enough to enjoy in almost the whole of Europe; but it was with considerable astonishment that I read of the curious happenings consequent on the performance, which happenings, considering the age in which we live, reflect but little credit on the intelligence and emotions of those responsible.[1]

The story of the creation has always been regarded as most sublime, and as one which inspires the utmost awe in mankind. To accompany this great occurence with suitable music could certainly produce no other effect than to heighten these sacred emotions in the heart of the listener, and to put him in a frame of mind where he is most susceptible to the kindness and omnipotence of the Creator. —And this exaltation of the most sacred emotions is supposed to constitute desecration of a church?

Have no fears about the outcome of this affair, for I am convinced that an intelligent consistory will learn a good deal from this apostle of peace and unity: it is not unlikely that the listeners went away from my Oratorio with their hearts far more uplifted than after hearing his sermons. No church has ever been desecrated by my *Creation*; on the contrary: the adoration and worship of the Creator, which it inspires, can be more ardently and intimately felt by playing it in such a sacred edifice.

If, however, this affair—which sounds completely ridiculous to every intelligent person—is not settled by the consistory, I am willing to place it before their Imperial and Royal Majesties, for Their Majesties have never heard this Oratorio without being deeply moved, and are quite convinced of the value of this sacred work. I am, Sir, most respectfully,

Your devoted servant,

[seal]   Joseph Haydn [m.p] ria.,

Doctor of Music.

Eisenstadt, 24th July 1801.
[Address:]   A Monsieur
        MONSIEUR CHARLES OCKL
        Rector in Plan

a

‿‿

PR. PILSEN   PLAN
               NÄCHST MIESS

    Receipt to be col-
lected

[1]The village of St. Johann near Plan intended to perform the *Creation*. Ockl, the local schoolmaster (*Rector*) and one of Haydn's admirers, applied *pro forma* to the consistory at Prague, and meanwhile all the necessary plans were made to perform the work in the parish church. Unexpectedly the consistory refused permission. The citizens then decided to perform the work in the open air, and erected a temporary platform which, however, proved hopelessly impractical. They therefore resolved to play the work in the church after all, and "kidnapped" the "rector", of whom they were fond, thinking that by removing him to another place he would not be present and would therefore have no responsibility. The priest misunderstood Haydn's name, and thought it was "Heiden," which in German means "heathens"; he rampaged from the pulpit, accusing St. Johann of playing oratorios by heathens in the parish church. Ockl, fearing for his position, then wrote to Haydn. See *Allgemeine Musikalische Zeitung* 1874, No. 3, pp. 41*f*.

[To HAYDN FROM A. BUYN (BUIJN?), "FELIX MERITIS" SOCIETY, AMSTERDAM, *Dutch*[1]]

To *Heer* Joseph Haydn.

Highly respected Sir,

I have duly received your letter, so very flattering to me, and see from it that you were gracious enough to accept the offer of the Society, and that you agree to become a member of it.

I thus fulfil a most pleasant duty in sending you the enclosed diploma and the membership rules of said Society, and wish you a happy future as a member.

It is with the utmost gratitude that I shall expect the 4 Seasons.[2]

I shall ask the Almighty to protect you, and subscribe myself, highly respected Sir, most respectfully,

Your most humble and obedient servant,
A. Buyn [Bujn?]
op den dam tot Amsterdam.

Amsterdam, 25th July 1801.

[1]A German translation of the year 1811 is included in the Esterházy Archives —see Sources.

[2]Haydn obviously promised to send them his new Oratorio as a token of his respect.

[To THE FRENCH MUSICIANS, PARIS. *French* (?)[1]]
[Answer to the letter of 20th July]

Vienna,[2] 10th August 1801.

Gentlemen,

It is the privilege of especially great artists to confer renown, and who can have greater claims to such a noble prerogative than you? You, who combine the most thorough and profound theory with

the most skilful and perfect execution, who cast a veil over the composer's deficiencies, and who often discover therein beauties which
the composer himself did not suspect. By thus embellishing the
Creation you have earned the right to share in the approbation with
which this composition was received. The public, too, echoes the
just tribute which I must pay to you here: their appreciation of your
talents is so great that your approbation ensures their own; and thus
your approbation in some measure indicates to those on whom it is
conferred the anticipated fame of posterity. I have often doubted
whether my name would survive me; but your kindness inspires me
with confidence, and the token of esteem with which you have
honoured me justifies my hope that perhaps I SHALL NOT WHOLLY
DIE. Yes, gentlemen, you have crowned my grey hairs, and strewed
flowers on the brink of my grave. My heart cannot express all that
it feels, and I cannot write to you my profound gratitude and devotion. You will know how to appreciate them, however: you,
gentlemen, who cultivate the arts from enthusiasm and not for gain,
and who regard the gifts of fortune as naught, but fame as everything.

I am, &c.

Joseph Haydn.

[1] Only the German version has survived: see Sources.
[2] Haydn was actually in Eisenstadt: see Pohl III, 185*f.*

[TO GEORG AUGUST GRIESINGER, VIENNA. *German*]

Well born,
Most highly respected Sir!

The short space of time I have in which to complete my new
Mass[1] does not permit me to write more than a few lines, to tell you
that at last I now have the honour of sending you the complete score
of the *Seasons.* I advise you to send it on to Herr Härtel [*sic*] as soon
as possible; but please give our porter a receipt for it. Meanwhile I
am, Sir, most respectfully,

Your most obedient servant,
Jos: Haydn.

Eisenstadt, 21st August 1801

[No address; on reverse side the following note in another hand:
"1801/ the 21st August" and to the right, "Eisenstadt / Haydn".]

[1] The *Schöpfungsmesse*: see *supra*, p. 183.

[TO AN AUSTRIAN OR GERMAN ARISTOCRAT, POSSIBLY GOTTFRIED
VAN SWIETEN. *German*]

Eisenstadt, 26th August 1801.

Excellency!

[Contents:]

The letter accompanied the shipment "by the diligence" of the score of the *Seasons.*

[Summary from "Katalog 1958", item 37,
Bayreuther Musikantiquariat.]

[TO THADDÄUS WEIGL,[1] VIENNA. *German*]

Dearest Friend!

I consider myself fortunate to be able to do you a small favour by writing you a certificate, the more so since, without any flattery, you really do deserve this important position more than anybody else, because of your many and varied merits, and your understanding of the subject. I congratulate you, and very much wish I could write more, but I'm a poor old fellow because of my new Mass,[2] which I'm just finishing, and which is to be performed the day after tomorrow. Meanwhile I hope to see you soon in Vienna, and remain, my dearest Friend, with every esteem,

Your most willing servant,
Joseph Haydn [m.p] ria.

Eisenstadt, 11th September 1801.

[No address; Weigl notes: "Father Haydn, from Eisenstadt/ 11th
Sept.801/received 14th Sept. 801".]

[1]Son of JOSEPH WEIGL (see *supra*, p. 8) Thaddäus—or, as he called himself in later years, Thaddé—was born about 1774 and died in 1844. In 1801, he applied for, and received, permission to open a music-dealer's business (*Kunsthändlerbefugnis*), and Haydn's letter and certificate were obviously written to help Weigl secure the necessary permit from the Vienna City authorities.

[2]The *Schöpfungsmesse*: see *supra*, p. 183.

[CERTIFICATE FOR THADDÄUS WEIGL. *German*]
[From an old copy]
Certificate

I, the undersigned, declare publicly and to all those whom it may concern that the music engraved under the supervision of Herr Thadäus [*sic*] Weigl distinguishes itself, over and above everyone else's, to his great advantage; which one would easily expect from such a man as Herr Thadäus Weigl, inasmuch as he himself is a composer, and possesses all the knowledge necessary to conduct such a business successfully. This is also to the obvious advantage of the state, since then it would no longer be necessary for our native composers to have their works sent abroad to be engraved.

At his request, and for his benefit, I have enumerated all these circumstances, which are entirely truthful, and set my hand and seal to this certificate.

Eisenstand [*sic*], 11th September 1801.   Joseph Haydn.

[TO HAYDN FROM PRINCE NICOLAUS II ESTERHÁZY. *German*]
To *Herr Kapellmeister* Haydn:

I urge you to bear in mind that the members of the band[1] must appear at all times with their uniforms clean and neat, and with powdered wigs. Disobedience will result in the offender being dismissed from the band.

Eisenstadt, 26th September 1801.   [Exp. Esterházy]

[1] A translation can hardly convey the arrogant German of "Chormusik Individuen"; Esterházy also used this expression in the letter of 14th August 1802.

[TO GEORG AUGUST GRIESINGER, VIENNA. *German*]
Well born,
Most highly respected Sir!

I, too, regret that I did not have the honour of seeing you, Sir, in Vienna last time, but I hope to wait on you there very soon. Meanwhile I am sending you, Sir, the proof-impression you wanted of the medal,[1] and trust that Herr Härtel will be satisfied with it. As far as the arrangement of the *Seasons* for quartet or quintet is concerned, I think that Herr Wranizky,[2] [*Kapellemeister*] at Prince Lobkowitz, should receive the preference, not only because of his fine arrangement of the *Creation*, but also because I am sure that he will not make use of it to further his own ends. In the near future you, Sir, will receive from Herr Baron von Swieten one or two sections of the *Seasons* with the English and French texts added. Meanwhile I have the honour to be, Sir, most respectfully,

Your most obedient servant,
Joseph Haydn.

Eisenstadt, 1st October 1801.

[1]The gold medal sent by the Parisian artists: see letter of 20th July 1801.
[2]ANTON WRANI(T)ZKY, Paul's brother (see *supra*, p. 150). Artaria had issued Wranizky's arrangement of the *Creation* for string quintet (2 V., 2 Ve., Vc.) in March (pl. no. 850).

[To GEORGE THOMSON,[1] EDINBURGH. *Italian*]

Eisenstadt, 7th October 1801.

Most esteemed Friend!

I send you herewith the violin accompaniment to the songs you requested, marked with the Numbers 1, 2, 3, 4, 5, 6, 7, 8, and trust that I have hit upon your taste. I have also altered the *ritornello* of No. 15, and added codas to Nos. 2, 9, 24 and 25, as you wished. I shall make every effort to satisfy you in the other songs, but you must be patient for a little while longer, and remember that I am now very old.

Send me the words of the 6 canzonettas, and I shall let you know in a short while how long it will take me to compose them; but I am not capable of composing the *Sonatine* for pianoforte and harp, for I am now too weak to do so.

I am eternally grateful to you for the handkerchiefs and for the beautiful snuff-box, which I treasure more than if it were made of gold. Please be good enough to mention to me someone in the Embassy who can take the place of Mr. Straton in respect of our negotiations.

Meanwhile, esteemed Friend, I am, most respectfully,

Your indebted servant,

Joseph Haydn.

[1]Concerning Haydn's dealing with Thomson, see Introduction.

[To THE "FELIX MERITIS" SOCIETY, AMSTERDAM. *German*]
[Answer to the letter of 4th May]

Learned Gentlemen!

I regard the generous approbation with which the efforts of my small talents have been hitherto received almost everywhere as a most beautiful reward, but also the only one I could have promised myself up to now. But when a company of men, who are brought together by no title other than that of true merit, decides to elect me to its distinguished circle, then I cast my eye over 70 full years of uninterrupted devotion to an art which now, in my old age, proves to be such a rich source of honour and delight. Yes, honourable Gentlemen, you fill my soul with the sweetest emotions, you revive an aged man and give him new strength; for you give me the flattering reassurance that, even if posterity does not cherish my works, my name, shining in the reflected brilliance of your own, will not wholly disappear in the stream of oblivion. As a result of this dignified public monument which you so nobly offer at the shrine of this art, posterity must ever be in your debt: for by your noble actions you awake sleeping talents. You show them the path, and also the reward which awaits them at the goal. Receive, therefore, the heartfelt assurance that my soul is filled with the deepest gratitude for the flattering marks of honour you have shown me. When my course is run, I shall pass on in complete peace of mind, filled with the happy thought that my place will never be empty, when true merits unite to guard and protect the art.

I have the honour to be, with every esteem,

Learned Gentlemen,

Your willing and obedient servant,

Joseph Haydn.

Eisenstadt, 18th October 1801.

[TO BARON GOTTFRIED VAN SWIETEN, VIENNA. *German*]

Excellence!

The great number of all sorts of works which had to be copied for the Princely band was responsible for the long delay.

I took the liberty of sending the whole score[1] to Your Excellency, because some of the things which I had added afterwards were not included, as Your Excellency will see by comparing the sign [left blank].

For rather a long time I have had no news either from Herr Hartel [*sic*] or from his business representative Herr von Griesinger, and I am very surprised at his announcement, for he promised to send the proofs to me, little by little, as they appeared. I would therefore beg Your Excellency to ask Herr von Griesinger to come to you, explain to him all the necessary points, so that Your Excellency will be satisfied. Next week I shall have the pleasure of waiting on you. Meanwhile I remain, with profound respect,

Your Excellency's

most humble and obedient servant,

Joseph Haydn.

Eisenstadt, 21st October 1801.

[No address; in another hand the following notes (German): "To the Baron van Swieten, Principal Imperial & Royal Librarian, and the author of the libretti of Haydn's *Creation* and *Seasons*".]

[1]This letter refers to the *Seasons*, the score of which Haydn had just sent to van Swieten.

[To George Thomson, Edinburgh. *Italian*]

Vienna, 27th October 1801.

Most esteemed Friend,

I now send you the arias you asked for, beginning with Number 14 and ending with No. 22. I sincerly hope that you will be satisfied with them. I could have made the *ritornelli* still longer, but the proportions of the songs do not allow it. I shall make every effort to complete all the others, and hope to send them in a little while. I would only ask you to designate another person to take Mr. Straton's place. Meanwhile I am, dear Friend,

Your most sincere friend and servant,

[signature forgotten].

[No address; Thomson's clerk notes: "Haydn / Vienne 27th Oct[r]. / 1801. — / With Symph[s] & Accp[ts] to 9 Scottish Airs".]

[To Georg August Griesinger, Vienna. *German*]

Vienna, 4th November 1801.

No copy available

[To George Thomson, Edinburgh. *Italian*]

Most esteemed Friend,

I now send you the rest of the songs, and I am quite convinced that they could not better be done: for I have taken great pains to satisfy you, and to show the world how far a man can progress in his art, especially in this *genre* of composition [*modulazione*], if he is willing to exert himself; and I wish that every student of composition would try his hand at this type of music. In time, the fruits of their efforts would surely be well rewarded.

I flatter myself that with this work I shall go on living in Scotland many years after my death. I would only ask you to send me a copy, when it is printed. In the hope of receiving your kind favour very soon, I am,

Dearest Friend,
Your sincere and most humble servant,
Giuseppe Haydn.

Vienna, 5th December 1801.
[Address:]   George Thomson. Esqr
            Trustees Office.   [Postal stamps indicating
               Edinburgh   date of arrival in England,
           North Britain.   and then in Scotland: "For-
   [With Haydn's seal "JH"]   eign Office De[c.] 28, 1801"
                           and "De[c.] 31, 1801"

[Thomson or Thomson's clerk notes: "Haydn / Vienna 5 Dec 1801/ With more Scotish [*sic*] /Airs harmonized etc./ by him—and men-/ tioning HIS HOPE THAT HIS NAME WILL BY MEANS OF THESE AIRS LIVE IN SCOTLAND LONG AFTER HIS DEATH."]

[TO BREITKOPF & HÄRTEL, LEIPZIG. *German*]
[Only the signature autograph]

I declare herewith that the firm of Breitkopf und Härtel in Leipzig is the only rightful publisher of my composition entitled *The Seasons* for the whole of Germany.

Joseph Haydn.

Vienna, 6th December 1801.

[LUIGI TOMASINI TO PRINCE NICOLAUS II ESTERHÁZY, PASSED ON TO HAYDN
    FOR RECOMMENDATION, WITH HAYDN'S ANSWER. *German*]
[Eisenstadt (?), *c.* 5th December 1801]

Your Highness!
The undersigned would certainly find it difficult to make this request, were not the greatly increased living costs—felt by everyone—such as to affect him and his

J.H.–P

family, and were he not in any case deprived of all extra benefits, also his usual winter trip which he has not been able to make for some years, and which used to be such a pleasant contribution to his well-being.

But convinced of his Prince's great generosity, judged merely by the many acts of kindness shown during these past years, and by the noble principle he has maintained in not letting anyone suffer:—convinced by all these noble-minded acts, he dares in all humility to request Your Highness in his graciousness to grant him a small increase in salary, which graciousness he will repay with gratitude and diligence to his duties.

Your Serene Highness'
most humble and most obedient
Louigi Tomasini.

[On the file's cover:]

To be sent to *Kapellmeister* Haydn for his opinion and report. Vienna, 7th December 1801.

Exp. Esterhazy.

[Haydn's answer:]

Inasmuch as His Serene Highness, our Prince, blessed by God, has in his graciousness assisted almost all the personnel serving His Highness during these highly expensive times, I would ask that the old Luigi Tomasini be supported in some small measure.
Vienna, 7th December 1801.

Jos. Haydn [m.p] ria.

[TO AUGUST EBERHARD MÜLLER,[1] LEIPZIG. *German*]

Well born,
Most highly respected Sir!

Again I admire your talent and the enormous energy which you have hitherto expended on such a difficult task. The arrangement is easy, and readily comprehensible throughout, especially the final fugue. But I must ask you to include the changes I have sent you, if at all possible. Apart from them, however, I rely entirely on your knowledge and your profound insight—even for improvements, should you perhaps still find a few small errors. I am too old and too feeble to be able to examine such a big work in detail, and the critics should therefore exercise a little forbearance. NOTHING IN THIS WORLD IS PERFECT. SED HOC INTER NOS.

N.B.: Since, because of the quick tempo, the storm in the 2nd part cannot possibly be played as it now stands, my suggestion would be to do it in the following way, so that the singers will find the right pitch more easily: *viz.*—you will see my suggestion on the enclosed sheet. I am so weak today that I cannot write more than this, but I hope soon to hear something from you, and also to see the results. I am, most respectfully,

Your wholly indebted servant,

Joseph Haydn [m.p] ria.

Vienna, 11th December 1801.

[Address:]   Monsieur

Monsieur Müller Maitre

de la Musique tres Célebre.

[The enclosed sheet, or rather the corrected proofs, have not survived in their entirety, but they included the following remarks: "No. 76, in the last line, the first bars should read as follows:

although they are not in the score. NB! This whole passage, with its imitation of the frogs, was not my idea: I was forced to write this Frenchified trash. This wretched idea disappears rather soon when the whole orchestra is playing, but it simply cannot be included in the pianoforte reduction."]

[1]AUGUST EBERHARD MÜLLER (1767–1817), composer and *Kapellmeister* at Leipzig, did the pianoforte reduction of the *Seasons*. The present letter is Haydn's comment on Müller's arrangement. Müller foolishly showed the passage in the enclosed sheet, quoted above, to the editor of the *Zeitung für die elegante Welt*, who promptly included it in support of his criticism of Swieten's wretched libretto. Swieten was enraged, and Griesinger reported that His Excellency "intends to rub into Haydn's skin, with salt and pepper, the assertion that he [Haydn] was *forced* into composing the croaking frogs." See Hase, pp. 33*f*. The passage in question occurs in No. 18 (*Gesamtausgabe*, Breitkopf & Härtel, Ser. XVI, Band 6/7, p. 197 at the bottom).

[TO HAYDN FROM THE INSTITUT NATIONAL DES SCIENCES ET DES ARTS, PARIS. *French*]

Institut National des Sciences et des Arts [letter-head]

à Paris, le 5 Nivose an 10 de la République

[Paris, 26th December 1801]

The President and the Secretaries of the *Institut National des Sciences et des Arts*, To *Monsieur* Haydn, celebrated composer of music in Vienna.

Monsieur,

L'institut National des Sciences et des Arts, in its plenary session held today, has voted to elect you a non-resident member of the section "Literature and Fine Arts".

We are persuaded that you will receive the notice of your nomination with pleasure, and we therefore hasten to inform you of it.

Please accept our sincere hommage, *Monsieur*, and be assured of our profound respect,

La Porte du Theil, *Secrétaire*
Villar, *Secrétaire*   Vincent
                                                             Président.
[For Haydn's answer, see letter of 14th April 1802]

[TO GEORGE THOMSON, EDINBURGH. *Italian*]
Most esteemed Friend!

I trust that you will have now received the remaining songs which I sent in two separate letters some time ago. I send you herewith the favorite song, THE BLUE BELL OF SCOTLAND[1] [*sic*], and would like to have this little song printed all by itself and dedicated in my name to the celebrated Mistriss Jordan, as a tiny, tiny token of my esteem for her; for although I have not the honour of her acquaintance, I have the most profound respect for her great virtue and reputation. I did not want to compose a more brilliant acompaniment, for that might have overpowered the expressive and beautiful voice of so delightful an artist.

I am very grateful to you for the handkerchiefs, which are most beautiful. Send me the words[2] as soon as possible, one after the other, so that I can give you a speedy reply whether I shall be able to satisfy you. Meanwhile I am, dear Friend,

                              Your most devoted servant,
                              Giuseppe Haydn.

I received the last package containing the rest of the songs.
[The following line is crossed out:] To tell you the truth, I am proud of this work.

Vienna, 2nd January 1802.

                                        [Postal stamps indicating
[Address:]   Georg Thomson Esqu^r   date of arrival in England:
             Trustees office,   "Foreign Office Fe[b.] 1,
             Edinburgh.   1802", "Feb. 1, 1802", *etc.*]
             North Britain.
        [With Haydn's seal "JH"]
[Thomson's clerk notes: "2^d Jan of 1802/ Haydn/ with Symph^s.

Accomp^s./ & Variations to the/ Blue bell — / And desiring Eng:
Verses to be sent to him as proposed —".]

¹*Recte*: "The Blue Bells of Scotland".
²The words to songs which Thomson wanted Haydn to compose.

[TO GEORGE THOMSON, EDINBURGH. *Italian*]
[Vienna, Middle of January 1802]¹

Most esteemed Friend,

Again I send you ten ariettas, and will deliver the rest in a little
while. I also trust that you will fulfil your promises, and am,

Your humble servant
Giuseppe Haydn [m.p] ria.

I AM PROUD OF THIS WORK.

[Address:]   George Thomson Esqr   [Postal stamps indicating
         Trustees Office   date of arrival in England,
         Edinburgh   "Foreign Office, Fe[b] 8,
         North Britain.   and then in Scotland:
[With Haydn's seal "JH"]   1802", "Fe[b] 11", *etc.*]

[Thomson, or Thomson's clerk notes: "Jan ./. 1802 rec^d. 11 Feb^y. /
Haydn/W^t. Symph^s & Accom^s. to 10 Airs — & ment^g./ THAT HE IS
PROUD OF THIS WORK! HE SAYS, MI VANTO DI QUESTO/LAVORO."]

¹The date of the letter can be judged from the postal stamps noting its
arrival in England.

[TO GEORG AUGUST GRIESINGER, VIENNA. *German*]
[Undated: Vienna, *c.* 20th January
1802¹]

Most esteemed Herr von Griesinger!

Yesterday evening I received a letter from Herr von Wassler concerning the transport of the plates and copies of the *Creation* to Herr
Hartel [*sic*] in Leipzig. I am very sorry to have to report that at
present I cannot serve Herr Hartel, because of a political reason
which I could not forsee, and that the whole affair will have to be
postponed. Meanwhile I am sending you the Mass,² which I would
like you to return to me in due course. Yesterday I also received a
letter from Music Director Herr von Müller, who would also like

to have one of my masses. If Herr Hartel can give it to him, I should
be glad; if not, I am sorry but I cannot help him. Meanwhile I am,

Your most indebted servant,

Giuseppe Haydn.

[1]On 23rd January Griesinger writes to Breitkopf & Härtel: " . . . Hn.
[Haydn] received a four-page letter with a 1 page postcript from Müller, but
read only the end, wherein he asks for a Mass. Müller wants to have a Mass
by Haydn as a relic to be kept in the Thomasschule [Leipzig], and this Mass
would also be performed on the great feast-days. The old Hiller is always
revived when he hears something by Haydn &c. &c. Haydn excused himself to Herr Müller by saying that business prevented him from not answering now (that means, in Haydn's case, *ad graecas latendas!*) . . ." (Brand,
p. 415). About Müller, see *supra*, p. 197 Johann Adam Hiller (1728–1804)
was the founder of the German *Singspiel* and Müller's predecessor as
Thomaskantor in Leipzig. The above letter deals with the transfer of the
Creation to Breitkopf & Härtel. Haydn procrastinated for months and
months, apparently on the advice of van Swieten, who thought it would
be degrading for Haydn to give up selling the work himself. Breitkopf
& Härtel did not get the plates until the Summer of 1803. See Hase, pp.
14*ff*.
[2]Probably the *Missa Sti. Bernardi de Offida* ("Heiligmesse", 1796), the first
of a series of Haydn masses which Breitkopf & Hätrel issued in full score.
The "Heiligmesse" was published in May, 1802.

[To George Thomson, Edinburgh. *Italian*]

Most esteemed Sir!

Today, the 29th of January 1802, I received your letter of the 28th
of December 1801, containing another 15 *canzonetti*, which—like
the others—I will make every effort to correct in the near future. I
trust, however, that you will have received thirty-two *canzonetti* by
now, which I have sent at various times. There now remain eight;
these are finished, and I shall put them in the mail today; you ought
to have them in 4 weeks.

You would do me a great favour if you would be kind enough
to arrange payment for them at once, a total of FORTY GUINEAS, which
is FOUR-HUNDRED FLORINS in Viennese currency. With this hope, I
remain, Sir, with every esteem,

Your most humble and devoted composer

and servant,

Giuseppe Haydn.

Vienna, 29th January 1802.

[Address, in Johann Elssler's hand:]
                    N°. 3
           George Thomson Esqr [Postal stamps indicating
                                          date of arrival in England,
                                          and then in Scotland: "Fo-
                                          reign Office Fe[b] 16 1802"
                                          and "Fe[b] 19, 1802", etc.]

           EDINBURGH
           North Britain.

    Joseph Haydn
    Gumpendorf N^{ro} 73 kleine steingasse
                    [seal]
[Thomson, or Thomson's clerk notes: "29 January 1802 /Haydn/ Of
his having received / the 15 Scottish Airs/last sent & that he/will
soon add Symph:/ & Accompts to them— / and desiring a remit-/
tance for those unpaid."]

            [TO F. S. SILVERSTOLPE,[1] VIENNA. *German*]
Well born,
Most respected Herr von Silverstolp!
    I take the liberty of enclosing 10 fl. for the kind *Mademoiselle*, and
would ask you, my dear Herr von Silverstolp, to send it to her as a
small token of my gratitude for the Quartets[2] she dedicated to me.
At the same time, however, I regret to have to tell her that I can not
fulfil her wish as far as selling the other copies to amateurs is concerned; for two very wealthy cavaliers (whose name I am ashamed
to mention, and to whom I sent the first violin part so that they
could look it over) said that they would not buy these Quartets until
they had played through them.
Since they have refused me, and because it is a delicate matter with
these gentlemen, I am afraid I shall have to forego helping the kind
Mademoiselle. I remain, Sir, most respectfully,
                        Your most obedient servant,
                              Joseph Haydn [m.p] ria.
[Vienna] From my home,
6th February 1802.

[1]See *supra*, p. 152.
[2]JOHAN WIKMANSON (1753–1800): *Tre Quartetter för Trå Violiner, Alt och
Violoncelle Tillägnade Joseph Haydn . . . Op. 1, Stockholm*, issued posthu-
mously by his daughter Christina. See Mörner, *Johan Wikmanson und die*

Brüder Silverstolpe, Stockholm, 1952, pp. 188*ff.*, 385*ff.* Title page reproduced on p. 189, Christina's dedication to Haydn on pp. 189*f.*

[TO HAYDN FROM AUGUST VON KOTZEBUE,[1] WEIMAR. *German*]

Weimar, 8th February 1802.

[Contents:]

Kotzebue wants to increase the value of his patriotic play, *Die Hussiten in Naumburg,* by having each chorus set to music by a different composer (Weber, Reichardt, Danzi, Schuster, Vogler &c.[2]), and asks Haydn if he would write the final chorus of the first act.

[HAYDN TO KOTZEBUE, WEIMAR. *German*]

[March or April 1802]

[Contents:]

Haydn is now in his seventies, and is generally ill. He does not dare to enter into a competition with such great masters, for he might easily be defeated by them.

[Griesinger, p. 76]

[1] The famous German dramatist (1761–1819) and opponent of Goethe.
[2] The young CARL MARIA VON WEBER, J. N. REICHARDT (1752–1814), FRANZ DANZI (1763–1826), JOSEPH SCHUSTER (1748–1812), GEORG JOSEPH (ABBÉ) VOGLER (1749–1814).

[TO HAYDN FROM PRINCE NICOLAUS II ESTERHÁZY. *German*]

Herr Kapellmeister Haydn!

Since Katharina Krines[1] of Eisenstadt, who has requested me to assist her while she is studying singing, has— according to the report of the tenor Haydn,[2] who was designated to examine her in this capacity—a most beautiful alto voice, and could become a right excellent alto singer, I expect from you a written report as to what fee one might give her, and with whom she might pursue her singing lessons.

Vienna, 4th March 1802.

Exp. Esterhazy.

[1] KATHARINA (or CATHARINA) KRINES' name does not appear on any of the musicians' lists known to me.
[2] JOHANN, tenor in the Esterházy choir.

[TO PRINCE NICOLAUS II ESTERHÁZY'S ADMINISTRATION. *German*]

Whereas His Serene Highness has ordered my brother to examine the musical talent of Catherina Krines, and he has found it very good, my humble opinion and request would be to give her, in

view of her alto voice of such rare beauty, and also my brother, for
his efforts up to now in teaching her, the sum of 4 fl. per month.

Joseph Haydn.

[Vienna], 10th March 1802.

[In the hand of a clerk: "vid. No. 592. 1802", referring to a parallel
file.] P. S. I shall undertake as soon as possible to find another clarinet
player to take the place of Werlam.[1]

[1]His name appears variously as Georg Warlan or Varlen.

[PRINCE NICOLAUS II ESTERHÁZY'S ANSWER TO THE ABOVE PETITION. *German*]
To the Director's Office: Since Katharina Krines, who is the suppliant of the
enclosed petition, has already been examined as to the possibilities of her musical
talent, and has been found capable of developing into an alto voice, the tenor
Haydn will give her lessons, and see to it that she becomes a real alto singer as
soon as possible, for which he is to be given four Gulden per month, which sum
shall be issued to him by my Director's Office.
Vienna, 13th March 1802

Exp. Esterhazy.

[TO PRINCE NICOLAUS II ESTERHÁZY. *German*]
[Vienna, March 1802]

Inasmuch as the alto singer Josepha Hammer[1] has made such
musical progress in a year that she is able to sing almost everything
correctly *a prima vista*, and since apart from this she has an alto voice
of such rare beauty, in my humble opinion Your Highness should
graciously grant her request.

Joseph Haydn [m.p] ria,
Kapellmeister.

[1]JOSEPHA HAMMER, from Pressburg, had made her debut in Haydn's *Missa
in tempore belli*, at a performance in Eisenstadt given in honour of the Archduke Karl on 29th September 1797. See Brand, pp. 264*f.*

[TO HAYDN FROM PRINCE NICOLAUS II ESTERHÁZY: ANSWER TO ABOVE PETITION.
German]
As a special act of grace, and taking into consideration all the other circumstances, the suppliant Josepha Hammer is granted—apart from her yearly salary—
an additional sum of one-hundred Gulden, which is to be paid to her by my chief
cashier.
Vienna, 24th March 1802.   Nicolaus Fürst Esterházy m.p.

[To L'INSTITUT NATIONAL, PARIS. *French*]
[Only the signature autograph]
[Answer to letter of 26th December 1801]
Vienna, 14th April 1802.

Joseph Haydn to the Citizen Vincent, President, and to the Citizens La Porte du Theil, and Villat, Secretaries of the *Institut National des Sciences et des Arts*, Paris.

Citizens,

The signal honour which the *Institut National des Sciences et des Arts* has shown me, by electing me a NON-RESIDENT MEMBER of the section "Literature and Fine Arts", is a reward so great that the value of my works—even considering the approbation which the public has seen fit to bestow on them—can never, in my opinion, be such as to deserve it.

I am keenly aware how flattering it is to have been admitted to a group which is so universally revered, and which has been so justly celebrated for so long a time. My future efforts will have no other goal than to justify this honour, and thus I wish to proffer to the Society, who has taken me into its illustrious ranks, the emotions of respect and gratitude with which my heart is filled.

I beg you, Citizens, to convey my respects to our colleagues, and to accept yourselves the assurance of my most profound esteem and most sincere regard.

Joseph Haydn [m.p] ria.

[To HAYDN FROM PRINCE NICOLAUS II ESTERHÁZY, VIENNA. *German*]
Dear *Kapellmeister* Haydn:

You are to intimate to the young Lougi Tomasini[1] that—inasmuch as his sojourn here is not only completely useless, but apart from that affords him the possibility of pursuing a frivolous existence—he is to proceed at once to Eisenstadt, where he is to take up his duties, unless he wishes, by his obstinacy and prolonged absence, to provide the reason for his no longer being regarded as a member of my music personnel; for no special prerogative attaches to his person, and he is under obligation to fulfil his duties in the same way as the other members of the music personnel.   Exp. F[ürst] Esterhazy m.p.
Vienna, 30th April 1802.

[1] ALOYSIUS (LUIGI) TOMASINI, son of the leader Luigi, was born on 17th February 1775. He and his brother Anton were engaged in 1796, when the Esterházy band was reconstituted, Luigi Jr. as violinist, Anton as violinist and viola player. See Pohl II, 382 (correcting the information found in I, 263*f.*). Luigi Jr. managed to stay in the band this time, but eventually he married a singer without the Prince's permission and was summarily dismissed.

[To Gottfried Christoph Härtel, Leipzig. *German*]

Vienna, 8th May 1802.

Kindest Friend!

Since I must accompany my Prince to Hungary at the end of this month, I should very much appreciate it if I could have the promised two-thousand-five-hundred Gulden[1] from Herr Kunze beforehand. Hoping to receive an answer in the affirmative I am, with my kindest regards to Herr von Griesinger, most respectfully,

Your most obedient servant,
Jos: Haydn.

[1]Payment for the *Seasons* (the first 2000 Gulden had been paid upon signature of contract, in July 1801).

[To Haydn from Prince Nicolaus II Esterházy. *German*]

[? Eisenstadt, *c.* 7th June 1802]

To Herr Kapellmeister Haydn:

You will be able to see from the enclosed sheet, on which the first bars of each piece are noted, which of your own Masses the Grand Duke of Tuscany already owns. I expect a further report from you, indicating which additional scores of your own compositions you had thought of giving to His Royal Highness, so that I can inform His Royal Highness thereof.

Exp. F[ürst] Esterhazy [m.p.].

[To Prince Nicolaus II Esterházy, Pressburg. *German*]

Most Serene [Prince],

From the list of music which the Grand Duke of Tuscany sent, I see that His Highness lacks only two of my masses: *i.e.* one of the earlier works and the last one,[1] which I wrote a year ago. But since Your Highness decreed that no one should have a copy of this Mass, I dared not to send it to him without previously informing Your Highness. Therefore I await your command whether I should have both these works copied and sent to Pressburg, where unfortunately they will be performed in my absence and thus (because they will lack finesse) lose much of their effect—and this will be greatly to the detriment of my industry, and will be most unpleasant for me. Meanwhile I am labouring WEARILY on the new Mass,[2] though I am ANXIOUS whether I shall receive any applause because of it.

Your most humble servant,
Joseph Haydn.

Vienna, 14th June 1802.

[1]The *Schöpfungsmesse* (1801).
[2]The *Harmoniemesse*.

[To HAYDN FROM PRINCE NICOLAUS II ESTERHÁZY, PRESSBURG. *German*]
To Herr Kapellmeister HAYDN:

I do not deny that it would be very difficult—especially in the case of new works—to perform music without the personal direction of the composer; but on the other hand, you need have no fears, particularly about the finesse, because in view of the worldwide fame of your celebrated works, you may be assured that these Masses will not lose their value in the eyes of the connoisseurs. Apart from this, I leave it to your own discretion what sort of answer should be given to a Grand Duke's request of this kind. But since there really seems to be no way to refuse his wishes, there is nothing to do but to have both Masses copied and sent to me at Pressburg.

By the by, since I have had no news from your brother, I would ask you to let me know if and when he will be coming from Salzburg.[1]

Pressburg, 21st June 1802.   Exp. F[ürst] Esterhazy, m.p.

[1]Michael had been offered the post of Assistant *Kapellmeister*. Esterházy had written to him on 18th January 1802 (Esterházy Archives, Acta Musicalia 1914): "Since I do not doubt that you have already made most of the preparations incident to your coming and settling here without further delay, I shall await your arrival with pleasure; and as a sign of your attention, I expect to receive from you, by August at the latest, a *Missa Solemnis* and a *Vesper de beata*." On 6th February Michael wrote that he will ask permission to leave Salzburg in June or July, to enter the Prince's service in August. In fact he was too attached to Salzburg to leave it.

[To ANTON STOLL,[1] BADEN. *German*]
                                        Vienna, 30th July 1802.
Dearest Friend!

Yesterday evening I had the pleasure of seeing my Prince in my humble cottage; he asked me to go to Eisenstadt next week, in order to rehearse under my direction various pieces of new music, *inter alia* two Vespers and a Mass by Albrechtsberger[2] and a Vesper by Fuchs.[3] Therefore I regret that I cannot go to Baden at present, and moreover, I am expecting the installation of an Assistant *Capellemister* in the place of my brother. I do not yet know who this will be. I thank you very much all the same for your kind offer to put me up at your house, and with a hearty kiss to your wife, I am, dearest Friend,

                                        Your sincere servant, Jos: Haydn

P. S. Herr von Albrechtsberger received a princely reward for his composition, and I was very pleased about this.

[Address:]   Herr v. Stoll
              Regens Chori
                   in
                 Baden.

[1]See *supra*, p. 157.
[2]See *supra*, p. 82.
[3]JOHANN NEPOMUK FUCHS, who was to be the Assistant *Kapellemeister*. See next letter.

[TO HAYDN FROM PRINCE NICOLAUS II ESTERHÁZY. *German*]
To *Kapellmeister* HAYDN:

Since, in view of his previous service to me, I have decided to appoint *Clavier-meister* Fuchs as Assistant *Kapellmeister* of my orchestra and church music, I wish to bring this fact to your attention, and at the same time ask you to introduce the newly appointed Assistant *Kapellmeister* to the assembled band and music personnel; except for Lougi Tomasini Senior[1], they are all ordered to defer to him with the proper subordination.

Just as the said Assistant *Kapellmeister* is now entrusted with the direction of the orchestra and church music in your absence, so the leader Lougi Tomasini is to assume the direction of the chamber music. Together with you, both of them, according to these circumstances, are to ensure that all the individual members of the band[2] show the proper obedience; whereby I insist that there will be no case of insubordination, and that the various duties be performed in an exemplary manner: this includes personal appearance, care of uniforms, and other tokens of good behaviour.

In this connection, the personnel is instructed to obey the following order: the whole band—male and female singers, without exception—is to hold a weekly rehearsal; their superiors will decide on which day it is to be held. They are likewise responsible for the music, and should draw up a catalogue under your supervision: the Assistant *Kapellmeister* the church music,[3] and the leader Lougi Tomasini the chamber music, with the stipulation that no one—under the most severe penalty—is to be allowed to copy or print either scores or other pieces which are part of our musical collection; a special room will be designated for this purpose.

For the rest, I have observed, not without displeasure, obvious proof of negligence of duty among certain members of the band: in future, a monetary punishment will be levied on any member of the band who absents himself from the [church] service; namely, one Gulden per person concerned, which is to be collected from anyone not having a proper excuse for being absent. The supervisors will be responsible for collecting such monetary punishments, and they will report to me about it from time to time.

Exp. F[ürst] Esterhazy, m.p.

Eisenstadt, 14th August 1802.

[1]The leader and violinist LUIGI [*recte*] TOMASINI, who had been engaged in 1762.
[2]"Musik Individuen": see comment to the letter of 26th September 1801.
[3]This part of the catalogue, beautifully written on small octavo paper and bound in red, is preserved in the Sándor Wolf Collection, Eisenstadt.

[TO BREITKOPF & HÄRTEL, LEIPZIG. *German*]
Eisenstadt, 22nd August 1802
[*No copy available.*]

[To Antonio Polzelli,[1] Vienna. *German, "Du" form*]

Eisenstadt, 28th August 1802

Dear Polzelli,

Please be good enough to send me the fugal Quartets by Gallus[2] which he dedicated to me, and which you know. They are lying on my pianoforte in the bedroom, or opposite, in the other room, on the cabinet. Also my calendar for this year, which my Johann[3] and I both forgot to take along with us; but take care that no piece of paper or memorandum drops out. Just tell my cook, to whom I send my regards: you must pack it very carefully and seal it up, and then give it to the driver Härtl. Lessel[4] wrote me yesterday that you are well and go to see him often: I'm glad to hear it, and please give him my regards. I hope that your Mama, too, is well; all the best to her. Today I also heard that everyone in my house is well. Please mail the enclosed letter on this coming Wednesday, for which I am your debtor and

Your sincere teacher,

Joseph Haydn.

Please also send me the German libretto of the *Seasons*, if you can find it.

[No address]

[1]Luigia Polzelli's youngest son, born at Esterháza in 1783. It was rumoured that Haydn was Antonio's father, but if this is true, neither Luigia nor Haydn ever admitted it. See Introduction.

[2]Johann Gallus (Mederitsch) (1752–1835), composer and member of the Vienna Court Theatre Orchestra. The works dedicated to Haydn were "Trois Quatuors ou Fantaisies pour deux Violons, Alto et Violoncello", Op. 6 (Artaria, pl. no. 1570), published in August 1802.

[3]Johann Elssler.

[4]Franz Lessel (1780–1838), born in Poland, came to Vienna in 1797 to study medicine; the next year he became Haydn's pupil and devoted his life to music. He remained in Vienna till 1810 and then returned to Poland. Artaria published two flute Duets and a flute Quartet by him.

[To Jean Phillip Krüger on behalf of the members of the *Musikverein* in Bergen, on the Island of Rügen, North Germany. *German*]

[Only the signature autograph]

Gentlemen,

It was indeed a most pleasant surprise to receive such a flattering letter from a part of the world where I could never have imagined

that the products of my poor talents were known. But when I see
that not only is my name familiar to you, but my compositions are
performed by you with approval and satisfaction, the warmest
wishes of my heart are fulfilled: to be considered a not wholly unworthy priest of this sacred art by every nation where my works are
known. You reassure me on this point as regards your fatherland, but
even more, you happily persuade me—and this cannot fail to be a
real source of consolation to me in my declining years—that I am
often the enviable means by which you, and so many other families
sensible of heartfelt emotion, derive, in their homely circle, their
pleasure—their enjoyment. How reassuring this thought is to me!—
Often, when struggling against the obstacles of every sort which
oppose my labours; often, when the powers of mind and body weakened, and it was difficult for me to continue in the course I had
entered on;—a secret voice whispered to me: "There are so few
happy and contented peoples here below; grief and sorrow are
always their lot; perhaps your labours will once be a source from
which the care-worn, or the man burdened with affairs, can derive
a few moments' rest and refreshment." This was indeed a powerful
motive to press onwards, and this is why I now look back with
cheerful satisfaction on the labours expended on this art, to which I
have devoted so many long years of uninterrupted effort and
exertion. And now I thank you in the fullness of my heart for your
kindly thoughts of me, and beg you to forgive me for delaying my
answer so long: enfeebled health, the inseparable companion of the
grey-haired septuagenarian,[1] and pressing business, deprived me till
now of this pleasure. Perhaps nature may yet grant me the joy of
composing a little memorial for you, from which you may gather
the feelings of a gradually dying veteran, who would fain even after
his death survive in the charming circle of which you draw so wonderful a picture. I have the honour to be, with profound respect,

> Your wholly obedient servant,
> Joseph Haydn [m.p] ria.

Vienna, 22nd September 1802.

[Address:]   de Vienne

[in another hand:] Portstrasse 21
b Dammas

A Monsieur
Monsieur Jean Phillip Krüger
Doctor Medicinae und königl. Assessor

des Collegii Sanitatis in Stockholm.

a

Bergen

auf der

Insel Rügen

IN SCHWEDISCH POMMERN

[1]On the left-hand margin, someone has written "geb[oren] 1732".

[TO FRAU NAUMANN,[1] DRESDEN. *German*]
[Only the signature and postscript autograph]

Well born,

Most esteemed Frau von Naumann!

Above all, I must beg your forgiveness a thousand times for the fact that my answer to your kind and esteemed letter arrives much later than duty and politeness would normally allow. My enfeebled state, and likewise pressing duties for my Prince, deprived me of this pleasure; perhaps I am now branded in your eyes as a heartless friend. Certainly, my esteemed lady, I feel to the depths of my heart the loss which you and the sweetest of all the arts have suffered in your husband's death, and irreplaceable is the position in which this noble priest served this beautiful godhead, to general applause. The whole of Europe had but one voice, and that was the praise and approbation which your late husband's undeniable merits inspired in everyone. It would be presumptuous of me to imagine that my voice could possibly add anything to the deceased's fame; it would be an echo of the opinion which every connoisseur and expert has already expressed about the immortal works of Naumann. This opinion founded his deserved reputation, and ensures that your late husband will continue to live forever. The general voice of opinion is the voice of God, and is more important than that of an individual, especially when the latter is in agreement with the general voice of opinion. The biographer has enough material to erect a worthy monument to the deceased without requiring my opinion; this monument will be based on the truth and the agreement of all the experts. I have the honour to be, with every esteem,

Your wholly obedient servant,

Joseph Haydn [m.p] ria.

Vienna, 22nd September 1802.

P. S. Her Majesty the Empress has demanded to see that most magnificent Opera, *Aci und Galatea*.[2] I will tell you more about this in my next letter.

[1]The widow of JOHANN GOTTLIEB NAUMANN, who had died at Dresden in October, 1801. She had asked Haydn to contribute an essay to Naumann's biography in the form of a musical judgement of his works.
[2]The full title of the Opera is: *Aci e Galatea, ossia, i cyclopi amanti.*

[TO HAYDN FROM CONCERT DES AMATEURS, PARIS. *French*]
Paris, 7th October 1802.

Monsieur,
The six months which have elapsed since our concerts of the past winter have not been able to make us forget the success which we gained by performing your sublime compositions, nor the promise you were kind enough to give us, that you would go to the trouble of writing a symphony for us, to the execution of which we would devote the care proportionate to our gratitude. It would be difficult indeed for us to pass over in silence a favour which would bring us such honour. The whole of Paris will soon know that you have flattered us with this hope: a hope which permits us to extend invitations to all those who wish to participate, and to those who ardently wish to attend. Consider, *Monsieur*, how many people you would delight if you were to respond to this universal enthusiasm by offering to the public, as the overture of our next concert series, a new *chef d'oeuvre* which would reassure them, and no less ourselves, as to the state of your health. We await a favourable answer with keen expectation.

Please forgive, *Monsieur*, this insistance, which would perhaps appear indiscreet if it were not the result of our love for that which counts the most in the art which is our profession, and the expression of our veneration for your genius.

We have the honour to be, with the highest esteem,

Monsieur,
The members of the committee of
the *Concert des Amateurs.*

de Bondy
Brollet [?]
Plantade

Frederic Rousseau
Brevas
Frederic Duvernoy

[TO JACOB HYRTL (HIERTL),[1] EISENSTADT. *German*]
Dearest Hiertl,   Vienna, 28th November 1802.
Yesterday I sent you a new military March[2] by my copyist Elsler,[3] but forgot to write you that in case the following passage

 *etc.*   should prove too difficult, you can

J.H.—Q

play it as follows  or ____. I leave it

[sic]

to your judgement, and recommend a good rehearsal; but you mustn't change anything in the clarinet part.

Meanwhile I remain your obedient servant,

Jos: Haydn.

[Address:]   [Haydn's seal "JH"]
                    Monsieur
           Monsieur HIERTL Musicien de
           S: Alt: Monseig. le Prince Esterhazy
                    a
                    Eisenstadt.

[1]JACOB HYRTL oboist in the Princely *Feldharmonie* (hunting wind-band).
[2]The March was entitled "Hungarischer Nationalmarsch" and is scored for wind band. The autograph is in the Esterházy Archives, Budapest.
[3]Johann Elssler (*recte*).

[TO IGNAZ PLEYEL, PARIS. *German, "Du" form*]
                              Vienna, 6th December 1802.
Dearest Pleyel,

The bearer of this letter is one of my pupils in composition, by the name of Haensel,[1] a charming young man of the best character, and also a good violin player. He has asked me to introduce him to you, so that if necessary you can lend him a helping hand. You will see how talented he is by examining his three new Quartets.[2] He is in the service of the Polish Princess Lubomirsky, and for that reason I suggest that you treat him kindly. Incidentally, I am much obliged to you for the exceptionally beautiful edition of the Quartets[3] which you sent by Herr Pichl:[4] because of their beautiful engraving, the paper—and the fact that they are so correct—as well as their general appearance, you will be remembered for them forever. It's only a pity that two sheets of the quartet version of the *Seven Words* in the small format, which I bought from Pichl for 52 fl., are wanting. I therefore asked Herr Pichl to write and ask you to replace the missing sheets. Recently I received still another proof of your industry from Herr Himmel[5] in Berlin: 3 Quartets and one Sinfonia in E flat in pocket size.[6] One can't imagine anything more beautiful and elegant; Heaven reward you for your pains! You thus increase my musical

talent, and yours! I only wish I could brush away 10 years of my old
age, so that I could still send you some new compositions of mine—
perhaps it will happen yet! Meanwhile farewell, and love your old
Haydn, who was always your friend, and always will be. Amen.

Joseph Haydn.

My compliments to your kind wife.

My Prince will arrive in Paris towards the end of this month: go and
see him. Please go and retrieve the letter, addressed to me, which
has been sitting in the post-office for a long time, and send it to me
here.

> [Address: this letter, on exhibition in the Maison Pleyel, Paris, is framed
> so securely that we could not, without destroying the frame, remove the
> letter to see the exact address. It is probably similar to that of 4th May 1801.]

[1] PETER HAENSEL (1770–1831), whose chamber music, published by Artaria
and others, achieved considerable fame in his lifetime.
[2] Probably Artaria's Op. 8 (pl. no. 865), in F minor, C and G, published—
with the composer's portrait—in 1801.
[3] Pleyel's collected edition of Haydn's Quartets in parts.
[4] WENZEL PICHL (1741–1805), a prolific composer whose works were
frequently confused with Haydn's. See Landon, Appendix II, Nos. 1, 61, 72,
85, 106—five spurious Haydn Symphonies written by Pichl.
[5] FRIEDRICH HEINRICH HIMMEL (1765–1814), composer and court conductor
at Berlin. He had conducted a performance of the *Creation* there on 5th
January 1801.
[6] Pleyel issued two Haydn Symphonies in miniature score: Nos. 99 and 103.
Probably Haydn saw the latter, which was the first of Pleyel's series. It is
hard to say which of the Quartets Haydn received.

[To Haydn from Concert des Amateurs, Paris. French]
Concert des Amateurs

We, the administrators of the *Concert des Amateurs*, declare that His Highness
Monseigneur le Prince d'Esterhazy had the kindness to deliver to us a letter and a
sealed package containing a Mass, an *Offertorium*, and a *Te Deum*[1] composed by
the celebrated Joseph Haydn; and that these three works will be deposited in our
archives as a souvenir, attesting to the token of esteem which the learned composer
has been kind enough to proffer our Society.

Paris ce Vingt un Nivôse an 11 [11 January 1803], de Sorie, Plantade, Brevas.
Frederic Duvernoy. de Bondy. Fr. Rousseau.

[1] Haydn received a medal from the *Concert des Amateurs*. The music was
probably the autograph of the *Schöpfungsmesse* (1801) and the autographs
or parts of the *Offertorio in stylo a capella* "Non nobis Domine" and the great
Te Deum in C of about 1799. See Brand, p. 413f. (I do not believe that the
Schöpfungsmesse can have been sent to the *Conservatoire*, which would
certainly have kept it in their archives until the present day. But if he sent it

to the *Concert des Amateurs*, it is quite likely that the autograph came into private possession after the *Concert* was disbanded. Breitkopf & Härtel bought it at a Paris auction in the middle of the nineteenth century.)

[DRAFT OF A LETTER TO HAYDN'S BROTHER, JOHANN MICHAEL, IN SALZBURG. *German.* "*Du*" *form.*]

Vienna, 22nd January 1803.[1]

Thank you so much for all the kind wishes which you sent me in your recent letter. I, too, wish it would be within my power to fulfil your wish about my wretched health, which has plagued me for so long. For the last 5[2] months I have been subject to a continual nervous weakness which renders me quite incapable of doing anything. You can easily imagine how terribly this miserable change of health has depressed me, but I am not entirely desperate and hope to God that when the weather changes, my precious health will be restored to at least half of what it once was.

Your decision, of which you wrote me, concerning His Royal Highness the Archduke and my Prince, is well thought out and bold, but it must cause not only me but the whole world regret.[3] Neither side can reproach you for having done anything wrong. Both are great, but the Archduke's love and understanding for music are greater than those of my Prince: your heart and your brain must make the decision here, to which of the two you give the preference. Meanwhile I wish you happiness, whichever choice you make, and I hope to hear your final decision as soon as possible. Till then, and as always, I am [end of draft].

[1]The date, "Vienna. 22.January 1803", suggests that Haydn started to write an Italian or an English letter, and then used the space to draft the above letter to Michael.
[2]Haydn originally wrote "7".
[2]Both Esterházy and the Grand Duke of Tuscany offered Michael Haydn lucrative and honourable positions. See also *supra*, p. 206. After endless procrastination, Michael decided to remain in his beloved Salzburg.

[TO JUSTIN HEINRICH KNECHT,[1] BRESLAU. *German*]

Vienna, 3rd March 1803.

. . . . You, Sir, did me the honour of sending me the *Blumenlese*, for which I am much indebted to you. I find in this journal, which is so important for music, nothing which is unworthy of the art, and I should very much like to be numbered among the competitors; but my age of 72 years [*sic*], and a rheumatic nervous fever which I have had for quite some time, deny me the necessary strength to do so. I am barely able to do even those services which my Prince requires for his establishment.

I do not yet disqualify myself from earning the laurel wreath which all the composers (especially, however, Knecht) deserve. God grant that my body be strengthened, and that nature will not extinguish in me those qualities with which she was hitherto so generous!. . . .

[1]JUSTIN HEINRICH KNECHT (1752–1817) was an organist and composer. He edited a musical periodical entitled *Die Schlesische Blumenlese*, which included songs &c. by leading composers of the day. Knecht had tried repeatedly to induce Haydn to write a piece for the *Blumenlese*, but without success.

[To GEORG AUGUST GRIESINGER, VIENNA. *German*]
Most esteemed Herr von Griesinger!

For various well-considered reasons, I have declined to send my songs[1] to the Russian Empress,[2] so that Herr Härtel, by publishing the works soon, can make his profit more quickly; please therefore inform him of this at your earliest convenience.

To you, kindest Herr von Griesinger, I must express my gratitude a thousand fold for all the pains you have gone to on my account, and am, most respectfully,

Your most obedient,
Joseph Haydn.

[Vienna], 13th March 1803.

[1]The three- and four-part songs with pianoforte accompaniment which Breitkopf & Härtel were about to publish.
[2]MARIA FEODOROWNA: see *supra*, p. 38 and also letter of 15th February 1805.

[To SIGISMUND NEUKOMM,[1] VIENNA. *German*]
Dearest Friend,   [Vienna, 3rd April 1803[2]]

Your servant Jos. Haydn urgently requests you to do the enclosed two Songs as soon as possible, and to tell my servant on which day he may come and get them—I hope perhaps the day after tomorrow.
[Address:]   To my dear Neukom [*sic*].

[1]SIGISMUND NEUKOMM (1778–1858), one of Haydn's favourite pupils, was in his day a successful composer. We shall hear of him again from Russia:

see *infra*, 3/17 April 1807. This present letter, tiny though it is, provides the key to the vast number of Scottish Songs which Haydn wrote for Thomson: When Silverstolpe became *chargé d'affaires* in St. Petersburg (see *infra*, p. 242), he met Neukomm and became friendly with him. Neukomm told him that he had written accompaniments for *seventy* Scottish Songs; Silverstolpe adds, "this perhaps explains why they have been so often criticized." I would go further: it is entirely possible that many of the Scottish Songs which Thomson published under Haydn's name are in fact compositions of various pupils. At any rate, that which one suspected musically is now supported by strong musicological evidence. *Caveat emptor!* (See Mörner, *op. cit.*, p. 404.)
[2]The date in Neukomm's hand.

[TO HAYDN FROM VIENNA CITY MAGISTRACY. *German*]
Well born,
Most highly respected Sir!
   In view of the many demonstrations of philanthropy by which you, Sir, have contributed to alleviate the pitiable condition of old and impoverished citizens of St. Marx, male and female, the Economic Committee of the Citizens' Hospital, established by the highest command [the Emperor], has felt obliged to inform us here of your high-minded actions, and has suggested to us that this act of charity should not go unnoticed.
   You, most esteemed Doctor of Music, undertook to conduct personally those Cantatas [*sic*], the justly admired masterpieces of your genius, and you conducted them many times without payment; as a result of this, many hearts were inspired to generosity, and the poor citizens of St. Marx received substantial sums. The Magistracy of this Imperial and Royal capital city, Vienna, has long waited for an opportunity to show in some manner its esteem for a man whose talents have made him immortal, and whom every educated nation has already showered with honours, and who brilliantly combines the advantages of the artist with the virtues of the citizen; it therefore takes advantage of the present occasion.
   In order to offer at least a modest tribute to you for this enduring act of merit, the Magistracy has unanimously voted to confer on you the present twelve-fold golden citizens' medal, as a small token of the gratitude felt by the poor male and female citizens of St. Marx whose spirits you have thus revived, and in whose name we venture to address you.[1]
   May it shine on your breast fully as long as these thankful hearts continue to pour forth their gratitude for your noble gesture! May you give us the opportunity whereby we may show you the esteem in which we hold you! In which hope we remain, Sir,

Your willing
Joseph Georg Hörl, Councillor to the Imperial and
Royal Lower Austrian Government, and Lord Mayor.
Stephan Edler von Wohlleben, Imperial and Royal
Councillor and Chancellor of the Exchequer.
Joh. Bapt. Franz, President of the Economic
Committee of the Citizens' Hospital

Vienna, 10th May 1803.

[1]The so-called "Salvator Medal" (from its title "Salvator mundi"). The "Cantatas" to which reference is made are, of course, the three oratorios, *Seven Words, Creation* and *Seasons,* performances of which Haydn had conducted for charity for several years past. Haydn was very much touched by the medal, and was more proud of it than of any of the other honours he had received. He said to Griesinger: "I thought to myself: *vox populi, vox Dei.*" (Griesinger, p. 80).

[To the Vienna City Magistracy. *German*[1]]
[Vienna, *c.* 15th May 1803.]

Most Worthy Magistracy,
Nobly born, most highly honoured Gentlemen,

When I endeavoured to help in the support of old and impover-ished citizens, by placing at their disposal my knowledge of the art of music, I esteemed myself very fortunate in having thus fulfilled one of my most agreeable duties, and could not flatter myself that the worthy Magistracy of the Imperial and Royal capital city would deign to bestow on me so distinguished a mark of their consideration, in return for my modest exertions.

It is not the noble gift alone, most highly respected gentlemen, much as I shall prize it as a mark of your favour during all the remaining days that Providence has seen fit to allot to me; but even more your kind letter, which so clearly bears the imprint of your noble convictions. My heart, deeply moved, is uncertain whether it should wonder more at your magnanimous conduct towards myself, or at the benevolent care you bestow on your citizens.

I wish here to express my profound gratitude for both; and allow me, esteemed gentlemen, to conclude by the fervent wish that, for the sake of this Imperial city, Providence may long preserve so humane a Magistracy.

I remain, most highly esteemed gentlemen, with profound respect,
Your obedient servant,
Joseph Haydn [m.p] ria.

[1]This letter was drafted by one of Haydn's friends, the *Abbé* Felix Franz Hofstätter, (librarian, 1741–1814) (Pohl III, 217).

[To Johann Nepomuk Fuchs,[1] Eisenstadt. *German, "Du" form*]
Vienna, 18th May 1803.

Dearest Fuchs!
Herr Diezl[2] has applied to me for permission to remain in Vienna

for a few more days, in order to finish some important business; he will certainly return to Eisenstadt before Whitsun. So please give him your kind blessing. Otherwise, I am told that you are exceptionally diligent, for which I heartily embrace your beautiful wife, and remain,

> Your old, but unfortunately useless friend,
> Joseph Haydn.

[1]See *supra*, p. 207.
[2]Johann Die(t)zl: see *infra*, p. 224.

[To JOSEPH ELSSLER JR.,[1] EISENSTADT. *German, "Du" form*]
> Vienna, 5th June 1803.

Dearest Elsler [*sic*]!

Please be good enough to send up to me, at the very first opportunity, the old Symphony (entitled *die Zerstreute*),[2] for Her Majesty the Empress expressed a desire to hear the old pancake. Thus I ask Herr Messner[3] to lend it to me for a few days: I won't damage it in any way. Otherwise, I should be happy to hear that everyone else is in good health; my compliments to all of them, especially my brother, Luigi, Fex, and his better half,[4] &c.

> Jos. Haydn m.p.

[Address:]

Haydn asks that this letter be expedited as soon as possible.
An Herrn Elsler, Oboist bey Sr. Durchl. Fürst Esterhazy,
> in
> Eisenstadt.

[1]Joseph was Johann's brother, and oboist in the *Feldharmonie*.
[2]Symphony No. 60 (incidental music to *Der* [*recte*] *Zerstreute*). The original copy, and the one Haydn made in 1803 (copied by Johann Elssler) are both preserved in the Esterházy Archives. A page of the 1803 copy is reproduced in Landon, p. 33 (facing).
[3]In charge of the music archives.
[4]Haydn's brother Johann (tenor); Luigi Tomasini; "Fex" (An Austrian expression which, in modern slang, might be translated as "nut") and "his better half" are Luigi's two sons, Luigi Jr. and Anton.

[To GEORGE THOMSON, EDINBURGH. *Italian*]
> Vienna, 30th June 1803.

Dearest Friend!

I send you herewith the remaining ariettas, and hope that you and all other lovers of music will be satisfied by this music. I only regret that in this world I am obliged to serve any gallant gentleman who pays me; and moreover, Mr. Whyte gives me two guineas for every single arietta,[1] that is to say, twice as much. My dearest Friend, I hope to be able to serve you on another occasion. Meanwhile I am, with the greatest esteem,

Your most sincere friend and servant,

Giuseppe Haydn [m.p] ria.

[Thomson's clerk notes: "30 June 1803/Haydn/ Vienna/ with a number/ of Airs harmo-/nized by him/ for me/ And that Mr White pays him 2 guineas/ for each air he has/ harmonized".]

[1]Haydn had sold a number of Scottish song arrangements to the Edinburgh publisher William Whyte, and Thomson was, not unnaturally, rather hurt and annoyed. Haydn's receipt to Whyte is reproduced in facsimile (see Illustration X.)

[To GEORGE THOMSON, EDINBURGH. *Italian*]

Most esteemed Sir!

I send you herewith forty new Scottish ariettas, and the rest will be finished shortly. I am most grateful to you for the payment of 120 gold ducats which I received not long ago[1] from Messrs. Fries & Co., and I embrace you, dear Friend, for the handkerchiefs, which are very beautiful, especially those intended for my poor wife. She lies buried these past three years, and so I have given them to a married lady who is most accomplished in the field of music. I hope you will agree with what I did. I am, with every respect, your most sincere friend, Giuseppe Haydn.

Vienna, 1st July 1803.

[Thomson's clerk notes: "Haydn / Vienna 1 July 1803 / W^t 40 Airs harmon-/ized p^e by him— /thanks for the money/ paid him & for In-/dia handkerchiefs."]

[1]The receipt (only signature is autograph) is dated 8th June: British Museum, Add. 35263, fol. 168.

[To GEORGE THOMSON, EDINBURGH. *French*]

[Only the signature autograph]

Mon très chère Amis!

I have received the money you sent me through the bankers Frise [Fries]: don't be angry at me for having to wait so long for the 25 songs, but they have been ready to be sent to you for 5 months. The Secretary of the Embassy, Sir Seward [Charles Stuart] has not known, or rather he hasn't told me, when he was to leave; till now I have not found an opportunity to send these and 14 more songs to you. I shall choose a safe way by which to send you the other 11 which I have yet to compose. I am much indebted to you for your gifts: I am having the handkerchiefs hemstiched.

The copy you sent me[1] is unparalleled, not only for its engraving but also for the beauty of the paper. I beg you to send me the 1st and 2nd volumes together with the 4th, for I admire this distinguished collection and the musicians who have worked on it. I shall be glad to pay for all of them, and am, with profound esteem, your most devoted servant,

Joseph Haydn [m.p] ria

Vienna, 6th July 1803.
[Thomson notes: " Haydn, Vienna 6 July 1803 acknowledging to have rec^d pay^t from Frise [*sic*] & Co. of the price of the Ritornelles & Accomp^ts soon to be sent me (120 ducats, or £ 59.1 3. 5) acking also to have rec^d. the presents I sent him and expressing his admiration of the manner in which the 3^d volume is printed— & requesting the other volumes. . . ."]

[1]The Third Volume of Scottish Songs (see Thomson's notes).

[To HAYDN FROM PRINCE NICOLAUS II ESTERHÁZY. *German*]
To *Kapellmeister* Haydn!
The distribution of uniforms, concerning which the wind band players and the tenor have petitioned in the enclosed *Suppliquen*, cannot be systematized into any category, and moreover was not included in the duly appointed salaries of these above-mentioned members of the band[1]—either in form of a uniform each year, or much less in form of a cash substitute; proof of this is seen in the fact that when one or the other of these members of the band leaves, some other member must take over his uniform; and when the wind band was formed, there was no uniform at all. Thus it is quite obvious that the suppliants are neither entitled to any compensation, nor is it intended that in their new contracts they should receive 400 Fl. instead of 300 Fl. annually.

To which end you will instruct the members of the band who petitioned, explaining fully all the circumstances enumerated above pertaining to the petition submitted.[2]

Eisenstadt, 13th October 1803.   Exp. Esterhazy

[1]"Musik Individuen".
[2]It is interesting to compare this rather grim document with a similar petition submitted to Nicolaus I: see letter written at the beginning of October 1789.

[To Madame Moreau.[1] *French*]
[Only signature autograph]

Vienna, 1st November 1803

Madame,

Prince Esterhazy did me the honour of informing me that you wish to have a Sonata of my composition. Nothing more than the ardent desire to please you would be necessary to incite me to begin this work; my age and my sicknesses have prevented me from accomplishing anything during the past two years, and I tremble that you may not perceive this fact: but indulgence is always the handmaiden of charm and talent, and I am sure that I may count on yours. My doctors lead me to hope for a mitigation of my ills; and I wish for nothing more, *Madame,* than to repair the weakness of my composition—a new work which I offer to you in reverence. I hope that it will be worthy of you and *M. le général* Moreau; I beg him not to judge me too sternly, and to remember that it was only Timotheus who had the privilege of singing in front of Alexander!

I have the honour to be, Madame, most respectfully,

Your most humble and most obedient servant,
Joseph Haydn [m.p] ria.

[1]The beautiful and talented creole wife of Jean Victor Moreau, the famous French general who refused to marry Caroline Bonaparte and thus earned Napoleon's undying hatred. Madame Moreau has been described as "Femme de grande distinction, parlant plusieurs langues, bonne musicienne, peintre de talent, elle exerçait une vivre séduction sur tous ceux qui l'approchaient" (J. Dontenville, *Le général Moreau* [*1763–1813*]. Paris, 1899, p. 142). Prince Esterházy seems to have thought it politic to have Haydn write her a new Sonata. Haydn, of course, did not dream of composing a new Sonata for her or anyone else, and gave her a copy of the pianoforte Trio No. 31 in E flat minor (1795), without the 'cello part. See Hoboken, p. 716, Pohl III, 213*ff.*, *etc.*

[To Prince Nicolaus II Esterházy. *German*]
[Text by Johann Elssler, the numbers filled in by Haydn and the signature also autograph]

[Beginning of November 1803][1]

In my humble but well considered opinion, all four suppliants deserve to have their requests granted, Barbara Philhofin [*recte*: Pilhofer[2]], discant, with an additional yearly allowance of 50 Fl., the other three with 25 each.

Haydn [m.p.] ria.
Kapellmeister

[1]Esterházy's answer is dated 18th November 1803 and names the other three suppliants: Johann Bader, bass; and Magdalena and Josepha Schöringer. Haydn's financial suggestions were accepted. (Esterházy Archives, Acta Musicalia Fasc. XXVII, 1988).
[2]BARBARA PILHOFER had been engaged as soprano in 1782; she was affectionately known as "Babette"—see also Haydn's will.

[TO GEORGE THOMSON, EDINBURGH. *Italian*]

Vienna, 18th December 1803.

My most esteemed Friend!

At last I can send you the thirteen songs you asked for, and hope that they will give equal pleasure to you and your dear—dearest— daughter, whose hands your good old Haydn kisses.——Some of these songs, contrary to my intention, turned out to be rather difficult, but when they have been more frequently played, they will be seen to have the same value as the others.——Many thanks for the 50 ducats which I received from Messrs. Fries et Comp.

Concerning that which you wrote me in your last letter—"in about a fortnight I shall write you about a composition of an entirely different sort"—I have not as yet heard anything further.

Since I have done so many Scottish songs for you, I am willing, if you so wish, to do another twenty-five more, and if your beautiful daughter wants some little English songs by me, with pianoforte accompaniment, I shall send them at once. It is enough if she will send me a little catalogue of those which she has already received from London. For the rest, I am as always, with the greatest esteem,

Your most sincere friend and servant,

Giuseppe Haydn [m.p] ria.

P.S.: Milord Minto will have seen my portrait *en buste*,[1] and not the medallion made by the famous Grassi in Vienna in a certain process rather like *terra cotta* porcelain;[2] the latter is very like me, and if the war does not prevent it, I shall try to send you one.

[Thomson notes: "18 Dec 1803 / Haydn/ with 13 Airs,/ chiefly Welsh,/ & Receipt for the/piece declaring these/to be my property &/ He agrees to do/more if wanted, &/ offers some Airs of his / comp[n] to my dau[r]."]

[Separate receipt:]

[English]

I acknowledge to have received of M[r] Georg Thomson Esq: of the City of Edinburgh in Scotland by the hands of Mess[rs] Fries et Comp:

per order of Mess^ers Thos Coutts et Comp: of London Fifty ducats
for composing Ritornelles et Accompaniments for the Piano Forte
etc: to twelve Welsh et Scottish Airs, and I declare these, in addition
to the 158 which I before composed for the Said G: Thomson to be
his sole property.—
Given under my hand at Vienna, the 18th of December 1803.
Dr Haydn [m.p] ria.
[Address in Elssler's hand, with postal stamp of foreign office indicating date of arrival: "JA[N] 11 1804".]

[1]Probably the lead bust, also by Grassi (reproduced in Landon).
[2]The splendid *terra cotta* bust, the original of which is reproduced in the
Musical Quarterly Vol. XVIII/2 (April 1932), facing p. 191.

[TO HAYDN FROM GEORGE THOMSON, EDINBURGH. *English*: FROM THOMSON'S
COPY-BOOK]
T.O. Edinburgh 20 Dec 1803.

To D^r. Haydn
   Vienna
(translated into Italian &
sent to M Coutts Trotter to
be transmitted through
Fries & C°.)
My dear Sir
[Copyist's hand:] Altho' I do not wish to harass you with more business than
may be agreeable to you, I must beg leave to send you [number added later:]
24 more Airs, WHICH WILL MOST CERTAINLY BE THE LAST. Your Ritornelles &
Accompaniments delight me so much, that I realy [*sic*] cannot bear the idea of
seeking an inferior Composer to finish a work already so nearly finished by you.
I do flatter myself therefore that you will not give me the pain & mortification of
a refusal. I ask it as a most particular favour, & I am willing to pay you [number
added later:] 4 ducats for each Air, & as the Airs are in general very short, they
will not ocupy [*sic*] much of your time. Let me beg you then that you will be so
good as to do them in your usual charming manner, as soon as you can, & if you
please to send me the one half without waiting till the other half is finished, I shall
be very glad to receive them. Messrs. Fries & Co: will pay the price of whatever
number you deliver to them on my account. I am expecting every day to receive
the Airs which I sent you on the 6th September last for the payment of which a
draft of 50 ducats was inclosed. I hope these airs are on the road to me.
    Allow me to mention, that if you find any of the Airs fit for an accomp^t
similar to that in your 1st Canzonet in C, published by Corri & Dussek,[1] I am
particularly fond of that kind of easy motion in accomp^t.
    I remain with Affectionate regard & the higest [*sic*] respect Dear Sir Yours
faithfully
    P.S. remember to send me your portrait [:] the one which Lord Minto saw in
Vienna which he told me is very like you.[2]

[1]"The Mermaid's Song" (Anne Hunter), the first of the "VI Original
Canzonettas" (see *supra*, p. 145), *Gesamtausgabe* Ser. XX/1, No. 25.
[2]See also previous letter: Thomson had obviously asked Haydn about the
portrait in an earlier letter.

[Undated letter from the Esterházy files of the year 1803]
[To PRINCE NICOLAUS II ESTERHÁZY. *German*]
My humble opinion would be to grant Madame Siess[1] an addi-
tional allowance of 50 Fl. per year, because of her especial diligence
and good conduct; and that you graciously heed the request of Jean
Dörzel,[1] who is the only good double-bass player in Vienna and the
whole of the Kingdom of Hungary.
                                Jos: Haydn [m.p] ria.
[On the cover of the file is the following pencilled note: "*Quoad*
RUMFELD none, Haidn should propose DÜZEL's additional allowance."[1]]

[1]MADAME SIESS was apparently a singer: nothing further is known of her.
Jean Dörzel (or Düzel) is apparently JOHANN DIETZL. Pohl and others have
confused the four Dietzls, who were: (1) JOSEPH, schoolmaster and tenor,
who died in 1777. See letter of 22nd Dec. 1768. (2) JOSEPH WOLFGANG, son
of the above, who was a horn player. He was engaged in the Esterházy
band in 1776, and died at Eisenstadt in 1795. (3) JOHANN, the double bass
player, who died at Eisenstadt in 1806 at the age of 52, and who was also a
son of the first. (4) JOSEPH, violinist, probably a son of Joseph Wolfgang.
He died in 1801. (Pohl I, 261, corrected by André Csatkai, 'Die Beziehungen
Gregor Josef Werners, Joseph Haydns und der fürstlichen Musiker zur
Eisenstädter Pfarrkirche', *Burgenländische Heimatblätter* I/1 [1932], p. 16.)
The "Rumfeld" mentioned on the cover of the file is the soprano Anna
Rhumfeld, who had been engaged in October 1797 (Pohl III, 133).

[DRAFT OF A LETTER TO KARL FRIEDRICH ZELTER,[1] BERLIN. *German*]
                                [Vienna, 25th February 1804]
Most esteemed Friend!
My extreme weakness does not permit me to write you more
than a few words, but they are words from my heart. You are one
of the few people who are thankful—you have shown this by the
beautiful biography of your teacher Fasch.[2] You are a man with a
profound knowledge of the science of music: this is evident from
your faithful analysis of my *Chaos*, which you could have composed
fully as well as Haydn did. I thank you for your interest, but posterity
will thank you even more for your attempts again to resuscitate the
half-forgotten art of singing by means of your concerts.[3] May God

preserve you for many years to come! Meanwhile I am, most respectfully,

Your indebted servant,

P. S. I am most grateful to you for the portraits you sent me, but there is a little mistake: 1733 should read 1732. It is [originally: "quite"] very like me. N.B. I was born in 1732, that means I am a year older.[4]

One thing more: I wish that my dear Zelter would go to the trouble of taking Gellert's *Abend Lied*, "Herr, der Du mir das Leben &c.",[5] from my score, and arrange it for his whole choir, alternating 4 soloists with the semi-chorus and full chorus. N.B. It is absolutely necessary, however, that the pianoforte accompaniment be included, JUST as it stands.

Address:[6]   A Monsieur
       Monsieur Zelter Maitre de la Musique
          tres Célebre

         a
        Berlin.

[1]This letter to Zelter (1758–1832), conductor of the famous Berlin *Singakademie* and friend of Goethe, is included in a series of drafts (see Sources). The page begins as follows: "Wienn, den 25^{tn} February 804 / Hochzu-Verehrende Frau! / Es gab eine Zeit" ("Most esteemed Lady. There was a time . . . "). The draft of the present letter begins just underneath. Obviously the date belongs to the letter written to the lady, but Zelter's letter was also drafted the very same day, as Zelter's answer shows.

[2]K. F. C. FASCH (1736–1800), composer, harpsichord player and Zelter's predecessor as director of the *Singakademie* in Berlin.

[3]The *Singakademie*.

[4]The portrait (the writer of these notes owns a copy) is at best quite (not "very"!) like Haydn, and is obviously based on the famous Hardy engraving (London 1792). It is marked "A Chaponnier del. Laurens sculp 1803" and, as Haydn points out, gives 1733 as the year of his birth.

[5]From Haydn's *Mehrstimmige Lieder* which Breitkopf & Härtel published. See also *supra*, p. 167.

[6]This draft of Zelter's address is preserved at the top of another set of drafts (Sándor Wolf Museum, Eisenstadt): see Sources.

[TO HAYDN FROM KARL FRIEDRICH ZELTER, BERLIN. *German*]
Berlin, 16th March 1804

I have not words, revered Master, to express the joy I felt on receiving your friendly letter of 25th February, which I shall bequeath as a relic, as a noble letter, to my eleven children. I know that I must ascribe such praise rather to your own kindness and goodness than to my merits; but praise from you is so precious that I shall in all seriousness strive earnestly to deserve it.

As I see, you are aware that I wrote the criticism of your masterpiece, and that long before this I fervently admired you; but to have written the work as you have done, great master, that I could not have done, and will never be able to. Your spirit has penetrated the sanctuary of heavenly wisdom: you have brought down fire from heaven, to warm and to illuminate our earthly hearts, and to lead them to a sense of the Infinite. The best which we others can do is simply this: to give thanks and praise to God, who sent you to us so that we may discern the miracles which He has revealed in this art through you.

What I wanted to have from you, my dear Friend, for my *Singakademie* (which now consists of two hundred voices, of which 160 may be regarded as energetic and useful) is one of your sacred compositions, and this I have wanted for a very long time; but it took 15 years before the funds of our institution were sufficient to afford the expense of such a masterpiece. I feel only too well how small is the fee we can offer you for a work of yours, which indeed no gold in the world can repay; and as a matter of fact I relied more on your love of art and the glory of God, than on our paltry money. I beg you then, if your physical strength permits, to undertake this work, so that your great name may resound in our circle to the glory of God and the honour of art; our circle has only one purpose, to preserve and revive CHURCH and SACRED MUSIC, HITHERTO SO SHAMEFULLY NEGLECTED.

In order to have at least something of yours, I took the liberty of arranging the two Gellert songs, "Herr, der Du mir das Leben" and "Du bist's, dem Ruhm und Ehre gebühret" for our choir. Thus your wish was fulfilled more than seven months ago; you will be able to judge from the accompanying whether I have done them properly, and I sincerly beg you to let me know any improvements you may suggest.

I do wish I could give you the pleasure of hearing your choruses sung here, and find edification in the peace, piety, purity and reverence with which they sing your beautiful chorus, "Du bist's dem &c.". The best and finest youths of Berlin assemble here with their fathers and mothers, like a heaven filled with angels, praising in joy and honour the glory of Almighty God, and practising the works of the greatest master the world has yet seen. Oh! come to us! Come! You will be received like a god among mortals; we will sing a *gloria* in your praise, so that your venerable grey hair will be transformed into a crown of laurel, for our teacher Fasch has taught us how to honour great men.

Farewell, dear and beloved master! May God long, long preserve you! You have not written a single work in which one notices your advanced age. Your *Seasons* is a work of youthful energy and venerable mastery. I commend you to God!

Your
Zelter.

[DRAFT OF A LETTER TO PRINCE NICOLAUS II ESTERHÁZY. *German*]
[Spring 1804][1]

The suppliant Joseph Richter,[2] tenor in the Princely choir, is a quiet and reserved man but also one of the most diligent in fulfiling his duties. Apart from this, he knows all the church ceremonies that occur throughout the year, understands and speaks Latin, and took the trouble to teach the proper pronunciation, especially in Graduals and Offertories, to all the other singers, male and female. He also understands the Gregorian chant and its declamation, and is eminently fitted to teach all 4 choir boys. Therefore I am so bold as to suggest that my gracious Prince help him by supporting his petition for a small bonus.

[1]Written on the same sheet as the letter to Zelter, but apparently a little later.
[2]Jacob Joseph Richter, who was probably the solo tenor in many of Haydn's late masses. See Brand, pp. 460f.

[To Prince Nicolaus II Esterházy. *German*]
[Spring 1804][1]
Inasmuch as in these expensive[2] times His Serene Highness has favoured almost all the individuals in His Highness' service in various ways; and since the suppliant Johann Fuchs[3] distinguished himself in various new compositions on the occasion of Your Serene Highness' happy return last year, my duty demands that I earnestly recommend him to Your Serene Highness.

Joseph Haydn,
Kapellmeister.

[1]Finished letter in the 1804 files of the Esterházy Archives: the draft, however, is written on the sheet containing the draft of Zelter's address (25th February).
[2]In the draft, "traurigen" (= "sad").
[3]Johann Nepomuk Fuchs, the Assistant *Kapellmeister*. For a description of the "various new compositions", see the contemporary report quoted in Pohl III, 220.

[To Haydn from Vienna City Magistracy. *German*]
Know all men by these presents that we, Lord Mayor and Councillor of the Imperial and Royal capital city of Vienna, inform the citizens as follows: The nobly born Herr Joseph Haydn, Doctor of Music, *Kapellmeister* to His Serene Highness Prince Esterhazy, member of the French National Institute of Science and the Arts, of the Royal Swedish Academy, and of the Musical Academy here, upon request of the Economic Committee of the Citizens' Hospital, assisted the impoverished citizens, male and female, of St. Marx by holding public performances of Cantatas [*sic*],[1] the proceeds of which were given to them; not only did he show great generosity in agreeing three different times to undertake to conduct the

J.H.–R

performance of his own justly celebrated musical compositions; for as a result of his presence, the number of persons attending the concerts was increased, and the proceeds for charity were thus greater; but he also showed himself at all times ready to give of his services freely and without remuneration, although these performances were a great strain to him.

By this remarkable and noble act of generosity, the citizens at the hospital, crippled by age, poverty and broken health, enjoyed for a considerable length of time comfort and relief from their fate. Through his exceptional talent, too, he has done much to raise the aesthetic taste of a large part of the community here. He has already received from abroad well-deserved marks of esteem and gratitude, in the form of honourable distinctions. In view of all these services, we have wished to show our gratitude in some form, also to posterity, and thus we, Lord Mayor and Councillor, have unanimously and with one mind voted that said Herr Joseph Haydn, Doctor of Music &c., should herewith receive, at the instigation of the Economic Committee of the Citizens' Hospital here, the honorary freedom of this Imperial and Royal capital city; he is thus invested with the rights of a citizen of the city of Vienna, and his name shall be incorporated in the citizens' land-registry office.

In witness and in affirmation whereof we have prepared this diploma, given under our hands and privy seals this First Day of April, 1804

Joseph Georg Hörl

Imperial & Royal Court Councillor and Lord Mayor.

Stephan Edler von Wohlleben,

Imperial & Royal, and Magisterial Councillor; and Chancellor of the Exchequer.

¹Sc.: Oratorios.

[Haydn's answer to this document has not been preserved. That given erroneously in Pohl III, 225, is the answer to the letter conferring the Salvator Medal: see *supra*, p. 217].

[To GEORGE THOMSON, EDINBURGH. *Italian*]

[Vienna] 6th April 1804.

Most esteemed Sir,

I have the honour of sending you twelve songs, and also the other two which I received a little while ago, with the one hope that they shall give the same pleasure as the others; in a little while you shall also receive the remainder.

Meanwhile I commend myself to your friendship, and kiss the hands of your dear and gracious daughter for her charming letter. I am, with every esteem and veneration,

Your most sincere and most humble servant

Giuseppe Haydn [m.p] ria.

I shall make every effort to procure
that little portrait of myself.

[Thomson notes: "Haydn/ Vienna 6 Ap¹. 1804/ With 14 Welsh airs/ more harmonized / by him."]
[Address no longer extant]

[TO GEORGE THOMSON, EDINBURGH. *Italian*]
Vienna, 10th May 1804.

Most esteemed Sir!

At last I send you all the remaining Scottish Songs, the composition of which has cost me great effort, for I have been very ill for some time now; but nevertheless I hope that all of them will give at least some pleasure, though it's difficult for a man of seventy-three to be able to satisfy the world. Well, be that as it may, I have done my very best not to disappoint my dear friend. In a little while I shall send my portrait in two different forms, both simple, to your dear and beautiful daughter, whose hands I kiss. God preserve every one of you, I love and esteem you all, though I have not had the honour of your acquaintance. Farewell. I am, and will always be,

dearest Friend,

Your most humble, most sincere friend and servant,
Giuseppe Haydn [m.p] ria.

[Thomson notes: "Haydn/ Vienna 10 May 1804/ With 11 other Welsh / airs harmonized / by him—".]

[DRAFT OF A LETTER TO THE BANKERS HAMMERSLEY & CO., LONDON. *German*]
[Vienna, May 1804¹]

Monsieur!

Yesterday I received a letter, dated 12th April 1804, from my friend Salomon in London, with the pleasant news that you have received on my behalf seventy-two pounds Sterling, eleven shillings and sixpence from Doctor Burney. Thus I would ask you to have this money transferred to me at your earliest convenience through a safe banker; I should prefer it to go through the bankers Fries & Compag. If you should be a lover of music, I shall be happy to send you something brand new, either by a courier or with the mail-coach. Meanwhile I am

¹Haydn would have received the letter of 12th April about four weeks later, if not a little sooner. The draft of the letter to Burney shows us to whom the present letter was addressed.

[TO CHARLES BURNEY,[1] CHELSEA. *German*]

[Vienna, May 1804]

Contents.[2] A thousand thanks, my dearest Friend, for having taken the trouble to collect on my behalf seventy-two pounds Sterling 11 sh. and sixpence, and for having given this sum to the bankers Hammersley, through whom I shall receive it quite safely. God preserve you and your good family many years—I had just written them a word of greeting myself. I am and will ever remain your admirer and sincere friend

D[r]. H

[1] See previous letter.

[2] Haydn must have translated the letter into Italian, the language in which he corresponded with Dr. Burney.

[TO HAYDN FROM *Hofrat* JÁNOS KARNER, *German*]

To *Herr Kapellmeister* Haydn:

Well born, most esteemed *Herr Doctor* of Music and *Kapellmeister*!

I had sincerely entertained the hope that you, as director of, and presiding official over your people, would, in profound gratitude and thankfulness over the success of the musicians' petitions, personally proffer your note of thanks, as is meet and proper in such cases. But since, however, such a tone has been wanting in your previous correspondence with me, you will please have the goodness to instruct the subordinate personnel accordingly; I myself shall not fail in the future to bring to your attention such official lapses of conduct among the members of the band, and I shall send you from here the necessary copies of such correspondence for your information.

In this connection, I have had prepared a new list of the salaries and number of persons in the choir and band [*Kammermusik*], because there have been various increases in salary and changes during recent times; I have enclosed this document for your information and use. Taking it as a basis, you are kindly requested to submit a report to His Highness not only concerning the petition—returned again—of Anton Tomasini, but also concerning the two petitions, herewith enclosed, of the leader Louigi Tomasini and the trumpeter Sebastian Binder, which His Highness ordered me to forward to you. Meanwhile I have the honour, Sir, of remaining, with every respect and veneration,

Your most obedient servant,
Exp. Karner.

1804 [date on the file], [probably May.[2]]

[1] KARNER seems to have been Prince Esterházy's Economic Administrator, a position similar to that of Rahier (see the letters of 1765 *et seq.*).
[2] See next letter.

[TO PRINCE NICOLAUS II ESTERHÁZY. *German*]

[Vienna, May 1804][1]

My humble recommendation for the leader Luigi Tomasini will

certainly not meet with my magnanimous Prince's disapproval, if, in view of his merits in so many and varied fields, I personally ask Your Serene Highness to support his request in some manner.

My recommendation for his son Anton Tomasini, however, who only five months ago received an additional yearly allowance of 40 Fl. and lodging money, depends entirely on Your Highness' generosity.

I suggest that in your graciousness you grant to the trumpeter Sebastian Binder, and to the trumpeter Michael Altmann, the modest extra allowances [*Deputat*] they ask for.

Joseph Haydn [m.p] ria,
Kapellmeister.

[1]The draft of this letter, in the Sándor Wolf Museum at Eisenstadt, is on the same page as that to the bankers Hammersley & Co. (see *supra*), and thus Karner's letter to Haydn, and Haydn's answer, may be dated with some certainty in the month of May 1804.

[To the father of one of Haydn's pupils. *German*]

[Vienna, (?) Spring or Summer 1804[1]]

Sir,

I am very sorry that in this short time I have not been able to give more than 30 lessons to your son, whom people here have robbed of the hope that he might ever learn how to compose. He is a good boy, I love him, and he has enough talent to prove to those gentlemen that they are wrong, and to show the world quite the contrary. His conduct, as far as I have observed it, is exemplary, but I, too, wish that he would better study, first, thorough bass; 2ndly, the art of singing; and lastly the pianoforte; for I assure you, dearest Friend, that by application and effort he can become a distinguished man yet.[2]

[1]There is no date on this draft, which is written on a smallish octavo sheet. The handwriting is similar to that of the drafts of May 1804, and I think it possible that someone (Johann Elssler?) happened to save all of them at once from the waste-paper basket. The dating of "Spring or Summer 1804" is therefore entirely conjectural, but the handwriting is certainly that of this late period.
[2]At the top of the letter "mit Fleiss und Mühe" (by application and effort). In the bottom left-hand corner the words "Emanuel Bach", underlined and then crossed out (possibly an indication that the young man should study

Bach's *Versuch über die wahre Art das Clavier zu spielen*). In the bottom right-hand corner the word "Wienn" (Vienna), preceded by a wobbly letter "W".

[TO PRINCE NICOLAUS II ESTERHÁZY (?)[1]. *German*]
[Only the signature autograph]
Your Serene & Princely Highness!

I must recommend the bearer of this letter, Herr Thieriot from Leipzig, to Your Serene Highness as a most talented man, and one who could perform with success at the greatest courts. His especially beautiful execution, the full tone of his violin playing, his beautiful *cantabile* and his great technical prowess have delighted as much as they satisfied me.

He was in Paris for a time, where he studied, and at present he wishes a satisfactory position. Since his personal character is particularly exemplary, I have taken the liberty of recommending this young man to Your Serene Highness' grace and favour.

In boundless admiration and indebted esteem,

> Your Serene Highness'
> humble
> Joseph Haydn [m.p] ria.

Vienna, 21st June 1804.

[1]There is no address, and it is just possible that the letter is addressed to another prince. PAUL EMIL THIERIOT (Leipzig, 1780—Wiesbaden, 1831) was not engaged in the Esterházy orchestra.

[TO PRINCE NICOLAUS II ESTERHÁZY. *German*]
[Letter in Johann Elssler's hand, only signature autograph]
Inasmuch as the Colonel's wife, Frau Spiellmann,[1] has had the kindness to recommend to His Serene Highness that the suppliant Anton Tomasini[2] receive an additional allowance, I, too, dare to add my humble petition for him.

Vienna, 6th July 1804.   Joseph Haydn [m.p] ria.

Remarks on the outside of the file: "2nd Aug. 1804" and "Since, by decree of 16th July 1804, the suppliant is to receive immediately an annual supplementary fee of 150 fl. for [teaching] 3 boy chorister apprentices, this petition is at present placed *ad acta*."]

[1]"Frau Obristin" ("Obrist" = obs. for "Oberst", or "Colonel"); apparently the Colonel was in one of the Prince's regiments.
[2]Luigi's son: see *supra*, p. 204.

[TO HAYDN FROM WILLIAM GARDINER, LEICESTER. *English*]

To Joseph Haydn, Esq., Vienna.

Sir,—For the many hours of delight which your musical compositions have afforded me, I am emboldened (although a stranger) to beg your acceptance of the enclosed small present, wrought in my factory at Leicester. It is no more than six pairs of cotton stockings, in which is worked that immortal air 'God preserve the Emperor Francis', with a few other quotations from your great and original productions. Let not the sense I have of your genius be measured by the insignificance of the gift; but please to consider it as a mark of the great esteem I bear to him who has imparted so much pleasure and delight to the musical world.

I am, dear Sir, with profound respect, your most humble servant,

William Gardner.

Leicester, Aug. 10, 1804.

[1]WILLIAM GARDINER, who printed this letter in his *Music and Friends*, adds: "The war was raging at this time, and as Mr. Salomon had no reply, we concluded that it never arrived at its place of destination. . . ". In a footnote Gardiner says: "The subjects quoted and wrought on the stockings were the following:—'My mother bids me bind my hair' [English canzonetta]; the bass solo of 'The Leviathan' [from the *Creation*]; the andante of the surprise sinfonia [No. 94]; his sonata 'Consumatum est' [from the *Seven Words*]; and 'God preserve the Emperor'." Gardiner owned the Salomon–Monzani & Cimador edition of the London Symphonies (Hoboken Coll.), and also annotated the English edition of Stendhal's piracy of Carpani's Haydn biography; the English edition was published in London in 1817 " . . . With notes by the author of the Sacred Melodies" (*i.e.*, Gardiner).

[TO A LADY. *German*]

Vienna, 14th September 1804.

[*Contents:*] The letter accompanied a present for a lady, and ends "Leben Sie ewig wohl".

[TO JOHANN NEPOMUK HUMMEL,[1] EISENSTADT. *German*]

Vienna, 28th September 1804.

Dearest Hummel,

I terribly regret that I cannot have the pleasure of conducting my little work for the last time, but on the other hand I am convinced that everyone (WITHOUT EXCEPTION) will do everything in their power to support their old Papa, especially since the worthy Hummel will be their guide.

Your most sincere

Joseph Haydn [m.p] ria.

P. S. My compliments to everyone.

[Address, in Elssler's hand:] A Monsieur
            Monsieur Jean Nep: Hummel
            Maitre de la Musique tres Celebre.
            au Service de S: Alt: Monseigneur
            le Prince d'Esterhazi
                    a
                    Eisenstadt.

    Jos. Haydn.
        [Haydn's seal "JH"]

[1]Hummel, now *Kapellmeister*, was about to conduct a performance of the *Creation* in Eisenstadt, on 30 September (libretto "Gedruckt von J. L. Stotz, hochfürstl. Buchdrucker"). Concerning Hummel, see also p. 124.

[To Haydn from J. N. Hummel, Eisenstadt. *German*]
                            Eisenstadt, 8th October 1804.

Most beloved Papa!
    Since, like an obedient son, I count on the kindly indulgence of the great musical father, I have dared to dedicate the enclosed little piece[1] to you. I was not moved to do so by any desire to shine; but rather the strong feeling of gratitude, of respect and of sincere love which I bear for you—these were the moving factors. If you continue to honour me with your kindly trust and benevolence, then I shall feel entirely happy as
                            Your devoted son,
                            Joh. Nep. Hummel, m.p.

[1]*Sonata pour le Pianoforte*, Op. 13, in E flat (Tobias Haslinger, Vienna): Hummel's first published piano Sonata.

[To George Thomson, Edinburgh. *Italian*]
                            Vienna, 17th October 1804.

Most esteemed Sir,
    In your last letter of July, you paid me many compliments about my *Creation of the World*. I esteem myself most fortunate that God gave me these little talents wherewith I can give satisfaction to the amateurs of music, the more so, because—as a result of that Divine grace—I can benefit my neighbour and the poor: now I should like to know whether they have given my *Creation* in London for the benefit of the poor, or for the benefit of the Professional Concerts, and how much money they made. With those two pieces of music, *i.e.* the *Creation* and the *Four Seasons*, I have made, here in Vienna over a period of three years, forty-thousand florins for our poor widows of musicians. I would be most grateful if you could let me have an answer on this point sometime.

I now send you these thirteen songs with the same hope that they will give pleasure; I should like before I die to finish twenty-five, or at any rate a dozen of these songs, but only for you, dear friend, for I can no longer take on anything larger than this—my old age makes me steadily weaker.

In the hope of receiving a short reply, I am, with every esteem,

Your humble servant,

Joseph Haydn.

I kiss the hand of your dear daughter.

[To George Thomson, Edinburgh. *Italian*]

Vienna, 30th October 1804.

Most esteemed Sir,

I now send you the piece you wanted, which I received three days ago. On this occasion I must thank you cordially for the payment, *viz.* fifty gold ducats,[1] which I received from Messrs. Fries. I want to see whether I am capable of satisfying your dear daughter, and should like her to choose two or three of the last Scottish canzonets, according to her taste, and then to send me a few bars of the vocal parts, so that I can make variations or rondos from them. For the rest, I am, and will always be, Sir,

Your most devoted servant, Giu. Haydn.

Today I feel very weak, but I hope that God will give me more strength. I kiss the hands of your dear daughter.

When the fourth volume is finished, I beg you to send me a copy; I shall very happily bear the expenses. *Addio.*

[Address, in Elssler's hand:]

Mr George Thomson Esqr

Trustees Office

Edinburgh,

in Scotland.

WIEN   [Postal stamps, indicating date of arrival in
                             England: "Foreign Office No[v] 19 1804"
Joseph Haydn   and "AO N[ov] 19 804"]
Gumpendorf Kleine-
Steingasse N° 73.   [Haydn's seal "JH"] [Thomson notes: "30th
                             Oct 1804/ Dr Haydn/ With a single Air,/ w^t
                             an easier Accomp^t/ thanks for the last/ 50
                             ducats paid to/him for 13 add^l Airs."]

[1]Haydn sent a receipt, written in English (only the signature, place and date are autograph), and signed "Vienna the 11th of June . . . 1804 Doctor Haydn". British Museum, Add. 35263, fol. 238.

[TO AN UNKNOWN GENTLEMAN]
Vienna, 5th November 1804.
[No copy of the letter available: last known whereabouts, New York City, 1915: see Sources]

[TO HAYDN FROM MARIA FEODOROWNA,[1] EMPRESS DOWAGER OF RUSSIA, ST. PETERSBURG. *German*]
Herr Kapellmeister HAYDN:

The letter and composition which your pupil Neukomm brought me gave me much pleasure, and I remembered with joy that I had met you personally in Vienna. This, and the flattering description of me you gave to the bearer, moved me to have him play it for me at once; and I did not fail to recognize his teacher in him. I do thank you so much for the beautiful songs that you sent me, and I hope with my whole heart that you will continue to enjoy good health, and that, for many years to come, you will earn the admiration of all music lovers through your exceptional talent and your masterpieces—an admiration which you so richly deserve. I hope that the musical public will be able to enjoy one of your beautiful works soon again, and I beg you to regard the enclosed remembrance as a token of my sincere good wishes, with which I am, as always,

Your ever well-disposed[2]
Maria.

St. Petersburg,
15th February 1805.

[1]See also *supra*, p. 215. The present letter was accompanied by a beautiful ring. For Neukomm, see *supra*, p. 215. Haydn had sent the Empress Dowager his edition (Breitkopf & Härtel) of the part songs, to which reference has been made above (see p. 167).
[2]"Wohl affektionierte".

[TO HAYDN FROM L'INSTITUT NATIONAL, PARIS. *French*]
Institut　　　　National
Classe des Beaux arts.　　　　[Letter-head]
Paris, le 1. Messidor an 13 de la République française [20th June 1805]

The permanent Secretary of the section [letter-head] to Mr. Haydn, composer, associated member of the *Institut National*.
Monsieur,

L'institut national de France elected you associated member; from the moment of its formation, it has considered this a tribute which it was pleased to have rendered to your deserved celebrity. The changes which have since taken place within the Institute are such as to increase substantially your ties with it; a musical section has been created, and it consists of dignified gentlemen who are the appreciators of your genius.

As a non-resident member, you have, in the capacity of a consultant, a voice in the Institute, the right to attend its assemblies, to wear its uniform—in short, you are part of it. In this capacity, then, I send you the medal which constitutes your right to the title, and the book containing our by-laws and likewise the names of our members. You will find yours in the article dealing with the section on the fine-arts.

I would wish, *Monsieur*, that you would show sufficient interest in the fine-arts section of the *Institut de France* for it to benefit from your wise observations on the art which is your profession, and with which you have gained such glory in Europe. I can assure you that it would receive this mark of your confidence with profound esteem. As for my own person, I regard as one of the most precious advantages of the duties with which I am honoured, that of corresponding with you, and of being able frequently to assure you of my profound respect.

I have the honour to greet you,

Joachim Le Breton.
Perpetual Secretary of the fine-arts section of the *Institut national de France*, member of the *Classe d'histoire*, the *Littérature Ancienne*, and *Légion d'honneur*.

[To Haydn from Conservatoire de Musique, Paris. *French*]
[Letter-head:] *Paris, le* [ink: "*7. messidor*"] *an* [ink: "*13*"]
de la République française
26th June 1805.

Le Conservatoire de France to Haydn:

The members of the *Conservatoire de France*, filled with the most profound sentiments of esteem and veneration for the immortal talent of Haydn, have the most fervent desire to inscribe the name of this celebrated artist in the annals of this institution.

The expression of this wish, carried to the celebrated Haydn by Chérubini,[1] could not but be received kindly; the members of the *Conservatoire*, thus filled with confidence, have charged their colleague to deliver to this great man, whom they consider to be one of their fathers in the art of music, the plans of the monument which the *Conservatoire* hopes to see erected in its midst, and of which the model has been chosen to celebrate the happy date of the foundation of this establishment.

Should this legitimate tribute of admiration to one of the greatest geniuses who have illuminated the republic of the arts be accepted by Haydn, it would represent to the *Conservatoire de France* a trophy which it would honour forever.

In the name of the members of the
Conservatoire de France

Méhul Gossec Cherubini Sarrette.[2]

[1] Luigi Cherubini (1760–1842), the famous composer, who had long been an ardent admirer of Haydn's, came to Vienna to conduct various works, including his new opera, *Faniska*. He brought Haydn this diploma, and a

medal which the Conservatory had struck in his honour. Haydn gave him
the autograph of the "Drum Roll" Symphony (No. 103).
²The leading French composers ÉTIENNE NICOLAS MÉHUL (1763–1817),
FRANÇOIS JOSEPH GOSSEC (1734–1829), and BERNHARD SARRETTE (1765–
1858), founder and director of the Paris *Conservatoire*.

[EXTRACT OF HAYDN'S ANSWER TO THE PARIS *Conservatoire*. *French*]
[Vienna, Summer of 1805]
. . . . I beg you, *Messieurs*, to accept my thanks, and to convey
them to the members of the *Conservatoire*, in whose name you had
the kindness to write.

Please be sure to add that, as long as Haydn lives, he will carry in
his heart the memory of the interest and consideration which they
have shown him. . . .

[TO ARTARIA & CO., VIENNA. *Italian*]
Most esteemed *Signor* Artaria,

I hope that for these twelve pieces of music¹ the old Haydn shall
have merited a small reward. Your sincere friend and servant,
Dʳ Haydn [m.p] ria.
[Vienna] 17th August 1805²
[Address in Elssler's hand:]
[Haydn's seal "JH"]   A
Monsieur
Monsieur d Artaria
& Comp:

¹It is hard to imagine what these "twelve pieces of music" were: the most
likely explanation is that they were autographs, for Artaria later owned
many Haydn autographs of pieces which the firm had never published.
²The date added by another (Elssler's?) hand.

[TO ?]
6th November 1805
"Fragment": *no copy available*. Last known whereabouts: Max
Friedländer, Berlin, 1892 (see Sources).

[TO BONIFAZIO ASIOLI,¹ MILAN. *Italian*]
My dear Colleague,

I should like Carlo Mozart to have the honour of being numbered among your pupils. I should congratulate him on having such a teacher as you, whose works and talents I very much admire.

Permit me to recommend this young man to you, as the son of my late friend, and as the heir to a name precious to all connoisseurs and friends of the art. I am sure that Carlo Mozart will prove himself worthy of all the goodness and trouble with which you will favour him, in order to make of him a person who will be a credit to his teacher and to his father. I pray you to forgive me if I, burdened as I am with the infirmities of old age, limit myself here to expressing the honour of subscribing myself, with every esteem and consideration,

Signore,
Your most humble and obedient servant,
Giuseppe Haydn [m.p] ria.

Vienna, 23rd April 1806.

[1]Asioli (1769–1832), a well-known composer, was professor of counterpoint at the Milan *Conservatorio*. Karl Mozart, Wolfgang's second son (born in 1784), went to study with Asioli and took this letter of recommendation with him. See also Walter Hummel, *W. A. Mozarts Söhne*, Kassel 1956, p. 37.

[To Prince Nicolaus II Esterházy. *German*]
[Letter in Johann Elssler's hand, only signature and title autograph]
Your Highness,

My experience of Your Highness has been not only that of the kindest of princes, but you have also earned respect as a most energetic patron of all that is beautiful and useful; and thus I humbly support the suppliant Herr Rupp's[1] request that, in your graciousness, his son be allowed to join the boys' choir. I can recommend this the more easily since the father has served many years, with every mark of distinction, as a horn player in Your Highness' band. Therefore I have considered it my duty to add my most humble plea to his, in the confident hope of your granting a request from which he would derive such advantages.

Your Highness'
most humble
Joseph Haydn [m.p] ria,
Kapell Meister.

Vienna, 3rd May 1806.

[On the outside of the file is the following pencilled note: "1° to Hummel for his information. 2° to Haydn, that at present no vacancy, however the matter will be noted". See next letter.]

¹J. Martin Rupp had been engaged as a horn player in 1777.

[TO HAYDN FROM PRINCE NICOLAUS II ESTERHÁZY. *German*]
To *Kapellmeister* von Haydn:
    As pleasant as it would be, in view of your written application, to appoint the son of J. Martin Rupp, court chamber-musician and horn player, to the boys' choir, yet I must inform you that this cannot be, for there is no vacancy there at present; but I shall take note of the matter and, when the time comes, give it favourable consideration.
    This is to inform you how matters stand. I am, with all esteem,
                                            Your most willing,
                                            Exp: Esterházy.
Vienna, 5th May 1806.

[TO THE VIENNA CITY MAGISTRACY. *German*; ARCHIVE COPY]
                    Vienna, 25th November 1806.
Worthy Magistracy!
    The undersigned has the honour to make the following statement regarding my late brother Michael Haydn¹ of Salzburg: he raises no objection to the widow being deemed without further ado the principal recipient of the testator's estate; and also that he and his brother had but 2 sisters, both of whom are deceased, and who left the following children: from the deceased sister, Anna Rafler— Anna Maria Moser, seamstress at Esterhasz in Hungary; Elisabeth Böheim, seamstress at Rohrau in Lower Austria; Theresia Hamer, schoolmistress at Garrhaus in Hungary; Mathias Fröhlich, farrier in Fischament; and Anna Loder, cobbler-mistress in Vienna. Further: from the deceased sister Franziska, there is only one daughter, by the name of Anna Wimmer, restaurant-keeper at Nikola in Hungary.
                                            Joseph Haydn,
                                    Kapellmeister to Prince Esterházy
                                        and Dr. of Music.

¹Died on 10th August 1806.

[TO HAYDN FROM PRINCE NICOLAUS II ESTERHÁZY. *German*]
Dear *Kapellmeister* Haydn!
    My dear wife, the Princess Maria, told me of your wish to receive from me six-hundred Gulden annually, in addition to your regular emoluments; she added

that the realization of this would be a great source of comfort and consolation to you. It is with great pleasure that I hasten to use this opportunity to show my esteem and friendship for you, and inform you herewith of my guarantee that you shall receive the sum of three-hundred Gulden semi-annually from my Court Treasury Office, whom I shall inform of this under separate cover.[1]

I hope that you continue to enjoy good health, and am your most willing

Fürst Esterhazy.

Vienna, 26th November 1806.

[1]The order to the Treasury Office is preserved in Budapest (Esterházy Archives, Acta Musicalia XXX,2226), and reads as follows: "Since I have decided to grant an additional yearly salary of six hundred Gulden to my worthy *Kapellmeister* and Doctor of Art [*sic*] Joseph Haydn, my Court Treasury Office is herewith notified to tender this sum in semi-annual instalments as of the 27th of the previous month, November. Eisenstadt, 1st December 1806. Exp. Esterházy."

[To Prince Nicolaus II Esterházy. *German*]
[Beginning of December 1806]

Most Serene Prince
and Gracious Lord!

I cannot find the words to express how touched and pleased I was to receive from Your Highness the most gracious note [*Hand billet*] addressed to me, for it went to my heart; and I am equally unable to describe my most heartfelt thanks for this most gracious of acts, extended to an old and enfeebled servant. Your Highness has thereby given me once again the proof that Your Highness is accustomed to reward an artist generously even when, because of his advanced age and weakness, he is no longer able to fulfil his duties.

May the Almighty grant me just enough strength, before my end, to enable me to express in music the emotions which this undeserved act of special grace has awakened in me.

I remain ever your most devoted, submissive and most obedient servant,

Joseph Haydn,
Kapellmeister to Prince Esterházy.

[To F. S. Silverstolpe,[1] St. Petersburg. *French*]
[Only the signature autograph]
Vienna, 30 December 1806.

Monsieur,

You will forgive an old man of nearly 75 if he makes use of a hand

other than his own to thank you, *Monsieur,* for your kind remembrance of me, and for the good tea which you were good enough to
send me. I never forget my friends, and I remembered you, *Monsieur,* as soon as I had opened your letter. Since the time when we
first met, my life has become more monotonous: I struggle against
the infirmities of old age, and I dare not occupy myself with my ar
any longer, for fear of injuring my health. Thus there is nothing tha
gives me more pleasure than to retrace past times, and to hear, from
time to time, that there are people in this world still interested in me

Please be good enough, *Monsieur,* to give my kind regards to our
good Neukomm;[2] I most sincerely wish him all the success which his
talent and his character deserve. The caravan-borne tea which you
were good enough to send me is the kind I prefer to all others. You
have guessed my taste exactly, and I promise you that I shall never
drink a cup without gratefully recalling the source from which
received it.

I remain, *Monsieur,* &c.,
Joseph Haydn.

[1]Silverstolpe (see *supra,* p. 152) had meanwhile become *chargé d'affaires* at the
Swedish Embassy in St. Petersburg. He noted the expenses for "2 canisters
of caravan-borne tea, a present for Haydn in Vienna, 10 roubles" (see
Mörner, *op. cit.,* p. 406, n. 3). Haydn included his famous visiting card,
with the *incipit* "Hin ist alle meine Kraft, alt und schwach bin ich," in the
above letter.

[2]See *supra,* p. 215.

[To Haydn from Johann Georg Albrechtsberger,[1] Vienna. *Latin,*
"Tu" form]

[Sometime during the year 1806
Pieridum Frater! qui dudum noster Apollo diceris: hunc Canonem fecit, dedicat
que Tibi vetus et sincerus Amicus Georg Albrechtsberger.

1806.

[Ad] Josepho Haydn

Canone perpetuo a 4 Voci in hypodiapente, et hypodiapson L'istesso Canone
in hypodiatesseron ed hypodiapson.

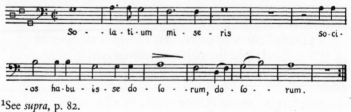

[1]See *supra,* p. 82.

[To Haydn from Sigismund Neukomm,[1] St. Petersburg. *German*]

St. Petersburg, 3 April 1807.
17

My dear Papa!

Yesterday I gave a concert here, the *affiche* of which I include. Your excellent choruses from *Tobia* were received with the great enthusiasm which I have always noticed, with deep satisfaction, is accorded to your unrivaled masterpieces whenever they are performed here. As No. 2 I chose the chorus, "Ah gran Dio! sol tu sei &c.",, as No. 4 "Odi le nostri voci &c." and as No. 6, "Svanisce in un momento" where, even at the end of the first part, they began to applaud with the utmost vigour. I conducted, and the excellent Court Chorus, combined with a selected band of large size, played with such affection that you certainly would have been completely satisfied with the performance, should we have had the good fortune to have had you with us.

I spared no costs to have my concert well cast, and thus I had expenses of more than 1100 roubles, but despite that, I made over 1200 roubles clear profit after deducting all expenses; and what increased my joy no end was that everyone went away from the hall satisfied.

I am writing you all this because I cannot show you my gratitude in any other way than to assure you that every stroke of good luck which will ever happen to me is only your doing.—You are my father and the creator of my luck.

How I envy Vienna for having the good fortune to have you within its walls! How often, dear Papa, I long to see you, even for an hour! Shouldn't this bliss soon be mine?

Let me know from time to time how you are, and no one will be happier than

Your grateful pupil,
Neukomm.

[1]See *supra*, p. 215.

[Haydn to Neukomm, St. Petersburg. *German*]

[? June] 1807.

[*Contents:*] Haydn congratulates Neukomm and encourages him in his work on the oratorio, *Tobia* [Neukomm was reorchestrating it, to bring it in line with "modern times"]. He relies on his pupil.

[Charavay's Catalogue of the Kafka Collection, Paris 1881 No. 32.]

[To Haydn from Société académique des enfans d'Appollon, Paris. *French*]

Paris, 30th December 1807.

Monsieur!

The French honour the immortal productions of your genius, because there are several things which you have composed for them. A grand concert in Paris does not seem to be complete unless one hears one or two of your symphonies.

Moreover, one may say, in all truth, that artists consider it a sacred duty to pay the utmost attention to their [the symphonies'] performance, fully assured of the taste and sensibility of the listeners, who always share their just enthusiasm.

Our Society has, among its members, your most zealous admirers. It enjoys a certain esteem. But it believes that this esteem would be better deserved, and the cult of Appollo more appropriately served, if it could be enriched by your companionship, and if it could inscribe your name in the list of its members.

Condescend, *Monsieur*, to accept this tribute! It would fain have the glory and the good fortune of your assent.

Please also accept with indulgence the attached copy of our statutes and by-laws, followed by a description of the Society, and likewise a gold medal, struck in the fashion of a voucher for attendance, which every member receives as a token of his right to attend each one of the sessions.

We have the honour to be, *Monsieur*, with every esteem, &c.

[For Haydn's answer, see 7th April, 1808]

[TO ANTONIO POLZELLI ON BEHALF OF THE ESTERHÁZY BAND,
EISENSTADT. *German, "Du" form*]
[Only the signature autograph]
Vienna, 20th March 1808.

My dear Son!

Your truly heart-warming remarks and those of all the members of the Princely Esterházy band, on the occasion of my name-day, moved me to tears. I thank you and all the others from the bottom of my heart, and ask you to tell all the members in my name that I regard them all as my dear children, and beg them to have patience and forbearance with their old, weak father; tell them that I am attached to them with a truly fatherly love, and that there is nothing I wish more than to have just sufficient strength so that I could enjoy once more the harmony of being at the side of these worthy men, who made the fulfilment of my duties so pleasant. Tell them that my heart will never forget them, and that it is the greatest honour for me, through the grace of my ILLUSTRIOUS PRINCE, to be placed at the head, not only of great artists, but of NOBLE AND THANKFUL HUMAN BEINGS.

Joseph Haydn [m.p.] ria.

[TO THE SOCIÉTÉ ACADÉMIQUE DES ENFANS D'APPOLLON, PARIS.
French]
[Only the signature autograph]
Vienna, 7th April 1808.

Messieurs,

The wish of the *Société académique des enfans d'Appollon* to inscribe my name on the list of its members is highly flattering to me, and I am most sensible of this honour. I assure them, through you, that they could not have thus honoured anyone more capable of appreciating their esteem, or of feeling the value of the honour conferred on me. I pray you, *Messieurs*, to allow my emotions to echo yours, and at the same time be the interpreters of my gratitude for the marks of distinction which you sent me—the copy of the statutes and by-laws, accompanied by a gold medal.

You, *Messieurs*, have strewn flowers on the path of life that yet remains for me to traverse. I am profoundly touched, and I feel keenly that though old age indeed numbs the faculties, it does not diminish my sensibility; for it is that which causes me to regret that my advanced age does not permit me to entertain the hope of ever being in your midst, of sharing in your labours, of cooperating in the cultivation of an art which constitutes the charm of society, or of participating in the celebrity which, because of its cherished and precious qualifications, the academy enjoys.

My infirmities force me to do without this comfort, and my regret is as lively as my gratitude is profound; pray receive this assurance, which is accompanied by the expression of my most sincere esteem. I have the honour to be, *Messieurs*, with profound respect,

Your most humble and most obedient servant,

Joseph Haydn [m.p.] ria.

[TO HAYDN FROM LUIGI CHERUBINI, PARIS. *Italian*]

Dearest and most esteemed Father. Forgive me for bothering you with my letter, but I have a favour to ask of you.

A merchant and music publisher in Paris has asked me to do a new edition of all your divine Quartets. Since the only way he can do this publication is by taking those [Quartets] found in various old editions, which are very incorrect, he has marked for me all the doubtful things which he thinks are incorrect in a little music copy-book, which please find enclosed. Now celebrated, and dear Father Haydn, please have the kindness to cast your eye over these fragments, in order to see if they are correct and conform to the originals, and if they are not, to correct the mistakes where you find it necessary to do so.

I do ask you to forgive me for taking this liberty, and for putting you to this trouble, and I beg you to consider the matter as soon as you can.

Now that I have got over the more disagreeable part of this letter, dear Father, I can add that I am unchanged, and still sick as a result of nervous attacks; and this has prevented me from working, and from trying to emulate you, OH! DEAR MASTER OF US ALL.

Here in Paris we heard with indescribable delight of the honours which were offered to you by the University of Vienna, on the day when they performed your immortal *Creation*.[1] I wept for joy at this news, and so much wanted to be there, in order to offer up my portion of incense, too.

Farewell, dearest Father, my wife embraces you tenderly. I do the same, and am, with respect and admiration,

Your affectionate son,
L. Cherubini.

Paris, 26th April 1808.
[Address:] Au très célébre [*sic*]

Joseph Haydn.
Die Kleine Steingasse
À VIENNE.

[1]The famous performance of the *Creation* which was given on 27th March 1808, and at which Haydn appeared in public for the last time.

[TO HAYDN FROM PHILHARMONIC SOCIETY OF ST. PETERSBURG. *German*]
Well born Sir,
Most esteemed *Herr Kapellmeister*,

The directors of the Philharmonic Society here hasten to fulfil a commission which they consider one of the most pleasant and most honourable of their lives. They are to deliver to the immortal composer of the most sublime music a token of the boundless admiration which inspires them, and every lover of music, upon the mention of the name Haydn; but this token is also one of gratitude, seldom better deserved and never proffered with more sincerety and emotion.

The Philharmonic Society owes its existence to the philanthropic zeal of a few admirers of music; they were fortunate enough to see even their most audacious hopes fulfilled more quickly and more beautifully than they could have dared hope. Thus an association came into being which has already been able to ensure an old age free of care to a by no means inconsiderable number of widows; and which, magnanimously supported by a philanthropically minded Imperial House and by a generous public, entertains the most optimistic hopes for the future.

And this wonderful success we owe to a masterpiece which is everywhere extolled; we owe it to—YOUR *Creation*! Please therefore, most honoured man, accept the enclosed medal of this Society as a token of our sincere and boundless gratitude. Receive it with the kindness which is characteristic of you, and of all great men, and bestow your good will and sympathy on an organization which you may regard as your own work; its beneficial effects will also call forth blessings on you in the serene evening of your life, devoted—as it was—to the joy of mankind. We sign, Sir, in the most heartfelt admiration,

Your most devoted servants,

Georg Johann Berwald. Epmatz. H. Czervenka. Dan. Gottlob Bachmann. Johann Gottfried Hartman.
St. Petersburg, 29th May 1808.[1]

[1]This letter was delivered by the Russian Ambassador in Vienna: see letter of 25th July 1808.

[To Haydn from Sigismund Neukomm, St. Petersburg. *German*]

St. Petersburg, 4 June 1808.
16

My dear Papa!

This is the last letter which I shall be writing to you from here; I leave the day after tomorrow, and hope to arrive in Vienna in September. I am making a very large detour, and will travel through a large part of Germany in a northerly -westerly- easterly direction. My trip to Germany will be of interest to me only because I shall be so delighted to see you again.

The Philharmonic Society in St. Petersburg has struck a medal in your honour, and sent it to you through the Russian Ambassador in Vienna. The directors of the Society wanted me to take it, but I refused, because I won't arrive in Vienna for three months, and because it is more dignified for you if it is presented by the Ambassador. The directors also asked me to tell you that the year 1802[1] is the year in which the Society was founded, and since your masterpiece, *The Creation*, which is admired by all, was the corner-stone of their building, the Society thought that this particular year, of such importance to them, could be thus best preserved for posterity. The medal wighs 42½ ducats.

Your diploma as honorary member of the Society has not yet been prepared.[2] Soon I shall be fortunate enough to see you again. Meanwhile farewell, my dear Papa, preserve your affection for me, which is the only thing which renders my lot an enviable one, and makes me one of the happiest inhabitants on this earth.

Always,
Your thankful son,
Neukomm.

[1]Engraved on the medal (it is reproduced in Griesinger, Appendix).
[2]Neukomm was not aware of the letter which the Society had already written.

[To Haydn from Prince Kurakin, Russian Ambassador at Vienna.
German]

Vienna, 25th July 1808.

The Philharmonic Society of St. Petersburg wishes to deliver the enclosed medal to the immortal Haydn, Doctor of Music, and Father of Harmony. It was with the greatest pleasure that I undertook to fulfil this task, which provided me with a happy opportunity to indicate my profound admiration and my boundless respect for the composer of the *Creation*, the *Seasons*, and so many other great works.

A. *Fürst* Kurakin.

[To the Philharmonic Society, St. Petersburg. *German*]
[Only the signature autograph]

Well born Gentlemen!

Most esteemed Directors of the Philharmonic Society!

It will be difficult for me to find words to express the profound

gratitude which your esteemed letter of 29th May, and the medal
sent with it, caused me to feel. Be assured that I am proud to know
that my works have been received with approbation also by the
inhabitants of your great and famous Imperial City, and that I attach
appropriate value to the testimonial with which your Society has
honoured me: a Society of connoisseurs and amateurs of the art to
which I have devoted my life. You have thus rejuvenated my waning
powers; and the realization that I have assisted—even if remotely—
in your efforts to comfort the unhappy and to dry the tears of the
widows and orphans, has provided me with many a happy hour in
my old age.

May an institution formed for such a worthy purpose continue in
ever increasing prosperity! May it succeed in developing talent, in
furthering the cultivation of musical art, and in encouraging men of
good will to further acts of charity!

With these sincere wishes, which I would ask you to communi-
cate to all the members of the Philharmonic Society, I remain,
worthy Gentlemen and Patrons,

Your grateful admirer,
Jos. Haydn.

Vienna, 28th July 1808.

[To Prince Nicolaus II Esterházy. German]
[Only the signature autograph]

Most Serene Highness,
Gracious Prince and Lord!

I humbly place myself at Your Serene Highness' feet for the
gracious approval of my request, whereby with the utmost kindness
you take over my yearly expenditures for the doctor and apothecary.
By this new act of generosity, Your Serene Highness has freed me
from a most pressing anxiety, and thus enabled me to await the end
of my earthly existence in peace and serenity. May Heaven grant my
zealous wish that Your Serene Highness live in everlasting well-
being and Your Gracious Highness' illustrious family in ever increasing prosperity! I remain ever your most devoted and

Your Serene Highness'
humble servant,
Joseph Haydn [m.p.] ria.

Vienna, 22nd December 1808.

THE LONDON NOTEBOOKS

[*German*]

HAYDN'S POCKET BOOK OF THE YEAR 1791 IN LONDON

Knitting needle[s], scissors and a little knife for Frau von Keess.
For Biswanger, spectacles for someone between 50 and 60 years
of age.
For Hamburger, nail-scissors and a larger pair.
A woman's watch chain.
For Frau von Gennzinger, various things.

FRAU VON KEES, the wife of Franz Bernhard: see *supra*, p. 94. Hamburger
was Haydn's landlord in Vienna: see *supra*, p. 120. Frau von Genzinger: see
Introduction.

[*English*]

Head of June, white Cornelian.	6 guinees
that other white red Cornelian	3½ guinees
6 Schirts – – – – –	8 —
12 deto – – – – –	12 —
watch from gold – – – –	30 —
the chen – – – – –	1 —

[*German*]

On 5th Nov.[1791] I was guest at a lunch given in honour of the
Lord Mayor. The new Lord Mayor and his wife ate at the first table
No. 1, then the Lord Chanceler and both the Scherifs, Duc de Lids
[Leeds], Minuster Pitt and the other judges of the first rank. At No. 2
I ate with Mr Silvester, the greatest lawyer and first Alderman of
London. In this room (which is called the geld Hall [Guild Hall]),
there were 16 tables besides others in adjoining rooms; in all nearly
1200 persons dined, all with the greatest pomp. The food was very

nice and well-cooked; many kinds of wine in abundance. The company sat down at 6 o'clock and arose at 8. The Lord Mayor was escorted according to rank before and also after dinner, and there were many ceremonies, a sword was carried in front of him, and a kind of golden crown, to the sound of trumpets, accompanied by a wind band. After dinner the distinguished company of [table] No. 1 retired to a separate room which had been chosen beforehand, to drink coffee and tea; we other guests, however, were taken to another adjoining room. At 9 o'clock No. 1 rose and went to a small room, at which point the ball began: in this room there is, *a parte*, an elevated place for the high *Nobless* where the Lord Mayor is seated on a throne together with his wife. Then the dancing begins according to rank, but only 1 couple, just as at Court on the King's Birthday, 6th January [*recte*: 4th June]. In this small room there are 4 tiers of raised benches on each side, where the fair sex mostly has the upper hand. Nothing but minuets are danced in this room; I couldn't stand it longer than a quarter of an hour; first, because the heat caused by so many people in such a small room was so great; and secondly, because of the wretched dance band, the entire orchestra consisting only of two violins and a violoncello. The minuets were more Polish than in our or the Italian manner. From there I went to another room, which was more like a subterranean cavern, and where the dance was English; the music was a little better, because there was a drum in the band which drowned the misery of the violins. I went on to the great hall, where we had eaten, and there the band was larger and more bearable. The dance was English, but only on the raised platform where the Lord Mayor and the first 4 numbers had dined; the other tables, however, were all occupied again by men who, as usual, drank enormously the whole night. The most curious thing, though, is that a part of the company went on dancing without hearing a single note of the music, for first at one table, then at another, some were yelling songs and some swilling it down and drinking toasts amid terrific roars of "Hurrey, H[urrey], H[urrey]" and waving of glasses. The hall and all the other rooms are illuminated with lamps which give out an unpleasant odour. It is remarkable that the Lord Major requires no knife at table, for a carver, who stands in front of him in the middle of the table, cuts up everything for him in advance.

Behind the Lord Mayor there is another man who, as is the custom, shouts out all the toasts as loudly as he can; after each shout come fanfares of trumpets and kettledrums. No toast was more

XXVII A page from a contemporary MS. copy of Haydn's String Quartets Op. XVII, with corrections and additions in the hand of W. A. Mozart. Discovered by Professor W. Senn in the Archives of the Heilig-Kreuz-Kirche, Augsburg (from Leopold Mozart's legacy).

Noyan wir gekündt. gekauft auß Musical=
nuß, Rhum, zucker. bond' u Martinique
aus west Indien francois gehörig.

my D: with this, you will receive the Soap,
I beg you a thousand Pardons for not Sending
it Sooner, I know you will have the goodness
to excuse me. — I hope to hear you are
quite well, and have Slept well _ I Shall be
happy to See you my D: as Soon as possible
I Shall be much obliged to you if you will
do me the favor to Send me twelve Tikets
for your Concert, may all Success atend you
my ever D: H: that Night, and always, is the
Sincere and hearty wish of your

James S: april 8th 792   Invariable and
                                truly affectionate

I am just return'd from from the Concert,
where I was very much charmed with
your delightful and enchanting Compositions. and your spirited and interesting
performance of them, accept ten
thousand thanks for the great

XXVIII Page from Haydn's Second London Notebook (1791–1792), showing a German
entry followed by Haydn's copies of letters sent to him by Rebecca Schroeter (Österreichische
Nationalbibliothek, Vienna).

applauded than that of Mr Pitt. But otherwise there is no order. This dinner cost £1600; half must be paid by the Lord Mayor, the other half by the two Sherifs. The Lord Mayor is newly elected every year. He wears, over his costume, a large black satin mantle, long and wide, in the shape of a domino cloak, richly ornamented in gold lace bands, especially round the arms. Round his neck we wears a large gold chain like that of our *Toison Order*; his wife has the same, she is Mylady and remains so. A new one is elected every year. The whole ceremony is worth seeing, especially the procession up the Tems [Thames] from Guildhall to Westmynster.

M^{tris} Schroeter. N° 6 James-Street Buchinghamgate [Buckingham Gate].

The national debt of England is estimated to be over two hundred millions. Recently it was calculated that if they had to make up a convoy to pay this sum in silver, the waggons, end on end, would reach from London to Yorck, that is, 200 miles, presuming that each waggon could not carry more than £6000.

Mr Hunter is the greatest and most famous surgeon in London. Leicester Square.

DR. JOHN HUNTER and his wife, Anne, became Haydn's friends. She wrote the words to some of his English songs. Shortly before Haydn left England in 1792, Dr. Hunter invited him to his house, and when he appeared, several strapping young men attempted to force Haydn into a chair, so that the famous surgeon could remove a polypus from his nose. Haydn kicked and struggled so violently that Dr. Hunter finally gave up the attempt, but (said Haydn later) "it seemed to me that he was sorry for me, for having refused him the great honour of experimenting with his talents on my person." (Dies, p. 124.)

N.B.: Mr Silvester, *valet de chambre* of the Duchess of York.

In France the girls are virtuous and the wives are whores; in Holland the girls are whores and the wives are virtuous: in England they stay proper all their lives.

que l'amitié Soit aussi Solide.   Sell Rak [?]
                          [*English*]
N.B. Lady Blake from Langham
                          [*German*]
On 3rd June 1792, I dined with *Mon*^r and M[a]^d Mara, Mr Kely
and M^dam Storace at her brother's Storace. *Sapienti pauca.*

"MARA", as she was called, was the brilliant dramatic soprano who en-
chanted London with her rich and powerful voice, which extended from
low g to e'''. Born Gertrud Elisabeth Schmeling in 1749, her career surpassed the wildest fiction. In 1773 she married the 'cellist Mara, whom she
divorced in 1799: the marriage was a farce even in the early 1790's (see
infra, p. 288. "Kely" = MICHAEL KELLY, the Irish tenor who, together with
NANCY STORACE, had sung in the first production of Mozart's *Figaro*. STEPHEN
STORACE was a well-known composer of English ballad operas.

On 30th [*recte*: 31st] May 1792, the grand Widows' Concert,
which was given for the last time a year ago in Westminster Abbey
with 885 persons, took place in St. Margaret's Church, because of
the great expense involved. There were 800 persons at the rehearsal
and 2000 at the actual performance. The King gave 100 guineas each
time.

Benefit Concert for the Royal Society of Musicians; the programme was
devoted to Handel's music.

Hastings' [Warren Hastings] trial which took place last week on
25th May 1792 was the ninety-second meeting in Westminster Hall.
Hasting [*sic*] has 3 advocates all to himself. Each of them gets 10
guinees on the day of the meeting. This trial began 4 years ago. It is
said that Hasting [*sic*] has a fortune of a million pounds Sterling.

On 15th June [1792] I went from Windsor to [blank = Slough]
to Doctor Hershel [Herschel], where I saw the great telescope. It is
40 feet long and 5 feet in diameter. The machinery is very big, but
so ingenious that a single man can put it in motion with the greatest
ease. There are also 2 smaller [telescopes], of which one is 22 feet
long and magnifies 6000 times. The King had 2 made for himself,
each of which measures 12 feet. He paid him 1000 guineas for them.
In his younger days Dr Hershel was in the Prussian service as an

oboe player. During the seven-years' war he deserted with his brother and went to England, where he supported himself as a musician for many years: he became an organist at Bath, but gradually turned more to astronomy. After having provided himself with the necessary instruments, he left Bath, rented a room near Windsor, and studied day and night. His landlady was a widow, fell in love with him, married him, and gave him a dowry of £100,000. Besides this he has a yearly pension for life of £500 from the King, and his wife, at the age of 45, presented him with a son this year, 1792. Ten years ago he had his sister come, and she is of the greatest assistance to him in his observations. Sometimes he sits for 5 or 6 hours under the open sky in the bitterest cold weather.

Today, 14th January 1792, the life of Madam Bilingthon [Billington] was published in print. Her life is exposed in the most shameless detail. The publisher is said to have gotten hold of her own letters, and to have offered to return them to her for 10 guineas; otherwise he intended to print them publicly. But she didn't want to spend the 10 guineas, and demanded her letters through the courts; she was refused, whereupon she appealed, but in vain; for even though her opponent offered her £500, he nevertheless issued this treasure of hers today, and you couldn't get a single copy after 3 o'clock in the afternoon.

It is said that her character is the worst sort, but that she is a great genius, and all the women hate her because she is so beautiful. N.B. She is said, however, to have written the most scandalous letters, containing accounts of her amours, to her mother. She is said to be an illegitimate child, and it's even believed that her own supposed father is involved in this affair.

Such stories are common in London. The husband provides opportunities for his wife so that he can profit from it, whereby he relieves his "brother-in-law" of £1000 Sterling and more.

ELISABETH BILLINGTON, *née* WEICHSEL (*c.* 1768–1818), was the most famous English soprano of her age. Haydn gave her his *Terzetto* for 2 sopranos, tenor, obbligato *cor anglais*, bassoon and French horn, with orchestra, "Pietà di me, benigni Dei" (see Landon, p. 861).

On 14th June [1792] I went to Windsor and from there 8 miles to Ascot Heath to see the races. These horse races are run on a large field, especially prepared for them, and on this field is a large circular track 2 English miles long and 6 fathoms wide. It is all very smooth and even, and the whole field has a gentle upward slope. At the summit the circle stops curving and becomes a straight line about 2000 paces long; along this straight line, stalls of various sizes, or rather an ampitheatre, have been erected, some of which hold 2 to 3 hundred persons. The others are smaller. In the middle there is one for the Prince of Wales and high personages. The places in these stalls cost from 1 to 42 shillings per person. Opposite the Prince of Wales' stall is erected a high platform with a bell over it, on which platform stand several persons who have been specially chosen and sworn, and they give the first signal with the bell for the performers to line up in front of the platform. When they are ready, the bell is rung a second time, and at the first stroke they ride off at once. Whoever is the first to traverse the circle of 2 miles and return to the platform from which they started, receives the prize. In the first Heeth [heat] there were 3 riders, and they had to go round the circle twice without stopping. They did this double course in 5 minutes. No stranger will believe this unless they have seen it themselves. The 2nd time there were seven riders; when they were in the middle of the circle, all 7 were in the same line, but as soon as they came nearer some fell behind, but never more than about [originally "20"] 10 paces; and just when you think that one of them is rather near the goal, and people make large bets on him at this moment, another rushes past him at very close quarters and with unbelievable force reaches the winning place. The riders are very lightly clad in silk, and each one has a different colour, so that you can recognize him more easily; no boots, a little cap on his head, they are all as lean as a greyhound and lean as their horses. Each one is weighed in, and a certain weight is allowed him, in proportion to the strength of the horse, and if the rider is too light he must put on heavier clothes, or they hang some lead on him. The horses are of the finest possible breed, light, with very thin feet, the hair of their neck tied into braids, the hoofs very delicate. As soon as they hear the sound of the bell, they dash off at once with the greatest force. Every leap of the horses is 22 feet long. These horses are very expensive. The Prince of Wales paid £8000 for one some years ago, and sold it again for £6000; but he won £50,000 with it the first time. Among other things a single large stall is erected, wherein the Englishmen place their bets. The King has his own stall at one side. I saw 5 heats on the first day, and despite a heavy rain there were 2000 vehicles, all full of people, and 3 times as many common people on foot. Besides this, there are all sorts of other things—puppet-plays, hawkers [*Ciarlatony*], horror plays [*Grusl Possen*]—which go on during the races; many tents with refreshments, all kinds of wine and beer, and many Io-players (in English it is written Eo), a game which is forbidden in London. This horse racing went on 5 days in succession. I was there on the 2nd day; the beginning was at 2 o'clock and it went on till 5, the 3rd day till half-past 6, though there were but 3 Heaths, because it happened twice that 3 riders came in first together, and thus they had to race four times to decide the winner.

If anybody steals £2 he is hanged; but if I trust anybody with £2000, and he carries it off to the devil, he is acquitted. Murder and forgery cannot be pardoned; last year a clergyman was hanged for the latter, even though the King himself did all he could for him.

The City of London consumes 8 times one hundred thousand cartloads of coal each year; each cart holds 13 sacks, each sack holds 2 dry measures [= 3.44 litre]: most of the coal comes from Newcastle. Often 200 loaded ships arrive at once. A cartload costs £2½. [The following sentence was added later, in another ink:] In the year 1795, the coal-measure [*Malten*] or dry-measure £7. Within the last 30 years, 38,000 houses were built.

If a woman murders her husband, she is burned alive, whereas the husband, on the contrary, is hanged.

The punishment of a murderer is increased, when sentence is passed on him, by the fact that his body is dissected after his death.

On 14th January 1792, the Pantheon Theatre burned down 2 hours after midnight.

On 21st [*recte*: 22nd] May [1792], Giardini's concert took place in Renalag [Ranelagh Gardens]. He played like a pig.

FELICE GIARDINI (1716–1796), a famous violinist and composer, had once been the darling of London musical Society. He had left London in 1784 and gone to Naples, where he had lived at the house of Sir William Hamilton. He returned to England some five years later, but never attained his former position. The concert Haydn attended was a benefit performance of Giardini's oratorio *Ruth*; Giardini, then 76 years of age, was a pathetic figure, whose violin playing was, of course, but a ghost of its former self. Haydn had wanted to meet Giardini, and "a Lord" (could it have been Lord Abingdon?) took Haydn with him one day to meet the old man. A servant let them into the antechamber, and while they were waiting they heard the loud voice of Giardini, through an open door, saying: "I don't want to meet the German dog." The Lord was horrified, but Haydn, reporting the story to Dies, found it only amusing; whenever Giardini's name was mentioned, after this occurrence, Haydn always "had to laugh" (Dies, pp. 105*f.*)

On 12th June [1792] Mara gave her benefit concert in the great Haymarket Theatre; they gave *Dido*, the music by Sarti. N.B.: Only the terzet, a few recitatives and a little aria were by Sarti, the rest was by 6 different other composers. The 1ma *Don[n]a* sang an old aria by Sacchini, *Son Regina etc.*

GIUSEPPE SARTI (1729–1802) and ANTONIO MARIA GASPARO SACCHINI (1734–1786) were leading operatic composers of their day. Haydn had performed operas by both in the Court Theatre at Esterháza.

Once, when an Archbishop of London asked Parliament to silence a learned public preacher of the Moravian religion, the Vice President answered that it could be easily done; just make him a Bishop, and he will remain silent the rest of his life.

Every canal-lock costs £10,000.

In Oxford Street I saw St. Peter engraved in copper; he was clad as a secular priest [*Weltbriester*] with outstretched arms. The glory of heaven shines on his right side, and on his left you see the devil, whispering in his ear, and with a wind-mill on his head.

On 1st June 1792 Mara gave her benefit concert. They played two of my Symphonies, and I accompanied her, all by myself at the pianoforte, in a very difficult English Aria by Purcell. The audience was very small.

Salomon was the leader, and Haydn "presided" at the harpsichord (pianoforte). Purcell's Song was "From rosy bower". See Landon, p. 501.

In the month of January 1792, a roasting chicken cost 7 shillings, a turkey 9 shillings, a dozen larks 1 crown. N.B.: a duck, if it is plucked, costs 5 shillings.

On 3rd June, that being the eve of the King's birthday, all the bells in London are rung from 8 o'clock in the evening to 9 o'clock, and so also in honour of the Queen.

On 8th Feb. 1792, the first Ancient Concert took place.
    [Space left for the programme, not filled in]

On 13th Feb. The Professional Concerts began.
    [Space left for the programme, not filled in]

On the 17th [Feb.] Salomon's Concert.
    [Space left for the programme, not filled in]

For the programmes of the Professional and Salomon's concerts, see Landon, pp. 472f.

ANECTOD: Just as the director of a grand concert was about to begin the first number, the kettledrummer called loudly to him and said he should wait a moment, since his 2 kettledrums were not yet tuned. The leader could and would not wait any longer, and said he should transpose in the meantime.

The little story of an errand boy who ate cow dung [*fessa*] [not filled in].

J.H.–T

When Mr Fox was seeking votes to elect him to Parliament, a citizen said he would give him a rope instead of a vote. Fox answered that he could not rob him of a family heirloom.

Duchess of Devonchire [*sic*], his protector. Anecdote about the foot under her petticoat.

N.B. from *Wurmland*:
Quoties cum stercore certo
vico nel vincor semper ego maculor.

Ex nihilo nihil fit.

Domine, praxis est multiplex, qui n'intellegit est simplex.

Stella a stella differt claritate, non eadem lux omnibus. Herr! Es ist nicht alles licht was lichtet [Lord! All is not light that lightens.].

Interesse toto mundo
Sin fronte colitur,
Sine satis, sine fundo,
Interque quaeritur.

Mel in ore, verba lactis.
Fel in corde, fraus in factis.
[Plautus, *Truculentus* 178]

Supernumerarius, das Fünfte Rad in Wagen [the fifth wheel of a waggon].

Mens, ratio, et consilium in senibus est.

Si nisi non esset, perfectus quilibet esset.

Raro sunt visi, qui carûere nisi.

8 days before Pentecost I heard 4,000 charity children in St. Paul's Church sing the song noted below. One performer indicated the tempo. No music ever moved me so deeply in my whole life as this devotional and innocent

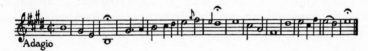

Adagio

N.B.: All the children are newly clad, and enter in procession. The organist first played the melody very nicely and simply, and then they all began to sing at once.

The chant was by JOHN JONES (1728–1796), organist at St. Paul's. The piece is actually written in D major (interested readers can find it in Pohl, H. in L., p. 214), which suggests that the organ at St. Paul's was pitched a note higher. Haydn's notation of bars 6 and 7 also differs from the printed version.

In the year 1791, 22 thousand persons died in London.

Lokhart [Lockhart], blind organist.

> Io vi mando questo foglio
> Dalle lagrime rigato,
> Sotto scritto dal cordoglio
> Dai pensieri siggillato
> Testimento del mio amore
> [Io] vi mando questo core.

On 13th February 1792, the first Professional Concert took place. [Space left for the programme, not filled in]

On 17th [February] Salomon's Concert.
[Space left for the programme, not filled in]

On 20th May 1792, there was a thunderstorm in the evening. An unusual thing in London.

An apprentice generally works the whole year round from 6 o'clock in the morning to 6 o'clock in the evening, and during this time he has not more than an hour and a half free time at his disposal. He gets a guinea a week, from which he must also feed himself. Many are paid by the piece, but every quarter of an hour of absence is docked.

Only the blacksmith's apprentices have to work an hour a day longer.

Today, 4th June 1792, I was in Vauxhall where the King's birthday is celebrated. Over 30,000 lamps were burning, but because of the severe cold there were very few people present. The grounds and its variety are perhaps unique in the world. There are 155 little dining booths in various places, most charmingly situated, each comfortably seating 6 persons. There are very large alleys of trees, which form a wonderful roof above, and are magnificently illuminated. Tea, coffee and milk with almonds [*Mandlmilch*] all cost nothing. The entrance fee is half a crown per person. The music is fairly good. A stone statue of Handel has been erected. On the 2nd inst. there was a masked ball, and on this evening they took in 3000 guineas.

Handel's statue, by Louis François Roubiliac, had been made in 1738. It is now in Novello's publishing house. See O. E. Deutsch, *Handel, A Documentary Biography*, London 1955, p. 456.

Singers, male and female, in London		*Composers*
Mara	Bacchierotti. Kelly	Baumgarten
Storace	Davide	Clementi
Billington	Albertarelli	Dussok—Dusseck
Cassentini	Dorelli	Girowetz

Lops NB   Lazarini, in the   Choris
                        Pantheon
Negri   Mazzanti   Chelsea Burney Dr
                                     College
Celestini   Morelli   Hülmandel
Choris   Calcagni   Graff
Benda   CROUTSCH   Diettenhoffer
Mrs Barthelemon   Harrison   Storace
   and her daughter
                   Simoni   Arnold
Schinotti
                   Miss Pool   Barthelemon

┌──┐
│ Maffei, bella, ma poco musica   │   Schield★
│ [pretty, but not very musical]   │
└──┘

Capelletti
                   Miss Barck   Carter★
Davis, detta Inglesina, la
quale Recitava a Napoli   Cramer
quando l'aveva 13ti anni[;]
ella è adesso vecchietta ma   Tomich
ha una buona Scola [called the
English girl, who at the age   ┌─────────────────────────┐
of 13 sang at Naples; she is   │ Frike Nro: 24   │
rather old now, but has a   │ BLANFORD STREET   │
good technique]   │ MANCHESTER SQUARE   │
                   Mtris Bland   └─────────────────────────┘
MAD: SECONDA *passabile*
Poet Badini   Callcot Scholar

                                    ┌─────────────────────────┐
                                  M │ la Trobe—dedicated   │
                                  o │ his piano Sonatas to   │
                                  r │ me   │
                                  a └─────────────────────────┘
                                  v
                                  i   Mazingi—at the
                                  a   pianoforte in the Pan-
                                  n   theon
                                      Friderici

                                    ┌─────────────────────────┐
                                    │ Burney   │
                                    │ Upper Titchfield   │
                                    │ Street   │
                                    └─────────────────────────┘

Singers: MARA (see p. 254); STORACE (see p. 254); BILLINGTON (see p. 255).

ANNA CASENTINI, who married Luigi Borghi (violinist and manager of the Italian Opera in London). LOPS (see p. 114). CRISTINA NEGRI, Luigia Polzelli's sister (see p. 116). CELESTINI: ? Choris = the soprano SOPHIA CORRI (later Mrs. Dussek). BENDA: ? MRS. BARTHÉLEMON, wife of the violinist and composer F. H. Barthélemon (1741–1808). Haydn became an intimate friend of the family. Their daughter was CECILIA MARIA (later *Mrs. Henslow[e]*). SCHINOTTI: ? MAFFEI, a soprano in Gallini's opera company. THERESA POGGI CAPPELLETTI, soprano in Gallini's opera company, who also sang in the Haydn–Salomon concerts. CECILIA DAVIES (*c.* 1750–1836), a relative of Benjamin Franklin, had toured the Continent with her parents and sister (MARIANNE, the celebrated player of the glass harmonica) from 1768 to 1773 (O. E. Deutsch, 'Neues von der Glasharmonika', *Oesterreichische Musikzeitschrift* IX [1954], Heft 12, pp. 380ff.). Seconda is probably MRS. SECOND from Bath, who sang in at least one concert in which Haydn participated (New Musical Fund Concert, 20th April 1795: see Landon, p. 544); she later sang in the first performance of Haydn's *Creation* in London (Pohl, H. in L., p. 316). BADINI (see p. 114). Bacchierotti = GAETANO PACCHIEROTTI, the castrato who scored such a success with Haydn's Cantata *Arianna* (Pohl, H. in L., p. 119; Landon, p. 443). KELLY (see p. 254). Davidde (DAVID: see p. 114). FRANCESCO ALBERTARELLI, who had been Mozart's Don Giovanni in the Vienna performance of 1788, was a member of Gallini's opera company and sang in the Haydn–Salomon concerts. DORELLI was a male singer in Gallini's company. LAZZARINI was a tenor who, apart from singing at the Pantheon, also sang in the Professional Concerts of 1792. FERDINANDO MAZZANTI. GIOVANNI MORELLI, member of the Italian Opera, had an exceptional bass voice; he sang in a Haydn Duet ('Quel tuo visetto amabile') at the composer's benefit concert of 1795. Croutsch = ANNE MARY CROUCH, whose recitative was said to equal that of Mara's. SAMUEL HARRISON, tenor. SIMONI was a tenor whom Salomon engaged in 1792; he had previously sung at the *Théâtre de Monsieur* in Paris (Landon, p. 492). CAROLINE POOL sang at the Haydn–Salomon concerts, and Haydn wrote an aria for her. Miss Barck = the MISTRESS PARK mentioned in one of Haydn's letters (see p. 144). MISTRESS BLAND was born Maria Romani and married George Bland. *Composers*: CARL FRIEDRICH BAUMGARTEN (*c.* 1740–1824). CLEMENTI (see p. 42). DUSSEK (see p. 131). ADALBERT GYROWETZ (1763–1850), who was engaged by the Haydn–Salomon concerts in 1791 and 1792. Choris = DOMENICO CORRI, the father of the Miss Corri mentioned under the singers. CHARLES BURNEY (see also *supra.* p. 145). NICHOLAS JOSEPH HÜLLMANDEL (Strasbourg, 1771—London, 1823). FRIEDRICH HARTMANN GRAFF (1727–1795), *Kapellmeister* at Augsburg, had received the honorary degree of D.Mus. from Oxford in 1789. DIETTEN-HOFER (see p. 119). STEPHEN STORACE (see p. 254). SAMUEL ARNOLD (1740–1802), organist at Westminster Abbey; see also *infra*, pp. 289f. F. H. BARTHÉLEMON: see *supra*, under singers. WILLIAM SHIELD (1748–1829): see also *infra*, p. 274 THOMAS CARTER (*c.* 1735–1804). J. B. CRAMER (1771–1858), son of Wilhelm, the leader of the Professional Concerts. FRANCESCO TOMICH, who later arranged many of Haydn's Symphonies for piano. PHILIPP JOSEPH FRIKE (or FRICK, as it was anglicized) (Würzburg, 1740—London, 1798). JOHN W. CALLCOTT (1766–1821), one of Haydn's pupils in composition. Rev. Christian I. Latrobe (1758–1836), whose *Three Sonatas for the piano forte* Op. III (J. Bland) were dedicated to Haydn. Joseph Mazzinghi (1765–1839). Burney's name is repeated here, probably because of the address in town.

Pianists	*Violinists*	*Violoncellists*	*Doctors*
Clementi	Salomon	Grosdill	Burney
Duschek	Giornovich	Menel	Hess in Oxford
Girowetz	Cramer	Mara	Arnold
Diettenhofer	Clement *petit*	Sperati	
Burney	Barthelemon	Schramb	Dupuis a great organist
Mis Burney	Schield		
Hüllmandel	Hindmarsh, Eng.	*Oboists*	
Graff, also	Scheener, Germ.	Fischer	
flautist	Raimondi, Ital.	Harrington	
Miss Barthe-	‖ Serra, from the	Lolli and his son came	
lemon	‖ Marquis Durazzo	from Stockholm.	
Cramer	Borghi		
Miss Janson	Gionovichi		
Humel from	Felix Janievicz		
Vienna	Jarowez		
Mrs Jansen	Giardini		
Lenz, still very			
young			

Clementi, Dussek, Gyrowetz, Diettenhofer and Burney: see previous note on composers. Miss Burney was his daughter, Esther (Hetty). Hüllmandel, see previous note on composers. J. G. Graeff (not to be confused with F. H. Graff, listed under composers) was a flautist who played in the Haydn-Salomon concerts of 1791–1792. Miss Barthélemon and J. B. Cramer: see previous note on composers. J. N. Hummel: see *supra*, p. 124. Therese Jansen was the pianist for whom Haydn wrote his last three pianoforte Sonatas (Nos. 50–52, London 1794). On 16th May 1795, she married Gaetano Bartolozzi, at which ceremony Haydn was a witness (W. Oliver Strunk, 'Notes on a Haydn Autograph', *Musical Quarterly* XX [1934] No. 2, pp. 192*ff*.). Lenz:? *Violinists*: Johann Peter Salomon, Haydn's impresario. Giovanni Mane Giornovichj (Jarnowik) (1745–1804). Wilhelm Cramer: see previous note on composers. Franz Clement 1780–1842), for whom Beethoven wrote his violin Concerto in D. Hindmarsh was violinist and viola player in Haydn's concerts; his wife was a singer. Scheener: appeared for the first time in London (spelt "Schenner") in 1781. Ignazio Raimondi (1733–1813) was also a composer: Haydn heard his 'Battle Symphony' in London (Landon, p. 471). Serra:? Luigi Borghi was also a composer. Felix Janiewiecz (1762–1848), famous violinist and composer. JAROWEZ:? Giardini: see *supra*, p. 257. *Violoncellists*: JOHN CROSDILL [*recte*] (1751–1825). MENEL first appeared as a 'cellist in London in 1789, SPERATI two years earlier. JOHANN MARA was the husband of the famous soprano (see *supra*, p. 254). Schramb: CHRISTOPHER SHRAM, who first played in London in 1792. *Doctors*: Charles Burney (see *supra, passim*). Hess: Dr. PHILIP HAYES (1738–1797), Professor of Music at Oxford University. THOMAS SAUNDERS DUPUIS (1733–1796), organist at the Royal Chapel. Sir George Smart, at the age of 90 (1866) told Pohl that he had once observed Haydn, listening with all his attention to Dupuis, as he played in the St. James Chapel; and when Dupuis left, Haydn fell on his neck and kissed him. "One man kissing another!" said Smart, who had never seen such a thing and was much shocked by it. (Pohl, H. in L., p. 203n.). *Oboists*: J. C. FISCHER (1733–1800), also a composer. HARRINGTON played at many of Haydn's concerts. ANTONIO LOLLI (*c.* 1730[1740?]–1802), well known both as a composer and as a violinist.

Krumpholz, l'Arpa. Mr Blumb imitated a parrot and accompanied himself admirably on the pianoforte.

Mrs de la Valle, a pupil of Krumpholz: plays rather less well than Madam Krumpholz. Also plays the piano. Her sister-in-law plays the violin very nicely.

MADAME KRUMPHOLTZ (*née* Meyer from Metz) married J. B. Krumpholtz, who had been in the Esterházy band from 1773–1776 and had studied composition with Haydn. His wife left him in 1788, and he committed suicide in Paris two years later. MADAME DELAVALLE (Delaval) played at the first Haydn-Salomon Concert of 1792.

M^r. Antis, Bishop and a minor composer.

Nicolai, *valet de chambre* of the King and a composer.

Hartman, flautist, had to leave England because of poverty, lost his wife by death, and ended up as a ne'er do well.

On 31st Dec. [1791] I was with Pleyel in the Pantheon Theatre. They gave *La Pastorella Nobile* by Guglielmi. Mad. Cassentini played the leading rôle and Laza[rini] the *primo huomo*; the thin Calvesi had *l'ultima parte*. The opera did not please. Neither did the ballet, even though the great Hillisburg danced.

Ignaz Pleyel, whom the rival Professional Concerts had engaged (see p. 127). For Anna Casentini and the tenor Lazzarini, see previous list of singers. Calvesi was possibly the tenor who had sung for many years at the Vienna Court Opera: in Haydn's absence he had sung once at Esterháza (Weigl's *Venere e Adonis*, 3rd August 1791: see Pohl II, 242), MADAME HILLIGSBERG [*recte*] was *prima ballerina*.

Ambassador, Count Stadion.
    Prince de Castelcicala of Naples.
    Marquis del Campo of Spain.
    My friend, you think I love you! In truth, you are not mistaken.

In solitude, too, there are divinely beautiful duties, and to perform them in quiet is more than wealth.

> Begehre nicht ein glück zu gross
> Und nicht ein weib zu schön,
> Der Himmel möchte dir di[e]s Loos
> Im zorne zugestehn.

(Do not desire too great happiness or too beautiful a wife: Heaven might, in anger, grant your wish!)

Wer mit Vernunft betracht' den wechsel aller Sachen,
Den kan kein glück nicht froh, kein unglück traurig machen.

(He who wisely observes how all things change cannot be made happy by good fortune or unhappy by bad.)

> INTRA IN GAUDIUM.
> HABEO, ET NON HABEOR.
> RESURGAM.
> IN COELO QUIES.

Chi ben commincia, ha la metà dell'opera, ne si commincia ben, se in dal cielo!

Gott im Herzen, ein gut weibchen in arm,
Jenes macht seelig, dieses gewiss—warm.

Mit eben einer wärme der ächten freundschaft empfilt sich zu beständigen angedenken [2. Version: "so viel zum angedenken Ihres"].

Kenne gott, die welt, und dich, liebster Freund, und denk an mich.

God in one's heart, a good wife on one's arm,
The one brings salvation, the second is—warm.

With just such a warmth of genuine friendship, I commend myself to your thoughts always [second version: "I commend myself this much to your thoughts, Your"]. [The text of the canon, which Haydn liked to present to his friends, might be translated: "Know God, the world, and thyself, dearest friend, and think of me."]

During the last 31 years, 38,000 houses were built in London.

M^r. Ott, and Guttenbrun.

Painters. A.M. Ott painted Haydn's portrait, which was then engraved by Bartolozzi; it appeared in 1791. J. A. GUTTENBRUNN's portrait belonged to Frau Haydn, and is now in possession of the von Karajan family in Graz; it was engraved by L. SCHIAVONETTI in 1792. Haydn thought it better than most of the others done in London, but was not satisfied with any except the profile by George Dance (Pohl III, 140, 153*ff.*).

CAPELLETTI

On 5th Nov. the boys celebrate the day on which the Guys set the town on fire.

This is Haydn's rather devious description of Guy Fawkes' Day. For Capelletti, see pp. 114 and 264.

On 9th Nov. [1791] I ate at the Lord Mayor's.
Kozwarra.

FRANZ KOTZWARA, a native of Prague, was engaged by Gallini as viola player in 1790 (he had been in Ireland previously). On 2nd September 1791, he visited a house of ill fame in Vine Street, St. Martin's, and paid a whore a guinea to hang him. His death caused considerable excitement in the Press (see *St. James's Chronicle*; Pohl H. in L., p. 136).

[*German*]

At the beginning of May 1792, Lord Barrymore gave a ball that cost 5,000 guineas. He paid 1,000 guineas for 1,000 peaches. 2000 baskets of gusberes [gooseberries], 5 shillings a basket.

The Prince of Wales' punch: 1 bottle champagne, 1 bottle Burgundy, 1 bottle rum, 10 lemons, 2 oranges, 1½ lbs. of sugar.

On 23rd June 1792, the Duchess of York gave a dinner for 180 persons under a large tent in her garden. I saw the same.

La riposta del S: Marchesi sopra una lettere del S: Gallini. Nell'anno 1791. "Ho ricevuto le sua gentilissima lettera, buona Notte.

Marchesi."

(Sig. Marchesi's answer to a letter from Sig. Gallini, in the year 1791: "I received your very kind letter. Good night. Marchesi.") For Gallini, see p. 67; LUIGI MARCHESI (1755–1829) was a famous castrato.

When a Quaker goes to Court, he pays the door-keeper to take off his hat for him, for a Quaker takes his hat off to no one. In order to pay the King's tax, an official goes to his house during the period when the tax is being collected, and in his presence robs him of as much goods as represent the tax in value. When the disguised thief leaves the door with his goods, the Quaker calls him back and asks him how much money he wants for the stolen things. The official demands just the amount of the tax, and in this way the Quaker pays the tax to the King.

Anno 1791 the last great concert, with 885 persons, was held in Westminster [Abbey]. Anno 1792 it was transferred to St. Margaret's Chapel, with 200 performers. People criticized this.

See also First Notebook, p. 254.

On 4th August [1791], I went to visit Herr Brassy, the banker who lives in the country, 12 miles from London. Stayed there 5 weeks. I was very well entertained. N.B.: Herr Brassy once cursed, because he had had too easy a time in this world.

NATHANIEL BRASSEY and his family lived at Roxford, about a mile from the village of Hertingfordbury in Hertfordshire; Haydn taught music to the daughter in London (see penultimate entry of this notebook). Brassey tried to shoot himself. See Dies, pp. 121*ff.*, Landon, pp. 464*f.* and Marion Scott, 'Haydn stayed here' (*Music & Letters* XXXII, 1951, pp. 38–44). Brassey died in 1798 and lies buried in the local parish churchyard.

In order to preserve cream or milk for a long time, one takes a bottle full of milk and puts it in an earthenware pot or copper vessel containing water enough to cover more than half of the bottle, and then places it over a fire and lets it simmer half-an-hour. Then one takes the bottle out and seals it securely, so that no air can escape, and in this way the milk will keep for many months. N.B.: The bottle must be securely corked before it is placed in the water.
This was told me by a sea captain.

The sea captain who keeps appearing in the stories of Haydn's English visits may have been the "CAPTAIN BLOUNT" who subscribed to the *Creation*, and whose name Haydn entered in his little subscribers' book.

On 26th March [1792], at Mr Barthelemon's Concert, an English clergyman was present who fell into the most profound melancholy on hearing the Andante:

 *etc.* [*Symphony No. 75 in D*, 2nd *movt.*]

because he had dreamt the previous night that this piece was a premonition of his death.—He left the company at once and took to his bed.

Today, the 25th of April, I heard from Herr Barthelemon that this protestant clergyman had died.

For Barthélemon, see *supra*, p. 264. The concert was actually Miss Corri's benefit concert. Barthélemon's Benefit Concert took place on 28th May 1792. Pohl, H. in L., p. 193; Landon, pp. 490*f.*

On 24th Nov. [1791], I was invited by the Prince of Wales to visit his brother, the Duc du York, at eatland [Oatlands]. I stayed there 2 days and enjoyed many marks of graciousness and honour, not only from the Prince of Wales but also from the Duchess, daughter of the King of Prussia. The little castle, 18 miles from London, lies on a slope and commands the most glorious view. Among its many beauties is a most remarkable grotto which cost £25,000 Sterling, and which was 11 years in the building. It is very large and contains many diversions, *inter alia* actual water which flows in from various sides, a beautiful English garden, various entrances and exits, besides a most charming bath. The Duke bought this country estate for some £47,000 Sterling. On the 3rd day, the Duke had me taken 12 miles towards London with his horse and carriage.

The Prince of Wales wants my portrait. For 2 days we played music for 4 hours in the evening, that is, from 10 o'clock till 2 o'clock in the morning, then we had supper and went to bed at 3 o'clock.

Cf. Letter to Genzinger of 20th December 1791.

On the 30th [November 1791], I spent 3 days in the country, 100 miles from London, at the house of Sir Patric Blak [Patrick Blake, who lived at Langham]; *en route* I passed through the little town of Cambridge. Saw the universities there, which are very conveniently situated, one after another, in a row, but each one separate from the other; each university has back of it a very roomy and beautiful garden, besides beautiful stone bridges, in order to be able to cross the circumjacent stream.—The King's Chapel is famous because of its stuccoed ceilung. It is all made of stone, but so delicate that nothing more beautiful could have been made of wood. It is already 400 years old, and everyone thinks that it is not more than 10 years old, because of the firmness and peculiar whiteness of the stone. The students there bear themselves like those at Oxford, but it is said that they have better teachers. There are in all 800 students.

Mr Fox's trousers. Story of a sedan-chair-bearer. He lost £4,000 but got them back by this clever [?] idea. [Story not continued.]

When 2 persons of opposite sexes receive permission to marry from the secular courts, the clergyman is forced to marry them as soon as they are in the church, even if they have loved without their parent's permission; if he doesn't, the bridegroom and bride have the right, as soon as the clergyman leaves the church, to tear his robes from his body. And then the clergyman is degraded and forever disqualified.   ·

The *obligation* for 1000 fl. deposited with Prince Esterhazi is dated 10th July 1791.

Covent-garden is the National Theatre. I was there on 10th Dec. [1791] and saw an opera called *The Woodman*. It was the very day on which the life story of Madam Bilington, both from the good as well as from the bad sides, was announced; such impertinent enterprises are generally undertaken for [selfish] interests. She sang rather timidly this evening, but very well all the same. The first tenor [space for name left blank] has a good voice and quite a good style, but he uses the falsetto to excess. He sang a trill on high C and ran up to G. The 2nd tenor tries to imitate him, but could not make the change from the falsetto to the natural voice, and apart from that he is most unmusical. He creates a new tempo for himself, now 3/4, then 2/4, makes cuts whenever it occurs to him. But the cahest [cast] is entirely used to him. The leader is Herr Baumgartner, a German who, however, has almost forgotten his mother-tongue. The Theatre is very dark and dirty, and is almost as large as the Vienna Court Theatre. The common people in the galleries of all the theatres are very impertinent; they set the fashion with all their unrestrained impetuosity, and whether something is repeated or not is determined by their yells. The parterre and all the boxes sometimes have to applaud a great deal to have something good repeated. That was just what happened this evening, with the Duet in the 3rd Act, which was very beautiful; and the pro's and contra's went on for nearly a quarter of an hour, till finally the parterre and the boxes won, and they repeated the Duet. Both the performers stood on the

stage quite terrified, first retiring, then again coming forward. THE
ORCHESTRA IS SLEEPY.

> *The Woodman* was by Haydn's friend William Shield (see *supra*, p. 264).
> The first tenor was Charles Incledon, and the second tenor was an Irishman
> named Johnstone (hence there is an Irishman in almost all of Shield's operas).
> Dr. Roger Fiske, who kindly supplied the above information, adds that
> "Haydn was not alone in finding Johnstone unmusical, but he had a way
> with him when it came to singing little Irish songs, and he was popular as a
> man." Dr. Fiske also discovered that there is in fact no duet in the original
> version of the third Act. What Haydn heard was "Together let us range the
> fields" from Boyce's *Serenata* "Solomon", which Mrs. Billington and
> Incledon had introduced into *The Woodman* soon after its first performance
> the previous February.

Mozard [*sic*] died on 5th Dec. 1791.

On 23rd Dec. [1791] Pleyel arrived in London. On the 24th I
dined with him.

The Duke of Cumberland had to pay £25,000 in an adultury
case.

Violin part. A work, vocal part and violin part.

> This cryptic notice probably refers to a projected composition.

Heymarket [*sic*] Theatre

It holds 4,000 persons; the pit, or parterre, alone holds 1,200; 10
persons can sit comfortably in each box. The *Amphy Theater* is
entirely round, has four tiers, and to light it there is a beautiful large
chandelier with 70 lights: it hangs suspended from the attic, pierces
the ceiling, and is situated in the middle of the *Amphy Theater*;
it illuminates the whole house, but there are also *a parte* small lustres
in the first and 2nd tiers, which are fastened outside the boxes half
an ell away.

I had to pay 1½ guineas for having the bells rung at Oxforth [*sic*]
in connection with my doctor's degree, and ½ a guinea for the robe.
The trip cost 6 guineas.

The City of London keeps 4,000 carts for cleaning the streets, and 2,000 of these work every day.

On 17th March 1792, I was bled in London.

In the month of August [1791] I lunched at noon on an East India merchantman with 6 cannon. I was given a magnificent meal.

In this same month I went with M^r [William] Fraser up the Tems [Thames] from Westminster Bridge to Richmond, where we ate on an island. There were 24 persons in our party, besides a *Feld Music* [wind band].

In England, a large man-of-war is reckoned according to the number of its cannon. Each cannon is estimated at 1,000 lbs.

Madam Mara was hissed at Oxford because she did not rise from her seat during the Hallelujah Chorus.

On 14th Sept. [1791] I dined for the first time at Mr Shaw's. He received me downstairs at the door, and then led me to his wife, who was surrounded by her 2 daughters and other ladies. As I was bowing round the circle, all at once I became aware of the fact that not only the lady of the house but also her daughters and the other women each wore on their headdress *a parte* over the front a most charming curved pearl-coloured band of 3 fingers' breadth, with the name Haydn embroidered therein in gold; and Mr Shaw wore this name on his coat, worked into the very ends of both his collars in the finest steel beads. The coat was made of the finest cloth, and with elegant steel buttons. The Mis^tris is the most beautiful woman I ever saw. N.B.: Her husband wanted a souvenir from me, and I gave him a tobacco-box which I had just bought brand new for a guinea; he gave me his instead. Several days later I visited him, and saw that he had had a silver case put over my box, on the cover of which was very elegantly engraved Apollo's harp and the following words: *Ex dono celeberrimi Josephi Haydn*. N.B. The Mis^tris gave me a stick-pin as a souvenir.

J.H.–U

In the 1st concert, only the Adagio of the new Symphony wa
repeated.

In the 2nd Concert, the Chorus and the above Symphony wer
given again, and the first Alle[gro] and the Adagio repeated.

In the 3rd concert, the new Symphony in B flat was given, and
the first and last Allegros encort [*sic*].

In Griesinger's quotation of this extract (p. 44), the first sentence reads
" . . . Symphony in D", information which Griesinger obviously re-
ceived orally. The concerts referred to are the Haydn-Salomon 1792 series:
the first was on 17th February, and the new Symphony was No. 93; the
Chorus is *The Storm*, first performed at the second concert, 24th February.
The third concert was on 2nd March, and the new Symphony was No. 98.
See Landon, pp. 473*ff*.

Lord Clermont [Claremont] once gave a large *Soupé*, and when
the King's health was drunk, he ordered the wind band to play the
well-known song, "God save the King" in the street during a wild
snowstorm. This occurred on 19th Feby 1792, so madly do they
drink in England.

The castle chapel at Windsor is a very old but splendid building
the high altar cost 50,000 fl. It shows the ascension of Christ in stained
glass. This year, 1792, in the side altar to the right, a smaller one
showing Christ appearing to the Shepherds, was completed. Thi
small one is valued more highly than the large one. The view from
the terrace is divine.

Hardy. Otto. Guttenbrun. Hoppener. Dassie, embossed in wax
[The following sentence was added later:] N.B.: The first 4 gentlemen painted my portrait, Dessie [*sic*] in wax.

The portraits of Otto and Guttenbrunn have been mentioned above (see
p. 268). THOMAS HARDY's portrait (1792) is now in the Royal College of
Music, London. John Bland apparently commissioned it, for the engraving, also made by Hardy, is described: "Painted & Engraved by T.
Hardy . . . From an Original Picture in the Possession [*sic*] of J. Bland.
London. Publish'd as the Act directs February 13.1792, by J. Bland, Nº45
Holborn." The HOPPNER portrait has been mentioned in connection with
a letter to Genzinger (see p. 124). The wax medallion by DESOIE [*recte*] seems
not to have survived.

[*English*]
THE THEATRE OF VARIETE'S AMUSANTES, IN SAVILLE-ROW.
[*German*]

On 23rd Nov. [1791] I was invited to go there. It is a marionette theatre. The figures were well directed, the singers were bad, but the orchestra was quite good.

Before she left for Italy, Mara sang 4 times at the Heymarcket [*sic*] Theatre in the English opera *Artaxerses* by Dᵣ Arnd [Arne]. Again she won roars of applause, and she was paid £100 for each appearance.

THOMAS ARNE (1710–1778) wrote his *Artaxerxes*, based on Metastasio's famous libretto, in 1762.

The larger traveller's lead pencil costs ½ a guinea.
The smaller one　　—　　—　　5 shillings 6 penz.
Pen　　　　　　　　　6　—　　　6 —

[*English*]

		schilling	penni
Stel Buttons —	£ 2 —	2	— 0
a steel girdl — —	1 —	4	— 0
a steel chain　—	1 —	11	— 6
2 Secissars 3 Sh: Each	—	6	–
3 —　at 6 Sh: Each	—	18	0
1 —　　at　—	—	7	— 6
1 —　　at　—	—	9	— 0
7 Penn Knifes　—	1 —	1	— 0

[*German*]

On 14th Nov. 1791, 2 Symphonies sent to Herr von Keess *per postam*, for which I paid 1 guinea 11½ shillings, and 3 shillings for 2 letters, and 1 guinea for the copying.

Symphonies Nos. 95 and 96. The two letters were to Herr von Kees and Frau von Genzinger. See also *supra*, p. 121.

Noyan, a drink. Squeezed from nutmeg, rum and sugar. Comes from Martinique in the West Indies, which belongs to France.

Oranges from Portugal arrive in the middle of November, but they are quite pale and not so good as they are later.

On 5th Dec. [1791] the fog was so thick that you could have spread it on bread. In order to write I had to light the lights at 11 o'clock.

On 18th May 1792, the last Salomon Concert was given at Hanover Square.

English Fanaticism. Miss Dora Jordan, a mistress of the Duc de Clarens [Clarence] and the leading actress at Drury Lane, wrote to the impresario one evening, an hour before the beginning of a comedy in which she was to play, that she had been taken ill suddenly and therefore couldn't act. When the curtain was raised in order to inform the public thereof, and to say that the management was inclined to give another piece [*Spectacul*], the whole public began to shout that the comedy which had been announced must be given at once, with another actress taking Jordan's rôle and reading with the part in her hand. At the beginning, the management took exception to this plan, but the public became stubborn and its wishes had to be satisfied. Miss Jordan made herself contemptible in the public's eyes because she drove barefacedly in Heÿ [Hyde] Park with the Duc. But she begged for pardon in all the newspapers, and people quite forgave her.

 *da Capo*

A gang of rowdy fellows sang this song with all their might. They yelled so loudly that you could hear them 1000 paces away from the street, in every nook and cranny.

Mr Bressy [Brassey] N^r 71 Lombard Street.

COESTHS:

REBECCA SCHROETER'S LETTERS TO HAYDN ARRANGED IN CHRONOLOGICAL SEQUENCE.

Abbreviations: "F." = Faithful; "M.D." = My Dear; "D." = Dear; "Dst" = Dearest; "M.Dst" = My Dearest; "H" and "Hn" = Haydn; "D.H." = Dear Haydn; *etc.*

[*English*]

Mrs Schroeter presents her compliments to Mr Haydn, and informs him, she is just returned to town, and will be very happy to see him whenever it is convenient to him to give her a lesson.

James St: Buckingham gate Wednesday
June the 29th 791.

Wednesday Feb: 8th 793.

M:D: Inclos'd I have sent you the words of the Song you desired. —I wish much to know, HOW YOU DO to day, I am very sorry to lose the pleasure of seeing you this morning, but I hope you will have time to come to morrow. I beg my D: you will take great care of your health, and do not fatigue yourself with to[o] much application to bussiness. My thoughts and best wishes are always with you, and I ever am with the utmost Sincerity M:D your F: et[c].

March 7th 92.

My D: I was extremely sorry to part with you so suddenly last Night, our conversation was particularly interesting and I had [a] thousand affectionate things to say to you, my heart WAS and is full of TENDERNESS for you, but no language can express HALF the LOVE and AFFECTION I feel for you, you are DEARER to me EVERY DAY of my life. I am very sorry I was so dull and stupid yesterday, indeed my DEAREST it was nothing but my being indisposed with a cold occasion'd my Stupidity. I thank you a thousand times for your concern for me, I am truly sensible of your goodness, and I assure you my D. if any thing had happened to trouble me, I wou'd have open'd my heart, & told you with the most perfect confidence. Oh, how earnes[t]ly [I] wish to see you, I hope you will come to me to morrow. I shall be happy to see you both in the Morning and the Evening. God Bless you my love, my thoughts and best wishes ever accompany you, and I always am with the most sincere and invariable Regard my D:

your truly affectio[nate]

My Dearest I cannot be happy
till I see you if you know,
do, tell me, when you will come

My D: I am extremely sorry I can not have the pleasure of seeing you to morrow, as I am going to Bleakheath [Blackheath]. if you are not engaged this Evening I shou'd be very happy if you will do me the favor to com[e] to me—and I hope to have the happiness to see you on Saturday to dinner. My thoughts and tenderest affections are always with you and I ever am most truly my D.

Your F: and etc.

April 4th $\overline{92}$.

My D: with this, you will receive the Soap, I beg you a thousand Pardons for not Sending it sooner, I know you will have the goodness to excuse me.—I hope to hear you are quite well, and have slept well—I shall be happy to see you, my D: as soon as possible. I shall be much obliged to you if you will do me the favor to send me twelve Tikets for your concert, may all SUCCESS attend you MY EVER D: H: that Night, and always, is the sincere and hearty wish of your

Invariable and

James S: truly affectionate

Aprill 8th $\overline{792}$.

James St: Thursday April 12th
M:D: I am SO TRULY ANXIOUS about YOU. I must write, to beg to know HOW YOU DO? I was very sorry I HAD not the pleasure of seeing you this Evening, my thoughts have been CONSTANTLY with you, and indeed MY D:L: no words can express half the tenderness and AFFECTION I FEEL FOR YOU—I thought you seemed out of Spirits this morning, I wish I cou'd always remove every trouble from your mind. be assured my D: I partake with the most perfect Sympathy in ALL YOUR SENSATIONS, and my regard for you is STRONGER EVERY DAY, my best Wishes always attend you and I ever am my D: H: most Sincerely your Faithful

et[c]

M: D: I was extremely sorry to hear this morning that you was indisposed, I am told you was five hours at your Study's yesterday, indeed MY D: L: I am afraid it will hurt you, why should you who have already produced so many WONDERFUL and CHARMING compositions, still fatigue yourself with such close application. I almost tremble for your health, let me prevail on you my MUCH-LOVED H: not to keep to your Study's so long at ONE TIME, my D: LOVE if you cou'd know how very precious your welfare is to me, I flatter myself you wou'd endeavor to preserve it, for my Sake, as well as YOUR OWN pray inform me how you do and how you have slept, I hope to see you to Morrow at the concert, and on Saturday. I shall be happy to see you here to dinner, in the mean time my D: my sincerest good wishes constantly attend you, and I ever am with the tenderest regard your most
J: S: Aprill the 19th 92.

Aprill 24th 792

My D.

I can not leave London without sending you a line to assure you my thoughts[,] my BEST WISHES and tenderest affections will inseperably attend you till we meet again.

The Bearer will also deliver you the March, I am verry sorry, I cou'd not write it sooner, nor better, but I hope my D: you will excuse it, and if it is not passable, I will send you the DEAR original directly: If my H: wou'd employ me oftener to write Music I hope I shou'd improve, and I know I shou'd delight in the occupation. now MY D:L: let me intreat you to take the greatest care of your HEALTH I hope to see you on Friday at the concert and on Saturday to dinner till when and ever I most sincerely am, and shall be your [etc.]

The March is probably the "March for the Prince of Wales" (Hoboken VIII: 3).

M:D: I am very anxious to know HOW YOU DO, and hope to hear you have been in good health ever since I saw you—as the time for your charming concert advances I feel myself more and more interested for your Success, and heartely WISH every thing may turn out to your Satisfaction. do me the favor to send me six Tickets more. on Saturday my D:L I hope to see you to dinner, in the mean while, my thoughts, my best wishes, and tenderest affections,

constantly attend you, and I ever am my D: H: most sincerely and
aff. [etc.]
J: S: May the 2ᵈ 792.

The concert referred to is Haydn's benefit concert of 3rd May.
The March is probably the *March for the Prince of Wales* (1792; Hoboken
VIII: 3).

James Sᵗ Tuesday May ye 8ᵗʰ
My Dᵗ I am extremely sorry I have not the pleasure Seeing you to
Day, but hope to see you to Morrow at one o'clock and if you can
take your DINNER WITH me to Morrow, I shall be very glad—I hope
to see you also on Thursday to dinner, but I suppose you will be
obliged to go to the concert that Evening, and you know the other
concert is on Friday, and you go to the country on Saturday, this
my Dᵗ LOVE makes me more solicitous for you to stay with me TO
MORROW, if you are not engaged, as I wish to have as much of your
company AS POSSIBLE. God Bless you my Dˢᵗ H, I always am with the
tenderest Regard

your sincere and
affectionate [etc.]

The concert on Thursday (May 10th) was probably a semi-private affair;
that of Friday (May 11th) was the eleventh Salomon Concert at Hanover
Square, in the second part of which Haydn's Symphony No. 97 was
probably played for the second time (Landon, pp. 495*f.*).

May 17ᵗʰ
M: D: Permit me to return you a thousand thanks for this Even-
ing's entertainment — where YOUR — SWEET compositions and your
EXCELLENT performance combine, it can not fail of being a most
CHARMING CONCERT, but independent of THAT, the pleasure of SEEING
YOU must ever give me infinite Satisfaction — Pray inform me HOW
YOU DO? and if you have SLEPT WELL? I hope to see you to morrow
my D: and on Saturday to dinner, till when and always I remain
most sincerely my D: L: most Faith[ful] etc.

Haydn seems to have given a musical party at Mrs. Schroeter's, or at one
of their mutual friend's.

M:D: If you will do me the favor to take your dinner with me to
Morrow, I shall be very happy to see you, and I PARTICULARLY wish

for the pleasure of YOUR company MY Dr LOVE BEFORE our other friends come. — I hope to hear you have SLEPT WELL to Night, and that you are in GOOD HEALTH, my BEST WISHES and tenderest Regards are your constant attendants and I EVER am with the FIRMEST Attachment my D^st H^n

> most Sincerely and Affectionately
> yours R S:

James S. Tuesday Ev: May 22^d

My D^r I beg to know HOW YOU DO? hope to hear you[r] Head-ach is ENTIRELY GONE, and that you have SLEPT WELL. I shall be very happy to see you on Sunday any time convenient to you after one o'clock— I hope to see you my D^r L on tuesday as usual to Dinner, [crossed out: "and all (?night ? p.m.) with me"] — and I shall be much obliged to you if you will inform me what Day will be agreable to you to meet M^r M^tris and MISS STONE at my house to Dinner, I shou'd be glad if it was either Thursday or Friday, whichever Day YOU PLEASE to fix, I will send to Mr Stone to let them know. I long to see you my D^t H, let me have that pleasure as soon as you can, till when and Ever I remain with the FIRMEST attachment My D^r L:

> most faithfully and affectionately
> yours [etc.]

Friday June ye 1st $\overline{792}$.

My D: I can not close my Eyes to sleep till I have return'd you ten thousand thanks for the inexpressible delight I have received from YOUR EVER ENCHANTING compositions and your INCOMPARABLY CHARMING PERFORMANCE of them. be assured my D H: that among ALL your numerous admirers NO ONE has listened with more PROFUND attention, and no one can have such high veneration for your MOST BRILLIANT TALENTS as I HAVE. indeed my D: L: no tongue CAN EXPRESS the gratitude I FEEL for the infinite pleasure your Music has given me, accept then my repeeted thanks for it, and let me also assure you, with heart-felt affection, that I shall ever consider the happiness of your acquaintance as one of the CHIEF Blessings of my life, and it is the SINCER wish of my heart to preserve[,] to cultivate and to merit it more and more. I hope to hear you are quite well. Shall be happy to see you to dinner and if you CAN come at three o'clock it would give me great pleasure, as I should be particularly

glad to see you my D: before the rest of our friends come — god
Bless you my D: I ever am with the firmest and most perfect
attachment

your et[c].

Wednesday night June 6ᵗʰ 9̄2.

"Mr. Salomon's last concert of the Season", held on 6th June, was the
concert to which Mrs. Schroeter refers (Landon, p. 502).

My Dˢᵗ Inclosed I send you the verses you was so kind as to lend
me, and am very much obliged to you for permitting me to take a
copy of them. pray inform me HOW YOU DO, and let me know MY
Dᵗ L: when you will DINE with me. I shall be HAPPY to SEE YOU to
dinner either to MORROW or TUESDAY whichever is most convenient
to you, I am TRULY ANXIOUS and IMPATIENT to SEE you, and I wish to
have as much of YOUR COMPANY as possible: indeed MY Dˢᵗ H: I FEEL
for YOU the FONDEST and TENDEREST AFFECTION the HUMAN HEART is
capable of, and I ever am with the FIRMEST attachment my Dᵗ Love

most Sincerely, Faithfully
and most affectionately yours [etc.]

Sunday Evening
June 10 792.

My Dearest
I hope to hear you are in good HEALTH, and have had an AGREABLE
Journey, that you have been much AMUSED with the Race, and that
EVERY THING has turn'd out to YOUR SATISFACTION pray MY Dᵗᵗ LOVE
inform me how YOU do? EVERY circumstance concerning you MY
BELOVED Hᵈⁿ is INTERESTING to me.—I shall be VERY HAPPY to SEE YOU
to DINNER TO MORROW and I EVER am with the sincerest and TENDER-
EST Regard my Dˢᵗ Hᵈⁿ

most faithfully & affectionately
yours R: S:

James S. Thursday Even: June yᵉ 14ᵗʰ 792

Haydn had attended the racing at Ascot (see *supra*, p. 255).

M:D: I was EXTREMELY SORRY, I had not the pleasure of SEEING YOU
TO DAY, indeed my Dʳ Love it was a very great disappointment to
me, as every moment of your company is MORE and MORE PRECIOUS

to me now your DEPARTURE is so near — — I hope to hear you are
QUITE WELL and I shall be very happy to see you my D^t H^n any time
to morrow after one o'clock if you can come but if not, I shall hope
for the pleasure of seeing YOU on MONDAY — you will receive this
letter to morrow morning [.] I wou'd not send it to Day, for fear you
shou'd not be at home, and I WISH to have your answer. God Bless
you my D^t Love, once more I repeat, let me SEE YOU as SOON as
POSSIBLE[.] I EVER am with the most INVIOLABLE ATTACHMENT my D^t
and most BELOVED H.

most faithfully and most affectionately
Yours
R Sch

Saturday,
June y^o 16th $\overline{792}$.

My D: I hope to hear you are in good HEALTH, and that you SLEPT
WELL last Night. I shall be VERY HAPPY to see you on Monday morning—permit me to remind you about Mr Frasers, and you will be so
good as to let me know on Monday how it is settled — God Bless
you my D: Love, my thoughts and best wishes are your constant
attendants, and I ever am with the tenderest Regard my D: H:

most et[c].

June the 26th $\overline{92}$.

Mr. Frasers is probably identical with the "Mr. Fraser" mentioned above
(see p. 275).

[*Undated letters*]

My Dearest,

I am quite impatient to know how you do this Morning, and if
you slept well last Night — I am much obliged to you for all your
kindness yesterday and heartely thank you for it. I earnestly LONG to
see you my D^t L: and I hope to have that pleasure THIS MORNING. my
THOUGHTS and best REGARDS are incessantly with you and I ever am
my Dst H:

most faithfully, and most
affectionately yours [etc.]

M: D: I was extremely sorry I had not the pleasure of YOUR company THIS MORNING as I most ANXIOUSLY wish'd to see you — my

THOUGHTS are continually with you, my beloved H: and my AFFEC-
TION for you INCREASES DAILY, no words can express half the TENDER
REGARD I feel for you —I hope my D^t L: I shall have the happiness of
seeing you to-morrow to dinner, in the mean time my best wishes
always attend you, and I EVER am with the FIRMEST ATTACHMENT MY
D. H. most et[c].

I am just return'd from from [sic] the Concert, where I was very
much charmed with your DELIGHTFUL and enchanting COMPOSITIONS,
and your spirited and interesting performance of them, accept
t[h]en thousand thanks for the great pleasure, I ALWAYS receive from
your INCOMPARABLE MUSIC. My D: I intreat you to inform me, how
you do, and if you get [sic] any SLEEP to Night. I am EXTREMELY
ANXIOUS about your health. I hope to hear a good account of it. God
Bless you MY H. come to me to morrow I shall be happy to see you
both morning and Evening. I always am with the tenderest Regard
my D: your
                                F: and aff.
Friday Night 12 o'clock.

M: D. I am heartily sorry I was so unfortunate not to see you,
when you call'd on me this morning, can you my D: be so good as
to dine with me TO DAY. I beg you will if possible — you can not
imagine how miserable I am that I did not see you — do come to
Day I intreat you — I always am M: D: with the tenderest Regard
most et[c].
Monday 2 o'clock.

THE THIRD LONDON NOTEBOOK (1794-1795)

[*English*]

M^ris Bindon　　　　　N° 19 great Pulteney
with two Daughters　　　　　Str.
　　　　　　　　　　　to Bath

To Honble M^ris Brown　　N° 3
Burlington Street.　Bath.　[*Cf.* p. 296.]

Dr Harlinghton　　　queen Square
　　Composer at Bath　　[*Cf.* p. 301.]

[In another hand:]
Mrs Carr — N° 2 Crescent
Miss Gubbins le meme Bath

[*German*]
On 11th June [1794] the whole city was illuminated because of
the capture of 7 French warships; a great many windows were
broken. On the 12th and 13th the whole city was illuminated again.
The common people behaved very violently on this occasion. In
every street they shot off not only small but also large guns, and this
went on the whole night. [*See* p. 292n.].

The 30th of May 1795 was such a bright day that you could read
anything at 9 o'clock in the evening.

[*English*]
When first I saw thee graceful move
Ah me! What meant my throbbing breast
Say soft confusion, art thou love?
If love thou art then farewell rest.

W. Barclay Squire tried to identify these English songs when Engl issued this notebook in 1909. Squire discovered that this song was one often performed in public gardens (it is known as early as 1750, in Signora Galli's setting), and which had been translated—or was it the original?—as "Se son Contana" in Hasse's "Twelve Duets". See Engl, p. 53.

[*German*]
Mr Orde *gouveneur* at Fernhall on the Isle of Wight, whose country house commands the most magnificent view over the ocean.

L'Isle of Whight [*sic*] is 64 miles in circumference.

Esse quam vedere [*sc.* videre]

On 24th March 1795, Mara, having returned from Bath, gave her Benefic-Music [benefit concert] in Hannovers Room [Hanover Square Rooms]. There were not more than 60 persons in the audience. It is said that she never sang better than at that time. Janiowick conducted.—Mr Clementi sat at the pianoforte, and conducted his new grand Symphony, without success. After the concert was over, Madam Mara gave a *Soupé* in the adjoining room. After 12 o'clock Mr Mara, very confident, walked in the door, came forward, and asked for a glass of wine. Since Madam Mara saw quite clearly that her husband was raging, and feared the consequences, she turned to her lawyer, who was at the table, and he said to Mr Mara: You know our laws; you will have the goodness to leave this room at once, otherwise you will have to pay £200 tomorrow. The poor man left the company. Madam Mara, his wife, went the other day to Bath with her *Cicisbeo*, but I rather think her obstinacy makes her despicable to the whole nation. N.B.: M. Florio.

About the unhappily married Maras, see p. 254. G. FLORIO was a flautist who first appeared in London in 1782. The son of Pietro Grassi Florio, former member of the Dresden band who left Dresden in 1756 to go to Paris and then London, Florio jun. was Madame Mara's *cicisbeo*. She took him to Germany in 1803 and performed several of his compositions. See Engl, p. 42 and Pohl, H. in L., p. 372.

On 30th March 1795 I was invited by Dr Arnold and his associates to a grand concert in Free Maisons [*sic*] Hall: one of my big symphonies was to have been given under my direction, but since they wouldn't have any rehearsal, I refused to cooperate and did not appear.

For the details of the concert, see Landon, pp. 540*f*. For Arnold, see also pp. 264, 290, 305.

The Mail Coach does 110 in 12 hours, that is, one-hundred-ten English miles.

Anno 1794 there was beautiful weather in the month of April as there can be in Germany in about the month of July. May, on the contrary, was very cold. Half of June and the whole month of July were very hot, and without any rain; people prayed for rain. In this great heat-wave, a great many people died in the Thames, because they went swimming in it. Some are capable of swimming 2 hours at a time, but when the tide catches them they're lost. Yesterday two fellows were bathing, and suddenly began to fight. They went on shore to box, and one of them received such a strong blow in the stomach that he gave up the ghost forthwith.

Every ship-of-the-line, or man-of-war, has 3 masts, likewise a Frigate.
Most of them have 3 decks.
A Brig has 2 masts.
A Cutter has only 1 mast.
Every ship-of-the-line must have at least 64 cannon.
A Cutter has but 14, at the most 16 cannon.
A fire-ship has 2 masts. In the middle of its sails it has 2 large and long cross-beams with round, pointed double irons:

ILLUSTRATION FROM THE ORIGINAL NOTEBOOK

When they come near an enemy ship, this iron grapples the rigging or even the sails, whereupon one sets the ship on fire, so that the other ship which is grappled to it has to burn, too. The crew saves itself in the little lifeboats which they take with them.

[*English*]
[The following written in pencil by another hand:]
Mr Hamilton
Rodney Place   Clifton Hill
near Bristol

Oh! fairest form of Natur, say
What lured thee from these vales away?
Was it new conquests to Explore?
The World my love, was thine before!

In the year 1794
Dr Haydn, Dr Arnold, Mr John Stafford Smith, and Mr Atterbury declared their readiness to cooperate with Dr Cooke, Dr Hayes, Dr Dupuis, Dr Parsons, Mr Calcott, the Rev^r Osborne Wight, Mr Webber, Mr Shield, and Mr Stevens in their Exertions towards perfecting a work for the Improvement of Parochial Psalmody.
as a Small Token of esteem for
his abilities and of gratitude
for his Services this Piece of
Plate is presented to Doctor Haydn
[in another hand:] by W. D. Tattersall.

The work described here was the Rev. William D. Tattersall's *Improved Psalmody. Vol. I* [all published] *The Psalms of David from a Poetical Version by James Merrick . . . with new music collected from the most eminent Composers,* printed by T. Skillern, London, 1794. For Arnold, Callcott, Shield: see Second Notebook, "Composers" (p. 264); for Hayes, Dupuis, see p. 266. JOHN STAFFORD SMITH (*c.* 1750–1836), organist and composer. Dr. BENJAMIN COOKE (1734–1793), composer and organist at Westminster Abbey. DR. (later SIR) WILLIAM PARSONS (1746–1817), pupil of Sacchini, was Master of the King's Band. SAMUEL WEBBE (1740–1816), organist and composer. RICHARD J. S. STEVENS, well known for his songs, glees, *etc.*

[The following notes are in pencil]
[*German*]
The Hospital was built in the year 1762.
At this time there were 1500 patients, among them 300 sailors
from the last naval battle. [*Cf.* also *infra*.]
Reid
Reed, port of war opposite Portsmouth.
RYDE

Ryde (Haydn finally got it right) is on the Isle of Wight.

A Cockswan [*sic*] is a kind of subaltern who, when his Capitain
[*sic*] goes to sea, stands at attention next to him. A capitain generally
has his special crew, all identically dressed, which he takes with him
to his port. At 12 o'clock I was in the neighbourhood of the fleet
when the 12 o'clock bells were rung. In July [there follow two or
three illegible words] I ate lunch [on a ship?].
[End of pencilled section]
Mister March is a dentist, *Carossieur* [*recte*: Carrossieur = coach-
maker] and dealer in wines all at the same time: a man 84 years old.
Keeps a very young mistress. Has a 9-year-old daughter who plays
the pianoforte quite respectably. I often ate at his house. N.B.: as a
dentist, he makes £2000 every year. Each waggon costs at least
£500. As a dealer in wines, I don't imagine his profits will be all
that large. He drags himself around on two crutches, or 2 wooden
feet.

Ebb-tide and flood-tide every 7 hours. In Spring the tide recedes
14 feet, during the rest of the season only 7 feet.

It is said that Juli[u]s Caesar, having had to flee, landed quite by
accident on this island, and is supposed to have said: this is the port
of the Gods. Godsport. There are 1500 patients in this hospital,
among them 300 sailors who were with Lord Howe in the last naval
battle.

Part of these notes already appeared in the pencilled section (see top of page).
Godsport, the harbour town opposite Portsmouth. Richard Lord Howe
(1726–1799), who had commanded the British fleet in North America
J.H.–X

during the Revolutionary War. In 1793, he had commanded the fleet in the British Channel, and on 1 June 1794, he won a great victory over the French at Quessant. (The first major entry of this notebook describes the excitement when he towed into Portsmouth six [not seven] captured French warships.)

On 9th July [1794(?)], I left at 5 o'clock in the morning for Portsmouth, 72 miles from London, and arrived there at 8 o'clock in the evening. Some small earthworks were thrown up 14 miles before Portsmouth; nearby there is a small camp of 800 men; one mile further, in the direction of the city, some 3,500 Frenchmen are quartered in barracks. I inspected the fortifications there, which are in good repair, especially the fortress opposite, in Godsport, which the *gubernium* [= the governors] had had constructed recently. I went aboard the French ship-of-the-line called *le just*; it has 80 cannon; the English, or rather Lord Howe, captured it. The 18 cannon in the harbour-fortress are 36-pounders. The ship is terribly shot to pieces. The great mast, which is 10 feet 5 inches in circumference, was cut off at the very bottom and lay stretched on the ground. A single cannon-ball, which passed through the captain's room, killed 14 sailors.

I met Lauterburg, the famous painter.

Engl (p. 23) read this as: "I met Famore, the painter, in Canterbury", but "Famore" is actually "Famose", and "Canterbury" is quite clearly "Lauterburg", *i.e.*, PHILIPP JAKOB LOUTHERBOURG, the younger (1740-1812), who had lived in England since 1771.

The Dockyard, or the place where ships are built, is of an enormous size, and has a great many splendid buildings. But I couldn't go there, because I was a foreigner. Hard by is a new and most splendid ship-of-the-line with 110 cannon, called the *Prince of Wales*. The King and his family stayed 3 days in the Dockyard at the *gouverneur*'s house.

On 15th July [1795(?)], I saw the Bank [of England]. There are, first, a *goveneur*, a Deputy or Vice *gouverneur*, 24 *Directores*, and a whole lot of other officials in the department. Mr Dea guided me, and showed me all the treasures. There is a very great fortune in gold ingots, most of which are worth £700 Sterling. There are over one-and-one-half millions in bank notes, some of which are £1000 notes. An enormous amount of Spanish taler. Most of the gold is underground in the vaults. In order to see the main cashier's office, 3 of the directors have to be present, each one of which has his own key. The vaults are exceedingly massive. There are also hidden vaults, which must be very useful in case of a rebellion. To write down all the bills they need 2000 large folio books every year, and on this account there is a very large library which is, however, apart from that very insignificant.

On 28th March 1795, I saw the Opera *Aci & Galathea* by Bianchi. The music is very rich in parts for the wind instruments, and I rather think one would hear the principal melody better if it were not so richly scored. The Opera is too long, especially since Banti has to keep everything going all by herself; for Brida is a good youngster with a beautiful voice but very little musical feeling; and Rovedino, and the good old Braghetti, and the wretched *Seconda Donna*—they all deserved, and received, not the least applause. The orchestra is larger this year, but just as mechanical and badly placed as it was before, and indiscreet in its accompaniments; in short, it was the 3rd time that this Opera was performed, and everyone was dissatisfied. It happened that, when the 2nd Ballet began, the whole public suddenly became dissatisfied and yelled "off - off - off", because they wanted to see the new Ballet which Madam Hillisberg had given at her *Benefice* 2 days earlier.—Everyone was embarrassed—there was an interval lasting half an hour — until at last a dancer came forward and said, very submissively: "Ladies and Gentlemen: since the performer Mr. Taylor cannot be found, the whole Ballet Company promises to perform the desired ballet next week, for which, however, the Impresario must pay Madam Hillisberg £300." That satisfied them, and they then yelled, "go on - go on"; and thus the old Ballet was then performed.

FRANCESCO BIANCHI (1752–1810) had been engaged to compose for the King's Theatre; he died in London. Banti = BRIGIDA BANTI-GIORGI (1759–1806), dramatic soprano with a big range who had been engaged at the King's Theatre; Haydn wrote his *Scena di Berenice* for her (see Fourth Notebook, p. 306). BRIDA (tenor), CARLO ROVEDINO (d. 1822; bass) and BRAGHETTI were members of the King's Theatre. HILLIGSBERG [*recte*] was the well-known *prima ballerina* (see also *supra*, p. 267). WILLIAM TAYLOR was not a "performer" but the director of King's Theatre.

A beer-brewer rented a house in Brighton opposite the Pavilion, for which he paid 27 guineas a week. N.B.: The Prince of Wales' mistress boarded there.

Madame Fizherbert [Fitzherbert] was divorced from the Prince of Wales in the month of July 1794. She received [an alimony of] £6,000 annually.

[Pencilled note:] On the way back [from Portsmouth] a good dinner at Farnham.

On the way to Portsmuth [*sic*] I saw the old Royal Castle at Hampton Court, which is very large and has a garden like that at Estoras, with three principal allées; there are various splendid statues in bronze, and very fine marble vases; especially beautiful the painting over the main staircase and the ceiling by the artist Verrio. This castle is mostly inhabited by aristocratic widows of the military.

On the preceding page Haydn wrote the notes for the above paragraph in pencil, and subsequently erased them (the words "Court", "Mahler" [painter], "Werrio . . . auf der Hauptstiege" [Werrio . . . over the main staircase] are legible). The King's Staircase in Hampton Court was designed by Christopher Wren, and Antonio Verrio painted the walls and ceiling in one huge composition. Sacheverell Sitwell, *British Architects and Craftsmen*, London 1945, p. 59.

SPECTAS, ET TU SPECTABERE is the inscription over the curtain in the Little Haymarket Theatre. I was there on 29th July 1794: they gave a National opera, N.B. a piece in Scottish costumes. The men were dressed in flesh-coloured breeches, with white and red ribbons twisted round their stockings, a short, brightly-coloured, striped masons' apron [*i.e.* kilt], brown coat and waistcoat, over the coat a large, broad ensign's sash in the same style as the apron, and black cap shaped like a shoe and trimmed with ribbons. The women all in white muslin, brightly coloured ribbons in their hair, very broad bands in the same style round their bodies, also for their hats. They perform the same abominable trash as at Sadlers Wells. A fellow yelled an aria so horribly and with such exaggerated grimaces that

I began to sweat all over. N.B. He had to repeat the aria. *O che bestie!*

Haydn saw *The Mountaineers* and *Auld Robin Gray* (*a pastorale*), both with music by Samuel Arnold. The date Haydn gives is wrong (it should be 28th July). Pohl, H. in L., p. 270.

Lord Littledon, a very rich and pious man, had the misfortune to be the father of only one very dissolute son, whom he tried to improve by every possible means.—Eventually he found a most charming wife for his son, but the latter lived with her only 3 months and then sent her back to his father. This behaviour caused the father's death a short while afterwards. But just before he died, the father wrote the son that the latter could sweeten his dying days if he [the son] would divorce his good wife before the father died; the son agreed to do this at once *in forma*, whereupon the old man died peacefully. Scarcely a fortnight went by, however, before the son had a dream, in which his father appeared to him, saying that the son would be a child of death within the very week; and so it happened. The young widow is still alive: but very sad.

On 2nd August 1794, I left at 5 o'clock in the morning for Bath, with Mr Ashe and Mr Cimador, and arrived there at 8 o'clock in the evening. It's 107 miles from London. The Mail Coach does this distance in 12 hours. I lived at the house of Herr Rauzzini, a *Musicus* who is very famous, and who in his time was one of the greatest singers. He has lived there 19 years, supports himself by the Subscription Concerts which are given in the Winter, and by giving lessons. He is a very nice and hospitable man. His summer house, where I stayed, is situated on a rise in the middle of a most beautiful neighbourhood, from which you can see the whole city. Bath is one of the most beautiful cities in Europe. All the houses are built of stone; this stone comes from quarries in the surrounding mountains; it is very soft, so soft, in fact, that it's no trouble to cut it up into any desired shape; it is very white, and the older it is, once it has been taken from the quarry, the harder it gets. The whole city lies on a slope, and that is why there are very few carriages; instead of them, there are a lot of sedan-chairs, who will take you quite a way for 6 pence. But too bad that there are so few straight roads; there are a lot of beautiful squares, on which stand the most magnificent houses,

but which cannot be reached by any vehicle: they are now building
a brand new and broad street.

Probably the flautist ANDREW ASHE, who had made his first London appearance at the second Haydn-Salomon concert of the 1792 season (Landon,
p. 476). CIMADOR was apparently the young violinist and composer who
later became a partner in the music publishers Monzani & Cimador.
VENANZIO RAUZZINI (1747–1810), the brilliant castrato for whom Mozart
had written the Motet "Exsultate, jubilate".

N.B. Today, on the 3rd, I looked at the city, and found, half-way
up the hill, a building shaped like a half-moon, and more magnificent than any I had seen in London. The curve extends for 100
fathoms, and there is a Corinthian column at each fathom. The
building has 3 floors. Round about it, the pavement in front of the
houses is 10 feet broad for the pedestrians, and the street as wide *a
proportione*; it is surrounded by an iron fence, and a terrace slopes
down 50 fathoms in successive stages, through a beautiful expanse
of green; on both sides there are little paths, by which one can
descend very comfortably.

Every Monday and Friday evening all the bells are rung, but
apart from this, you don't hear many bells being rung. The city is
not thickly populated, and in Summer one sees very few people; for
the people taking the baths don't come till the beginning of October,
and stay through half of February. But then a great many people
come, so that in the year 1791, 25,000 persons were there. All the
inhabitants live off this influx, without which the city would be very
poor: there are very few merchants and almost no trade, and everything is very dear. The baths are by nature very warm; one bathes in
the water, and one also drinks it—generally the latter. And one pays
very little: to bathe it costs 3 shillings at all times. I made the acquaintance there of Miss Brown, a charming person of the best *conduit*; a
good pianoforte player, her mother a most beautiful woman. The
city is now building a most splendid room for guests taking the cure.

MISS BROWN, apparently the daughter of Abraham Brown (Browne), who
had often appeared with Handel. (Engl, pp. 48*f.*; Deutsch, *Handel*, p. 581.)
The "most splendid room" was to be the Pump Room, completed in 1796.

On the 6th I went from Bath 11 miles to Pristol [*sic*], to visit M^r
Hamilton. The city is very large and half of it, too, is built on a rise.
The River [blank: = Avon] flows through the middle of the city,

and many hundred merchant ships lie at anchor in the river. There is a great deal of trade, because the open sea can be reached a few hours. The city is also very heavily populated, but otherwise rather dirty; very small streets; a lot of building going on, especially on the hill, which commands the most magnificent views. The churches — there are a great many — are all in the old Gothic style, as they are at Bath, too. In Bath, I saw a vehicle in the form of two sofas for 4 persons; N.B.: 2 persons on each side with their backs diagonally opposite to each other. The drinking and bathing water is especially beneficial for lameness and rheumatism; in Pristol for hectic and consumption. The drinking water at Pristol is very sweet and pleasing. The guests go to Pristol in the Summer, and to Bath in the Winter. The trip there and back cost me 75 Viennese Gulden.

I left Cowes at 4 o'clock in the afternoon for Southampton where I spent the night. It is a little town on a peninsula.

From there to Winschester [*sic*], where there is a beautiful Gothic Cathedral Church, the altar-piece BY WEST.

These notes again refer to Haydn's trip to (or rather from) the Isle of Wight. BENJAMIN WEST (1738–1820), the American artist who went to Rome and then to London, where he became Reynolds' successor as President of the Royal Academy of Art.

On 23rd July 1794, fire broke out in a master shipwright's dock above London Bridge; the fire spread to a ship with a cargo of nitre, which was docked nearby, and driven by a very strong wind, the fire reached such proportions that it consumed over [at first: "500"] 1200 houses. It lasted from 4 o'clock in the morning to the morning of the next day. The damage is immeasurable, since one single dealer in sugar by the name of Mr Whiting lost £40,000. They are raising a general subscription for the unfortunates. The City Council has had 120 tents erected there as shelters for the poor inhabitants. It is not yet known how many people lost their lives.

By the end of July they have now raised a collection of £10,000 Sterling for the unhappy people.

The *Entrepreneur* of the Haymarket Theatre, of which the Duke of Pedfort [Bedford] is the principal figure, pays that miserable cur

Taylor £21,000 Sterling every year for the expenses of the opera house; which sum is never sufficient, so that a group of various Lords, bankers, merchants &c. (but in all more than 200 of them) helps out. Moreover the house brings in not less than [at first: "two hundred"] £500. The present contract was established in 1791 and lasts for 17 years. Each backer gets 15 percent annually, but he loses the capital entirely after the 17 years are up.

For Taylor, see also p. 293.

1794

Milord Chatam [*sic*], President [*sic*] of the War Office and brother of Minister Pitt, was so drunk for 3 days that he couldn't even sign his name, and thus occasioned that Lord Howe couldn't leave London, and together with the whole fleet couldn't sail away.

Haydn has confused the two brothers, sons of WILLIAM PITT, SR. (died in 1778): (1) SIR JOHN, 2ND EARL OF CHATHAM, was first Lord of the Admiralty in 1794, though changing to Privy Seal in December of that year; (2) WILLIAM JR. was Prime and War Minister in 1794. Haydn thus gives the name of John but the office of William. Mr. O. W. Neighbour, who kindly supplied this information, adds that "presumably Howe might have felt the effects of either's drinking."

In the month of Sept. 1794, there was an attempt to assassinate the King. The principal murderers were very young, one was a clock-maker, the other a chemist. They constructed a kind of blow-pipe from which a little poisoned arrow was to kill the King in the Theatre. The understanding was to start a brawl right under the King's box, during the course of which each of the gang was to raise his stick in the air and threaten to beat the other, whilst the principal rogue was to shoot his arrow at the King. They have discovered another two participants, one of them a bookseller. The clock-maker's name is La Maitre, presumably a Frenchman; the chemist, Higgins. The bookseller is named Joh[n] Smith, the 4th man, Upton. The clock-maker invented the murder weapon.

[German:] The trip into [!] Jersey, or divorce à la mode. [English:] Trip to JERSEY, or — divorce a la mode. [German:] Jersey is the name of the Prince of Wales' new mistress. THAT'S WHAT THEY SAY: *relata reffero* [*sic*].

> Salomon und David waren grosse Sünder,
> Hatten schöne weiber, machten viele kinder.
> Da Sie nicht mehr konnten und kamen in das alter,
> macht der Eine Lieder, und der andere Psalter.

(Salomon and David were great sinners / had beautiful wives and made many children./ When they couldn't do it any more and grew old,/ the one wrote songs and the other wrote psalms.) The play on names (Salomon = Haydn's impresario; David = the famous tenor, DAVIDDE, who was always referred to as David in England) is obvious. The poem is written down with many corrections and improvements, which suggests that Haydn was probably the author (or translator?).

N.B. Lord Avington set it to music, but miserably; I did it a bit better.

THE EARL OF ABINGDON, a great musical enthusiast, had been in correspondence with Haydn before he came to England. Haydn wrote various things for Lord Abingdon, *inter alia* a Trio for 2 flutes and 'cello (Hoboken IV:2) and part of an oratorio (*Mare Clausum*). Together, they issued "Twelve Sentimental Catches and Glees"; the melodies were by Abingdon and the accompaniments by Haydn.

On 8th April 1795, the Prince of Wales married the Princess of Brunswick. On the 10th I was at the Covent Garden Theatre —to see the big Spectacul [*sic*]—WINDSOR CASTLE, THE MUSIC BY SALOMON QUITE PASSABLE. The decorations — costumes — scenery, and the enormous amount of people on the stage are exaggerated. All the Gods of Heaven and Hell, and everything that lives on the earth are in the piece.

The Overture was "composed expressly for the occasion by Dr. Haydn" (*Overture to an English Opera*): see Landon, pp. 541f.

Lord Macartney was sent as Ambassador to China.
Pekin [*sic*] is the capital — Gehol the Emperor's residence, 150 miles from Pekin. The wall of Pekin is 2,000 miles long. The city is not paved. The longest street is 6 miles long and 130 feet broad. The wall is 26 feet high and some 15 feet broad, at the base 20 feet.

Every 150 paces along this wall there is a tower 15 feet high and 45 feet long; there are 45,000 of them in all. The present Emperor is 83 years old. Everyone prostrates himself at his feet.

The King of England wanted to open commercial intercourse with China, but he received a negative answer. The Emperor sent George some verses which he himself had written in his [the King's] honour.

The Castle at Newport has a well 300 feet deep which is driven by a mule. Newport is a nice little town; the people look just like the Germans and mostly have black hair

Again a reference to the Isle of Wight, of which Newport is the capital.

Bartholomew Fair is generally held at the cattle-market, in the City; it goes on for 3 days. There are Berchtesgaden wares [toys] to be had there, and all sorts of plays are given, little comedies, juggling, tight-rope-walking, hawkers [*Carlatonerey*], dentists; and all sorts of riff-raff are there.

The cattle-market was then held at Smithfield.

A very good English toast, or drink-your-health: the first 2 words of the 3rd Psalm, "Lord! How" *etc*: [are they increased that trouble me!], that is, Lord Howe, the great English soldier.

On 9th Sept. 1794, I travelled with a bridal pair. The man was named Lindley, organist, 25 years old; his wife 18, with very good features — but both of them stone-blind. The old proverb, "Love is blind", does not apply here. He was poor, but she brought him a dowry of £20,000 Sterling. Now he doesn't play the organ any more.

Lord Avington [Abingdon] had an organ built in the church on his estate. When the Archbishop of the diocese heard about it, he wrote a letter reproving him for having done this without his knowledge, inasmuch as one cannot do such a thing without previously informing the authorities. He got an answer: "The Lord gave it, and the Lord can take it away again." This is most ambiguous, but very good.

Banti, Rovedino, Morichelli, Morelli, Brida, Braghetti, Bianchi, Martini, Ferlendis, Dragonetti, Harrington; Taylor, impresario. GLUCK's *Alceste*, BIANCHI's *Semiramide*. S:[ig.] Neri, *povero castrato*.

Mostly members of the Italian Opera at the King's Theatre. Bianchi (see p. 293) and MARTIN (Vincente Martin y Solar, 1754–1806) were the composers engaged. Banti (see p. 293), Rovedino (see p. 293), Morichelli (see p. 68), Morelli (see p. 264), Brida (see p. 293) and Braghetti (see p. 293) were singers. GIUSEPPE FERLENDIS, formerly at the Salzburg Court, was an oboe and English horn player (see also *infra*), D. DRAGONETTI was a famous double-bass player. Dr. HENRY HARINGTON (on the first page of this Notebook Haydn spells him Harlinghton) was a composer who lived at Bath; Haydn wrote a song for him, "What Art expresses". For Taylor, see also pp. 293 and 298. Neri was a second-rate castrato.

L'Isola del piacere BY MARTINI

The Overture from *L'Arbore di Diana*, a lot of old stuff from *Cosa rara*; and he had a very unsuccessful benefit concert.

Ferlendis, oboe player, is mediocre.

[*English*]
O spare that dreadful thought,
If I shou'd leave thee!
May I all pleasure leave
Lass — when I leave thee.

Field a young boy, which plays the pianoforte Extremely well.

JOHN FIELD (1782–1837), who later created the Nocturne.

LOVE
When I know that your heart is another's
That our wishes can never agree
That a flame in your Bosom still burns
That never was kindled by me,
One should think, that your Friendship's soft Balm,
Unasisted [*sic*] by love['s] ardent Sigh
Might ev'ry disquietude calm
And wipe off the tear from my eye.

[*Latin*]
"Excitat, mulcet, ut Magus"

Hor:[atius].

[*German*]
On 24th March 1795, Mara gave her Benefice Music [benefit concert] in Hanover Square. Yaniewish [*sic*] conducted; Clementi sat at the pianoforte. She had to bear the expense. [*Cf.* p. 288.]

[*English*]
SONG

1.
Guardian Angels now protect me[,]
Send, Ah send the youth I love,
Deign O Cupid to direct me[,]
Lead me to the myrtle grove.

2.
Bear my Sighs of floating Air,
Say I love him to dispair[,]
Tell him it is for him I grieve[,]
For him alone, I wish to live.

[An old song, perhaps by Thomas Carter]

ON MELODY
Oh! pour thy Spirit o'er my lays,
Coelestial MELODY inspire!
Sweet as the Royal Psalmists lyre
That I with THEE my ——— his praise.

THE SIGH OF A DISCARDED LOVER
Go gentle Zephyr, go and bear,
The tenderest Sigh to Kitty's Ear,
In wispers [*sic*] soft ah tell my pain,
Tell how I love but dar'nt complain.

THE LADIES LOOKING GLASS.

Trust not too much to that Enchanting Face [,]
Beaty's [*sic*] a charm, but soon that charm will pass.

Haydn's setting of this song has survived only in his autograph (National-bibliothek, Vienna): the melody, which is perhaps an English folk song, also appears in one of the Divertimenti for two flutes and violoncello.

SONG

Ah stay! Ah turn! ah whither would you fly?
Too charming, too relentless Maid[!]
I follow not to conquer, but to Die,
You of the fearful are afraid.

[*German*]

Madam Mara gave a 2nd concert under the auspices of the flautist Ashe. The house was quite full; I sat at the pianoforte.

The concert was held on 8th June 1795 at the King's Theatre; it was possibly the last public concert in England in which Haydn participated. For details of the programme, see Landon, p. 550.

[*English*]

[Pencilled note:]   Turk was a Faithful Dog
                     and not a Man.
                     Alfred Str.

The text of a canon which Haydn wrote for the dead dog of V. Rauzzini in Bath, and probably an address there.

[*Latin and German*]

CURAS CITHARA TULLIT.   On a house in Pristol [*sic*]
MORS JANUA VITAE

Suaviter in modo.   ⎫
fortiter in Re.   ⎬   The rascal beat the boy terribly.
                    ⎭

[Claudio Aquaviva (1543–1615)]

VIRTUTE PARTA.

[*French*]

tiens ta Foy.

[Extracts from the biographies of Dies and Griesinger,
here arranged in chronological order]

[*German*]
On 26th Aug. 1794, I went to Waverly [*sic*] Abbey, forty miles
from London, to visit Baron Sir Charles Rich, quite a good 'cello
player. Here there are the remains of a monastery which has already
been standing for 600 years. I must confess that whenever I looked
at this beautiful wilderness, my heart was oppressed at the thought
that all this once belonged to my religion.

[Griesinger, pp. 100*f.*]

Waverley Abbey is in Surrey, three miles away from Farnham, where on
a previous journey Haydn had had "a good dinner" (see *supra*, p. 294).
LADY RICH later subscribed to the *Creation*.

On 14th Nov. 1794 I went with Lord Avingdon [Abingdon] to
Preston, 26 miles from London, to visit the Baron of Aston; he and
his wife love music.   [Griesinger, pp. 50*f.*]

SIR WILLOUGHBY ASTON, Bart., lived at Preston, near Hitchin in Hertfordshire. Haydn wrote one of his Trios for 2 flutes and 'cello (C major, Hoboken IV: 1) for Sir Willoughby. Since one of the other "Divertimenti" (as
Haydn called them) for this combination was written for Lord Abingdon,
it may be that both were written at the same time for this week-end party.
See also *supra*, p. 299.

On 15th Dec. 1794, I visited Mr. Baze, who conducts the Ancient-
Concert from the organ and plays quite well; his wife has a very
pleasant, flexible voice, her pitch is very true and her pronunciation
clear; she has Bachierotti's [Pachierotti] way of singing, but her
shake is a little too rapid.   [Griesinger, p. 48.]

JOAH BATES (*c.* 1740–1799), a great admirer of Handel's music, also conducted the mammoth performances at Westminster Abbey. His wife, *née*
Harrop, died in 1811. (Pohl, H. in L., pp. 277*f.*)

On 21st Jan. 1795, I dined with Dr. Parsons. There arose an argument which of the Doctors, Parsons, Dupuis, or Arnold, should conduct the orchestra for the Handel Antiphon at the Prince of Wales' marriage. Dr. Parsons is Master of the King's Band, the other two are Court Organists. In England, however, the organist is the head in all the churches, and the singers are subordinate to him. Each of the three wanted to be the principal conductor. When I was forced to express my opinion, I said: The youngest organist should play the organ; the other should conduct the singers who are subordinate to him; and Dr. Parsons should conduct the Instrumental Performers; and since the singers always have the preference over the instrumental players, one of them should place his chorus on the right, the other on the left. They didn't want that, however, and so I shook the dust off my feet and went home. [Griesinger, p. 49.]

For Dr. Parsons, see p. 290; Dr. Dupuis see pp. 266, 290; Dr. Arnold, pp. 264, 290. The marriage took place on 8th April. The music included Handel's "Sing unto God" (Wedding Anthem, which had been written for George III's father, then [1736] Prince of Wales), and the arrangement of the performers turned out to be that suggested by Haydn: Dr. Parsons directed the King's Band (leader: Wilhelm Cramer) and was principal conductor; Arnold and Dupuis conducted the choir, and Dupuis also played the organ. (Pohl, H. in L., p. 299.)

On 1st February 1795, I was invited by the Prince of Wales to attend a musical soirée at the Duke of York's, which the King, the Queen, her whole family, the Duke of Orange &c. attended. Nothing else except my own compositions was played; I sat at the pianoforte; finally I had to sing, too. The King, who hitherto could or would only hear Handel's music, was attentive; he chatted with me, and introduced me to the Queen, who said many complimentary things to me. I sang my German song, "Ich bin der verliebteste". On 3rd Feb., I was invited to the Prince of Wales'; on 15th, 17th and 19th Apr. 1795, I was there again, and on the 21st at the Queen's in Buckingham Palace. [Griesinger, p. 50.]

Haydn enlarged upon these notes to Griesinger (pp. 57ff.)—see Landon, pp. 532f. for translation and contemporary newspaper report.

On 8th Apr. 1795, the marriage took place between the Prince of Wales and the Princess of Brunswick. On the 10th, I was invited to a musical soirée at the Prince of Wales' in Carlton House. An old

Symphony was played, which I accompanied on the pianoforte; then a Quartet; and afterwards I had to sing some German and English songs. The Princess sang with me, too; she played a Concerto on the pianoforte quite nicely.   [Griesinger, pp. 49*f.*]

For a contemporary newspaper report, see Landon, p. 541.

On 4th May 1795, I gave my benefit concert in the Haymarket Theatre. The room was full of a select company. a) First part of the Military Symphony; Aria (Rovedino); Concerto (Ferlandy) for the first time; Duet (Morichelli and Morelli) by me; a new Symphony in D, the twelfth and last of the English; b) Second part of the Military Symphony; Aria (Morichelli); Concerto (Viotti); *Scena nuova* by me, Mad. Banti [*English:*] (She song very scanty). [*German:*] The whole company was thoroughly pleased and so was I. I made four thousand Gulden on this evening. Such a thing is only possible in England.   [Griesinger, p. 53.]

The Military Symphony is No. 100, in G. The Concerto was played by Giuseppe Ferlendis, probably on the *cor anglais* (it was the concerto which was played "for the first time", not the duet). The Duet was "Quel tuo visetto amabile" from Haydn's *Orlando Paladino* (1782); Haydn had rewritten the work with new words ("Quel cor umano e tenero"), in which form it was played in Da Ponte's *Il burbero di buon cuore* (Act II, Scene 3) on 17th May 1794, also with Morelli and Morichelli. For some reason, however, Haydn chose to perform it at his benefit concert with the original text, as the only extant copy of the hand-bill (in possession of Albi Rosenthal, Esq., Oxford) clearly shows. The new Symphony in D was No. 104, Haydn's last work in the form. The "Scena nuova" was the *Scena di Berenice*, Haydn's greatest work of this kind. For Rovedino, see p. 293; Ferlendis, p. 301; Signora Morichelli, p. 68; Signor Morelli, p. 264; G. B. VIOTTI (1753–1824) was the famous violinist and composer who had just taken London by storm; for Signora Banti, see p. 293.

[Undated entries]

Dr. Arnold composed an opera for the Drury Lane Theatre; since the backers were afraid that it would not be successful, Dr. Arnold agreed to give it three times at his own expense. He spent over seven-hundred pounds on it; the backers, however, payed a lot of people each time to hiss the opera. Finally Arnold let the backers have the opera and the costumes for two-hundred pounds, and they thereupon performed it, with some alterations—better costumes and

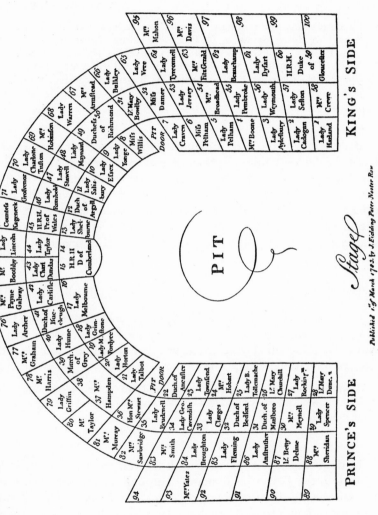

Published 1st of March 1783 by J. Fielding Pater-Noster Row

11. THE KING'S THEATRE, 1783

Interior plan of The King's Theatre, Haymarket, 1783, from a woodcut in *The European Magazine* reproduced in Terry's *John Christian Bach.*

scenery—and earned twenty-thousand pounds with it in the course of one year; the publisher alone earned some five-thousand pounds, and the poor composer lost five-hundred. O, what swindlers!

[Griesinger, pp. 47f.]

> Haydn has the essence of the story right, but the wrong theatre. Samuel Arnold (see also p. 264) wrote *The Banditti* for Covent Garden in 1781. The opera failed; Covent Garden staged it the next year as *The Castle of Andalusia*, and it then stayed in the repertoire for a good half century with no benefit to the composer. I am indebted to Dr. Roger Fiske for this information.

If a singing-, pianoforte-, or dancing-master asks half a guinea per lesson, he demands that an entrance fee of six guineas be payed at the first lesson. This is done because during the winter many Scots and Irishmen take pride in having their children study with the best teachers, only to find that at the end they cannot pay the fee. The entrance fee is dispensed with if the teacher charges a guinea, but the guinea must then be paid at every lesson.   [Griesinger, pp. 48f.]

[The following extracts from Dies are quoted in the third person]

On the very day that Haydn left Bath, a French emigrant sent him a laurel wreath. This wreath was accompanied by four poems which express nothing other than good will but are simply too poor to deserve quotation. [Dies, p. 155.]

> Haydn's sojourn at Bath is described in the Third Notebook (see p. 295). One of the poems was printed in *The Bath Herald and Register*, and reprinted in Pohl III, 82f.

In the company of several friends, Haydn went to see the wild animals in the Tower [of London]. Through carelessness the keeper had left the trap-door to the tiger's cage open. Madame Donelli was fortunate enough to discover this in time, though the keeper rushed to the scene just at the very moment when the tiger had already reached the trap-door. [Dies, p. 155.]

> Donelli may be a misprint for DORELLI, in which case MADAME DORELLI was probably the wife of the singer in Gallini's company (see also *supra*, p. 264).

[Catalogue of all the works Haydn wrote in and for England
between 2nd January 1791 and 1795]

[English]

Orfeo, opera seria.[1]	110	sheets
6 Symphonies.[2]	124	—
Concertant Symphonie.[3]	30	—
The Storm. Chor.[4]	20	—
3 Symphonies.[5]	72	—
Aria for Davide.[6]	12	—
Maccone for Gallini.[7]	6	—
6 Quartettes.[8]	48	—
3 Sonates for Broderip.[9]	18	—
3 Sonates for Preston.[10]	18	—
3 Sonates for Miss Janson.[11]	10	—
1 Sonate in F minore.[12]	3	—
1 Sonate in g.[13]	5	—
The Dream.[14]	3	—
Dr. Harringtons Compliment.[15]	2	—
6 English songs.[16]	8	—
100 Scotch songs.[17]	50	—
50 Scotch songs (for Nepire).[18]	25	—
2 Flüte divert.[19]	10	—
3 Symphonies.[20]	72	—
4 Song for Thattersal[21]	6	—
2 Marches.[22]	2	—
1 Aria for Miss Poole.[23]	5	—
1 God save the King.[24]	2	—
1 Aria con Orchestra.[25]	3	—
Invocation of Neptun.[26]	3	—
10 Commandments (Canons).[27]	6	—
March—Prince of Wales.[28]	2	—
2 Divertimenti a più voci.[29]	12	—
24 Minuets and german dances.[30]	12	—
12 Ballads for Lord Avingdon.[31]	12	—
Different songs.[32]	29	—
Canons.[33]	2	—
1 Song with the whole orchest.[34]	2	—
Of Lord Avingdon.[35]	2	—
4 Contrydances [sic][36]	2	—
6 Songs.[37]	2	—

Overtura Coventgarden [*sic*][38]	6	—
Aria per la Banti.[39]	11	—
4 Scotch songs.[40]	2	—
2 Songs.[41]	1	—
2 Contrydances.[42]	1	—
3 Sonates for Broderip.[43]	[see note]	

Summa 768 sheets.

The catalogue is reproduced in Dies in the original English, but without the number of sheets, and with various cryptographic abbreviations ("for P—"). Griesinger prints the list in German, but with the number of sheets ("Blätter") and with the names written out. Differences between the two sources are noted below. For purposes of comparison, Carpani's biography (in the English translation of the Stendhal piracy) occasionally proved useful (Carpani's Italian biography, *Le Haydine* . . . Milan 1812 = Stendhal, *Vie de Haydn* [published under pseudonym, L. A. C. Bombet], Paris 1814; English translation, *The Life of Haydn*, London 1817, pp. 328*f*.). The number of sheets which Haydn lists is often inaccurate. Sometimes Haydn seems to mean four pages for a sheet: the *Scena di Berenice* (= Aria per la Banti, 39) has in fact 11 double sheets, or 44 pages. At other times, however, this four to one relationship does not apply. The *Sinfonia Concertante* (2) is listed as having 30 sheets. The autograph has 40 sheets (80 pages).

1 *Orfeo*, or as its actual title reads, *L'anima del filosofo*, was composed in the first six months of 1791.
2 Symphonies Nos. 93–98 (1791–1792).
3 *Sinfonia Concertante* in B flat (1792).
4 The autograph is entitled *Madrigal* (1792).
5 Presumably Symphonies Nos. 99–101 (1793–1794).
6 The aria is lost.
7 The *Maccone* is either lost or unidentified.
8 The so-called Op. 71 & 74 (a silly method of identification, inasmuch as all six were written at one time and as an entity), Vienna 1793.
9 Haydn wrote three sets of pianoforte Trios (they were published as "Sonatas") for Longman and Broderip: Nos. 18–20 (published in 1794), Nos. 24–26 (published in 1795) and Nos. 27–29 (published in 1797).
10 Pianoforte Trios Nos. 21–23 (published in 1795). In Dies "P—".
11 In Griesinger "zwey Sonaten" (two Sonatas). Probably pianoforte Sonatas Nos. 50–52, but possibly the pianoforte Trios Nos. 27–29, which are dedicated to her. Stendhal also lists "3", not 2 works.
12 The so-called *Andante con varizioni*, the autograph of which is entitled *Sonata* (1793). For pianoforte solo.
13 The pianoforte Trio in G, Hoboken XV: 32, published by Preston in 1794. For years this work has been considered a violin Sonata, but

the authentic Preston edition shows clearly that Haydn wrote it as a Trio.

14 This piece, called "Jacob's Dream", was for violin and pianoforte; it seems to be lost.

15 Haydn wrote this piece in Bath for Dr. Henry Harington, who had composed the poem, "What Art expresses", in Haydn's honour. The work is written in a rather curious form: voice and pianoforte, then a mixed chorus, and finally variations for pianoforte solo. See Haydn *Gesamtausgabe* (B. & H.), Ser. XX, Band I, p. xv, n. Clementi found this procedure very amusing, and wrote: "The first doctor [Harington] having bestowed much praise on the second doctor [Haydn], the said second doctor, out of doctorial gratitude, returns the first doctor thanks for all favour received, and praises in his turn the said first doctor most handsomely." See Geiringer, *Haydn*, London 1947, p. 133. See also *supra*, p. 301.

16 Probably the first set of *VI Original Canzonettas* (see *supra*, p. 145), published in June 1794.

17 The Scotch songs for Napier, the first set of which included 100 settings. They appeared in the autumn of 1791.

18 The bracketed part appears only in Griesinger "(für Nepire)". The 50 songs constituted a second volume (see 17). Cecil Hopkinson and C. B. Oldman, 'Haydn's Settings of Scottish Songs in the Collections of Napier and Whyte' (*Edinburgh Bibliographical Society Transactions*, Vol. III, Part 2, pp. 85*ff*).

19 Two *Divertimenti* for 2 flutes and 'cello: Haydn wrote three such works in 1794: Hoboken IV: 1–4 (of which No. 4, containing one movement, obviously belongs to another work).

20 Presumably Symphonies Nos. 102–104 (1794–1795).

21 In Dies "4 Song for S-", in Stendhal "4 Songs for F.", in Griesinger "Vier Gesänge für Thallersal". I presume Griesinger misread Haydn's handwriting, and have therefore simply altered the "ll" to "tt". See *supra*, p. 290, for a description of the hymns which Haydn arranged.

22 The Marches for Sir Henry Harpur. See Carl Haas, 'Haydn's English Military Marches' (*The Score*, No. 2, Jan. 1950, pp. 50*ff*.).

23 In Dies " . . . for Mss. P—". The Aria is lost.

24 Haydn's setting is lost.

25 The Aria cannot be identified, and is presumably lost.

26 Aria and chorus from an unfinished Oratorio, *Mare clausum*, which Haydn started to write for Lord Abingdon in 1794. Autograph in the B.M.

27 These Canons were written for the Saxon minister in London, Count Brühl. The autograph in the Gesellschaft der Musikfreunde is in my opinion a copy Haydn made for himself.

28 This March, Haydn's best, survives in two versions, one for wind band (the Prince of Wales' version) and one for orchestra (the version Haydn made for the Royal Society of Musicians).

29 Haydn here appears to count two arrangements of Notturni which he wrote for the King of Naples in 1790; in fact Haydn rewrote

about six such Divertimenti, and played them in the Salomon concerts of 1791 and 1792.

[30] As I have said elsewhere (Landon, p. 563), these 24 Minuets and *Deutsche Tänze* are probably identical with the Redoutensaal dances of 1792: see also *supra*, p. 139.

[31] Dies " . . . for Lord A—". The pieces have been mentioned above (see p. 299).

[32] The "Different songs" cannot be identified.

[33] It is almost impossible to say which canons Haydn refers to: possibly the canon he wrote for his Doctor's degree at Oxford ("Thy voice, O Harmony, is divine"), and the German Canon which he entered in one of the London Notebooks (see p. 268).

[34] The "Song" cannot be identified.

[35] Dies " . . . Lord A." Probably songs, or one of the Divertimenti for 2 flutes and 'cello (see also 19 and p. 299).

[36] The "Contrydances" are apparently lost.

[37] Probably the second set of *VI Original Canzonettas*, published in the Autumn of 1795.

[38] The Overture to Salomon's *Windsor Castle* (first edition, edited by the writer of these notes, published by the Universal Edition, Vienna). Haydn's *Entwurf-Katalog* lists the work as "Musik zu einer Englischen opera, 1994" (*i.e.* 1794), but *Windsor Castle* was first performed in the Spring of 1795. See also *supra*, p. 299.

[39] The *Scena di Berenice*, 1795.

[40] The "4 Scotch songs" cannot be identified.

[41] The "2 Songs" are possibly "O Tuneful Voice" and "The Spirit's Song", English Songs which are not part of the twelve Canzonettas.

[42] The two Dances are lost.

[43] This entry is missing in Griesinger, but it appears in Dies and also in Stendhal ("3 Sonatas for Broderich"): see note 9.

APPENDIXES

THE SOURCES

Sources: The use of → simply indicates that the autograph passed from one known place, collector or bookseller to another; it does not necessarily indicate that the recipient acquired it directly from the owner previously listed. Antiquarian booksellers often acquire and sell such letters without listing the autographs in any catalogue. In addition to the abbreviations used throughout the book, the following appear below:

Libraries and Manuscripts

Artaria Archives = Archives of the firm of Artaria & Co., Vienna. When Pohl was alive, the firm owned most of the letters Haydn had written to them; later they gradually sold many of the letters. After the First World War the owners then began to repurchase them from antiquarian booksellers, and the firm managed to re-collect a sizable amount. Unfortunately, the entire collection was sold in 1953 and is now in a private library.

Budapest = Those Haydn letters owned by the National Museum, Budapest, which are not part of the Esterházy Archives.

B.M. = British Museum, London.

Esterházy Archives = Now in the National Museum, Budapest.

Prince Esterházy's Coll. = A kind of semi-private collection of Haydniana which the various Princes Esterházy kept separate from the "Acta Musicalia". The material in this private collection was for the most part left to Prince Nicolaus II in Haydn's will. It was kept at Eisenstadt until the First World War, and is now in the National Museum, Budapest.

Harburg Castle = The Archives of Prince Oettingen-Wallerstein, Harburg Castle (Bavaria).

IMBA = Internationales Musiker-Brief-Archiv, Berlin.

Pohl MS. = A collection of Haydn letters copied by C. F. Pohl during the preparation of his Haydn biography; Gesellschaft der Musikfreunde, Vienna, $\frac{9076}{108}$.

VNat = National Library, Vienna (Österreichische Nationalbibliothek, Wien).

Antiquarian Booksellers[1]

Artaria & Co., Vienna (after cessation of music publishing business, Artaria continued to sell engravings, maps. &c.: occasionally it sponsored auctions, in some of which Haydn letters appeared).

Mary Benjamin, New York City (director of firm of Walter Benjamin).
M. Bermann, Vienna.
Richard Bertling, Dresden.
C. G. Börner, Leipzig.
Martin Breslauer, London.

Étienne Charavay, Paris.
Gabriel Charavay, Paris.
Noël Charavay, Paris.
Albert Cohn, Berlin.
Friedrich Cohen, Bonn.

Heinrich Eisemann, London.

R. Geering, Basel.
Gilhofer und Ranschburg, Vienna.
Lucien Goldschmidt, New York City.
Paul Gottschalk, Berlin.
Franz Gräffer, Vienna.

Otto Haas, London.
V. A. Heck, Vienna.
K. E. Henrici, Berlin.
Hermann, London.
Heinrich Hinterberger, Vienna.

M. Lengfeld, Cologne.
Leo Liepmannssohn, Berlin.
List und Franke, Leipzig.

Thomas Maddigan, New York City.
Maggs Brothers, London.

Gustav Nebehay, Vienna.

J. Pearson, London.

Gerd Rosen, Berlin.

David Salomon, Berlin.
Walter Schatzki, New York City.
Hans Schneider, Tutzing über Munich.
O. A. Schultz, Leipzig.
Ignaz Schwarz, Vienna.
Sotheby, Wilkinson & Hodge, London.
Sotheby & Co., London.
J. A. Stargardt, Berlin (later Marburg on the Lahn).

T. Tausky, Paris.

R. Zeune, Berlin.

[1]For the period up to 1909, I have relied mainly on Ignaz Schwarz, 'Verzeichnis der bisher im Handel vorgekommenen Haydn-Briefe. Ein Versuch.' (in Gilhofer und Ranschburg Cat. No. 92, Vienna 1909).

German Abbreviations used in Connection with Antiquarian Booksellers' Catalogues, &c.

Auk. = Auktion (Auk.-Kat. = Auktions-Katalog);
Auction (Auction-Cat.);
Facs. = facsimile;
Jg. = Jahrgang (*i.e.* Vol. no. or rather "year");
Kat. = Katalog (Catalogue);
Lager-Kat. = Lager-Katalog (Cat. of material in stock);
Nachlass (Legacy; From the legacy of . . . &c.);
Samml. = Sammlung (Collection);
Verst. = Versteigerung (Auction);
Verst.-Kat. = Versteigerungs-Katalog

Literature (under "Printed Sources")

An attempt has been made to list the first publication, so far as it is known. Certain letters have been reprinted many times, and no attempt has been made to list every publication, especially since most of them derive from one principal source, *e.g.* Karajan or Nohl. The list given below is intended primarily to give readers a chance to consult the best printed text of a given letter in its original language; thus, the Genzinger letters are all printed very accurately in Karajan, and therefore a reference to Nohl, wherein the texts are modernized, was considered superfluous. The following additional abbreviations have been employed:

A. Csatkai = 'Aus dem Haydnzimmer der Wolfsammlung' (*Burgenländische Heimatblätter*, Jg. 1, Heft 1, pp. 31*ff.*).

A. Diemand = 'Joseph Haydn und der Wallersteiner Hof' (*Zeitschrift des historischen Vereins für Schwaben und Neuburg*, Band 45 (1920–1922), pp. 1*ff.*).

K. Geiringer = *Joseph Haydn*, Potsdam 1932.

Geiringer MQ = 'Haydn and the Folksong of the British Isles' (*Musical Quarterly* XXXV/2 [April 1949], pp 179*ff.*).

Mörner = C.-G. Stellan Mörner, *Johan Wikmanson und die Brüder Silverstolpe*, Stockholm 1952.

Sandberger = A. Sandberger, *Gesammelte Aufsätze zur Musikgeschichte*, Munich 1921.

Sandys-Forster = W. Sandys and S. A. Forster, *The History of the Violin*, London 1864.

Schmid = E. F. Schmid, *Joseph Haydn, Ein Buch von Vorfahren und Heimat des Meisters*, Kassel 1934.

Valkó = Arisztid Valkó, 'Haydn Magyarországi Müködése a Levéltári Akták Tükrében' (*Kodály Zoltán 75. születésnapjára* [Zenetudományi Tanulmányok VI], Budapest 1957, pp. 627*ff.*).

THE SOURCES

Letter	Autograph	Printed Source(s)	Source used
9 Sept. 1765	Esterházy Archives Acta Musicalia I, 49	Valkó, pp. 643f.	Autograph
Rahier to Esterházy (13 Sept. 1765)	Esterházy Archives Acta Musicalia	none	Marton copy in VNat.
Prince Esterházy to Haydn [Oct. or Nov. 1765]	Esterházy Archives, Acta Musicalia I, 346	Pohl I, 247 (incomplete)	Autograph
5 Dec. 1766	Esterházy Archives Acta Musicalia I, 53	Valkó, p. 647	Autograph
20 March 1768	Esterházy Archives Acta Musicalia I, 56r	Valkó, p. 651	Autograph
Applausus letter (1768)	Gesellschaft der Musikfreunde, Vienna	R. Haas, *Aufführungspraxis*, Potsdam 1931, pp. 238/240 (lacking one sentence); other printed sources (Pohl, Geiringer, *etc.*) are incomplete.	Autograph
22 Dec. 1768 to Prince Esterházy	Esterházy Archives Acta Musicalia I, 57	Valkó, p. 652 (incompl.)	Autograph
22 Dec. 1768 to Scheffstoss ("cover"-letter for above)	Esterházy Archives Acta Musicalia I, 47	Valkó, p. 652	Autograph
Autumn 1770	Esterházy Archives Acta Musicalia I, 50	Valkó, p. 653	Autograph
21 Dec. 1771	Esterházy Archives Acta Musicalia	none	Marton copy in VNat.
9 Jan. 1772	Esterházy Archives Acta Musicalia I, 51	Valkó, p. 653	Autograph
1773 (undated) application and receipt for 400 fl.	Esterházy Archives Acta Musicalia 625 & 626	none	Autographs
[c. 18 March 1774]	Esterházy Archives Acta Musicalia	none	Marton copy in VNat.
[March] 1776	Formerly Esterházy Archives (at present not yet located)	Pohl II, 23 (extracts)	Pohl

Letter	Autograph	Printed Source(s)	Source used
6 July 1776	(1) autograph, Esterházy Archives; (2) old copy, Budapest (cat. Ep. Mus. 287; (3) fair copy (not aut.), probably the copy sent for publication: Stargardt Cat. (Meyer-Cohn) No. 3068→Hans Schneider→Hoboken Coll., Ascona	F. Weigl, *Wiener Zeitschrift für Kunst, Literatur und Mode* 1836/IV, p. 1241 (inaccurate) [Pohl, *etc.* follow this source]; Erich Prieger, Programme notes to Rosé Quartet's Concert at Bonn, 15th February 1912 (based on source 3): facsimile of this in Willi Kahl, *Selbstbiographien deutscher Musiker des XVIII. Jahrhunderts,* Cologne 1948, pp. 83/86	Autograph (1) and fair copy (3)
1 June 1777	Esterházy Archives Acta Musicalia, 1036	none	Copy kindly made for me by Dénes Bartha.
4 Feb. 1779	Formerly Tonkünstler-Societät, now disappeared	E. Hanslick, *Signale,* 23. Jg. No. 47 (1865); Pohl, *Tonkünstler,* pp. 21f.; Pohl II, 84/86; Nohl, *Addenda* (LI-LIII)	Hanslick & Pohl.
31 Jan. 1780	Mayeda Foundation, Tokyo. (Leo Liepmannssohn, 8 May 1929)	none	Autograph
8 Feb. 1780	? (Formerly Artaria Archives)	Nohl, p. 82; Artaria-Botstiber, p. 8 (based on Nohl).	Nohl
25 Feb. 1780	Friedrich Cohen, Cat. Posonyi No. 470→ National Museum, Budapest, Ep. Mus. 286/1	Nohl, pp. 82f. (incompl.); Artaria-Botstiber (based on Nohl)	Autograph
20 March 1780	Heinrich Hinterberger (1953)→ ?	none	Autograph
29 March 1780	?(Formerly Artaria Archives)	Artaria-Botstiber, p. 10	Artaria-Botstiber
7 Nov. 1780	Esterházy Archives Acta Musicalia I, 52	Valkó, pp. 655f.	Autograph (facs. Valkó)
27 May 1781	? (Formerly Artaria Archives)	Nohl, pp. 83/85; Artaria-Botstiber, pp. 11/13	Nohl

Letter	Autograph	Printed Source(s)	Source used
23 June 1781	Heinrich Hinterberger (1953)→ ?	Nohl, pp. 86*f.*; Artaria-Botstiber, pp. 15*f.* (from aut.)	Artaria-Botstiber.
20 July 1781	Artaria Archives→Leo Liepmannssohn Cat. 4 Nov. 1907 No. 88→ Coll. Heyer, Cologne→ Coll. Arthur Hill, London→Sotheby (Hill Coll. Cat., lot 290) 17 June 1947 [with wrong date: 1789 instead of 1781]→ Otto Haas (£90)→ Rudolph Kallir, New York City	Nohl, pp. 87*f.* (incompl.); Artaria-Botstiber, *Addenda* (from aut., then at Coll. Heyer)	Artaria-Botstiber
18 Oct. 1781	Artaria Archives→ Kästner Museum, Hanover	Nohl, *Addenda* (LIII–LIV); Artaria-Botstiber, p. 18	Autograph (IMBA)
3 Dec. 1781 [Lavater]	Zürich Univ.-Bibliothek, Cat. Lav.-Br. Bd. 11, No. 264, MSS. 511	Isler, *Neue Züricher Zeitung*, 31 Mar. 1932 No. 503; Sandberger, *Peters-Jahrbuch* 1933, pp. 28*f.*	Sandberger
3 Dec. 1781 [Prince Oettingen-Wallerstein]	Harburg Castle	Sandberger, p. 224	Autograph
4 Jan. 1782	Heinrich Hinterberger (1953)→ ?	Nohl, p. 88 (incompl.); Artaria-Botstiber (from aut.), pp. 19*f.*	Artaria-Botstiber
20 Jan. 1782	Artaria Archives→ Leo Liepmannssohn Cat. 713 (1901), No. 132→ Otto Haas→ Coll. Richard Franko Goldman, Amawalk, New York.	Nohl, p. 89 (without address &c.); Artaria-Bostiber, pp. 20*f.*	Autograph
15 Feb. 1782	Artaria Archives→K. H. Henrici Auk.-Kat. 152 (10/11 May 1929) No. 485→ Sotheby 1 Aug. 1939, lot 705→ Hermann (£11.10)→ Otto Haas→ Coll. J. E. Kite, Hove (Sussex)	Nohl, p. 89; Artaria-Botstiber, pp. 21*f.*	Autograph

Letter	Autograph	Printed Source(s)	Source used
8 Feb. 1782	Harburg Castle	Sandberger, p. 225	Sandberger
16 Aug. 1782	Berlin Staatsbibliothek (now Library of Congress, Washington)	Artaria-Botstiber, pp. 23*f*.	Autograph
[*c.* 25 Aug. 1782]	Friedrich Cohen, Cat. Posonyi No. 471→ National Museum, Budapest, Ep. Mus. 286/2	Nohl, p. 90 (in compl.); Artaria-Botstiber, pp. 22*f*. (from Nohl)	Pohl MS. & collation with aut. (Dénes Bartha)
29 Sept. 1782	Heinrich Hinterberger (1953) →?	Nohl, p. 91; Artaria-Botstiber, pp. 24*f*. (from aut.)	Artaria-Botstiber
20 Oct. 1782	Heinrich Hinterberger (1953)→ ?	Nohl, p. 91; Artaria-Botstiber, p. 25 (from aut.)	Artaria-Botstiber
27 Jan. 1783	K. E. Henrici Auk.-Kat. CXXVI (15 Dec. 1927)→ Heinrich Hinterberger (1953)→ ?	none	Autograph
20 March 1783	Artaria Archives→ Theodor Petter, Vienna → Albert Cohn Cat. 194, No. 196→ Coll. Robert Ammann, Aarau (Switzerland).	Artaria-Botstiber, pp. 26*f*.	Autograph (facs., without address, in R. Ammann, *Die Handschrift der Künstler*, Bern 1953—plate 86); Pohl MS.
3 April 1783	Friedrich Cohen, Cat. Posonyi No. 472→ National Museum, Budapest, Ep. Mus. 286/3	Nohl, p. 92 (incompl.); Artaria-Botstiber, pp. 27*f*. (from Nohl)	Pohl MS. & collation with aut. (Dénes Bartha)
18 June 1783	Heinrich Hinterberger (1953)→ ?	Nohl, p. 92 (incompl.); Artaria-Botstiber, pp. 28*f*. (from aut.).	Autograph
5 July 1783	Coll. Sir Ian Malcolm → Sotheby 28 Jan. 1949, lot 159→ Martin Breslauer (£58); Breslauer Cat. 71 (1950) No. 39→ T. Tausky→ ?	none (summaries &c. in above cats.)	Part of autograph (facs. p. 1 in Sotheby Cat.)
3 Feb. 1784	*Finanzrat* Schaffer, Schärding→ Heinrich Eisemann (for Coll. Dr. Manning, London)	Artaria-Botstiber, p. 30	Autograph
4 Feb. 1784	?	Dies, p. 70	Dies

Letter	Autograph	Printed Source(s)	Source used
1 March 1784	Haydn Museum, Vienna (stolen in 1945); wrongly listed in cat. as 1 May	Nohl, p. 93 (incompl.); Artaria-Botstiber, pp. 29f. (from Nohl)	Pohl MS.
5 April 1784	Leo Liepmannssohn Cat. 18 Nov. 1895, No. 1167→ ?	Nohl, p. 94 (very incompl.); Artaria-Botstiber, p. 31 (from Nohl)	Pohl MS.
8 April 1784	Roger Barrett, Chicago	none	Autograph
18 May 1784	Formerly Artaria Archives→ Heinrich Hinterberger (1953)→ ?	Artaria-Botstiber, pp. 31f.	Autograph (complete facs. in Artaria-Bots.)
25 Oct. 1784	?	C. A. Mangold in *Neue Zeitschrift für Musik*, IX (28 Aug. 1838), p. 72; Nohl, p. 94	Mangold
20 Nov. 1784	Coll. H. Gouin, Royaumont (France).	Artaria-Botstiber, pp. 32f (incompl.).	Autograph
29 Dec. 1784	Haus-, Hof- und Staatsarchiv, Vienna (files of Freemasons' Lodge □).	O. E. Deutsch, "Abendausgabe" of *Neue freie Presse*, Vienna, 14 March 1933, p. 6; Brand, pp. 209f.	Autograph (IMBA)
2 Feb. 1785	? (Formerly Alexander Count von Apponyi)	Pohl II, 208 (extracts)	Pohl
1 Sept. 1785	? (1) An old copy, private coll. in Basel, possibly used for engraving of (2) printed foreword of Mozart's Quartets Op. X, Artaria (pl. no. 59)	*Inter alia* Pohl II, 212; Köchel 3rd ed. (Einstein), pp. 506f., &c., &c.	Photograph of old copy (1), shown to me by O. E. Deutsch, and Artaria (facs. in Haas, *Mozart*, p. 113, &c.).
26 Nov. 1785	Paul Gottschalk Cat. 2, (1909), No. 63→ K. E. Henrici Auk.-Kat. I (1910), No. 451→ Aut.-Samml. Auk. C. G. Börner, 3–6 May 1911, No. 981→ K. E. Henrici Lager-Kat. 23 (1927?), No. 268→ Heinrich Hinterberger (1953)→ ?	none	Autograph

Letter	Autograph	Printed Source(s)	Source used
10 Dec. 1785	Frau Ida Konrat, Vienna →K. E. Henrici Auk.-Kat. CXX (27/28 May 1927), No. 557→ Westley Manning Coll. → Sotheby 12 Oct. 1954, lot 204→ H. J. Laufer (£125)→ Mrs. Marguerite Manley, Scarsdale, N.Y.	Nohl, pp. 94f.(very incompl); Artaria-Botstiber, pp. 34f. (from Nohl)	Autograph
May 1786	? (Formerly Alexander Count von Apponyi)	*Signale*, Jg. 92, No. 41 (1934), p. 558	Pohl MS. and *Signale*
1786 (undated)	B.M. Eg. 2380, f.12	Sandys-Forster, pp. 302ff.	Autograph
1 Feb. 1787	Artaria Archives→ O. A. Schultz Cat. 19	Artaria-Botstiber, pp. 36f. (from Pohl MS.)	Pohl MS. and Artaria-Botstiber
4 Feb. 1787	Cat. Donebauer 1894, p. 54→ Stargardt Cat. Donebauer (6 Apr.1908) No. 376→ C. G. Boerner Cat. XVI (1910), No. 151 (with facs.)→ V. A. Heck, Cat. 42 (April 1928), No. 54 (with 1st p. in facs.)→ Burgenländische Landesregierung (from a grant by Sándor Wolf): now Sándor Wolf Museum, Eisenstadt	Artaria-Botstiber, p. 37	Autograph
7 Feb. 1787	Leo Liepmannssohn Cat. 21 Nov. 1887, No. 126→ S. L. Courtauld, Imbeza Valley, S. Rhodesia	Nohl, pp. 95f. (incompl.), Artaria-Botstiber, pp. 38f. (from Pohl MS.)	Autograph
March 1787	Friedrich Cohen, Cat. Posonyi No. 473→ National Museum, Budapest, Ep. Mus. 286/4.	Nohl, p. 96 (incompl.); Artaria-Botstiber, p. 39 (from Nohl)	Pohl MS. and collation with aut. (Dénes Bartha)
April 1787	B.M. Eg. 2380, ff. 1–2	Pohl, H. in L., p. 355	Autograph
1 April 1787	?	*Wiener Zeitung*, 6 June 1787, p. 1355; Dies, p. 71; see Hoboken, p. 408	*Wiener Zeitung*

J.H.–Z

Letter	*Autograph*	*Printed Source(s)*	*Source used*
26 April 1787	Artaria Archives→ Heinrich Hinterberger (1953)→ ?	Nohl, p. 97; Artaria-Botstiber (from aut.), p. 48.	Artaria-Botstiber
2 May 1787 [Artaria]	Friedrich Cohen, Cat. Posonyi No. 474→ National Museum, Budapest, Ep. Mus. 286/5	Nohl, pp. 98f. (incompl.); Artaria-Botstiber, pp. 49f. (from Nohl)	Pohl MS. and collation with aut. (Dénes Bartha)
2 May 1787 [Eybler]	New York Public Library	none	Autograph
19 May 1787	Maggs Bros. Cats. 353 (1917) No. 353 [sic] with facs., 411 (1921) No. 1867 with facs., 449 (1924) No. 217 with facs.→ K. E. Henrici Auk.-Kat. XCVII (Nov. 1924), No. 52→ V. A. Heck→ Heinrich Hinterberger (1953)→ ?	none (facs. in K. Geigy-Hagenbach, *Handschriften berühmter Personlichkeiten*, Basel 1925, p. 247.)	Autograph
10 June 1787	Coll. Arthur Hill→ Sotheby Cat. 16–17 June 1947, lot 235 (with facs.)→ Maggs Bros. (£72)→ ?	none	Autograph (facs. in Sotheby Cat.)
21 June 1787	Artaria Archives→ Heinrich Hinterberger (1953)→ ?	Nohl, pp. 99f. (incompl.); Artaria-Botstiber, pp. 40f. (from aut.)	Artaria-Botstiber
23 June 1787	Artaria Archives→ Heinrich Hinterberger (1953)→ ?	Artaria-Botstiber, pp. 41f. (from aut.)	Artaria-Botstiber
28 June 1787	B.M. Eg. 2380, ff. 3–4	Sandys-Forster, pp. 302ff.	Autograph
12 July 1787	Artaria Archives→ Heinrich Hinterberger (1953)→ ?	Artaria-Botstiber, p. 42 (from aut.)	Artaria-Botstiber
19 July 1787	Sotheby Wilkinson & Hodge, 2 March 1905, lot 569→J. C. Murray (£10.5)→ Sotheby 6 Feb. 1920 lot 206→ Lacroix	none except Sotheby 1905	Sotheby 1905 (an almost complete translation)
28 July 1787	Geheimes Staatsarchiv Berlin (Rep. 110 B59-b)	Sandberger, *Zeitschrift für Musik* 105 Heft 12 (Dec. 1938.)	Autograph (IMBA)

Letter	Autograph	Printed Source(s)	Source used
Aug. 1787	Artaria Archives→ Heinrich Hinterberger (1953)→ ?	Artaria-Botstiber, pp. 5of. (from aut.)	Artaria-Botstiber
Aug. 1787	B.M. Eg. 2380, ff. 5-6	Sandys-Forster, pp. 302ff.	Autograph
6 Sept. 1787	Emilia Succi, Bologna (Mostra Internazionale 1888, No. 507)→ Leo Liepmannssohn 6 May 1889, No. 505→ Coll. Floersheim-Koch, Muzzano-Lugano (Switzerland)	none	Autograph
10 Sept. 1787	B.M. Eg. 2380, ff. 7-8	Sandys-Forster, pp. 302ff.	Autograph
Oct. 1787	Artaria Archives→ Heinrich Hinterberger (1953)→ ?	Nohl, p. 100; Artaria-Botstiber, pp. 43f. (from aut.)	Artaria-Botstiber
2 Nov. 1787	Artaria Archives→ C. G. Börner Cat. XXVI No. 345→ Artaria Archives (re-bought!)→ Heinrich Hinterberger (1953)→ ?	none	Autograph
7 Nov. 1787	Artaria Archives→ Heinrich Hinterberger (1953)→ ?	Nohl, pp. 100f.; Artaria-Botstiber, pp. 44f. (from aut.)	Artaria-Botstiber
Dec. 1787	?	Niemetschek, Mozart, Prague 1797, pp. 51f.; Allgemeine Musikalische Zeitung I (19 Dec. 1798), pp. 182f.; &c., &c.	Niemetschek (the only complete text).
Feb. 1788	Harburg Castle	Diemand, pp. 31f.	Diemand.
6 Feb. 1788	Max Friedländer (1909) → Leo Liepmannssohn Verst.-Kat. 63 (9 Dec. 1932) No. 72→ ?	Nohl, p. 102 (incompl.); Artaria-Botstiber, pp. 46f. (from Nohl)	Autograph (facs. in Schmidt, Joseph Haydn, Berlin 1898, p. 60).
18 Feb. 1788	B.M. Eg. 2380, ff. 9-10	Pohl, H. in L., p. 357.	Autograph
2 May 1788	?	Nohl, p. 103; Artaria-Botstiber, p. 47	Nohl, Artaria-Botstiber.
10 Aug. 1788	Haydn Museum, Vienna (stolen in 1945)	Nohl, p. 103 (incompl.); Artaria-Botstiber, pp. 51f. (from Nohl).	Pohl MS.

Letter	*Autograph*	*Printed Source(s)*	*Source used*
17 Aug. 1788	Coll. Kafka (*c.* 1870)→ B.M. Add. 29804, f. 1	Nohl, p. 104; Artaria-Botstiber, p. 52	Autograph
29 Aug. 1788	Gabriel Charavay Cat. 14 Feb. 1887, No. 159	none	no copy available
22 Sept. 1788	S. Tauber, Vienna (1870)→Leo Liepmannssohn 20 Jan. 1902, No. 28→ Therese Liebig, Vienna→ Verst.-Nachlass Liebig, Artaria, 22 March 1934, No. 625→ ?	Artaria-Botstiber, pp. 54f. (from Pohl MS.)	Artaria-Botstiber (collated with Pohl MS.)
26 Oct. 1788	Artaria Archives→ Heinrich Hinterberger (1953)→ ?	Nohl, pp. 104f. (no address); Artaria-Botstiber, pp. 52f. (from aut.)	Artaria-Botstiber
16 Nov. 1788	Formerly Artaria Archives	Artaria-Botstiber, p. 54 (from Pohl MS.)	Artaria-Botstiber (collated with Pohl MS.)
8 March 1789 [Traeg]	Historical Society of Pennsylvania	none	Autograph
8 March 1789 [Artaria]	Artaria Archives→ Heinrich Hinterberger (1953)→ ?	Nohl, p. 105 (incompl.); Artaria-Botstiber (from aut.)	Artaria-Botstiber
22 March 1789	*Hofrat* Viktor Keldorfer, Vienna	none (Pohl II, 249: extracts)	Autograph
29 March 1789	Artaria Archives→ Ludwig Zatzka, Vienna (1920)→ II. Aut. Auk. Dorotheum (Vienna), 6–10 June 1922, No. 155 (with extracts, corr. Artaria-Botstiber). An old "archive copy" formerly in Artaria Archives.	Nohl, pp. 33f. (no address); Artaria-Botstiber, pp. 56f. (from old copy)	Nohl, Artaria-Botstiber, Cat. Dorotheum 1922
5 April 1789 [Breitkopf]	Goethe-Schiller-Archiv, Weimar	none	Autograph (IMBA)
5 April 1789 [Sieber]	Maggs Bros. Cats. 425 (1922), No. 1285; 473 (1926), No. 263 (with facs. p. 2: this facs. in all other Maggs Cats.); 504 (1928), No. 1048; 512 (1928), No. 420; 538 (1930), No. 254→ ?	*Signale*, Jg. 92, No. 41 (1934), p. 558	Autograph (p. 2 only—from Maggs Cats.) and *Signale*.

Letter	Autograph	Printed Source(s)	Source used
6 April 1789	Artaria Archives→ Albert von Franck, Graz (1870)→Leo Liepmannssohn 3 Mar. 1886, No. 480→ Coll. Heyer, Cologne→ V. A. Heck 5 Sept. 1927→ G. Nebehay→Artaria Archives (rebought!)→ Heinrich Hinterberger (1953)→?	Artaria-Botstiber, pp. 57f. (no address)	Autograph (IMBA)
10 June 1789	VNat, Cod. 14300	Karajan, p. 57	Autograph
14 June 1789	ditto	Karajan, p. 58	Autograph
5 July 1789	Friedrich Cohen, Cat. Posonyi No. 475→ National Museum, Budapest, Ep. Mus. 286/6	Nohl, pp. 108f. (incompl.); Artaria-Botstiber, pp. 58f. (from Nohl)	Pohl MS. collated with autograph (Dénes Bartha)
27 July 1789	Pearson Cat. 12, No. 165 (c. 1900?)→Maggs Bros. Cat. 320 (1914), No. 328 (with facs. of p. 2).	none	Autograph of p. 2 and summary of rest of contents in Maggs Cat.
28 Aug. 1789	Yemeniz Coll.→ Alfred Morrison Coll. (Catalogue of the Collection . . . London 1885, II, p. 245)→ Arthur Hill Coll.→ Sotheby 17 June 1947, lot 291→ Walter Schatzki (£75) →?	none	no complete copy available (extracts from Morrison and Sotheby Cats.)
[Beginning of Oct. 1789]	Esterházy Archives, Acta Musicalia XIX, 1266	none	Autograph (from a copy kindly provided by Dr. Valkó)
[c. 17 October 1789]	Harburg Castle	Diemand, p. 33	Diemand
29 Oct. 1789	VNat. Cod. 14300	Karajan, p. 59	Autograph
7 Nov. 1789	ditto	Karajan, p. 60	Autograph
12 Nov. 1789	ditto	Karajan, p. 61	Autograph
15 Nov. 1789	Formerly Artaria Archives→ Friedrich Cohen, Cat. Posonyi No. 476→ National Museum, Budapest, Ep. Mus. 286/7	Artaria-Botstiber, pp. 60f. (from Pohl MS.)	Artaria-Botstiber collated with Pohl MS. and aut. (Dénes Bartha)

Letter	Autograph	Printed Source(s)	Source used
18 Nov. 1789	VNat. Cod. 14300	Karajan, p. 62	Autograph
29 Nov. 1789	Harburg Castle	Sandberger, p. 226; Diemand, p. 34.	Autograph
11 Jan. 1790	Artaria Archives→ Heinrich Hinterberger (1953)→ ?	Nohl, pp. 154f. (as 10 Jan. 1799) Artaria-Botstiber, p. 61 (from aut.)	Artaria-Botstiber
13 Jan. 1790 [Receipts] [See note at top of p. 95]	Two copies 1909 in Artaria Archives; one or more of these or possibly a third: V. A. Heck 2 May 1938→ Schmahl; Therese Liebig→ Verst.-Nachlass Liebig, Artaria, 22 Mar. 1934 No. 626	Artaria-Botstiber, p. 62 (from auts.): two versions	Artaria-Botstiber
23 Jan. 1790	VNat. Cod. 14300	Karajan, p. 64	Autograph
3 Feb. 1790	ditto	Karajan, p. 65	Autograph
9 Feb. 1790	ditto	Karajan, pp 66–68	Autograph
14 Mar. 1790	ditto	Karajan, pp. 69–71	Autograph
13 May 1790	ditto	Karajan, pp. 72f.	Autograph
30 May 1790	ditto	Karajan, pp. 74f.	Autograph
6 June 1790	ditto	Karajan, p. 76	Autograph
7 June 1790	Dr. Pölchau, Hamburg (1886)→ ?	La Mara, *Musikerbriefe* . . . . Leipzig 1886, I, pp. 246f. (from aut.)	La Mara
8 June 1790	VNat. XXXIII, 109-1 (gift of Eybler)	none	Autograph
20 June 1790	VNat. Cod. 14300	Karajan, pp. 77f.	Autograph
27 June 1790	ditto	Karajan, pp. 79f.	Autograph
4 July 1790	ditto	Karajan, pp. 81f.	Autograph
11 July 1790	ditto	Karajan, pp. 83f.	Autograph
31 July 1790	Esterházy Archives Acta Musicalia	none	Marton copy in VNat
[15 Aug. 1790]	VNat. Cod. 14300	Karajan, pp. 85f.	Autograph
22 Nov. 1790	2 copies, both formerly in Artaria Archives: (1) Friedrich Cohen, Cat. Posonyi No. 477→ National Museum Budapest; (2) Mary Benjamin (1955)→ ?	Pohl II, 249 (one version); Artaria-Botstiber, p. 63 (from Pohl)	Pohl MS. of both versions, collated with the aut. in Budapest (Dénes Bartha).
31 Dec. 1790	VNat. Cod. 14300	Karajan, p. 87	Autograph

Letter	Autograph	Printed Source(s)	Source used
8 Jan. 1791 [Genzinger]	ditto	Karajan, pp. 88–91	Autograph
8 Jan. 1791 [Esterházy]	Esterházy Archives Acta Musicalia I, 55	Valkó, p. 658	Autograph
14 Mar. 1791	Albert Cohn, Cat. Paar No. 1551→ private coll. in New York City (1958).	Pohl III, 19 (with wrong date: 4 instead of 14 March; Hoboken has checked the date of the aut., which I have not seen)	Pohl III, with corr. supplied by Dr. van Hoboken
c. 25 May 1791	?	Jackson's *Oxford Journal* of 28 May 1791; Mees, *The oldest Music Room in Europe*, London 1911, pp. 134f.; Pohl III, 24f.	Jackson's *OJ* (collation kindly made by Charles Humphries)
4 Aug. 1791	Leo Liepmannssohn, Cat. Bovet (24 Nov. 1902) No. 492→?	Pohl III, 29	Pohl III
7 Sept. 1791	VNat. Cod. 14300	Karajan, pp. 92–94	Autograph
13 Oct. 1791	ditto	Karajan, pp. 95–97	Autograph
7 Nov. 1791	ditto	Karajan, pp. 98f.	Autograph
13 Dec. 1791	Harvard College Library	Pohl III, 34 (inaccurate and incomplete)	Autograph
20 Dec. 1791	VNat. Cod. 14300	Karajan, pp. 100–103	Autograph
January 1792	?	Nottebohm, *Mozartiana*, Leipzig 1888, p. 10 (incompl.)	Nottebohm
4 Jan. 1792	Stargardt Cat. Donebauer (6 Apr. 1908), No. 377→Maggs Bros. Cats. 512 (1928), No. 419; 538 (1930), No. 253; 565 (1931), No. 811; 568 (1931), No. 1043; 586 (1933), No. 573; 601 (1934), No. 809; 616 (1935), No. 944 [the latter with substantial reduction in price]→ Heineman Foundation, Greenwich, Conn. (U.S.A.)	Pohl III, 34ff (incompl.)	Autograph
7 Jan. 1792	VNat. Cod. 14300	Karajan, pp. 104–106	Autograph

Letter	Autograph	Printed Source(s)	Source used
2 Feb. 1792	ditto	Karajan, pp. 107f.	Autograph
26 Feb. 1792	?	Grove's *Dictionary* (1st ed., 1879) I, 474 (Eng.); Pohl III, 9n	Pohl III
2 March 1792	VNat. Cod. 14300	Karajan, pp. 109–111	Autograph
10 Apr. 1792	Esterházy Archives Acta Musicalia I, 54	Valkó, p. 658	Autograph (facs. in Valkó)
24 Apr. 1792	VNat. Cod. 14300	Karajan, pp. 112f.	Autograph
Apr. 1792	?	*The Morning Herald,* 27 Apr. 1792; Pohl, H. in L., p. 194n.	*Morning Herald* (collation by Charles Humphries)
22 May 1792	Sotheby Wilkinson & Hodge Cat. 2 Mar. 1905, No. 568→ Maggs Bros. Cats. 394 (1920), No. 1366; 433 (1922), No. 3317→?	Pohl III, 59	Pohl III
13 June 1792	Sotheby Wilkinson & Hodge Cat. Huth Coll. (12–13 June 1911), No. 104→ Neumayer (£24) → Heyer Coll., Cologne→?	Pohl III, 59f.	Pohl III
4 Aug. 1792	VNat. Cod. 14300	Karajan, p. 114	Autograph
22 Oct. 1792	V. A. Heck Cat. 46, No. 322 (30 Oct. 1928) → Artaria & Co.→?	Pohl III, 66f. (incompl.)	Autograph (facs. in *Musical Quarterly*, Apr. 1932)
13 Nov. 1792	VNat. Cod. 14300	Karajan, p. 115	Autograph
7 Dec. 1792	Artaria Archives→ Heinrich Hinterberger (1953)→?	Artaria-Botstiber, p. 66 (from aut.)	Artaria-Botstiber
20 June 1793	Rudolf Brockhaus, Leipzig (1886)→ K. E. Henrici, Verst.-Kat. 155 (July 1929), No. 45→ Otto Haas Cat. 7 (Mar. 1938) No. 71→?	Pohl III, 70f.	Pohl III
14 Aug. 1793	Haydn Museum, Vienna (archive copy)	none	Archive copy
23 Nov. 1793	Haus-, Hof- und Staatsarchiv, Vienna, Fasz. 148–177	F. Reinöhl, *Neues Beethoven-Jahrbuch* VI (1935), pp. 36ff.	Autograph
23 Dec. 1793	ditto	ditto	Autograph

Letter	Autograph	Printed Source(s)	Source used
11 Jan. 1794	Private coll. Vienna→ V. A. Heck Cat. 69, No. 45a→ Stanford Memorial Library	Pohl I, 266	Autograph
22 Oct. 1794	Stargardt Cat. 534 (8 Nov. 1957), No. 421 (with facs.)→ Coll. Hoboken, Ascona	none	Autograph
[undated: to Holcroft]	Mary Benjamin (1957) → Coll. Hoboken, Ascona	none	Autograph
[undated: to Burney]	Stargardt Cat. 314 (24 Nov. 1930), No. 105 → ?	none (extracts in Stargardt Cat.)	Autograph (IMBA)
13 Aug. 1795	Sotheby Wilkinson & Hodge Cat. 2 Mar. 1905, No. 564→ Morton (£3.12)→ B.M. Add. 38071, f. 5	none	Autograph
27 Feb. 1796	Sotheby Wilkinson & Hodge Cat. 2 Mar. 1905, No. 565→Ellis (£6.5)→ Maggs Bros. Cats. 394 (1920), No. 1367; 433 (1922), No. 3318→ Library of Congress, Washington	*Musical Quarterly,* April 1932 (facs. with transl.)	Autograph
25 Mar. 1796	Leo Liepmannssohn Cat. 141, No. 597→ private coll., Louisville, Kentucky	none	Autograph
15 April 1796	W. Westley Manning → Sotheby Cat. 11/12 Oct. 1954, lot 205→ (£36) Dr. Schilling→ Hugo von Mendelssohn-Bartholdy, Basel	none (extract in Sotheby Cat.)	Autograph (Herr von Mendelssohn-Bartholdy kindly supplied a photograph)
16 Apr. 1796	Senator Gwinner, Frankfurt/M.→ O. A. Schultz Cat. 15, No. 107→ Coll. Floersheim-Koch, Muzzano-Lugano (Switzerland). Old copy in B. & H. Archives, destroyed in air raid of 4 Dec. 1943	Hase, p. 6	Autograph

Letter	Autograph	Printed Source(s)	Source used
9 Nov. 1796	Paris Conservatoire	Tiersot, *Lettres des musiciens*, Turin 1924, pp. 72*f.*	Autograph
[End of 1796]	? Old (contemporary) copy in VNat. Cod. 15391: date "Im Januar 1795" added later, in the same handwriting.	Nohl, pp. 151*f.*	Old copy in VNat.
20 Jan. 1797	Formerly Tonkünstler-Societät, now disappeared	Pohl, *Tonkünstler*, p. 41.	Pohl
[28 Jan. 1797]	VNat. XXXIII No. 109 -2	Nohl, p. 153	Autograph
1 June 1798	Gesellschaft der Musikfreunde, Vienna	none	Autograph
[End April 1799]	Kungl. Bib., Stockholm	none	Autograph
18 May 1799	Gesellschaft der Musikfreunde, Vienna	none (facs. in biogr. by Schmidt, Geiringer [Eng. ed. of *Haydn*, London, 1947])	Autograph
12 June 1799	K. E. Henrici Auk.-Kat. CXII (1926), No. 1001 → V. A. Heck→ Stadtbibliothek, Vienna (40. 044)	Griesinger, pp. 122*f.* (incomplete and with sentence added by G.)	Autograph
15 June 1799	?	*Allgemeine Musikalische Zeitung* (Intelligenzblatt, XV, 1799); Hase, pp. 10*f.*	AMZ
25 June 1799	B.M. Add. 33965, f. 205	none	Autograph
5 July 1799	Berlin Staatsbibliothek, stolen in 1945	none	Autograph (from a copy kindly provided by Dr. van Hoboken)
12 July 1799	Leo Liepmannssohn Cat. 20 Jan. 1908, No. 28a→ Paris Conservatoire	Nohl, *Addenda*, pp. LIV–LV; Artaria-Botstiber, p. 73 (from Pohl MS.)	Autograph
18 July 1799	Esterházy Archives, Acta Musicalia XXVI, 1854	none	Autograph (from a copy kindly provided by Dr. A. Valkó)

Letter	Autograph	Printed Source(s)	Source used
Between middle of July and September 1799]	Esterházy Archives, Acta Musicalia XXVI, 1855	none	Autograph (from a copy kindly provided by Dr. A. Valkó)
20 July 1799	Gabriel Charavay Cat. Kafka (1881), No. 30 → Alfred Morrison (*Catalogue of the Collection* . . . London 1885, II, p. 245)→ Sotheby (1917)→ Maggs Bros. Cat. 405 (1921), No. 925→ ?	Artaria-Botstiber, p. 74 (from Pohl MS.)	Autograph (photograph kindly supplied by Dr. van Hoboken)
24 July 1799	?	Pohl III, 150f.	Pohl III
10 Aug. 1799 Brühl]	Felix Salzer, New York City	none	Autograph
10 Aug. 1799 Knoblich]	Verst. Ignaz Schwarz 10 June 1918, No. 167 → O. A. Schultz Cat. 27, No. 276 → Musée de Mariemont (Belgium), cat. 1109 A / 3	*Neue Musikzeitung* (Stuttgart) 27 May 1909, p. 371; Pohl III, 151	Autograph (no address)
15 Aug. 1799	Artaria Archives→ Heinrich Hinterberger (1953)→?	Nohl, pp. 156f. (incompl.); Artaria-Botstiber, pp. 74f. (from aut.)	Artaria-Botstiber
19 Aug. 1799	?	*Harmonicon* V (1827), p. 63; Pohl H. in L., pp. 358–360.	*Harmonicon*
24 Sept. 1799	Stanford Memorial Library	none (Eng. transl. in Cat. of Stanford Memorial Library)	Autograph (IMBA)
21 Sept. 1799	Formerly Theodor Breusnig, Osnabrück	Nohl, *Addenda*, p. LV	Nohl
23 Sept. 1799	? (Formerly E. L. Gerber)	Gerber, *Neues historisch-biographisches Lexikon* . . . II (1812), p. 553	Gerber *Lexikon*
30 Sept. 1799	From Briefcopierbuch of Simrock (now IMBA)	none	Briefcopierbuch (IMBA)
Nov. 1799	? (Formerly Breitkopf & Härtel)	none	Autograph (facs. in Hase, facing p. 12)

Letter	Autograph	Printed Source(s)	Source used
[24 March 1800]	Archiv für Nieder-österreich, Vienna.	R. F. Müller, *Die Musik* XXII/2 (1929)	Autograph
11 May 1800	Aut. Samml. Verst. C. G. Börner 3–6 May 1911, No. 982→ Sotheby Cat. 27 June 1932, No. 127→ Lambert (£21)→ ? [in Sotheby Cat. the letter is listed as addressed to Griesinger]	none	Copy by E. von Mandyczewski (Gesellschaft der Musikfreunde. Vienna)
23 May 1800	Archiv des Landesgerichtes, Vienna	Pohl II, 92	Autograph
16 June 1800	Artaria Archives→ Heinrich Hinterberger (1953)→ ?	none	Summary kindly provided by Herr Hinterberger
1 July 1800 [Griesinger]	? (Formerly Coll. Heyer, Cologne)	none	no copy available
1 July 1800 [Breitkopf & Härtel]	Archives of B. & H.→ Leo Liepmannssohn Cats. Verst.-Kat. 52 (16–17 Nov. 1928), No. 248; Verst.-Kat. 56 (15–16 Nov. 1929), No. 248→?	Hase, pp. 20*f.*, 24, 42 (incompl.)	Hase
7 July 1800	Leo Liepmannssohn Cats. 174, No. 841; 39th Aut.-Verst. (17–18 Nov. 1911), No. 334→ Maggs Bros. Cat. 278 (1912), No. 208 (with facs.)→ Sotheby Cat. 26 July 1938, lot 608→ Otto Haas (£17)→ Maggs Bros. Cat. 825 (1954), No. 443→ Mary Benjamin→ Coll. Hoboken, Ascona	Pohl III, 158 (extracts)	Autograph (kindly placed at my disposal by Dr. van Hoboken)
18 July 1800	Briefcopierbuch, Breitkopf & Härtel, Leipzig (destroyed during World War II)	Sandberger, *Peters-Jahrbuch* 1933, pp. 28*ff.*	Sandberger
2 Aug. 1800	?	Extracts in Pohl III, 162 and *Musical Quarterly*, April 1932, p. 214 (English)	Pohl III & *MQ*

Letter	Autograph	Printed Source(s)	Source used
3 Aug. 1800	Artaria Archives→ Gabriel Charavay Cat. Kafka (1881), No. 31→ Noël Charavay Cat. 8 June 1900, No. 90→ Pearson *Cat. of Rare & Valuable Letters* Part I, No. 270 (£15.15)→ Sotheby Cat. 27–28 Nov. 1913, No. 172→ Maggs Bros. Cats. 320 (1914), No. 329; 337 (1915), No. 757; 360 (1917), No. 1850; 381 (1919), No. 1847; 417 (1921), No. 2788→ Henrici Auk.-Kat. 76, No. 282→J. A. Stargardt Kat. 337 (8 Feb. 1933), No. 93→Leo Liepmannssohn Verst.-Kat. 64 (23–24 May 1934), No. 700→?	none	Pohl MS.
11 Aug. 1800	Friedrich Cohen, Cat. Posonyi No. 478→ K. E. Henrici Auk.-Kat. LXXXVIII, No. 184→ V. A. Heck Cat. 4 Sept. 1925→Thomas Maddigan→Heinrich Hinterberger Cat. XX (Oct. 1937), No. 215 (with facs.)→Harvard College Library	Artaria-Botstiber, p. 79 (from Pohl MS.)	Autograph
22 Aug. 1800	? (Formerly Artaria Archives)	Nohl, p. 157; Artaria-Botstiber, p. 80 (from Nohl)	Pohl MS.
28 Aug. 1800	Karolina von Schubert, Graz (1892)→ *Studienprofessor* F. Boccali, Kempten (Allgäu)	none	Autograph
3 Sept. 1800 [Artaria]	Friedrich Cohen, Cat. Posonyi No. 479→ Gilhofer & Ranschburg Cat. 27 Oct. 1908, No. 470→Coll. Geigy-Hagenbach, Basel.	Nohl, p. 158; Artaria-Botstiber, pp. 80f. (from Nohl)	Autograph

Letter	Autograph	Printed Source(s)	Source used
3 Sept. 1800 [Wrani(t)zky]	W. La Croix→ VNat. XXXIII No. 109-3	Nohl, p. 159	Autograph
6 Oct. 1800	Artaria Archives→ Heinrich Hinterberger (1953)→ ?	Artaria-Botstiber, pp. 82f. (from aut.)	Artaria-Botstiber
16 Oct. 1800	Historical Society of Pennsylvania	none	Autograph

[Letters of Johann Friedrich Wagner (Danzig), 1 July 1800 and 30 Sept. 1800: formerly Artaria Archives→Heinrich Hinterberger (1953)→? The summaries kindly provided by Herr Hinterberger.]

[Oct. or Nov. 1800]	Esterházy Archives Acta Musicalia 1876	none	Autograph
10 Dec. 1800	Esterházy Archives, Acta Musicalia XXVI, 1880	none	Autograph (from a copy kindly provided by Dr. A. Valkó
[Undated: c. 1800]	R. Geering Cat. 402, No. 1212	none	Contents from Geering Cat.
30 Mar. 1801	Esterházy Archives Acta Musicalia	none	Marton copy in VNat.
28 Apr. 1801	E. Charavay Cat. Fillon, No. 2416→ M. Lengfeld Cat. 42, No. 395→ Coll. Geigy-Hagenbach, Basel.	none	Autograph
4 May 1801 [Pleyel]	? (Formerly Maison Pleyel, Paris)	Weckerlin, *Musiciana*, Paris 1877, pp. 291f. (French).	Weckerlin
4 May 1801 [Felix Meritis Society, open letter]	Prince Esterházy's Coll. (National Museum, Budapest, An. Mus. Ha. I, 2; Ger. trans., dated 1811, Ha. I, 3) (Draft in Gemeente-Archief Amsterdam, Archief Felix Meritis No. 74–78)	Pohl III, 182 (German)	Autograph (& Draft)
4 May 1801 [Commissioners' of "Felix Meritis" Society]	Esterházy Archives, Varia, Fasc. 2432/3, pp. 3f. German translation of the year 1811 in Fasc. 2432/3, pp. 7f.	none	Autograph (from a copy kindly provided by Dr. A. Valkó)
20 May 1801	1904: Allgemeiner Konzertverein, Barmen	*Allgemeine Musikzeitung* XXXI (1904), pp. 372f.	Autograph (facs. in *AM*)

Letter	Autograph	Printed Source(s)	Source used
2 June 1801	Esterházy Archives, Acta Musicalia XXVI, 1894	none	Autograph (from a copy kindly provided by Dr. A. Valkó)
1 July 1801	Leo Liepmannssohn Verst.-Kat. 56 (15–16 Nov. 1929), No. 89→ Sándor Wolf Museum, Eisenstadt	Csatkai, p. 33	Autograph
3 July 1801	? (Formerly Breitkopf & Härtel Archives, Leipzig)	Hase, pp. 24ff.	Hase
10 July 1801	ditto	Hase, pp. 26f.	Hase
20 July 1801	?	Allgemeine Musikalische Zeitung No. 51 (1801), pp. 842f.; Griesinger, pp. 72f.; Dies, pp. 175f.	AMZ, Griesinger
21 July 1801	Breitkopf & Härtel→ Coll. Julius Rietz, Dresden→ List & Franke Cat. 7 Dec. 1887, No. 556→ Coll. Julius von Herz, Vienna (1892)→ C. G. Börner Cat, 3–6 May, 1911, No. 983→ Coll. Heyer, Cologne→?	Nohl, Addenda, p. LVI	Nohl, collated with MS. copy by E. von Mandyczewski in Gesellschaft der Musikfreunde in Vienna
24 July 1801	? (Formerly Coll. Nadler, Plan [Bohemia])	Deutsche Zeitung Vienna 1873 (23 Dec., p. 3); Pohl III, 187; &c.	Autograph (facs. in Vienna Stadtbibliothek, 99282)
25 July 1801	Esterházy Archives, Varia Fasc. 2432/3, pp. 1f. German translation of the year 1811 in Fasc. 2432/3, p. 7	none	Autograph (from a copy kindly provided by Dr. A. Valkó)
10 Aug. 1801	?	Dies, pp. 176f. (German, n.d.); A. Reissmann, Joseph Haydn, Berlin 1879, pp. 225f. (German, with date)	Dies; Reissmann

Letter	Autograph	Printed Source(s)	Source used
21 Aug. 1801	K. E. Henrici Auk.-Kat. CVII (22–23 Feb. 1926)→ Captain Nydahl, Stockholm	none	Copies of the autograph kindly made by Paul Badura-Skoda & Count C.-G. Mörner
26 Aug. 1801	Bayrenther Musik-antiquariat, "Katalog 1958", item 37	none	Summary from Catalogue
11 Sept. 1801 [Letter]	C. G. Börner Auk. 118 (7 June 1913) No. 164→ K. E. Henrici Verst. L (1919), No. 71→?	Pohl III, 181	Autograph (IMBA)
11 Sept. 1801 [Certificate]	? (Old copy in Artaria Archives→Heinrich Hinterberger [1953] →?)	none	Old copy, kindly placed at my disposal by Herr Hinterberger
26 Sept. 1801	Esterházy Archives Acta Musicalia	none	Marton copy in VNat.
1 Oct. 1801	Historical Society of Pennsylvania	Pohl III, 190f.	Autograph
7 Oct. 1801	K. E. Henrici Lager-Kat. 7, No. 47→?	Merker, Jg. 1 Heft 19, p. 771 (Botstiber: German)	Merker
18 Oct. 1801	? (Dutch Translation in Gemeente-Archief Amsterdam, Archief Felix Meritis No. 74–78)	Pohl III, 182f. (original German)	Pohl collated with Dutch copy (photograph kindly provided by Dr. van Hoboken)
21 Oct. 1801	David Salomon Cat. 10, No. 90 (with facs.) → C. F. Peters, New York City	Pohl III, 191	Autograph
27 Oct. 1801	B.M. Add. 35263, f. 130	Merker, Jg. 1 Heft 19, p. 771 (Botstiber: German)	Autograph
4 Nov. 1801	?	Mentioned in Pohl III, 191	no copy available
5 Dec. 1801	B.M. Add. 35263, ff. 136–137	Merker, Jg. 1, Heft 19 (Botstiber: German); Geiringer MQ, p. 185 (English).	Autograph

Letter	Autograph	Printed Source(s)	Source used
6 Dec. 1801	Aut. formerly in B. & H. Archives, Leipzig, destroyed in an air-raid on 4th Dec. 1943	*Allgemeine Musikalische Zeitung*, Intelligenz-Blatt V, Dec. 1801, p. 1	AMZ
[*c*. 5 Dec. 1801] 7 Dec. 1801	Esterházy Archives, Acta Musicalia XIX, 1308-1309	none	Autograph (from a copy kindly provided by Dr. A. Valkó)
11 Dec. 1801	R. Zeune Cat. 20, No. 81→ Coll. Floersheim-Koch, Muzzano-Lugano (Switzerland)	none	Autograph
26 Dec. 1801	Prince Esterházy's Coll. (National Museum, Budapest, An. Mus. Ha. I, 4)	Dies, pp. 183*f*. (no signatures); Pohl III, 193 (wrong date)	Autograph (photograph R. Forstner, Eisenstadt)
2 Jan. 1802	BM. Add 35263, ff. 138-139	*Merker*, Jg. 1, Heft 19 (Botstiber: German); Geiringer *MQ*, p. 186—Eng. incompl.	Autograph
[Middle of Jan. 1802]	K. E. Henrici Lager-Kat. 7, No. 48→ Sotheby Cat. 17 June 1930, lot 225→ Masters (£7)→ Coll. Elizabeth Firestone, Akron, Ohio. [In Sotheby Cat. the letter is (wrongly) dated, "27 January".]	Geiringer *MQ*, p. 186 (English)	Autograph (photograph kindly sent to me by Dr. Geiringer)
[*c*. 20 Jan. 1802]	Deutsche Staatsbibliothek Berlin	none	Autograph
29 Jan. 1802	B.M. Add. 35265, ff. 140-141	*Merker*, Jg. 1, Heft 19 (Botstiber: German); Geiringer *MQ*, pp. 186*f*. (extract)	German
6 Feb. 1802	Näs Castle, Sweden	C. F. Hennerberg, *Bericht des III. Kongress der I.M.G.*, Vienna-Leipzig, 1909, p. 430.	Autograph (facs. in Mörner, p. 387).
8 Feb. 1802 Haydn's answer March or Apr. 1802) J.H.–AA	?	Griesinger, p. 76 (extracts)	Griesinger

Letter	Autograph	Printed Source(s)	Source used
4 March 1802	Esterházy Archives, Acta Musicalia XXVI, 1919	none	Autograph (from a copy kindly provided by Dr. A. Valkó)
10 March 1802	Esterházy Archives Acta Musicalia 1952	none	Autograph
13 March 1802	Esterházy Archives, Acta Musicalia XXVII, 1953	none	Autograph (from a copy kindly provided by Dr. A. Valkó)
[March 1802]	Esterházy Archives Acta Musicalia 1920	none	Autograph
24 March 1802	Esterházy Archives Acta Musicalia 1315	none	Autograph
14 April 1802	Boston Public Library	none	Autograph
30 April 1802	Esterházy Archives Acta Musicalia 1926	none	Autograph
8 May 1802	? (Formerly Breitkopf & Härtel Archives, Leipzig)	Hase, p. 28	Autograph (facs. in Hase, p. 27).
[c. 7 June 1802]	Esterházy Archives Acta Musicalia 1931	none	Autograph
14 June 1802	Esterházy Archives Acta Musicalia 1933	Pohl III, 200f.	Autograph
21 June 1802	Esterházy Archives Acta Musicalia 1934	Pohl III, 201 (incompl.)	Autograph
30 July 1802	L. C. Seydler, Grätz→ V. A. Heck Cat. XXVI, (1926) No. 45 (with facs.)→ A. C. Meyer →?	Wiener Allgemeine Musikalische Zeitung 1847, No. 132; Nohl, pp. 167f.	Autograph (facs. in Heck Cat. without the address)
14 Aug. 1802	Esterházy Archives Acta Musicalia 1937	none	Autograph
22 Aug. 1802	? (Formerly Breitkopf & Härtel Archives, Leipzig)	none (mentioned in Hase, p. 28)	no copy available
28 Aug. 1802	Gilhofer & Ranschburg Cat. 21 Feb. 1898, No. 260→ Stadtbibliothek Vienna, 99474	none	Autograph
22 Sept. 1802 [Krüger]	J. A. Stargardt Cat. 23 Nov. 1908, No. 1328→ Coll. Hoboken, Ascona	Pohl III, 203f. (without address)	Autograph

Letter	*Autograph*	*Printed Source(s)*	*Source used*
22 Sept. 1802 [Naumann]	Berlin Staatsbibliothek (now Universitätsbib. Marburg/Lahn)	Pohl III, 208	Autograph
7 Oct. 1802	Count Harrach, Rohrau & Vienna (now Österreichisches Staatsarchiv, Vienna: Harrach-Archiv, Karl 773, ff. 1–2)	none	Autograph
28 Nov. 1802	Haydn Museum, Vienna	Pohl III, 204	Autograph
5 Dec. 1802	Maison Pleyel, Paris	Comettant, *Un Nid d'autographes,* Paris 1885, pp. 9–11 (French), with facs.	Autograph
11 Jan. 1803	Count Harrach, Rohrau & Vienna (now Österreichisches Staatsarchiv, Vienna: Harrach-Archiv, Karl 773, ff. 3–4).	Mencik, *Beiträge* (Musikbuch aus Österreich 1909); Pohl III, 216 (wrong date)	Autograph
22 Jan. 1803	Sándor Wolf Museum, Eisenstadt	Csatkai, p. 33	Autograph
8 March 1803	?	*Schlesische Provincialblätter,* Breslau 1803; *Echo,* Berliner Musikzeitung, Jg. 6, No. 48; Pohl III, 210	*Echo* & Pohl III
13 March 1803	A. Cohn Cat. 173, No. 1066→ ?	Pohl III, 210*f.*	Pohl III
8 April 1803	J. A. Stargardt Cats. 24 Mar. 1902, No. 642; 513 (1954), No. 550	none	Copy kindly provided by Dr. van Hoboken
10 May 1803	?	*Allgemeine Musikalische Zeitung* No. 40 (1803), pp. 669–672; Griesinger, pp. 80–82; Dies, pp. 188*f.* (without signatures &*c.*)	AMZ, Griesinger
[*c.* 15 May 1803]	Coll. Floersheim-Koch, Muzzano-Lugano (Switzerland)	*Allgemeine Musikalische Zeitung (ibid.);* Dies, pp. 189*f.*; Pohl III, 217*f.* Nohl, p. 170	Autograph

Letter	Autograph	Printed Source(s)	Source used
18 May 1803	?	Pohl III, 218f.	Pohl III
5 June 1803	? (Formerly W. Taubert, Berlin [1873])	Nohl, *Addenda*, pp. LVI–LVII	Nohl
30 June 1803	B.M. Add. 35266, f. 170	*Merker*, Jg. 1, Heft 19 (Botstiber: German); Geiringer *MQ*, p. 188 (English)	Autograph
1 July 1803	ditto f. 171	ditto (*Merker*, p. 775, *MQ* p. 187)	Autograph
6 July 1803	ditto ff. 172–173	*Merker* (as above); *MQ* only extract	Autograph
13 Oct. 1803	Esterházy Archives, Acta Musicalia XXVII, 1976	none	Autograph (from a copy kindly provided by Dr. A. Valkó)
1 Nov. 1803	*Cantor* F. Dietrich, Berlin (1856)→ Prof. H. Rauscher (1932)→ priv. coll. in Basel. A draft (not aut.) in Paris Conservatoire.	Sandberger, *Peters-Jahrbuch* 1933, pp. 28 ff. (the draft). Facsimile of aut. printed in Nadermann's edition of Haydn's pianoforte Trio No. 31 in E flat minor (see Hoboken, 715); text in *Echo*, Berliner Musikzeitung 1856 No. 11, p. 81	Facs. of autograph (Vienna Stadtbibliothek 3079) & draft.
[Beginning of Nov. 1803]	Esterházy Archives Acta Musicalia XXVII, 1984	none	Autograph
18 Dec. 1803	B.M. Add. 35266, ff. 196–197	*Merker*, Jg. 1, Heft 19, p. 776 (Botstiber: German); Geiringer *MQ*, p. 189 (Eng.)	Autograph
20 Dec. 1803	B.M. Add. 35266, f. 17 (Thomson's Copy Book)	Extracts in Geiringer *MQ*, p. 188.	Autograph
Undated 1803 letter:			
Re Madame Siess, &c.	Esterházy Archives Acta Musicalia 1982	none	Autograph
25 Feb. 1804	Draft in VNat. XXXIII, No. 109-4 (from antiquarian bookseller Bader)	Nohl, p. 171	Autograph

Letter	Autograph	Printed Source(s)	Source used
16 March 1804	Coll. Kippenberg, Düsseldorf	Dies, pp. 100–102	Copy of autograph (IMBA)
[Spring 1804] [Re Richter]	Draft in VNat. XXXIII, No. 109–4	none	Autograph
[Spring 1804] [Re Fuchs]	Esterházy Archives Acta Musicalia	none	Marton copy in VNat.
[Draft for above	Sándor Wolf Museum, Eisenstadt	Csatkai, pp. 33f.	Autograph
1 April 1804	Prince Esterházy's Coll. (National Museum, Budapest, An. Mus. Ha. I, 1)	Pohl III, 224f.	Autograph
6 April 1804	B.M. Add. 35265, f. 225	Merker, Jg. 1, Heft 19 (Botstiber: German)	Autograph
10 May 1804 [Draft for above	ditto, f. 233 VNat. XXXIII, No. 109–4	⌠Pohl III, 226 (draft) ⌡	Autograph Autograph
[May 1804] [Hammersley]	Draft in Sándor Wolf Museum, Eisenstadt	Csatkai, p. 34	Autograph
[May (?)] 1804 (Karner)	Esterházy Archives, Acta Musicalia XXVII, 2002	none	Autograph (from a copy kindly provided by Dr. A. Valkó)
[May 1804] [Burney]	ditto	ditto	ditto
[May 1804] [Tomasini]	Esterházy Archives Acta Musicalia 2005	none	Autograph
[Draft for above	Sándor Wolf Museum, Eisenstadt	Csatkai, p. 34	Autograph
[? Spring or Summer 1804]	Draft in Sandor Wolf Museum, Eisenstadt	Csatkai, p. 34	Autograph
21 June 1804	Autograph ditto (Bought from K.E. Henrici Auk.-Kat. CXLII, No. 21)	ditto, p. 33	ditto
6 July 1804	Esterházy Archives Acta Musicalia 2034	none	Autograph
10 Aug. 1804	? (Gardiner kept copy)	Gardiner, Music & Friends, 1838, I pp. 362f.; O. E. Deutsch, Music Review IV/3 (1943), pp. 161f.	Gardiner

Letter	*Autograph*	*Printed Source(s)*	*Source used*
14 Sept. 1804	? (1932: President Kux, Vienna. I wrote to Mr. Kux, who is now in Switzerland, and received the answer that he had given the letter to a refugee in 1938 and could no longer remember the recipient's name)	none	no copy available
28 Sept. 1804	Margarete Hummel, Florence	Pohl III, 230 (no address, wrong date)	Autograph
8 Oct. 1804	? (Copy in Aloys Fuchs' notebook, "Miscellania", Göttweig Abbey).	*Allgemeine Theaterzeitung* No. 103 (Vienna, 1841)	Fuchs' copy
17 Oct. 1804	? (Formerly owned by Miss Emilie Schaup, Vienna [1931])	*Merker*, Jg. 1, Heft 19, p. 777 (Botstiber: German); Italian original in Leo Grünstein, *Das Alt-Wiener Antlitz*, Vienna 1931, I, pp. 138*f*. (wrongly noted as being to Bridi)	Grünstein
30 Oct. 1804	B.M. Add. 35263, ff. 244–245	*Merker*, Jg. 1, Heft 19; Geiringer *MQ*, p. 189 (Eng.)	Autograph
5 Nov. 1804	? (Auction Anderson Galleries, New York City, 3 Nov. 1915, No. 512)	none	no copy available
15 Feb. 1805	?	Pohl III, 236*f*.	Pohl III
20 June 1805	Prince Esterházy's Coll. (National Museum, Budapest, An. Mus. Ha. I, 5)	Dies, pp. 184*f*.; Pohl III, 193*f*. (wrong date)	Autograph (facs. in Geiringer, p. 28)
26 June 1805	(National Museum, Budapest, An. Mus. Ha. I, 6)	Dies, pp. 185*f*.; Pohl III, 243*f*. (incompl.)	Autograph (facs. in *Bulletin* de Soc. Inter. de Mus. VI, No. 1 [1910], p. 79).
[Haydn's answer	?	*Bulletin* (see 26 June 1805): extract.	*Bulletin*

Letter	Autograph	Printed Source(s)	Source used
17 Aug. 1805	? (Formerly Artaria Archives)	Artaria-Botstiber, pp. 88f.	Autograph (facs. in Artaria-Botstiber)
6 Nov. 1805	? (Formerly Coll. Max Friedländer, Berlin [1892])	none	no copy available
23 April 1806	Private possession in Italy; an old copy in Conservatorio "G.B. Martini", Bologna, Ms. UU/12: Gaetano Gasperi, Miscellanea Musicale, Tomo II, p. 791.	A. Coli, *Vita di Bonifazio Asioli* . . . Milan, 1834, p. 50 (incompl.)	Old copy in Bologna (kindly copied for me by L. F. Tagliavini)
3 May 1806	Esterházy Archives Acta Musicalia 2153	none	Autograph
5 May 1806	ditto	none	Autograph
25 Nov. 1806	Landesregierungsarchiv Salzburg, File 430: an archive copy, not aut.	Schmid, p. 259	Archive copy (Salzburg)
26 Nov. 1806	? (Probably a draft is in the Esterházy Archives)	Dies, p. 144	Dies
[Beginning of Dec. 1806]	Esterházy Archives Acta Musicalia	Pohl III 252f.	Marton copy of aut. (VNat.) collated with Pohl III
30 Dec. 1806	Näs Castle, Sweden	*Några anteckningar om adliga ätten Silfverstolpe*, Stockholm, 1884, pp. 200f.	Copy kindly prepared by Count C.-G. Mörner.
Undated, 1806	Prince Esterházy's Coll.	Pohl III, 248	Autograph
3/17 Apr. 1807	(National Museum, Budapest, An. Mus. Ha. I, 19)	Dies, pp. 150f.	Dies
June 1807]	Gabriel Charavay, Cat. Kafka (1881), No. 32 → ?	none	Extracts (contents) from Charavay
30 Dec. 1807	?	Dies, pp. 167f.	Dies
20 March 1808	Arno Wotke, Berlin	none (mentioned in Pohl II, 96)	Autograph (IMBA)
7 April 1808	Gerd Rosen Auk. XI, No. 27→Lucien Goldschmidt→Dr. Max Thorek, Chicago.	Dies, p. 168f.	Autograph

Letter	Autograph	Printed Source(s)	Source used
26 April 1808	J. A. Stargardt Cat. Donebauer (6–8 Apr. 1908), No. 385→ C. G. Boerner Cat. XVI (1910), No. 153→ Library of Congress, Washington	Pohl III 269 (no address)	Autograph
29 May 1808	?	Griesinger, pp. 83 *ff*.; Dies, pp. 171*f*. (no signatures).	Griesinger
4/16 June 1808	?	Dies, pp. 170*f*.	Dies
25 July 1808	?	Dies, p. 171	Dies
28 July 1808	Formerly (1884): Archives of Philharmonic Society, St. Petersburg	Pohl III, 271	Pohl III
22 Dec. 1808	Esterházy Archives Acta Musicalia XXIV, 2564	Pohl III, 273 *f*.	Autograph

THE LONDON NOTEBOOKS

I (1791–1792)	VNat. Cod. 15391	Extracts in Dies, Griesinger, Pohl, H. in L. and Pohl III; nearly complete Eng. translation in Krehbiel, *Music & Manners*, New York 1898	Autograph
II (1791–1792)	ditto	ditto	Autograph
III (1794–1795)	Salzburg Mozarteum	Nearly complete but very inaccurate: J. E. Engl, *Handschriftliches Tagebuch aus der Zeit seines zweiten Aufenthaltes in London*, Leipzig 1909	Autograph
IV (1794–1795)	lost	Extracts in Dies and Griesinger	

INDEXES

These indexes do not include material in the Preface, Introduction or Source List.

Index of Haydn's Works Mentioned in this Book

NOTE: Symphonies are identified by the standard numbers in the Breitkopf & Härtel *Gesamtausgabe*, Quartets by the traditional opus numbers, piano Sonatas by the chronological list in the Breitkopf & Härtel *Gesamtausgabe* (Ser. XIV), piano Trios by the chronological list in Larsen's *Drei Haydn Kataloge* (Copenhagen, 1941). Other works are listed by their title and, in brackets, the number of Hoboken's *Haydn-Verzeichnis* (Mainz, 1957), in so far as it includes the work in question (the first volume of the *Verzeichnis* contains only the instrumental music).